Italy Today

Italy Today represents one of the most comprehensive examinations of contemporary Italy. It is a provocative and innovative collection that aims to highlight the current 'crisis' of the country through an analysis of several 'dark shadows' of contemporary Italian society.

Italy has had a long history of 'unresolved' issues; several chronic problems and contradictions that have been ignored for a very long time, during which time they have assumed dramatic proportions and gravity. The peninsula has now become the 'Sick Man of Europe', a country facing a veritable decline also caused by apparent incapacity and difficulties of the ruling economic, political and social elites.

Discussions include:

- An evaluation of the current predicaments of the political system
- Analysis of emerging mafias, including new powerful crime organizations such as *'Ndrangheta*
- Issues surrounding the ongoing presence of Fascism
- Examination of the recent xenophobic tensions
- Discussion of problems associated with the missed opportunity of the EU funding, and the increasing regional economic gaps
- Outline of the systemic troubles of Italy's economic and industrial systems

Written by leading experts in the field and covering a wide range of topics, this collection is essential reading for all those seeking to understand the issues and problems that are facing contemporary Italy.

Andrea Mammone is a Lecturer in Modern History at Kingston University, London. He has previously held visiting research and teaching positions at NYU Florence, State University of New York at Stony Brook, and the Università di Siena, Italy.

Giuseppe A. Veltri is currently a scientific fellow at the European Commission JRC Institute of Prospective Studies (IPTS), Spain. His research interests are in behavioural economics and social psychology of economic life and public understanding of science.

"Faced with the attention-seeking antics of Silvio Berlusconi and his political allies, increasingly the temptation is not to treat Italy seriously. The great achievement of the contributors to this excellent volume is to reach behind the façade of political posturing to show that Italy does matter, because the failure of Italy's political system to come up with solutions to the chronic problems facing the country today poses questions that are relevant to all advanced democracies. Italy today, but where next?"

John Davis, *University of Connecticut, USA*

"Written by well known specialists and young researchers from Italy or outside, this book is dedicated to Contemporary Italy, considered as the sick man of Europe. All the aspects of its decline are studied in an interdisciplinary approach."

Marc Lazar, *Sciences Po, Paris, France*

Italy Today

The sick man of Europe

**Edited by Andrea Mammone and
Giuseppe A. Veltri**

Routledge
Taylor & Francis Group

LONDON AND NEW YORK

First published 2010
by Routledge
2 Park Square, Milton Park, Abingdon, Oxon, OX14 4RN

Simultaneously published in the USA and Canada
by Routledge
270 Madison Avenue, New York, NY 10016

Routledge is an imprint of the Taylor & Francis Group, an informa business

Typeset in Times by
HWA Text and Data Management, London
Printed and bound in Great Britain by
CPI Antony Rowe, Chippenham, Wiltshire

British Library Cataloguing in Publication Data
A catalogue record for this book is available from the British Library

Library of Congress Cataloging in Publication Data
Italy today : the sick man of Europe / edited by Andrea Mammone
and Giuseppe A. Veltri.
    p. cm.
  1. Italy–Politics and government–1994. 2. Italy–Economic conditions–1994.
  3. Italy–Social conditions–1994. 4. Berlusconi, Silvio, 1936.
  I. Mammone, Andrea. II. Veltri, Giuseppe A.
  DG583.5.I87 2010
  945.093–dc22   2009031310

ISBN10: 0–415–56159–0 (hbk)
ISBN10: 0–415–56160–4 (pbk)
ISBN10: 0–203–85963–4 (ebk)

ISBN13: 978–0–415–56159–4 (hbk)
ISBN13: 978–0–415–56160–0 (pbk)
ISBN13: 978–0–203–85963–6 (ebk)

For Angelo, Lia, Liliana, Luca, Franco,
Vanessa, and Mariangela and Valeria

Contents

Figures

Tables

Contributors

Felia Allum is a Lecturer in Politics and Italian at the University of Bath (UK).

Percy Allum is an Honorary Senior Research Fellow at the University of Reading (UK) and former Professor of Political Science at the Università di Napoli l'Orientale (Italy).

Joshua Arthurs is an Assistant Professor of Modern European History at West Virginia University (USA).

Martina Avanza is an Assistant Professor in Political Sociology at the Université de Lausanne (Switzerland).

Stefania Bernini is a Lecturer in European History at the University of New South Wales (Australia).

Carlo Carboni is a Professor of Economic Sociology at the Università Politecnica delle Marche (Italy).

Anna Cento Bull is a Professor of Italian History and Politics at the University of Bath (UK).

Nicolò Conti is a Post-Doctoral Fellow of Political Science at the Università di Siena (Italy).

Paul Corner is Professor of European History at the Università di Siena (Italy).

Eva Garau is a Teaching Fellow in European Studies at the University of Bath (UK).

Chris Hanretty is a PhD Researcher in Political and Social Sciences at the European University Institute in Florence (Italy).

Alfonsina Iona is a Lecturer in Finance at Aston University (UK).

Leone Leonida is a Lecturer in Economics at Queen Mary University of London (UK) and at the Università di Messina (Italy).

Andrea Mammone is a Lecturer in Modern History at Kingston University London (UK).

Simona Milio is the Associate Director of the Economic Social Cohesion Laboratory, London School of Economics and Political Science (UK).

Raoul Minetti is an Associate Professor of Economics at Michigan State University (USA).

Catherine Moury is an Advanced Research Fellow at CIES-ISCTE Lisbon (Portugal), and Guest Assistant Professor of Political Science at ICHEC Brussels (Belgium).

Ercole Giap Parini is a Lecturer in Sociology at the Università della Calabria (Italy).

Christophe Roux is an Assistant Professor of Political Science at the Université de Montpellier I (France).

Nando Sigona teaches Refugee Studies at Oxford Brookes University (UK) and is a Research Officer at the Refugee Studies Centre at the University of Oxford (UK).

Marco Simoni is a Lecturer in European Political Economy at the London School of Economics and Political Science (UK).

Giuseppe Sobbrio is a Professor of Public Economics at the Università di Messina (Italy).

Giuseppe A. Veltri is a Research and Scientific Fellow at The Institute for Prospective Technological Studies (IPTS), (Spain).

Foreword

Paul Corner

One does not have to be particularly old to be able to remember the smiling face of a triumphant Bettino Craxi when, in 1987, he announced to the press that Italy had 'overtaken' Britain and become the world's fifth largest industrial power. The claim hit the headlines and seemed to confirm the image of an Italy back on track after the dark years of the 1970s, when terrorism and industrial unrest had interrupted the progress of the nation of the economic 'miracle'. If the *sorpasso* was contested at the time (by the British, understandably, but also by some Italians) and if it was not true in every respect, there was clearly enough justification in the claim to warrant Craxi's radiant smile. The passage of twenty years has changed the picture dramatically. In the midst of the current financial crisis it is difficult to know what the position is at present – sometimes it looks very much like a race to the bottom – but, until little more than a year ago, there could have been few doubts that the Italian 'overtaking' of Britain had been reversed almost at the outset and that Italy has been falling behind not only Britain, but most other European competitors for many years. The heady days of the expansion of Italy's famous small industries – something that seemed a model for the world – have long passed, and the cult of 'Made in Italy' has to some extent lost its sheen. Certainly, lifestyle, food, fashion and culture keep Italy in the forefront of popular perceptions, but the image of Italy portrayed by the world press, in political and economic terms, is now almost universally that of a country in slow but very steady decline, moving not towards the economic levels of France, Germany and Britain but towards those of Greece and Portugal. There is an undoubted element of journalistic exaggeration in the phrase, but for the foreign press Italy has become, as the title of this volume indicates, very much 'the Sick Man of Europe'.[1]

It is tempting to explain this decline with reference to the more evident short-term factors. Very predictably the controversial figure of Silvio Berlusconi, who has in many ways dominated the history of the so-called Second Republic, is often at the centre of such explanations. Berlusconi is better known outside Italy for his gaffes than for any great speeches and he undoubtedly makes for good press copy. Foreign correspondents are able to point to a whole list of questions relating to the Italian Prime Minister which suggest an unusual political situation in Italy, to say the least. These range from the more substantial issues concerning Berlusconi's conflict of interest through his very extensive control of the media, his often apparently undemocratic attitudes, his self-protecting legislation, his alleged bribery of judges and corruption of witnesses, down to the more 'colourful' questions about why showgirls become government ministers, and exactly what goes on in his private villa in Sardinia. Some of this is serious, some only semi-serious, but in the context of Italian decline, the overall impression communicated by many foreign journalists is that of imperial decadence, with Nero fiddling as Rome burns.

The centrality of Berlusconi to Italian decline must be questioned, however. Certainly his governments may not have managed to reverse the trend of decline, but it must be recognized that the downward slide has been fairly constant since about 1990 – that is, well before Berlusconi could exercise any influence on affairs. Other recent governments – Dini, Ciampi, Prodi, D'Alema, Amato – seem to have been equally powerless to restore Italy's relative position. Clearly Berlusconi is not the only – perhaps not even the main – culprit; other forces have been at work. In fact, one only has to look over the annual reports of the Governor of the Bank of Italy to understand that the Italian economy is suffering from serious structural weaknesses, the origins of which go back several decades. Small firms have signally failed to grow as they were supposed to; productivity remains an enormous problem and the public debt continues to be alarmingly high. But the problems are not all economic. Many Italian institutions are clearly very much in need of an overhaul. The political system remains complex, fragmented and lethargic. The slowness of the legal system is legendary, as is that of the bureaucracy. Italian universities are grossly underfunded by European standards; within them they have certain areas of undoubted excellence but, in most of the tables of world rankings, it is difficult to find an Italian university inside the top two hundred. Italian researchers figure as one of the largest categories of emigrants from Italy and the knock-on economic costs of this emigration are all too obvious. Nor would it be right to neglect the governments' failure to deal with the problem of organized crime in Italy – still thought to be responsible for about 10 to 15 per cent of Italian Gross Domestic Product. As anyone who has read (or seen) *Gomorra* will know, organized crime has a very high social cost within Italy itself, but it is also damaging to national interests on a much wider scale. In an age of globalization of investment, it is not hard to find foreign industrialists who will tell you that they are unwilling to invest in Italy, not only because it takes them weeks to get a telephone line, months to get a local government permit and years to get a legal judgment, but also because they fear the long arm of a flourishing criminal sector. Rankings of countries in terms of suitability for business activity find Italy a long, long way from the top.

Italy Today directs its attention to some of these more general, long-term questions of Italian politics and society which may have had a hand in provoking relative decline. It is a very timely attempt to look beyond the immediate polemics of Italian politics towards underlying issues that dictate the progress of Italian society and which may help to explain the current phase of indisputable difficulty that Italy is experiencing. Some of the issues are very long-term indeed. Those that relate to questions of national identity clearly go back as far as Italian unification, and even beyond, as do those concerned with the relationship between North and South. Others involve the question of the way in which Italian society is articulated and of the relations between different groupings; sometimes it seems that the clan rather than the nation might be the more appropriate frame of reference. More than one contributor here makes clear how, within a generally corporative structure of interest groups, for many Italians the distinction between the concepts of 'public' and 'private' remains hazy, reflecting the great difficulties still existing in the formation of a sense of collective identity and in the creation of a collective civic ethic. As the well-known Italian sociologist Giuseppe De Rita wrote recently, 'for the average Italian, the others don't exist' (*La Repubblica*, 10 May 2009).

The general context in which most of the contributions presented here are placed is, of course, that of a society which, until the 1950s, was predominantly rural and was also very poor, and which has witnessed a pace of change comparable with that experienced by contemporary China. This poses the problem, very evident in Italy, of the relationship between the traditional – the family and the church, for example – and the new. To many non-Italians the juxtaposition of elements of the traditional society and those of the new – the latter often dramatically accentuated because of their relative novelty – represents one of the most fascinating aspects of present-day Italy. Within this framework the traditional has proved surprisingly resistant to change, but the tensions are unmistakable. It is very obvious that Italian society continues to face the pressures of modernization rather uncertainly. To give just one example, a traditionally welcoming Italian society has reacted badly to both European and non-European immigration, permitting the rapid development of a generalized sense of insecurity, amply encouraged, it must be said, by a largely xenophobic press and television. On a different plane, even the famous Italian family – the absolute kernel of Italian society – is feeling the pressures of change as, very slowly and with some notable delay in respect of Northern Europe, rates of divorce and illegitimate births begin to rise.

The essays in this volume invite the reader to look beyond Berlusconi, therefore, and to consider the wider issues relating to a variegated society in once-rapid, now not-so-rapid, transition. In many different ways they chronicle the difficulties of a society in which there seems often to be an extremely uneasy relationship between the old and the new, with a clear conflict between the straitjacket imposed by the traditional methods of organizing and running society and the requirements of a wider world that finds these methods inadequate to modern purposes. The recent discussion in Italy about the absence of a genuine meritocracy is emblematic in this sense. In principle everyone is in favour of meritocracy, but open competition remains anathema in many areas when it comes down to selection processes.[2] This is only one area where Italy seems to lag behind others in Europe, preferring the security of set ways and guarantees to the uncertainty of a truly competitive system. The need for major reforms to free-up the system is widely recognized; the problem is that reforms hurt vested interests and threaten consolidated positions and, as a result, can be politically counter-productive. In this sense one of the major criticisms to be levelled at Berlusconi might be less about what he has done than what he has not done. The great danger for Italy is that it emerges from the world financial crisis with exactly those same structural weaknesses it had when the crisis began. Indeed it is the lack of prospect of change which constitutes perhaps the most alarming aspect of the Italian crisis.

The old, condescending, journalistic chestnut about Italian crises was that the situation was always grave, but never serious. Perhaps that has done its time. The seriousness of the crisis facing Italy at the moment is unquestionable. The chapters in this volume attempt a diagnosis of this crisis and try to explain what has happened to the optimism and dynamism that so characterized Italy in the two decades following the end of the Second World War. Of course, 'Italy in crisis' is hardly a new headline and, paradoxically, this gives ground for hope. Experienced observers of Italy are used to what has always been an extremely resilient and resourceful Italian society bouncing back from the edge of disaster with renewed force and energy. This collection of essays may help us to understand whether this picture is also finally outdated. One can only hope not – there is still much about Italy that gives good reason for hope. And, after all, given the right diagnosis, sick men often get better.

Università di Siena
Siena, 15 June 2009

Notes

1   The honour does the rounds. The same title was awarded to Britain in the late 1970s and to France in the mid 1990s.
2   In this respect it may be no coincidence that the most successful Italian manager of the moment, Sergio Marchionne of Fiat-Chrysler, grew up and was educated in Canada.

Acknowledgements

Italy Today saw its light after the passionate and long discussions that we had in our native Calabria, in Southern Italy (and, incidentally, other contributors come from the same area, or, more generally from the Mezzogiorno). It was incredible for us – at that time still research students in the UK – that in Italy only a few in the media, some intellectuals and citizens were aware of the worrying downturn of Italian society, let alone that the situation was worsening, a decline that was not in keeping with the global financial crisis. In this context, we felt the need to move away from some stereotypical analyses or images of Italy *tutta pizza e mandolino*.

The first research step in this direction was a special edition of the *Journal of Modern Italian Studies* (JMIS, available at www.informaworld.com), entitled 'Italy in Chiaroscuro: The Dark Shadows of Modern Italian Society', from which this book originates. Since the beginning of the special edition editing process, it was clear that a single journal issue was not going to be enough to present the complex array of deficiencies of contemporary Italy. Hence, this volume is the offspring of that initiative and it has benefited from the feedback received for the special issue of JMIS and it has been enriched by the contribution of a wider range of scholars (whom we thank). We are thus strongly indebted to Prof. John Davis and JMIS (and Taylor & Francis Ltd) for the republication of some material that now appears in *Italy Today*. Similarly, we want to thank Prof. Paul Corner who has kindly and constantly supported this enterprise from its early stages.

We also owe a big debt of gratitude to artist Attilio Lauria who generously designed the image used on the front cover.

We are similarly very grateful to editors Craig Fowlie and Nicola Parkin at Routledge for their suggestions and advice (and, of course, patience) during the editorial and publishing process.

However, no one deserves more gratitude than our families in Calabria, as well as Mariangela and Valeria; they have always supported us, even when they were not fully conscious of what we were really doing or when our lives were crossing national borders. It is to them that this volume is dedicated.

Andrea Mammone and Giuseppe A. Veltri
Rome, 27 July 2009

Abbreviations

AN	Alleanza Nazionale (National Alliance)
CEI	Conferenza Episcopale Italiana (Italian Episcopal Conference)
CGIL	Confederazione Generale Italiana del Lavoro (General Italian Confederation of Labour)
CISL	Confederazione Italiana Sindacati dei Lavoratori (Italian Confederation of Labour Unions)
DC	Democrazia Cristiana (Christian Democratic Party/Christian Democrats)
DIA	Direzone Investigativa Antimafia
DS	Democratici di Sinistra (Left Democrats)
EC	European Commission
EMU	Economic and Monetary Union
EU	European Union
FI	Forza Italia (Go Italy)
GDP	Gross Domestic Product
IDV	Italia dei Valori (Italy of Values)
LN	Lega Nord (Northern League)
MSI	Movimento Sociale Italiano (Italian Social Movement)
PCI	Partito Comunista Italiano (Italian Communist Party)
PD	Partito Democratico (Democratic Party)
PDL	Popolo della Libertà (People of Freedom)
PDS	Partito Democratico della Sinistra (Democratic Party of the Left)
PSI	Partito Socialista Italiano (Italian Socialist Party)
RAI	Radio Televisione Italiana (Italian Radio Television)
RC	Rifondazione Comunista (Communist Refoundation Party
RSI	Repubblica Sociale Italiana (Italian Social Republic, also known as the Republic of Salò)
UDEUR	Unione Democratici per l'Europa (Union of Democrats for Europe)
UIL	Unione Italiana del Lavoro (Italian Union of Labour)

Map of Italy's regions

1   A 'sick man' in Europe

Andrea Mammone and Giuseppe A. Veltri

THE MAKING OF THE SICK MAN[1]

In October 2006 the popular TV programme *Le Iene* (The Hyenas) scheduled a documentary on the Italian Members of Parliament (MPs) and their use of cannabis and cocaine. About 50 MPs (secretly and involuntarily) were tested by *Le Iene* journalists, and 32 per cent appeared to use these illicit drugs. However, the Italian Privacy Authority refused permission to screen it, and the Public Prosecutor's office in Rome confiscated all the material – including the drug tests. A few days later, the 'revenge' of *Le Iene* was to test MPs' general culture knowledge:

Who is Nelson Mandela?
'I am not really aware of this'; 'There are different opinions on Mandela's figure'; '[He is] the South-American President [...], he is Brazilian.'
What is Guantanamo? Have you ever heard about Guantanamo?
'No.'
Where is Guantanamo?
'In Afanistan.'[2]
Where?
'In Afanistan!'
Who is Venezuela's current President?
'Gomez.'
Who?
'Comez.'
Where is Darfur?
'It is the Lebanon's issue.'
And what about the Darfur drama?
'Unfortunately this is not an Italian "moda" [fashion] [...]. We [Italians] should not have it. We are a country of "style", a country of good food [...]. [The Darfur] is a lifestyle, a type of behaviour [...], [the Darfur] is for food.'

Such striking answers were provided by some MPs interviewed in front of the national parliament in Rome.[3] With the exception of a few newspaper articles, not many questioned the surprising lack of knowledge of part of national party representatives.

This peculiar 'status' of the parliamentary elite echoes some of its historical precursors. In Liberal Italy, as Christopher Duggan reminds us, 'a Tuscan, Ferdinando Martini, was horrified by the ignorance of his fellow deputies and recalled an occasion when the Minister of the Interior, Giovanni Nicotera (a southerner and a former Mazzinian revolutionary), repeatedly referred to "King Teodoro" of England in a speech after misreading a note that had been slipped to him about "the Tudors"' (Duggan 2008: 311).

Yet, Italy's problems go much deeper than its parliamentarians' lack of knowledge. In general, this country – well-known as a nation of art, culture and beautiful landscapes – has a long history of unsolved issues and long-term problems that still characterize its relatively young democracy. For instance, Italy is known as a country with a weak sense of nationhood, a high degree of politicization of social life, a multitude of quarrelsome political parties, unstable or unproductive government coalitions, constant inequalities between regions, the dramatic presence of powerful crime organizations, widespread corruption in public life, and growing xenophobic stances. The wide array of these and other critical issues seems to have reached a critical mass that has transformed Italy into the 'sick man of Europe': a country still struggling between modernity and backwardness, between the need/will to change and the fear of losing some local or specific privileges.[4] In such a context, Italy, as already noted, became an interesting 'laboratory' for democracy as it copes with a series of political and social challenges that have a wider, European significance (Lazar 1997: 4).[5]

The country is therefore facing a tangible decline to which its economic, social and political elite have no answers. These ruling elites do not seem ready to cope with the crisis of Italian society and politics. They are distrusted by most of its citizens and affected by a worrying lack of renewal and meritocracy. Linked to this last point, it is clear that many of these elites are selected through a self-referential process which influences access to several professions, including journalism, public service and bureaucracy, university professors, and professional politicians (Floris 2007b; Iezzi 2009; Carlucci and Castaldo 2009); and it is often regulated by personal networks or political links rather than proven and effective know-how.

This naturally developed an in-group narrow mentality, one in which the *raccomandazione*, the 'preferential' treatment, is the only certain way of getting a job, social position and favour. Journalist Giovanni Floris, for instance, called it *Mal di Merito* and highlighted the social impact of this system (with the inherent loss of human capital) as well as the 'epidemic of recommendations which is paralyzing Italy' (Floris 2007a). A recent survey by the Luiss University of Rome showed that the economic impact of this non-meritocratic system costs each Italian citizen between €1,080 and €2,671 each year (Iezzi 2009: 23). This obviously contributes to an overall inefficiency and to the low growth of the economy, but it also affects the quality of the education system. For example, the 2006 Programme for International Student Assessment – which tests the knowledge and skills in mathematics, science and literature of 15-year-old pupils in 57 countries –from the Organisation for Economic Co-operation and Development (OECD) certified that 50.5 per cent of Italian students are unable to understand what they read (the average in the OECD area is 42.2 per cent). While some countries showed significant improvements in student performance since 2000, Italy had a further drop of 5 per cent. If the best expertise and 'brains' are thus 'lost' due to the *raccomandazione* system, who is consequently dealing with the most crucial issues and domestic predicaments?

Some of these crucial issues should be pressing enough to stimulate an open public debate involving all political, social and intellectual forces. Yet, this debate is simply not taking place.[6] There is instead a superficial, and often demagogic, discussion in which chronic problems are mainly used as rhetorical tools for one party or another. Similarly, mass media are hardly shaping this debate – and this is by no means surprising as, according to several international bodies, Italy does not allow the mass media enough freedom. The perverse outcome of this is that the intellectual (academic) milieu, or other non-leading opinions, which have no real party or media links are often confined to the local or marginal press. Although there is an understandable and justifiable tendency to associate Italy's lack of media freedom with the figure of an industrialist such as Prime Minister Silvio Berlusconi, this is instead another 'legacy' and traditional negative domestic feature.[7]

One of the rhetorical tools often used as an alleged solution for current national troubles is the creation of a stronger executive branch and the weakening of the powers of elective Chambers. Recently Berlusconi similarly questioned the usefulness of parliaments with a large number of deputies, and seemed to suggest a re-balance of power in favour of the government as well as a new institutional structure. To balance the failure of Liberal Italy and the outcomes of the First World War, some thought the solution to the domestic quandaries lay with the implementation of a fascist dictatorship. Obviously, those were different historical times and conditions, though Fascism still remains alive in the Italian collective memory, architecture and politics (Mammone and Veltri 2007; Mammone 2006). Indeed, setting aside the controversial approach of the now extinguished Alleanza Nazionale (AN), deputies like Alessandra Mussolini, the well-known granddaughter of Benito and leader of the neo-fascist and anti-immigrant Azione Sociale (Social Action) or newly elected MPs like the editor Giuseppe Ciarrapico never denied their respect for the Duce or the fascist regime.[8]

This is particularly worrying in a country that is currently facing an alarming rise of far-right culture and so-called soft-core racism, including citizens' (and some neo-fascist) squads against local crime (mainly attributed to immigrants), the proposed fingerprinting of gypsies (including children) living in camps, the violence against the Roma population,[9] or the creation of separate school classes for young non-Italians. Recently, a group of parents in Rome proposed to withdraw their children from the local school because 'there are too many immigrants', but glossing over the fact that these *immigrati* were, in reality, born in Italy and speak perfect Italian, and are thus completely integrated into the local community (Martini 2009: 20). Rather than criticizing this, some leading politicians and ministers similarly affirmed that a multi-ethnic Italy 'is not our idea' or proposed that 'some Milan Metro carriages should be reserved for Milanese only' (Owen 2009), declared that the government will send boats full of immigrants back to the African coasts (De Zulueta 2009), and even argued that the United Nations High Commissioner for Refugees (UNHCR) displays an 'inhuman and criminal behaviour' (Ruotola 2009: 4).

As one of *Italy Today*'s editors recently suggested, these events are showing a deeper trend, as the

> focus on immigration encourages the distraction of public opinion from an economy in serious trouble, and politics and society in general in crisis.
>
> In Italy, crimes committed by immigrants can be discussed for weeks. Yet in May 2008, some neo-fascists in Verona murdered an Italian because he refused to give them a cigarette. This story disappeared from most newspapers after no more than a few days. *Il Giornale*, a daily newspaper which supports Berlusconi, even disputed that those arrested belonged to the far right […].
>
> The night before Obama's capture of the White House, a group of young neo-fascists burst into the Rome headquarters of the RAI, the Italian public television station, to threaten journalists who had reported on violent attacks by neo-fascist thugs on high school students demonstrating against the government's education policy […].
>
> In such a climate, with mainstream politicians apparently unwilling or unable to stand up to racist violence and xenophobia, and some even prepared to justify these reprehensible acts, it is hardly surprising that right-wing extremists are not afraid or embarrassed to show their true, violent faces […]
>
> (Mammone 2009: 15)

Despite this, groups like the Lega Nord or politicians like Alessandra Mussolini are not perceived as potential threats to the functioning of an Italian society that is increasingly becoming multi-ethnic and multicultural. The most controversial point is that these forces are currently governing the nation. The same grand-daughter of the Duce can even proudly claim that, along with her neo-fascist party, she is one of the founders of the recent Popolo della Libertà (PDL), the biggest Italian party, led by Silvio Berlusconi.[10] A rightist bloc was thus created without any serious internal debate but only on the base of the leader's will (it also includes the 'post-fascists' of the AN). Outside Italy, this overall process and strategy looked so worrying that a much respected British newspaper wrote the headline, 'Fascism's shadows', and commented that:

> Mr Berlusconi has used his political career and power to protect himself and his media empire from the law [...]. The Italian left, in particular, has failed to mount an effective opposition. Yet Mr Berlusconi's latest action – the merger into his new People of Freedom bloc [...] of his own Forza Italia party with the Alleanza Nazionale which derives directly from Benito Mussolini's fascist tradition – may leave a more lasting mark on Italian public life than anything else the populist tycoon has done.
>
> Unlike Germany, postwar Italy never properly confronted its own fascist legacy. As a result, while neofascism has never seriously resurfaced in Germany,

in Italy there were important continuities [...]. Those continuities have just become stronger. It is a day of shame for Italy

(The Guardian 2009: 30)

The Italian Ambassador in London protested against this article. In his view – and despite widely accepted evidence – it was generally false that Italy has been unable to cope with its fascist legacy and criticisms towards Berlusconi were mainly based on ideology, because he 'was democratically elected three times' (Aragona 2009: 35).

Thus, there should be a direct legitimization of the leader that comes from the popular will, roughly as a modern monarch is legitimized by a religious divinity. This should prevent others from criticizing the personalization of party politics, the governmental political strategies, the erosion of some basic constitutional rights, the lack of media freedom, the continuous attacks of the judicial system or, given the perceived weakness of the state, the alarming tendency to recognize the need of a 'holy saviour' for Italy's problems.

Studying the *Italia malata*

Italy has also been under the spotlight of the international mass media for quite some time now: its economic decline or the political predicaments united with the flamboyant figure of Berlusconi and the recent 'daily racism' constituted an easy target for a wide array of (foreign) critics. At the same time, some scholarly production focused on some of these themes, with the addition of the always-salient one of Italian organized crime. Such attention has been welcomed and has served the function of unveiling some 'shadows' affecting Italian society, but at the same time it constitutes a constraint to a more holistic approach to the current crisis of the whole country.

Setting aside these few studies, there is, nonetheless, little scholarly literature systematically dedicated specifically to Italy's 'shadows'. On the one hand, traditional studies tend to focus on elections or political actors and systems. On the other hand, after the *tangentopoli* (Bribesville) scandal in the 1990s, operation Clean Hands, and the collapse of the so-called Prima Repubblica (First Republic) and existing party system – due to political corruption, widespread bribes and illegal financing of parties, as well as the 'hubris, excess and venality of its leaders' (Gilbert 1995: 1) – much of the literature focused on the scandals and the political and institutional 'transition' to the Seconda Repubblica (Second Republic). A good example of this is the special edition of *West European Politics* edited by Martin Bull and Martin Rhodes in 1997 and entitled 'Crisis and Transition in Italian Politics',[11] or Routledge's edited volume on *The New Italian Republic* by Stephen Gundle and Simon Parker in 1996. At that time, public expectations were high, and most Italians were optimistic that a new and much better phase in Italy's political history was about to begin. Indeed, *tangentopoli* and the *witch hunt* of 1992–1994 looked like real earthquakes and the only comparable, even if approximate, event seemed to be the fall of France's Fourth Republic which 'occurred in the context of a colonial crisis and potential civil war' (Gundle and Parker 1996: 1). Yet Bull and Rhodes (2007: 659) made it clear that the:

> [A]pparent or real overhaul of parties and political alliances that accompanied the *tangentopoli* corruption scandals was a critical moment to be sure; but in and of itself it could not have resolved the crisis. Rather, it changed the guard – which had been part agent and part victim of the system's problems – and raised the prospect that a new modernising political class might emerge to manage the structural crisis and steward a wider-reaching process of reform.

This alleged transition thus turned into a never-ending process that has led to a general sense of disillusionment. It is now 'fair to speak of a feeling of dashed expectations. The much-vaunted "Second Republic" has clearly not arrived, even if the "First" is apparently clearly no longer with us' (Bull and Rhodes 2007: 660).[12]

In sum, in the early 1990s it seemed that the birth of a new and unstoppable political and ethical renovation was on the horizon, but in reality the 'new politics' never started, or at least not as desired or claimed. In its political scandals the new Republic revealed dangerous continuities with the pre-*tangentopoli* system. The crisis of the early 1990s did not bring a genuine change, and many of Italy's most serious structural and civic–cultural problems remained unsolved. These are the shadows that continue to hang over Italian society (and which obviously have not come from out of the blue).

Some of these shadows were partially highlighted in a comparative study of Italy and Japan edited by Jean-Marie Bouissou and Marc Lazar and published in the *Revue Française de Science Politique* in 2001.[13] Their key idea was that despite different geographical locations and culture, Italy and Japan shared many traits such as political fragmentation, corruption, *clientelismo*, the de-legitimization of ruling elites, popular dissatisfaction with politics and organized crime. The contributors carefully rejected the sort of exceptionalist approaches that would portray the two countries as anomalies or deviations from an idealized model of North American democracy. Instead, they considered Italy and Japan as genuine, fully legitimized and effectively operative political systems (Bouissou and Lazar 2001: 533). Similarly, even if form our standpoint Italy appears to be suffering from a specific 'malaise', we reject a narrow analytical framework or parochial reading of local history. What we do argue is that Italy shows some particular and specific features that can certainly be compared with similar countries, but which nevertheless appear to be incongruous to most other functioning Western democracies.

Particularly scarce also is the Italian academic production on contemporary domestic problems. The ground is indeed left to investigative journalists and that is also the reason why they are here often quoted as primary sources of Italian current affairs. One might even argue that this is in itself a 'dark shadow'. Indeed, one of the greatest shortcomings of public debate in Italy is the very limited contribution of the academic community, and in particular of social scientists.

The result is that these complex problems are often addressed in superficial and rhetorical terms. The academic community might instead have an important role to play in proposing effective solutions and helping policy-makers make informed choices for the several problems that still afflict society, politics, collective memory and the economy.

However, what appears clear is that the whole country for a long time was not aware of its own difficulties and decline. Indeed, even when the current world financial crisis was coming to the fore, many (Italian) politicians instead called for an unclear Italian 'exceptionalism' – and specifically to some economic and financial strengths. Although in the early 1970s a former social-democrat minister had already published a book with the title *Italia malata* (Preti 1972), it is only in the past ten years that the image of a country 'in trouble' and faced by constant difficulties as well as an 'agitated' political history became more recurrent, and book titles frequently refer either to a population of 'discontents' (Ginsborg 2003), or to a 'dark' national 'heart' (Jones 2003), or else suggest that Italy is 'not a normal country' (Andrews 2005) and faces a range of negative legacies (Stella and Rizzo 2008). The word 'decline' has consequently (but confusingly) been at the centre of public debate in both the 2006 and 2008 Italian elections. All parties and candidates acknowledge – often only in a populist and propagandist way – the particular difficulties facing Italy; and in the foreign press Italians were then described as depressed or too worried about the present to think about the future of their country (Owen 2007; Lachman 2006; Singer 2007).

In sum, a remarkable process seems to have occurred in public debate in Italy. First, in the last twenty years, Italian society has experienced a condition that in the case of individuals is known as 'cognitive polyphasia' (Moscovici 1961), that is to say the co-existence of rarely compatible representations. What was generally perceived to be an exceptionally high standard of living co-existed with an awareness that long-term problems and contradictions that have been ignored for a very long time were actually assuming dramatic new proportions and gravity (this produced a variety of Italian paradoxes, including that of having one of the highest turnouts in a general election in Europe and at the same time one of the most chaotic and inefficient political systems in the EU). However, setting aside the non-academic accounts or a general growing 'hostility' towards politicians, in part due to the increasingly wide coverage of political scandals in the Italian press (Cepernich 2008), a systematic public discussion about the most serious of these problems has never really taken place. Indeed, the most frequent reaction has simply been to blame Italy's decline on external factors without taking account of Italy's failure to address the long-term problems that it seems unable to shake (Tremonti 2007).

It is hard to deny the role of global economic and social processes in shaping the fortunes of each nation, and globalization has certainly played a role in the Italian economic crisis. Indeed, Italy's decline is generally analyzed only in economic terms or linked to the incapacity of national capitalism to face the challenges of globalization (see for example Galli 2006; Petrini 2004; Toniolo and Visco 2004). The loss of competitiveness of the Italian industrial system and the below-average growth of the GDP compared with the rest of the EU have also attracted much attention. And for the first time since the flamboyant and 'swinging' (Italian) 1980s and the confused, hectic and uncertain 1990s, an awareness of political, economic and social decline has spread like wildfire as have perceptions of a sudden fall in the quality of life (see Bastasin 2007; Cerruti 2007; D'Argenio 2007; Floris 2007a; Masci 2007).

Globalization should not, nevertheless, account for the wider chronic 'fatigue' that seems to afflict Italian society. Symptomatic of such fatigue is the never-ending story of underdevelopment of Southern Italy. The so called Mezzogiorno has lost centrality in national politics, which are more interested in supporting federalist reforms or, in the case of parliamentary opposition, the re-conquest of the lost 'northern' votes (Mammone 2008). A Mezzogiorno in which the billions of euros provided by the European Union for the period 2007–2013 appears like the very last chance to fill the gap with other EU areas (but only the 36.5 per cent of former financed EU projects have been realized: see also La Spina 2007).

This part of the country is (unfortunately) appearing in the international headlines only for the dramatic rise of its organized mafias. This is the case, for example, of Calabria's virtually unknown (outside Italy) but very powerful *'Ndrangheta* that has become a genuine global illegal enterprise with ramifications in Northern and Continental Europe (see the famous Duisburg's killings in Germany) and Latin America; or the violence and *degrado* developed by the more famous Neapolitan Mafia, namely the Camorra, described in Roberto Saviano's highly acclaimed *Gomorrah*. So, how can we explain the ongoing predicaments of a significant Italian territory still influenced by political corruption, unclear links between mafia and politics, managerial inefficiency, and where, in Sicily, the job of magistrate (a category generally and often criticized by Italy's prime minister) is so unpopular and risky that only four people applied for the 55 unfilled positions?[14] Can we blame this on external factors or globalization, or should we simply believe that organized crime is no longer *the* central problem in contemporary Italy?

In such a context, like the damage produced by the circulation of unrestrained toxins, the old (and new) problems have weakened Italian society's capacity to react to the new challenges posed by global socioeconomic processes as well as to its own internal conflicts.

Beyond Berlusconi

This book aims to provide an overview of the systemic crisis of Italy. The idea behind this volume was to collect a number of studies that would tackle chronic or relatively new critical issues that have been usually scarcely investigated, at least as a whole. Some of them have played an important part in shaping and influencing the construction of contemporary Italian identities, politics and society – and, once more, they can also help to explain the crisis the country is facing.

A quick look at the table of contents shows Silvio Berlusconi as the 'ignored elephant in the room' of this volume. This is in spite of the fact that the rise of this media magnate represents probably the main, and most controversial, change in domestic society since Fascism, and his 'figure' and presence well reflects the current 'drift' of a country with an 'unpredictable' future (Lazar 2006: 142). Indeed, his impact on the Italian peninsula is sharply described as another local anomaly (Stille 2007). Beside the several significant accounts of Berlusconi's biography and rise to power (Ginsborg 2005), it is the explanation of his popularity in contemporary Italy that should also represent another crucial issue. The most acclaimed explanation is that the current Prime Minister is benefiting from a long-term influence on the views of Italians gained through thirty years of mass-media dominance. This is what has been labelled as 'Berlusconismo' – or the invasion of what Perry Anderson (2009b) has rightly defined as 'the cultural counter-revolution of Berlusconi's television empire, saturating the popular imaginary with a tidal wave of the crassest idiocies and fantasies'. According to *The Economist* (2009), for example, Berlusconi's control and ownership of media has 'changed attitudes and even the meaning of words. When he entered politics in 1994, few gave credence to his claim to be a victim of conniving communist judges; now it is widely believed'. Hence, the Berlusconization of Italy and its culture is, in reality, an object of study in itself. On the other hand, to fully understand this phenomenon as well as the 'environment' which allowed its growth, it is equally important to uncover and map the number of unsolved problems that helped to shape what is contemporary Italy.

Thus, by not denying the importance of an analysis of Berlusconi and of Berlusconismo – and with the partial exception of this introductory chapter – *Italy Today* decided to focus on something else to avoid the strong and recurrent temptation to place all of Italy's faults on Berlusconi's shoulders. It is now clear that, to use Lazar's (2006: 138) metaphor, the 'doctor Berlusconi' has not helped to recover this key *malade* of Europe, and one might pertinently wonder if this Mediterranean *sick man* has worsened since his arrival. But, although there are few doubts that Berlusconi's major conflicts of interest and influence might have aggravated some of the dark shadows over the country, many such problems were already part of the Italian social fabric (in this sense, there is no need for a sterile repetition of an already widely studied phenomenon). For example, Berlusconi has often been accused of being more interested in preserving his financial empire than in governing the country. However, to some degree, it was already clear in 1992 that Italy was emerging as a modern 'cleptocracy': 'a state whose leading political figures were running the country into the ground for their own profit' (Gilbert 1995: 5). Assuming Berlusconi's interest is only in his own personal business (Anderson 2009a: 3), would this politician's approach be a new 'phenomenon' or simply an unfortunate repetition of some (recent) historical patterns? Further, Romano Prodi's short-lived and quarrelling centre-left government did not perform any better than previous centre-right executives. Setting aside a few positive results, it did not represent a real break from 'Berlusconistan' – as Italy was recently labelled by some of the foreign media – at least not in people's eyes. To use Alexander Stille's (2008: 59) spiky words:

One of the few things Prodi managed to pass was an amnesty for criminals that had been pushed heavily by Berlusconi and that was designed quite clearly to keep Berlusconi's chief corporate lawyer, Cesare Previti, who had been convicted of bribing judges, out of prison. And so, early in Prodi's tenure, the Italian public watched the unedifying spectacle of 26,000 criminals going free, many of whom returned quickly to stealing, raping, and killing [...].

Similarly, the Prodi government passed another law, again with the enthusiastic help of Berlusconi and the right, to make it illegal for prosecutors to use criminal evidence gathered against members of parliament who turned up on police wiretaps. [...].

Thus an administration that had promised a clean-government alternative to Berlusconi appeared no more willing than its predecessor to take on corruption or the system of patronage or Mafia infiltration of the state. [...].

Disillusioned, many Italian voters concluded that there was little difference between the politicians of the left and the right and that taken together they were simply a corrupt, self-perpetuating 'caste'; not only did its members enjoy extraordinary privileges and absurdly high salaries, they appeared to be not merely useless but a significant drain on public resources as well.

In such a frame, Berlusconi's figure, with all its contradictions and oligarchic tendencies, often diverted the attention from deeper and older issues affecting Italy, a country that has never been an outstanding example of a widespread sense of civic duty and democratic maturity. Similarly, as the cover image of this volume shows, Berlusconi is only a piece of a wider puzzle.

Italy Today: an overview

To summarize, this volume generally represents an example of different methodological frameworks – often cross-disciplinary – applied to the study of social phenomena, organizations, political parties, governments, economic systems, cultures and sub-cultures, and collective memory that are among the key topics in many of the social sciences and the humanities. But, as suggested, the specific rationale behind *Italy Today* is that the Italian decline can be understood only through systematic analysis of some concrete problems – even if for space constraints we left out other critical issues, such as the predicaments of the national health system, the somewhat Jurassic judiciary system, the politicization and violence of some *Serie A* stadiums, or the regrettable *fuga dei cervelli* ('brain drain').

Although far from exhaustive, *Italy Today* tries to offer a wide range of these critical 'shades'. These are divided into macro- and micro-areas whose boundaries are not fixed and therefore the chapters interact with each other. Politics deserve a special mention because it is from there that we are supposed to derive solutions to most of the country's problems – and politics is often the backdrop of the stories told by contributors. Within this context, Roux challenges the use of federalism as a solution for Italy's problems, showing its paradoxes and arguing that it is not a popular demand but rather a process driven by the elite. Political elites and coalitions also often converge in strategies and programmes regardless of their ideological pledges, according to Conti's chapter. In spite of this, Moury argues that the performance of Italian politics is controversial, with a lack of governance. But domestic politics also contains an increasing populist and xenophobic element as well, as illustrated by the example of the Northern League analyzed by Avanza. This somewhat institutional(-ized) racism is an element that is recurrent in the recent debate about Roma and Sinti communities as argued by Sigona, and also, as Garau suggests, in the controversial approach of some of the Catholic Church.

Collective memory and the reconstruction of national history play a fundamental role in contemporary times. Cento Bull argues that the country's inability to successfully complete the transition from the First to the Second Republic and renew its political institutions is, at least in part, due to the country's failure to deal with its problematic legacy of (terrorist) conflicts and ideological confrontation of the 1960s and 1970s. Another example of unsolved conflicts in collective memory is Fascism, and Joshua Arthurs' contribution examines the presence of the Fascist past in Italy through the lens of the built environment, focusing on the case of the Foro Italico in Rome.

If politics and collective memories look problematic, society appears equally affected by a certain 'illness'. In general, Carboni argues, the ruling elite are more and more mistrusted and a democratic 'malaise' is affecting Italian society: this is consequently leading to a widespread pessimism and cynicism that creates a vicious cycle. As such, the Italian public sphere is not only influenced by some ineffective leading elites, but is also shaped a by a bizarre mass media system with a peculiar 'history' that goes beyond Berlusconi and that is here analyzed by Hanretty. Similarly, the public sphere along with policies, social structures and people's every day lives, are also strongly influenced by the powerful presence of the Vatican, as highlighted in Bernini's chapter.

When talking about politics and society, it would be impossible to overlook the never-ending troubles of Southern Italy. The focus in *Italy Today* is on the most dramatic presence of organized crime, but also on the missed opportunity of economic development. The Allums, for example, give a detailed historical account of the rise and fall of 'hopes' following the election of Antonio Bassolino as the mayor of Naples: the reality is that not a lot has changed and crime and 'clientelism' has gained strength. Linked to this, this volume offers one of the few accounts of what Italian police consider as the dominant Mafia, namely the *'Ndrangheta* from Calabria. Parini analyzes its structure and its ability to forge alliances with corrupt politics, economies and various professions.

The troubles of economic development of Southern Italy are also crucial in two other chapters. Iona, Leonida and Sobbrio show that the Italian economy has 'two long-run equilibriums', which are essentially due to the different level of industrialization between the regions located in the centre-north with respect to those located in the Southern regions. On the other hand, Milio's contribution focuses on the use of European Union structural funds and shows the significant differences between Italian regions in their implementation. However, the analysis of economy is not confined to the Mezzogiorno. Simoni, for instance, offers an analysis of the alliance between the centre-left and organized labour (in order to gain a wider popular consensus on hard-to-swallow economic reforms). However, the increased segmentation of the labour market, which resulted from economic restructuring, played against its main actors. Finally, Minetti focuses on another traditional feature of capitalism Italian-style, notably its family dimension. In the past this was regarded as a successful model of corporate organization, but it now seems unable to face mounting global competition.

Many of these contributions share the common theme of a sense of *incompletezza* that affects Italy, of the lack of planning, of the general tendency of starting and never finishing important reforms and changes, and, in general, of a country which has become the 'sick man of Europe'.

Notes

1 We wish to thank Dr Imogen Long for her help with copy editing this chapter.
2 Please note the mistake with the pronunciation of the word 'Afghanistan'.
3 For the interview see: www.youtube.com/watch?v=R0x-fmqSXms.
4 Stille (2008: 59) recently summarized the state of art of the peninsula, which is perceived as 'deeply at odds with itself, paralyzed and dysfunctional, angry, fearful, intensely dissatisfied but unwilling to undertake any changes that threaten the fragile privileges of this or that protected group. It is a country that is sick of high taxes but sits by when Berlusconi blocks the sale of the national airline, Alitalia, even though it is hemorrhaging taxpayer money; a country that hates government but expects free education and free health care and takes advantages of the opportunities of a vast government patronage system; a country that clings to its high standard of living and generous welfare state but fantasizes about kicking out millions of foreign workers who now produce close to 10 percent of the gross domestic product and whose presence in the workforce is the only realistic hope for maintaining a national pension system for Italy's aging population.'
5 Marc Lazar, a well-known French scholar, in his recent pamphlet *L'Italie à la dérive* (2006), by looking at Berlusconi's phenomenon, further develops this concept of Italy as a 'laboratory' for other European democracies and societies.
6 The recent exception of an interesting special edition of the geo-political magazine *Limes* ('Esiste l'Italia? Dipende da noi', No. 2, 2009) on some national critical features, cannot yet represent a change of this 'silent' trend.
7 In any case, it is an almost ironic fact that Berlusconi, the media mogul, after the NATO Summit of Heads of State and Government (3–4 April 2009) accused some Italian journalists of being 'enemies of Italy'. Berlusconi considered himself as 'working' for Italy, while these journalists were allegedly working 'against Italy', and as he argued, 'I do not talk with people which work against Italy' (Luzi 2009: 6). This was for the excessive light given to his gaffes rather than to his international achievements. The prime minister added that he was tempted to adopt 'strong measures' against some members of the press (Luzi 2009: 6). Criticisms are also made to the foreign media, at times accused of being influenced or manipulated by the (Italian) left and communists.
8 Before the 2008 election when a journalist asked Ciarrapico why there were pictures of the Duce all over the walls in his newspapers' quarters, he simply replied: 'Bellissimo' (Caporale 2008). Mussolini similarly argued that she is 'with pride on the wrong

side' (Schianchi 2008: 10). This 'wrong side' meant Fascism and the Italian Social Republic.

9 *The Economist* on 28 May 2009 aptly headed: *Rome v Roma*; Alfredo Guardiano, a Neapolitan judge, suggested how the burning of Roma's camps might metaphorically represents the burning of the whole legal system (Guardiano 2009). In general, the Roma issue created controversies with both the EU and countries such as Spain which criticized Italy (Caprara 2008).

10 On the website of the *Azione Sociale* it is possible to download the program of Berlusconi's Popolo della Libertà as well as the list of the 113 delegates that represented Mussolini's extreme-right movement at the PDL founding congress. For the full list see: www.azionesociale.net/index.php?option=com_content&task=view &id=1011&Itemid=1.

11 It is worth noting that before this 1997 contribution, the last special issue of *West European Politics* entirely devoted to Italian politics only harked back to 1979; and, ironically, it similarly referred to 'Italy in Transition' (Lange 1979).

12 A similar view on the relative failure of this 'transition' is also embodied in Gundle and Parker (1996: 15). Ten years later, Bull and Rhodes argued that Italy was then dealing with 'a post-crisis process of institutional (re-)stabilisation and negotiated change in which the 'new' (or at least substantial parts of it) looks remarkably similar to the "old"'(Bull and Rhodes 2007: 662).

13 In late 2008, Lazar edited another interesting special edition ('Italie: la présence du passé') of the journal *Vingtième Siècle* which focused on some Italian historical developments, culture, and a few critical features. This was also to provide French readers with the latest developments on Italy and its historiography.

14 On this (in English) see also Kingston 2009.

Bibliography

Anderson, P. (2009a) 'An entire order converted into what it was intended to end', *London Review of Books*, 31(4): 3–8.

—— (2009b) 'An invertebrate left', *London Review of Books*, 31(5). Online. Available: www.lrb.co.uk/v31/n05/ande01_.html.

Andrews, G. (2005) *Not a Normal Country: Italy after Berlusconi*, London: Pluto Press.

Aragona, G. (2009) 'Antifascism guides Italian political life', *The Guardian*, 31 March.

Bastasin, C. (2007) 'L'anno della fiducia. Gli Italiani non credono nelle potenzialità del loro Paese', *La Stampa*, 31 December.

Bouissou, J.-M. and Lazar, M. (2001) 'Comparer deux "démocraties hors norms"', special edition: 'Italie et Japon aujourd'hui: deux "démocraties hors norms" à l'épreuve de la crise', *Revue Française de Science Politique*, 51(4): 531–43.

Bull, M. and Rhodes, M. (2007) 'Introduction – Italy: a contested polity', special edition: 'Italy: A Contested Polity', *West European Politics*, 30(4): 657–69.

Caporale, A. (2008) 'Ciarrapico: "Io con Silvio ma resto sempre fascista"', *La Repubblica*, 10 March. Online. Available: www.repubblica.it/2008/03/sezioni/politica/verso-elezioni-9/ciarrapico-fascista/ciarrapico-fascista.html

Caprara, M. (2008) 'E il caso Rom arriva all'Europarlamento', *Corriere della Sera*, 20 May.

Carlucci, D. and Castaldo, A. (2009) *Un paese di baroni. Truffe, favori, abusi di potere. Logge segrete e criminalità organizzata. Come funziona l'università italiana*, Milan: Chiarelettere.

Cepernich, C. (2008) 'Landscapes of immorality: scandals in the Italian press (1986–2006)', *Perspectives on European Politics and Society*, 9(1): 95–109.

Cerruti, G. (2007) 'Una Milano da sberle. Dagli appalti truccati ai manager incompetenti', *La Repubblica*, 16 May.

D'Argenio, A. (2007) 'Italia ventunesima in Europa', *La Repubblica*, 27 February.

De Zulueta, T. (2009) 'A cruel end for Italy's asylum-seekers', *Guardian.co.uk*, 16 May. Online. Available: www.guardian.co.uk/commentisfree/2009/may/16/italy-asylum-seekers-berlusconi

Duggan, C. (2008) *The force of Destiny. A History of Italy since 1796,* London: Penguin.

Editorial. (2009) 'Fascism's shadow', *The Guardian*, 30 March.

Floris, G. (2007a*) Mal di merito. L'epidemia di raccomandazioni che paralizza l'Italia*, Milan: Rizzoli.

—— (2007b) '"Ecco l'Italia dei raccomandati"', *La Stampa*, 4 November.

Galli, G. (2006) *Poteri deboli. La nuova mappa del capitalismo nell'Italia del declino*, Milan: Mondadori.

Gilbert, M (1995) *The Italian Revolution: The End of Politics, Italian Style?*, Boulder, CO: Westview Press.

Ginsborg, P. (2003) *Italy and Its Discontents. Family, Civil Society, State. 1980–2001*, London: Penguin.

—— (2005) *Silvio Berlusconi: Television, Power and Patrimony*, London: Verso.

Ruotola, G. (2009) 'Accuse all'Onu, bufera su La Russa', *La Stampa*, 19 May.

Guardiano, A. (2008) 'Con i roghi nei campi rom anche il diritto rischia di andare a fuoco', *Corriere del Mezzogiorno*, 20 May.

Gundle, S. and Parker, S. (eds.) (1996) *The New Italian Republic. From the Fall of the Berlin Wall to Berlusconi,* London: Routledge.

Iezzi, L. (2009) 'L'Italia che non premia il merito ci costa 2.500 euro a persona', *La Repubblica*, 18 April.

Jones, T. (2003) *The Dark Heart of Italy: Travels Through Time and Space Across Italy*, London: Faber and Faber.

Kington, T. (2009) 'Mafia-hunter who needs protection to visit his office coffee machine', *The Observer*, 29 March.

Lachman, D. (2006) 'Italy Follows Argentina Down Road to Ruin', *Financial Times*, 16 March.

Lange, P. (ed.) (1979) 'Italy in Transition: Conflict and Consensus', *West European Politics*, 2(3).

La Spina, L. (2007) 'È a Bruxelles la capitale del Sud. Un fiume di soldi dall'Europa al Meridione: 100 miliardi in 7 anni', *La Stampa*, 4 May.

Lazar, M. (1997) 'Introduction: Comprendre l'Italie politique', in I. Diamanti and M. Lazar (eds.) *Politique à l'Italienne*, Paris: Presses Universitaries de France.

—— (2006) *L'Italie à la dérive. Le moment Berlusconi*, Paris: Perrin.

Luzi, G. (2009) 'Berlusconi minaccia la stampa', *La Repubblica*, 5 April.

Mammone, A. (2006) 'A daily revision of the past. Fascism, anti-fascism, and memory in contemporary Italy', *Modern Italy*, 11(2): 211–26.

—— (2008) 'Il "malessere" del Sud e la Calabria dimenticata', *Il Ponte*, LXIV(10): 35–8.

—— (2009) 'The reality of racism in modern Italy', *Tribune*, 73(11): 14–5.

—— and Veltri, G. (2007) 'La memoria daltonica del fascismo', *Il Ponte,* 62(3): 89–97.

Martini, E. (2009) 'La scuola dei G2', *Il Manifesto*, 24 March.

Masci, R. (2007) 'Al Nord-Est la scuola migliore. Il rapporto Ocse: solo lì si supera la media europea. Allarme Italia: uno su due non capisce quello che legge', *La Stampa*, 5 December.

Minello, B. (2009) 'D'Alema striglia Chiamparino. Dario lo consola', *La Stampa*, 19 May.

Moscovici, S. (1961) *La psychonalyse son image et son public*, Paris: Presses Universitaires de France.

Owen, R. (2007) 'La dolce vita turns sour as Italy faces up to being old and poor', *The Times*, 22 December.

—— (2009) 'Silvio Berlusconi under fire over anti-immigration remarks', *Times Online*, 10 May. Online. Available: www.timesonline.co.uk/tol/news/world/europe/article6261408.ece.

Petrini, R. (2004) *Il declino dell'Italia*, Rome-Bari: Laterza.

Preti, L. (1972) *Italia malata*, Milan: Mursia.

Scianchi, F. (2008) 'Figli contro padri. È guerra dentro An', *La Stampa*, 18 September.

Singer, P. (2007) 'In a funk, Italy sings an aria of disappointment', *The New York Times*, 13 December.

Stella, G. A. and Rizzo, S. (2008) *La Deriva. Perche' l'Italia sta naufragando*, Milan: Rizzoli.

(2009) 'The Berlusconisation of Italy', *The Economist*, 30 April. Online. Available: www.economist.com/world/europe/displayStory.cfm?story_id=13576329.

Stille, A. (2007) *The Sack of Rome*: *Media + Money + Celebrity = Power = Silvio Berlusconi*, London: Penguin.

—— (2008) 'Italy Against Itself', *New York Review of Books*, LV(19): 59–62

Toniolo, G. and Visco, V. (2004) *Il Declino economico dell'Italia*, Milan: Bruno Mondadori.

Tremonti, G. (2007) *La paura e la speranza*, Milan: Mondadori.

Part I
Politics and society

2 Elites and the democratic disease

Carlo Carboni

Summary

This chapter takes into account not only the Italian economic decline but also its democratic malaise. Obviously, this democratic malaise is connected to the reciprocal mistrust that exists between the mass of people and the few elites. It is also linked to a social disease that mediatized, professionalized and financed politics has difficulty in interpreting as a crisis of Italian social democracy. We place this democratic malaise right in the centre which attacks an affluent society like Italy and invades its political, social, cultural and economic dimensions. It is a malaise whose causes are related to representative and pluralistic democracy (such as the leading classes) on the supply side as well as the social demand side. At present, we have an Italy that is dominated by cynicism and mistrust, and pessimism amplified by the strategy of fear and (later) by the financial crisis. This is certainly not a good starting point. Italians should give greater importance to what is positive both in the society as well as in the ruling classes. Above all, they should have the strength to change, especially in Southern Italy, in order to find the spirit of national community once again. A ruling class should be one that leads by example of merit and responsibility, capable of making decisions and with a vision of the future.

Introduction: democratic malaise

Complex and slippery concepts like the ones concerning the elite and society are talked about in a very casual way. For instance, the term *elite* is ordinarily substituted with 'leading class', establishment, ruling class, political class or dominating class, terms that are very similar to each other but not the same, as Aristotle would have observed. Society has become 'liquid' in Bauman's (2000) perspective or has actually 'disappeared', as reported in a recent book by Touraine (2004). Thus, there is the need to have more analytical information on the elite and society and prepare case studies, like the Italian case, which is always peculiar and in ferment. Italy is one of the European countries that is endowed with its own ambiguous personality having roots in its historical leading role in the 'Old World'. Indeed, it was sometimes a cynical country; in other words, a nation that has been strong and harsh with the weak but not with the powerful. On the other hand, it has been also a *civic* nation because of its kindness and hospitality and, especially because of its lifestyle in its main cities of art.

This chapter is divided into two parts. The first part focuses on the Italian elites, whereas the second part is an outline of the continuing social mutation, as 'seen from above'. The theme that connects these two parts is a set of theses and hypotheses that I present in the next paragraphs (Carboni 2007a and 2008a).

The Italian elites mirror the society: the former being self-referential, the latter, cynical; both of them male chauvinists, aged and provincial. Italy is a country without great economic and financial centers, but it is also without any real political-social hegemonies where rules are gotten around or broken and where they are never abreast of the ongoing changes in the country and around the world. It is a nation where the state has always struggled on the grounds of credibility and reliability and where general interest has always been crowded out by specific, territorial or categorical interests, whatever they may be. Italy is also a Nation of co-optations, shortcuts and various 'wise guys of the neighborhood'[1] where the country's semi-modernization and indecisiveness of the elites have laid the path for the penetration of the occult and Mafia forces. This fact cannot be hidden or forgotten.

In the Italian context, the phenomenon of separation of public life from private life has matured just as in other developed democratic and economic societies. The lack of a new link between these two spheres has brought forth a prevalent idea of public life as a mere function of private and individual interests. The part of the Italian society which functions and which has modernized itself, at both ruling class and active and competent citizenry levels, remains a minority.

All this leads us to consider first a relative decline of national economy which has grown at less than one-third of the EU economy in the past eight years (Nardozzi 2004), and second a *democratic malaise* that can be observed from three negative trends in the past 25 years: political party members; reliability rate on main institutions; falling trend in the voter turnout rate (IDEA 2008).

Obviously, this democratic malaise is connected to the reciprocal mistrust that exists between the mass of people and the few elite. It is also linked to a social disease that mediatized, professionalized and financed politics has difficulty in interpreting as a crisis of our social democracy. We do not have just a simple representative institutional democracy, but whether one likes it or not, we also have a social democracy, which is a product of institutionalization of individual spheres of life in the context of a model of *social capitalism* that has long been followed by the European nations and now by the EU. I would place this democratic malaise right in the centre which attacks an affluent society like Italy and invades its political, social, cultural and economic dimensions. It is a malaise whose causes are related to representative and pluralistic democracy (such as the leading classes) on the supply side as well as on the social demand side.

Are the best in power?

Who runs and governs Italy? Who are the Italian elites? There have not been many empirical studies on Italian elites before I conducted research in 2004 on more than 5,500 famous and powerful personalities in Italy (Carboni 2007a).[2] Let us consider some main characteristics of the elites that have emerged out of of this research.

Italian elites are of 'one gender' only. There is an accentuated male dominance in our elite: almost nine out of ten (88 per cent) are men. In the past 15 years, women have gone up in number very slowly: famous and powerful women moved from 8 per cent in 1990 to 9 per cent in 1998 and to 12 per cent in 2004. Women are younger than men. They are mostly present in show business and café society and are a little less educated. A recent survey on the fame of national leaders of Europe shows that the importance of Italian female personalities (17.2 per cent) is close only to that of the 'pink' Spanish power (19.6 per cent), which is definitely less than that of the British leaders (43.3 per cent) and the French leaders (36.4 per cent) (Carboni 2008b: 76–83).

Italian elites are 'gerontocratic'. They are, on average, sixty years old, and the trend shows that they are getting older at a constant pace (Figure 2.1). In fact, in about fifteen years, the average age of the famous and powerful personalities in Italy has gone up by about four years: from 56.8 years in 1990 to 58.8 in 1998, and reaching 60.8 in 2004. These data reinforce the impression that we are facing a ruling class that is characterized by a low capability of generational change. In comparative terms, in Europe, leaders are older in Italy (with an average age of 69.4 years) and in Germany (68.2 years) compared to the UK (64.8 years) and Spain (65 years) (Luiss Report 2008: 72–5).

Italian elites are 'provincial'. The past fifteen years have brought about a change in a ruling class that is definitely more educated than it was in the past: only two out of three (66 per cent) famous and powerful personalities were university graduates in 1990, this rose to 78 per cent in 1998. In mid-2000, this percentage came close to almost 90 per cent. However, the curricula of our top

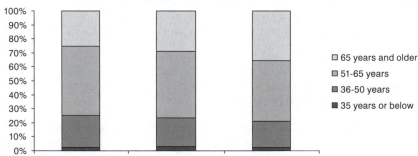

Elites by age classes (%)

1990 (mean age 56.8) 1998 (mean age 58.8) 2004 (mean age 60.8)

□ 65 years and older
▨ 51-65 years
▪ 36-50 years
■ 35 years or below

Figure 2.1 The aged Italian elite

leaders seem to be limited in terms of studies or work done abroad (less than one-third of the elite).

Entrepreneurial leadership stands out among the Italian elites. Analysis by sector of origin shows that the majority of the Italian elite (42 per cent) belong to a professional and cultural domain; 26.3 per cent of them belong to the political-institutional domain, 18 per cent to the economic domain and 14 per cent to sports and show business. These data show that the changes that have occurred in the Italian society in the past 15 years or so have also transformed the structure of the top of the ruling classes and their ways of accessing power. In fact, if in the early 1990s access to power came about especially through the narrow door of economic wealth; in the past ten years, prestige seems to have been gained mainly by possessing intangible elements such as professional and cultural-communicative skills and knowledge. However, in Italy, in comparative terms, there is a very significant incidence of entrepreneurs and managers in the most limited component, which is second (22 per cent) only to the one corresponding to Germany (26 per cent; while the UK is 15 per cent) (LUISS Report 2008).

Italian elites are strong in agreement but weak in competence. An analysis of professions leads us to point out that the growth of new cultural-professional vocations are preferred to the most traditional ones, and the presence of managers, and engineers or people with a technical expertise (*tecnici*) remains low.

Italian elites are central-northerners and metropolitan. The geography of power in Italy shows a strong correlation between the territorial distribution of places of birth and the residence of famous and influential people and the most general distribution of economic wealth and social wellbeing in Italian society. As a consequence, Southern Italy (the Mezzogiorno) shows a large lag in terms of contribution to national elites, more than all the other macro-areas of Italy. In addition, power is essentially a metropolitan phenomenon. At the national level, Rome and Milan play a central and growing role in the morphology of Italian power and they represent the two main 'poles of attraction' of the elites.

Italian elites are ubiquitous and they are almost always the same ones. Apart from their omnipresence, which is characterized by their continual conflicting interests, one of the salient features of the Italian elite is their duration and stability in the past few years: two-thirds of the powerful and famous personalities that were present in our 2004 research were there even in 1998, constituting a relatively wide nucleus of personalities who have consolidated the foundation of their power over the course of time.

Decision, merit and sense of responsibility: between desire and reality of the Italian elites

Our more recent research (Carboni 2007b and 2008b) has been focusing on the reputation of the elites in the population and of some Italian leading classes. Our interviews have raised some interesting results. The first one is the differences between the ruling class that Italians would like to have and the one they actually have. According to 88.6 per cent of the population, the ideal leading class is supposed to have foresight and decision-making capabilities. They should be chosen on the basis of their merit and competence (92.7 per cent) and should demonstrate a sense of responsibility and transparency (89.8 per cent). On the contrary, the Italian ruling class, according to Italians, has long been affected by indecision. It has been chosen on the basis of its economic wealth (68 per cent) and good relations (54.2 per cent), regardless of merit. Merit, which does not distinguish the ruling class, is considered an important criterion for the nation – a good medicine for its malaise. But it also creates a kind of embarrassment when it is applied to oneself. In that case, one starts to reason that merit is an abstract concept (56 per cent of the Italian population) and that everyone follows his or her own interests starting from the ruling classes (80.6 per cent).

However, Italians recognize merit and innovative capabilities in the entrepreneurial and professional world (51.6 per cent), in the school system (49.6 per cent) and in culture. The group most responsible for Italian evils are politicians (78.5 per cent), especially national ones. These, together with civil servants, are seen as a way of gaining social status without merit or capacity for innovation. However, according to 84 per cent of the Italian population, politicians are also considered fundamental for pulling the country towards a revival, especially at this time when we are undergoing a fiasco in the stock market. As such, there is a need for a different and better politics rather than anti-politics.

This kind of ruling class chose to support special interests, rather than to lead and rule generally. As a self-referential elite, it has taken care to preserve the mechanisms of patronage. The fact that it was not able to lead can be seen from the insufficient maintenance of Italian human and social capital, or from the incapacity to establish an economic and industrial policy, starting from the peculiarity of the Italian economic structure. It can also be seen from the undeserved incomes that come from the welfare system and from the 'outcomes' of patronage policies.

Italian elites struggle with the idea that globalization would first require a cancellation of these 'incomes' and other privileges. They do not face this so that the complicated mechanisms of political patronage and favouritism can remain intact. The narrow political classes do not make decisions that will last, instead surrounding themselves with and co-opting those who are loyal rather than those who are deserving. Thus, there is a problem of renewal of the elites and of their being persistent with 'traditional aggregates' (i.e. the tendency of traditions to self-preservation) as affirmed by Vilfredo Pareto (1916). In many cases, for example in the political-institutional class, there is a lack of transparency, competition and merit – fundamental ingredients *of* and *for* social mobility, and especially of the ruling class.

It is true that we seem to be sailing towards private life and individualism which is often cynical, but it is also true that there is a great disenchantment towards public life, managed by a professional political class that is self-referential and fleeting in its decisions. In brief, the Second Republic has been a period of broken promises and great disillusion. Italians are paying off years of unfulfilled promises. The mistrust of the Italians towards their main institutions has increased. This same feeling is also shared by other European countries, but is more pronounced in Italy due to the specific political crisis as well as to the general economic decline (Table 2.1).

What is Italian citizenry doing for the quality of its democracy?

Plato said that to better appreciate the quality of democracy, check if the best are in power and if the citizenry gives its attention and energy for the public good. I would like further examine the second part of the matter – as did J.F. Kennedy – of Plato's idea. What does the citizenry do for the quality of its democracy? How has the social demand changed in comparison with the political institutions? Italian society is not at all liquefied - to use Bauman's definition (see Bauman, 2000) - for the weakening of social ties. The traditional collectivistic structures have become weak but their decline has not left us with a completely jumbled and elusive social scenario.

The civil society has not disappeared, but it has changed. In particular, several organizations, associations and the intermediate groups between society and democratic institutions, become weaker. Marxist philosopher Antonio Gramsci (1973) considered such social entities as an important collective framework for industrial democracy: however, today these intermediate groups have been transformed by the mechanisms of delegation of powers and representation (i.e. professionalization, personalization and mediatization).

Thus the Italian society has been affected by several changes, and one needs to observe it in both its socio-economic morphology and in its civic sense as well in its territorial disparities.

In terms of social stratification or socio-economic morphology, the principal transformations, in addition to those already manifested in the world of work (i.e. flexible job contracts and a considerable increase in freelancers), are:

- A progressive loss of income and wealth by the 40 per cent less affluent Italian families, 'compensated' by a consistent increase in income and wealth held by 20 per cent of the more affluent Italian families;[3]
- A crisis in the traditional middle class as an effect of the increase in the aforementioned inequality. Middle class employees are the ones that are most distressed;
- The return of the importance of the economy is bringing work back to the centre of changes, even if the study of cultural *habitus*, lifestyles and consumption remains essential in social stratification, especially now that society is in the danger of becoming a market accessory.

With regard to the civic domain, individual values do not always go along with collective moral ones, as the latter are always more fleeting. Even the Italian society that has long been *familistic*, is now becoming a 'society of individuals' whose values often have difficulties adapting themselves to moral ones. In Italy, this individualization is often experienced with a 'sense of guilt' (towards the family, party, civil commitment) that, instead of taking an individual on the path of emancipation, makes him fall back on the short-sighted security of amoral

Table 2.1 Trust in institutions by population in seven European countries (2006–2007) (%)

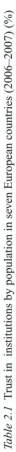

	France		Germany		Italy		Poland		Spain		Sweden		United Kingdom		EU	EU 25 2006
	2007	Change 2067–2007 %	2007	Change 2006–2007 %	2007	Change 2006–2007 %	2007	Change 2006–2007 %	2007	Change 2006–2007 %	2007	Change 2006–2007 %	2007	Change 2006–2007 %	EU 27 2007	
European Union	51	+11	56	+18	58	+10	68	+10	65	+13	56	+18	36	+10	57	45
European Central Bank	40	+3	65	+5	52	+12	50	+10	55	+13	60	+1	30	+3	53	46
EU Parliament	54	+4	58	+4	60	+4	60	+1	58	+7	58	0	33	+8	56	52
National Parliament	44	+17	51	+20	39	+8	15	+4	52	+15	70	+9	41	+12	43	33
National Government	36	+12	49	+22	37	+8	18	+3	52	+12	55	+9	34	+10	41	30
Press	53	0	45	+3	46	+7	42	-3	59	+2	35	-6	18	-1	47	44
Radio	63	0	69	+3	58	+9	62	0	67	0	80	0	62	0	66	63
TV	44	+4	62	+6	47	+6	57	+4	56	+6	68	-1	51	-3	58	53
Internet	36	+4	33	+4	41	+6	42	+10	43	+2	33	+1	32	+2	39	35

Source: Author's calculation on Eurobarometer (2006, 2007), Nos. 66 and 67

and cynical individualism and, with disenchantment and disinterest, leads him to appoint a body of professionalized politicians in political intermediation (and in *nepotistic shortcuts*). This position of indifference towards public life seems strongly related to the liberal one that gives an increasing importance to independence of private life: a community of individuals who are intent on, and absorbed by, exercising their own autonomy; Émile Durkheim's 'democracy without consensus' and the 'passive loyalty' of the Frankfurt School (from Theodore Adorno to Jurgen Habermas).

What has just been mentioned above gives an understated description of the society in many respects. It is functional with a concept of *minimum democracy* as defined by Colin Crouch. Developed market societies have almost abandoned the idea of a real democracy that provides for a responsible participation of the citizens and of their associations in order to make public decisions and choices. What prevails is minimum democracy which is marked by a gap between politics and the citizenry (Crouch 2004).

Finally, there is the aspect of territorial dimension, important in an Italy that is trying to regain an awareness of national community in a fiscal federalism that will not hesitate to point out the economic-financial fragility of the southern regions (except for the GDP produced by the criminal organizations). As both Avanza and Roux underline in this volume, Umberto Bossi's Northern League party, particularly, insists on a federalist perspective that would grant them a crucial role in Northern Italy. It should be highlighted that the local and municipal dimension has continued to play a decisive role for many centuries. Also in Italy, in the past fifty years, local economic development of industrial and tourist districts, especially in central-north-east Italy, has turned out to be crucial for the socio-economic affluence of the entire nation (Bagnasco 1988; Trigilia 2005; Carboni 2009). The gathering of a political consensus takes place through the circulatory system of the local district. The local district is so important that it has been able to split a European country like Italy, if not in three, at least in two very different societies in terms of regulatory systems. The North has already been living with global integration at an economic and social level. It is going through the pangs of the market. In some respects, this is also true for Central Italy. On the contrary, Southern Italy is mainly regulated by a patronage political market, which has always focused on 'familism' and localism. Integration at an international level takes place more in the criminal market than on the institutionally recognized market (see in this volume the chapters by the Allums and Parini).

A bird's eye view of the society

Picturing the society from a socio-political scenario is, however, quite different. In our case, the scenario has been 'infected' by our latest research on the Italian ruling classes.[4] The picture, in a certain sense, is upside down. In fact, it is a bird's eye view of the society, an approach that was developed by Charles Wright Mills. The picture that it represents is similar to a flying disc whose command module is at the centre, raised, or at the top of six important circles that descend from the top.

The scenario represents concentric circles, starting from the smallest and central ones, i.e. narrow circles of the elites, to the wider ones of the 'mass society'.

In the first circle, the smallest one, there are around 2,000 leaders that represent big institutions and economic, political, cultural and professional associations (Figure 2.2). The leading players who have a penchant for leadership (fame and charisma) are entrepreneurs, opinion makers, the clergy, national and European parliamentarians. Their image is greatly mediatized.

The first circle forms part of a second wider and lower circle made up of 6,000 excellent leading players whose strength lies in creating top organizational resources. If the first circle is made up of 'lions', the second one is made up of 'foxes' at the top of the trust-based systems of the country. This is the circle of the leading elite on whom all decisions are dependent, including the decision to 'make the ruling class', i.e. they function as a guide to the whole nation also at a moral level. It is the decisive circle within which the transversal equilibrium of the elite is created and broken, within which top level agreements and pacts are made and erased.

The third circle is made up of 17,000 people. It includes policy-making elites and territorial elites, who, different from the aforementioned elites, are vision bearers and those who hold resources and partial, sectorial and corporate competences. There is the public ruling class, which is mainly political-administrative, as well as the geographical distribution of Italian local/regional power. This circle is also 'extendable', in the sense that lowering the threshold of our selective criteria, more than 50,000 individuals could be included.

The fourth circle numbers around two and a half million individuals and possibly their family members. The circle includes the bourgeoisie class, the only class that has perhaps survived the old classist and industrial social order. This class in itself mobilizes between five and six million Italians and benefits from

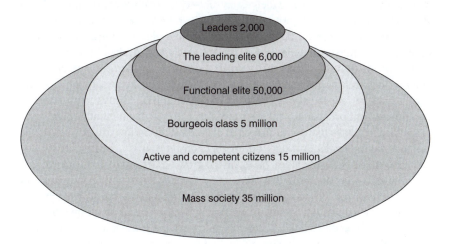

Figure 2.2 A bird's eye view of the Italian society

40 per cent of the national wealth. As a result, it has notably and surprisingly become wider in the past twenty-five years. At least one million professionals have become part of the traditional bourgeois sector and there has also been an increase in 'intellectual professions'. However, this class is always hit by strong conflicting interests and, as such, it is made up of many weaknesses (capitalism without capital in a country without real hegemonies).

In the fifth concentric circle, there is an area that is always very decisive in terms of the socio-political fate of Italy: the competent citizenry, the potential tank for replacing the ruling class. They are about 15 million people who have higher levels of education, who obtain information from newspapers and TV, read books, use the Internet and, in some cases, volunteer. Above all, they are interested in politics even when the elections are not near (but more so when they are). This class being middle, intellectual and autonomous is a kind of middle-class citizenship; it is the most modern part of the society. The competent citizenry is made up of the highest aggregate of significant values, connected to the development of the autonomy of individual choice. It asks for more participation and for institutional policy reforms, such as less waste and irrationality, and for more moderation and severity. It considers democracy not only in its representative form of socio-economic interests, but above all in its professional and rational dimension. It is a crucial sector that aims at sharing a change that, above all, concerns self-reform of the institutional and political system. If we need to start filling civic 'emptiness', this is the audience to which the political class should first turn.

In the sixth circle is the majority of the citizenry, which is the large body of the Italian society. It is a network of relationships that is still an orphan of the old society of the industrial mass even though it is gaining new values and new socio-cultural aggregations. The remaining Italian society is gravitating towards it. We have already talked about the unstable morphology of this majority, of this area of passive loyalty that widely represents conservativeness of the Right and the Left. It is a social majority that is blocked by low mobility that is reaching out and asking for greater flexibility. It has become old, 'sectionalistic' and often corporative. It mirrors the majority of our ruling classes. At the same level, it is an orphan of the three big pacts that marked the growth of the economy and of the country: between politics and economy, between the political and public system and, lastly, the 'consociationalism pact' (Rebuffa 2007). Always more plural, its social stratification is complex, with areas of extreme socio-cultural lags. It is a circle that coincides more with an area of disinterestedness towards politics. A third of them are interested in it only during election time. It is a mass society whose resistance to a system of values, based on the growing decision-making capabilities and new individual opportunities, takes on the wrong path of amoral individualism. The society is just an accessory to the market. While waiting to establish and promote new values of a society of knowledge and of equal opportunities, in the absence of leadership, Italian society is going off the track towards a traditional individualism that is often riotous when facing change. This naturally mirrors the egoistic and cynical self-reference of the same Italian (ruling) elites. These cultural lags of our society have essentially been encouraged by the Left that is deprived of old social blocks and of class party,[5] and by the Right which is an orphan of the traditional family (see also Bernini's chapter here).[6] In fact, it hides the attention given to growth in individual autonomy and freedom, and as a result, care towards maintaining good human and social capital was overlooked – factors that were important for economic growth and social development.[7] In brief, it is hard for our mass society to take the right path. Therefore, the strength to turn around will not come from below, from the pressure exerted by the majority, but it will eventually be determined by the competent citizenry minority that we mentioned before.

Cynic or civic

When the great social movements became rare, the same mass society, in its economic and social affluence, streamed into 'singularization' (individualization), into its legitimate representation (representative democracy), into its mediatization, transfused in public opinion. Among the debris of old collectivism, two correlated social phenomena made their way: a social fragmentation and atomization (the society of individuals) and a more distinct division between the public and private sector. This division has created distance between the governed and the governing – between freedom and authority – and it has been filled and substituted by public opinion that broadcasts the life and activities of the political class and of the elite with great media exposure.[8] With the advent of commercial media and information communication technology (ICT), the processes of social integration and control reposition themselves on the individuals, on the mediatized processes of individual differentiation. There is not just a mediatized policy (see Hanretty's chapter), but there is also an educated and mediatized society. The country's training flows through the controversial labyrinths of the media (television as a collective mind) and through the education system (requiring maintenance), which, in recent years, has released a mostly educated mass (accessories to the market) trapped in the autonomy of the private sector/life, where cynical behaviour and amoral individualism in its disillusion has grown. It is an Italy that is looking for shortcuts, trying to imitate the dealings of wise guys of the neighbourhood, trying to come out at any cost and hopefully with just one sling shot. This is Guicciardini's 'particularistic' Italy, one that is viscous, one that, in order to last long, is indecisive and creates obstacles, one that hides itself cynically in nepotistic protection, one that holds dear to the income and privileges arising from the protective niches of the political market. At least before the financial crisis we could see an Italy that 'was enjoying itself', attracted by exclusive and luxurious consumption, while half of the country was hard up and tightening its belt. It is the same cynical Italy that is strong with the weak and weak with the strong. There is also a part that represents countless consumers, many of whom are the victims of consumption credit, but also many who are victims of themselves. In fact, there is a big part of the Italian society whose education follows the footsteps of the media, of commercial television from which *habitus* and behaviour is extracted and recommended in the daily lifestyle. The list of cynical Italy gets longer when we add to it tax evaders, 'hooligans' and an Italy that does not respect rules and takes advantage of the inefficiency of the law. In addition, there is also an Italy whose modernity has cynically remained 'halved', i.e. an Italy of great abasement that, with rubbish and a concrete jungle, has defaced cities and brought eternal damage to nature. We have an Italy where we are seeing growing violence against women and the family, an Italy that is feeding criminal and Mafia organizations. It is therefore inevitable to open our eyes to the inert, cynical and even the cloudy and illegal side of our social fabric.

However, Italy is not just this. The quality of social life has improved enormously in the past fifty years. Education, information and welfare have forged a competent society that has a high level of education, and keeps itself informed by watching TV news, reading newspapers and books, surfing the Internet, viewing cultural and political debates. The citizenry is attentive and interested in new and good politics that wants to influence decisions regarding their lives. Currently, it is a little more than a third of the population which can be an incubator for a better society in the future and potentially constitutes a competent, plural, multicultural centre of gravity for a positive change in our civic and social mindedness. It is this part that can guarantee dynamism to democracy and get in tune with the innovative components of the ruling classes; but on the contrary, it can also flow again, due to resentfulness, toward the non-voting area or toward the protesting parties voting area (such as Bossi's Northern League and Italy of Values led by 'Clean Hands' ex-prosecutor, Antonio Di Pietro). In all these spheres, Italian dualism comes forth; in terms of character, one can go from a talented and creative Italian to the stereotypical sly and cynical Italian; in terms of territory, the north and the south; in terms of socio-economic dimension, winners and losers; in civic terms, between competent citizenry and mass society.

All this brings forth democratic malaise that is only partially related to relative economic decline. The quality of democracy depends only to a certain extent on the per capita GDP. Beyond a certain threshold of economic wealth there are other factors that affect a country's democracy. Values, studied especially by Inglehart and Welzel (2005), and civicness, sustained by Almond and Verba's (1963) work and some more recent studies by Putnam (1996), are two dimensions which, to a great extent, can explain both democratic malaise and paradoxical co-existence in a society that lacks public interest, on the one hand, and with a part of the citizenry that is emotively involved by policies meant as public good, on the other. This attentive and competent citizenry shows new sensitivity on matters of public spirit and values. It demonstrates this sensitivity through the radical citizens movements such as Girotondi's in 2002–2003 or the gatherings of Beppe Grillo more recently, which have centred around ailing Italy's democracy and justice (Orazi and Socci 2008).

Individual, democratic and social capitalism

Today, people are free to make choices in their everyday life. This freedom is an indication of what has been produced by social democracy, that is from that slow drawing near of the society towards the goal of democracy of equals – of citizens with equal rights, duties and opportunities. This process, which is contradictory to autonomy and to social democracy, obtained through institutionalization of the spheres of everyday life, seems always more disconnected from collective democracy and more associated with the fragmentariness of individual experiences of life. All this is usually interpreted as degenerating and liquefying social life. However, this detachment of the individual from the collective, in the long term, should be meant – in the sense of emancipation for the individual – as a real progressive strengthening of freedom and personal responsibility. What is required is not just greater political participation. It would instead require a political class that is capable of directing the democratic values of the country, of creating equal opportunities and raising the quality of merit in schools, institutions, services, workplaces. It would require a policy that knows how to push our social democracy but whose quality is considered among the last in Europe (Dalton 2004; Skidmore and Bound 2008). On the contrary, unfortunately, in Italy's case, the political class is an opaque power. This means that there is a lack of transparency which is a proof of weakness as far as merit criteria and social responsibility are concerned. This 'halved' modernization of our country has led to the encouragement of hidden forces and degeneration of the prosperity of *casematta* of the Mafia counter-forces in the South which is finding itself in great difficulty.[9] Although it is hard to assess the real impact, these hidden and secret illegal forces are able to influence the political power, especially in Southern Italy (once more see the chapters of Parini and the Allums).

The threat rather than a crisis of a real economic depression requires an urgent in-depth reconsideration of the model of European social capitalism. The reconsideration of social capitalism from a European viewpoint must focus on 'singularization' as an effect of social democracy and as a product of a problematic freedom of the individual in an administered society. Moral guidance and the national leader seem to be an important key for a real change.

Next, the leading classes have to be reconsidered. Not creating them *in vitro*, the crucial aspects must be constituted by a strengthening of academic merit and better rules for practical merit, transparency and necessary replacement that, in part, is regulated. The new ruling classes must give shape to big projects for Italy (see also the chapters Milio as well as Iona *et al.*), especially in the South that has an average per capita income less than that of Portugal (slightly more than €17,000 per annum), while in the centre-north it is above €29,000 per annum, about €1,500 more than the UK. On the other hand, Lombardia is among the richest regions of Europe. The Southern issue is a black hole that attracts all national problems, from the ruling classes to unemployment, to public inefficiency determined by mass patronage, by Neapolitan refuse (see also Percy and Felia Allum's chapter), to the Mafia's connivance in the public healthcare system in Calabria (see the analysis on '*Ndrangheta* by Parini), to Sicily's over 35,000 employees, around five times more numerous than those of the most-populated Lombardia.

At the moment, it seems that the political class is not able to offer anything other than Berlusconi's contested populism, clearly the leader of the Second Republic. The new Democratic Party (PD) is not able to propose a convincing political platform that can be shared by the most active and competent citizenry. The same 'justicialist' opposition of Di Pietro's IDV party, which is gaining success in recent surveys, seems like it is concentrating excessively on anti-Berlusconi propaganda rather than reflecting on the silent metamorphosis that Italy and, in part, Europe is experiencing with it. At present, we have an Italy that is dominated by cynicism and mistrust, and pessimism amplified by the strategy of fear and lately by the financial crisis. Italians should give greater importance to what is positive in the society as well as in the ruling classes. Above all, they should have the strength to change, especially in the South, to find the spirit of national community once again. The next ruling class should be one that exemplifies merit, responsibility, decision-making capability and that has a vision of the future.

Notes

1 These *ragazzi* (guys), such as Stefano Ricucci, Gianpiero Fiorani, Giovanni Consorte, Danilo Coppola and Giuseppe Statuto, were called 'furbetti del quartierino' since they have tried to take over the most popular Italian newspaper *Il Corriere della Sera* (RCS Group) as well as the Banca Nazionale del Lavoro and Antonveneta. They were impeached in 2006 with regard to both the illegal methods they used and the large financial resource that they have abruptly build up.
2 I completed my first research on elites in 1990 and I did another one in 1998 (Carboni 2000).
3 Gini Index is 33 in Italy, compared to 28 in Germany and France (23 Sweden and 34 UK) (European Union Survey 2007).
4 I am referring to those carried out in 1990, 1998 and 2004 at the Interdepartmental Centre of Marketing and Communication of the Marche Polytechnic University and those carried out by Luiss 'Guido Carli' between 2006 and 2007 (Carboni 2007b and 2008b).
5 In 2006 the Left Democrats had a little more than one-third of the members registered with the old Italian Communist Party.
6 In the 1994–2004 period, marriages came down by 14 per cent, while divorces went up by 80 per cent.
7 The disappointing results of our use of human capital, including productivity, can be seen in Ederer 2007 (especially Chapter 2).
8 In addition, I have had the opportunity to highlight the relationship between the media class and the political class and the emergence of 'mediocracy' (Carboni 2008b).
9 'Casamatta' is Gramsci's (1973) concept that underlines the existence of counter powers which are disseminated within civil society.

Bibliography

Almond, G. and Verba, S. (1963) *The Civic Culture: Political Attitudes and Democracy in Five Nations,* Princeton: Princeton University Press.

Bagnasco, A. (1988) *La Costruzione Sociale Del Mercato,* Bologna: Il Mulino.

Bauman, Z. (2000) *Liquid Modernity*. Cambridge: Polity

Becattini, G. and Sengenberger W. (1990) *Industrial Districts and Inter-firm Cooperation in Italy*, Geneva: Ilo.

Bergami, M. (2007) 'La percezione del proprio ruolo da parte della classe dirigente', in Rapporto LUISS, *Generare classe dirigente.Un percorso da costruire*, Milan: Il Sole 24 ore.

Carboni, C. (2000) *The Power Elites: Chi Comanda Nella Società Della Comunicazione*, Rome: Ediesse.

—— (2005) 'Innovazione e competenza nella società della conoscenza e della tecnologia', *Lavori*, 2: 7–17.

—— (ed.) (2007a) *Elite e Classi Dirigenti in Italia*, Rome-Bari: Laterza.

—— (2007b) 'La percezione della classe dirigente da parte della popolazione', in Rapporto LUISS, *Generare classe dirigente. Un percorso da costruire*, Milan: Il Sole 24 ore.

—— (2008a) *La Società Cinica. Le Classi Dirigenti Nell'epoca Dell'antipolitica*, Rome-Bari: Laterza.

—— (2008b) *Il posizionamento all'interno delle classi dirigenti Europee*, in Rapporto LUISS, *Generare classe dirigente*, Milan: Il Sole 24 ore.

—— (ed.) (2009) *Governance e sviluppo locale*, Bologna: Il Mulino.

Crouch, C. (2004) *Postdemocracy*, London: Polity.

Dalton, R. (2004) *Democratic Challenges–Democratic Choices: The Erosion of Political Support in Advanced Industrial Democracies*, Oxford: Oxford University Press.

Ederer, P. (ed.) (2007) *European Human Capital Index*, Lisbon Council Policy Brief, Brussels, Belgium.

European Union Survey (2007) *Survey on Income and Living Conditions*, Brussels, Belgium.

Gramsci, A (1973) *Scritti Politici*, Rome: Editori Riuniti.

Inglehart, R. and Welzel, C. (2005) *Modernization, Cultural Change and Democracy, The Human Development Sequence*, New York: Cambridge University Press.

International Institute for Democracy and Electoral Assistance (IDEA) (2008). Online. Available: www.idea.int.

Nardozzi, G. (2004) *Miracolo e Declino. L'Italia Tra Concorrenza e Protezione*, Rome-Bari: Laterza.

Orazi, F. and Socci, M. (2008) *Il Popolo di Beppe Grillo*, Ancona: Catterale.

Pareto, V. (1916 [1988]) *Trattato di Sociologia Generale*, Turin: Utet.

Putnam, R. (1996) *La Tradizione Civica Nelle Regioni Italiane*, Milan: Mondadori.

Rebuffa, G. (2007) 'Gli antichi vizi del corporativismo italiano', *Il Mulino*, (1):14–20.

Skidmore, P. and Bound, K. (2008) *The Everyday Life Democracy Index*, London: Demos.

Touraine, A. (2004) *Un Nouveau Paradigme. Pour Comprendre le Monde Aujourd'hui*, Paris: Fayard.

Trigilia, C. (2005) *Lo Sviluppo Locale. Un Progetto per l'Italia*, Rome-Bari: Laterza.

3 Common manifestoes and coalition governance

How political leaders missed the window of opportunity

Catherine Moury

Summary

This chapter looks at the double role of common electoral platforms in Italy: the role of informing voters about future government policies, and that of facilitating coalition decision-making. The overall conclusion of this study is that political leaders have not used common manifestoes in a very efficient way to fulfil the two functions cited above. First, the governments examined only fulfilled half of the most important pledges in their entirety – a proportion that includes certain laws which did not produce the desired outcome. Second, a significant majority of inter-party conflicts over issues included in the common manifestoes were not followed by a concrete resolution. Generally, the main problem of Italian governance (particularly where centre-left governments are concerned) has been the absence of a strong party that is able to coordinate intra-coalition bargaining and thus impose a commitment over the deals included in the programme.

Introduction

When forming the governments of the First Republic, party leaders usually dedicated much more attention to the allocation of ministries than the definition of policy – unsurprising, given the inability of the executive to control its own majority and adopt significant reforms (Di Palma 1977).

Things started to change when the new mixed electoral system was adopted in 1993.[1] In all of the succeeding elections, two coalitions (centre-left and centre-right) have been presented to the voters, often with a common electoral platform.[2] These common programmes, which in most countries with coalitions facilitate inter-party decision-making, opened a window of opportunity for Italian political leaders. However, they failed to use these documents in an efficient way, and hence let the opportunity slip by. To demonstrate my point, this chapter will show that common manifestoes in Italy serve two essential purposes very poorly: that of informing the voters about government decisions and that of facilitating the resolution of inter-party conflicts.

With regard to the informative role, electoral programmes are persuasively assumed to be the best indicators of what parties communicate to the voters, not so much because voters read it, but because they determine the political discourse of party officials during the electoral campaign (Klingemann *et al.* 1994: 6; Costello and Thomson 2008).[3] Pledges in common manifestoes, as an indicator of what parties promise, should be implemented; otherwise, there is lack of accountability vis-à-vis the voters. Recent studies have shown that the majority of policy pledges are fulfilled by European coalition governments (Costello and Thomson 2008; Thomson 2001; Moury 2005), but this chapter demonstrates that Italian ministers and members of parliament do not satisfactorily fulfil the main pledges included in their manifestoes.

In a coalition, the common electoral programme also serves a second purpose: it lists the policy intentions on which the parties in the coalition agree. These policies may be the result of an attempt at some overall balance or may contain single deals on which the degree of concession varies between parties. That is to say, parties anticipate conflict and commit themselves collectively to deals on major policy topics while maintaining the ability to differentiate their party positions over issues not included in the agreement. While in most countries common policy platforms effectively help coalition parties to accommodate their differences and produce policy decisions (De Winter *et al.* 2000; Timmermans 2006), Italian parliamentary parties do not consider themselves committed on the issues included in the manifesto.

To prove my case, I consider three former Second Republic governments which, before election, had drafted a common manifesto (i.e. Prodi I, Berlusconi II and Prodi II). I first focus on the coalition formation process and the content of common manifestoes and then assess whether these manifestoes are implemented – or are even relevant to the management of policy disputes.

Common manifestoes in Italy: case studies

Despite the reform introduced in 2005, which almost brought back proportional representation,[4] the Italian political system became bipolar with the electoral reform of 1993 (Bartolini *et al.* 2004). Since then, there have been five general elections – 1994, 1996, 2001, 2006 and 2008. This chapter will specifically focus on the three former governments which, before election, had drafted a common electoral manifesto: Prodi I, Berlusconi II and Prodi II.

Prodi I (1996–1998) – After losing the 1994 election, the Left Democrats moved towards an 'opening to the centre' and accepted Romano Prodi's proposal in 1995, that the party of the left should join a government coalition, the Ulivo (Olive Tree), on the understanding that he would be Prime Minister in a possible future government. Several small parties decided to join the Ulivo (e.g. Popolari, Democratici-Patto Segni, Alleanza Democratica and Socialisti Italiani) (Virgilio 1996: 535). Six months before the elections, in November 1995, Prodi and what was called the group of seven 'wise men' started to formulate the common electoral programme: the so-called tesi dell'Ulivo. This ambitious programme, covering a broad range of arguments, was presented to the congresses of the coalition parties for ratification. Three small parties rejected it: the Verdi (Green

Party), not convinced by its environmental policies, and Patto Segni and Socialisti Italiani (socialists), which were opposed to the institutional reforms proposed. These parties, nevertheless, stayed in the pre-electoral coalition and had a seat in government. The elections did not give Ulivo an overwhelming victory: it obtained a small majority in the Senate, but needed the votes of Rifondazione Comunista to obtain a majority in the Chamber of Deputies.[5]

Berlusconi II (2001–2005) – A few months before the next general election in June 2001, six parties formed the Casa delle Libertà (House of Freedoms) coalition. Three parties had already participated in the 1996 elections, notably Berlusconi's Forza Italia (FI), the 'post-fascist' National Alliance and the Christian Democratic Biancofiore.[6] They were joined by the right-wing 'ethno-regionalist' Northern League, led by Umberto Bossi (on this party see both Avanza and Sigona in this volume), and two other very small parties (the socialist Nuovo PSI and the Republicans). The centre-right coalition represented various electoral programmes, including 'a letter to the Italian people', sent to all centre-right activists and published on the website of FI, and the 'contract with the Italian people', signed on television, with its five broad pledges and Berlusconi's commitment to leave political life in the case of non-fulfilment. A few days before the elections, the FI website also published the 'government plan for the parliamentary term', only one week after centre-left politicians had accused the House of Freedoms of not having a programme. All the parties in the coalition recognized it afterwards as their official manifesto. Journalists reported a pact between Berlusconi and Bossi – a means to convince the latter to support the government. Indeed federalization of the country (the so-called 'devolution'), Bossi's central claim, was included in the programme (for more details on federalism see Roux's chapter), along with certain elements of the other parties' manifestoes. But, for all this agreement, the document was never formally ratified by the coalition as a whole. In the elections of 13 May 2001, the centre-right coalition won a large majority in both chambers.

Prodi II (2006–2008) – In 2005, the centre-left parties felt they had a chance of winning the upcoming elections, in 2006, on condition that they would tow the line. Prodi returned from the European Commission and proposed that he should retain the leadership – that is, lead a centre-left coalition. There was an awareness of the need for Rifondazione Comunista participation, to avoid the 1998 scenario (i.e. the fall of the government after a lack of support from this party). The first 'Grand Democratic Alliance', which became the Unione (Union) a few months later, was built as a coalition between the Ulivo partners and other parties. It contained as many as nine parties, ranging from the communists to the centre-left Catholics. Though Prodi's leadership met with resistance, he was ultimately accepted and promptly announced he would write the manifesto. Finally, one year before the elections, he started to coordinate workshops preparing a draft programme, which was finally amended during meetings between Prodi, party leaders and specialists from the party. The Laic party (the Rosa nel Pugno), refused to ratify it. On 17 May, the Union won the elections, but with a tight majority of votes in the Assembly and seats in the Senate.

Table 3.1 Process of drafting the common manifesto

	Parties	Duration of manifesto drafting process (in days)	Future ministers involved in the drafting (considering only ministers with portfolios)	Coalition parties which ratified the manifesto
Prodi I	DS, PPI, RI, UD, Verdi	180	7/22	4/5
Berlusconi II	FI, AN, LN, CDU-UDC	7	4/22	0/4
Prodi II	DS, Margherita, Verdi, Italia dei Valori, MRE, PCI, RC, UDEUR, Rosa nel pugno	350	10/27	8/9

Abbreviations: DS: Democratici di Sinistra (Left Democrats), PPI: Partito Popolare Italiano (Italian People's Party), RI: Rinnovamento Italiano (Italian Renewal), UD: Unione Democratica (Democratic Union), FI: Forza Italia, AN: Alleanza Nazionale, LN: Lega Nord, CDU-UDC: Cristiani Democratici Uniti – Unione Cristiana Democratica (Christian Democrats), Margherita (Daisy), Verdi (Greens), Italia dei Valori (Italy of Values), MRE: Movimento Repubblicani Europei (European Republican Movement), PCI: Partito dei Comunisti Italiani (Italian Communist Party), RC: Rifondazione Comunista (Communist Refoundation Party), UDEUR Unione Democratici per l'Europa (Democratic Union for Europe), Rosa nel Pugno.

Table 3.1 summarizes the previous sections: it presents the duration (in days) of the drafting of the coalition agreement, the number of ministers and the number of parties that officially ratified the document.

Negotiation of the common manifestoes

The short description given above shows that the process of negotiating the common manifesto is quite different from what happens elsewhere. First, in most countries with coalitions, the principal negotiators for the coalition agreements are party leaders, accompanied by party experts in different policy domains, who are subsequently given cabinet portfolios (Müller and Strøm 2000). The resulting document is then presented to the parties for ratification. Two virtuous consequences come out of this process: first, the drafters of the coalition agreement, as party leaders, are in a position to impose commitment to the ratified document; second, ministers who participate in the drafting of the document have the opportunity to 'internalize' the deals made (Timmermans 2006).

As we have seen above, the process does not happen this way in Italy. The common manifesto of the Prodi I government was drafted by Prodi himself and the group of 'wise men' did not include the party leaders, though they all became ministers. The negotiators may well have 'internalized' the policies included in a document that they themselves had drafted; but it was much less likely that they would have the authority to impose a strong commitment to these deals.

Moreover, the seeds of disloyalty were sown when some coalition parties refused to ratify the resulting manifesto.

Berlusconi II had an agreement that was mainly drafted by Berlusconi's collaborators, though it included certain deals conceded to by some of his party champions, who also entered the cabinet. The results were not formally ratified by the parties. Also, the very short time (7 days) in which the coalition agreement was drafted does not inspire much confidence regarding the care associated with its drafting.

The formulation of the Prodi II common manifesto resembled northern practice more closely, as it involved experts and party leaders, most of whom took a seat in the government. The very long time (one year) spent preparing the programme shows that the drafting was addressed with care. However, as happened during the first Prodi government, some parties (here La Rosa nel Pugno) refused to ratify the resulting document.

Description of common manifestoes

What are these three common platforms like, exactly? (For further treatment of this point, see Conti, in this volume). Here I examine the word count, completeness and precision of the common manifestoes, in the manner developed in a previous article (Moury and Timmermans 2008). Counting the number of words is a clear-cut process. To measure *completeness*, Moury and Timmermans compared the range of policy fields included in the agreement in relation to the set of cabinet portfolios. Our measurement for completeness varies from 1 (when the common manifesto contains intentions in *all* fields of government policy with which portfolios are associated) to 0 (where there is no written common manifesto). *Precision* is about the feasibility and applicability of intentions. We based the work on a distinction made by Royed (1996) between the types of policy pledges, and counted the proportion of each type of pledge in the common manifesto, thus building an index of completeness, as follows:[7]

Precision = (% of precise pledges *1) + (% of imprecise pledges *0.5) + (% of rhetorical pledges *0)

Table 3.2 shows the content features of each of the three governments' common manifestoes. We see that Prodi's common manifestoes are very long, particularly the one for the Prodi II government (92,000 words or the equivalent of a 150-page book), whereas the Berlusconi II programme was much shorter. This large difference in length between common centre-left and centre-right manifestoes illustrates a very different approach in addressing the voters: in the first case, voters are presented, long before the elections, with a book-length document – obviously very difficult to read and understand in its entirety; in the second, a few days before the vote, they receive a short and well-structured programme through the mailbox. Nevertheless, even the common manifesto produced by the

Table 3.2 Properties of the common manifestoes of the three governments

Government	Parties	Size	Completeness	Precision
Prodi I (1996–1998)	DS, PPI, RI, UD, Verdi	41,500	0.90	0.50
Berlusconi II (2001–2006)	FI, AN, LN, CDU-UDC	9,600	0.80	0.30
Prodi II (2006–2008)	DS, Margherita, Verdi, Italia dei Valori, MRE, Pci, RC, UDEUR, Rosa nel Pugno	92,200	0.80	0.50

Berlusconi coalition was not that brief: it contains 9,600 words (almost double the number in this chapter).

Not surprisingly, long documents like these are also complete, and all the common manifestoes score at least 0.8 on the completeness scale. Italian common programmes, however, are not very precise. This low level of preciseness has to do with the reluctance of the coalition parties to shed too much light on their disagreements and publicize unpopular policy deals: these particular manifestoes avoided or remained very vague on several contentious subjects. For example, the Berlusconi II coalition agreement mentioned the 'devolution' (further federalization) aspired to by the Lega Nord (LN) (but disputed by the Christian Democrats), while it remained very vague about its implementation. In a similar vein, the Prodi II coalition agreement mentions something about 'transport infrastructure' without explicitly referring to the contentious subject of the high-speed rail link in the North. However, all three coalition agreements also contain their own set of precise points and deals, including relatively contentious ones. The Prodi II coalition agreement, for example, included a law on civil unions; and the common manifestoes for the Prodi I and Berlusconi II governments contained specific economic and social policies that were far from consensual (i.e. budget cuts and pension and school reforms).

Implementation of pledges

I now propose to check whether what Italian parties promise their voters is consistent with what they do once they are in power. After identifying the twenty principal common manifesto pledges that are testable (i.e. excluding rhetorical pledges that are not objectively testable, e.g. the pledge 'to increase social harmony'), I then proceed to ascertain whether we can find a government decision that is congruent with the proposal in the pledge.[8] A distinction is made between 'fully fulfilled' or 'partially fulfilled' pledges.

It is important to note two important limits on this analysis. First, this measurement does not include a qualitative assessment of each government decision or an assessment of its implementation once the bill was passed by Parliament. These two points are developed in the following tables (Tables 3.3–3.5).

Table 3.3 Main pledges fulfilled, Prodi I government

Main pledges	Fulfilled (Yes – No – Partially)
Reform of Public Administration	Yes
State reform	No (Failure of Bicamerale)
Reform of penal system	Partially
Legal reform	No (Defeated in Parliament)
Participation in EMU	Yes
Enlargement of NATO	Yes
Reduction in public deficit and public debt	Partially
Reduction in tax evasion	Partially
Introduction of regional tax	Yes
No increase in taxes	No
Creation of specific 'Authorities' and an anti-trust body	Yes
Privatisation	Partially
Market liberalisation	Partially
Pension reform	Yes
Reform of immigration rules	Yes
Actions for the South	No
School reform	Yes
Parity between public and private schools	Yes
University reform	Yes
Transport measures	No
Total	*10 Yes, 5 Partially, 5 No*

As we can see in these three tables, only half of the pledges were fully fulfilled by the Prodi I and Berlusconi II governments, and 45 per cent by the Prodi II government. Without doubt, many important pledges were addressed by each of the governments studied. For example, the Prodi I government managed to get Italy into the Economic and Monetary Union (EMU) and reformed the immigration laws and school system; Berlusconi introduced further federalization, reformed the labour laws, decreased the taxes on investment and reformed the pension system; finally, Prodi II liberalized important sectors, introduced the 'class action' system, reduced corporate taxation and decreased the public deficit.

However, every government could have done much more: important pledges that were emphasized during the electoral campaign were not fulfilled. For example: the promised reform of the state, the executive and the legal system was not carried out by the Prodi I government, which also increased taxes when the manifesto had explicitly promised not to; Berlusconi did not pass measures

Table 3.4 Main pledges fulfilled, Berlusconi II government

Main pledges	Fulfilled (Yes – No – Partially)
E-government	Yes
Reform of Public Administration	No
Devolution	Yes
Stronger government	Yes
De-regulation	Partially
'Obiettivo' Law	Partially
Reduction in taxes on firms' corporate benefits	Yes
Investment for the southern regions	No
Reduction in taxes on earned income	No
Tax reductions	Partially
Fight against tax evasion	No
Legalization of capital held abroad	Yes
Flexibility of working conditions	Yes
Increase for those on low pensions	Partially
Pension reform	Yes
Fight against illegal immigration	Yes
Separation of judges' careers	Partially
School reform	Yes
Liberalization of energy	Yes
Total	*11 Yes, 5 Partially, 4 No*

to reform the executive or fight tax evasion; and the Prodi II government did not substantially reform immigration laws, the labour laws or the law on civil unions.

Moreover, as said earlier, in this analysis we only count the fact that the law was passed, without considering whether it was implemented or whether it achieved the desired goal. However, two examples illustrate very well that passing a law does not always mean solving a problem. The first example concerns the so-called 'conflict of interest', i.e. the potential conflict between the public and private interests of those in government. As is known, this risk was particularly acute for Berlusconi, who controls half the television channels, a substantial slice of the dailies and magazines published and, through his influence on the advertising market, a good number of periodicals that are nominally independent (see also Hanretty, Chapter 7). Because an electoral victory would also give him control, as prime minister, of public broadcasting, Berlusconi repeatedly promised during the campaign that he would solve this problem once in power. After a few months in office, Frattini indeed presented a bill addressing the issue. However, it is doubtful

Table 3.5 Main pledges fulfilled, Prodi II government

Main pledges	Fulfilled (Yes – No – Partially)
Increase in school independence	Yes
Law on conflict of interest	No (never became law)
Decrease in corporate taxation	Yes
Consumer protection	Yes
Decrease in delays in the legal system	Partially
Spending for the South	No
Development of renewable energies	Partially
Increase in family allowances	Partially
Reform of citizenship rules	No (never became law)
Decrease in the public debt	Yes
Fiscal federalism	Yes
Local autonomy code	No
Law on civil unions	No (never became law)
New electoral law	No (never became law)
Withdrawal of troops from Iraq	Yes
Graduation for pension age	Yes
Integration in new transport networks	Yes
Fight against precarious labour	Partially
Fight against tax evasion	Yes
Liberalization of energy	No (delegating law never passed)
Total	*9 Yes, 4 Partially, 7 No*

whether the legislation – which introduced the principle that only managers, not owners, may be supposed to have interests as far as a given firm is concerned – provided a genuine solution to Berlusconi's conflict of interest. A second example relates to the bill on the liberalization of certain sectors (e.g. insurance, banking, pharmaceutical services, retailing and taxi services) that were obstructing competition, to the detriment of consumers. The law was successfully passed, but some of the relevant provisions needed to be implemented by local and regional administrations. The resistance of the sectors in question was sometimes able to block implementation, partially annulling the effect of the law and provoking widespread disappointment.

Finally, it is worth noting that looking at the proportion of pledges fulfilled is not the only way to check whether a government is accountable. We should also look at the policies adopted that are not based on the programme (Moury 2010). As Frognier puts it, parties must adopt the kind of policies that pursue the 'common good' and not the personal interest of ministers (Frognier 2000). Though the notion of the 'common good' is undoubtedly difficult to define, it is clear that some of the bills adopted by recent Italian governments do not come close to this concept. In particular, the Berlusconi government passed laws that were mainly relevant to its Prime Minister's legal position (i.e. the laws changing the definition of such crimes as false accounting, the procedures for the acceptability of evidence in court, and the law on letters rogatory). There is also widespread consensus on the effects of the so-called Indulto, the reform introduced by Mastella under the Prodi II government. It had a seriously negative impact on public opinion as it emptied the jails (25,000 inmates were released) without adopting long-term reforms that would reduce the prison population (Paolucci and Newell 2008).

Common manifestoes: a tool for coalition governance

As suggested, some important problems regarding accountability remain. I will now turn to the second function of a common manifesto: its capacity to facilitate coalition governance. To do so, I have considered all of the major policy controversies that emerged between the coalition parties during the life of the three governments in question. I first checked if these could be traced back to the common manifesto and then examined the way they were resolved (i.e. by means of a decision or not).

Anticipation of conflicts

Table 3.6 presents the number of conflicts faced by each government, distinguishing between those not mentioned in the common manifesto and those included, a subset of which are the conflicts on which the agreement contained precise deals. Table 3.6[9] shows that more than two-thirds of all conflicts were on matters on which the common manifesto contained some kind of deal. This means that common manifestoes include potentially controversial issues, but it also shows that these documents do not remove conflict. The fact that half of the conflicts relate to the imprecise part of the common manifesto shows that the relative impreciseness of some policy deals is a good indicator of the disagreement of the

Table 3.6 Conflicts on issues mentioned and not mentioned in the common manifesto

	Conflicts	Not in common manifesto	In common manifesto	Precise in common manifesto
Prodi I	11	5	6	2
Berlusconi II	14	4	10	4
Prodi II	7	1	6	1
Sub-total	32	10 (31%)	22 (69%)	7 (22%)

parties over these policies. For example, the following conflicts were over policies imprecisely defined in the programme: the conflict between the coalition parties in Parliament on constitutional reform and the reform of the legal system (Prodi I), the conflict within the Council of Ministers on the issue of anti-trust authorities (Prodi I); the deep dissension in the Council of Ministers and Parliament, on how to pursue the federalization of the state, how to reform immigration and whether to decrease taxes (Berlusconi II), and the divergence within the Parliamentary majority over the railway in Valle d'Aosta, the law on civil unions and electoral reform (Prodi II).

Conflict resolution

Was conflict over issues contained in the agreement resolved in different ways than that over issues not mentioned in any pre-existing deals? I have distinguished two types of conflict resolution: those resulting in a decision and those resulting in non-decision.[10] By comparing conflict resolution on issues included and not included in the common manifesto, it is possible to see whether the agreement in some way facilitated conflict resolution and, indeed, committed the parties.

We see in Table 3.7 that solving conflict by a decision is the most frequent type of conflict resolution (75 per cent of the cases), but we also observe strong variations among the governments. Indeed, the level of non-decision is relatively high for the first Prodi government (36 per cent) and very high for the second (43 per cent), while non-decision occurred very rarely during the Berlusconi II government (in only 7 per cent of the cases).

A closer look at the particular conflicts shows that the main origin of non-decision was not the incapacity of ministers to decide, but rather the difficulty of centre-left governments to get their bills through Parliament. For example, the Prodi I government drafted a bill on state reform and legal reform and the Prodi II government prepared legislation providing for electoral reform, the much-advertised DICO (law on civil unions), and reform of the rules on citizenship and conflicts of interest. None of this legislation was ever passed by Parliament.

Figure 3.1 illustrates the weak discipline of centre-left Parliaments. On the basis of the data available at the Assembly website, I present the proportion of government bills passed by Parliament. We can see that the two Prodi governments

Table 3.7 Types of result in conflict management (N=76)

	Conflict over issue included in agreement		Conflict over issue not included in agreement		Total	
	Decision	Non-decision	Decision	Non-decision	Decision	Non-decision
Prodi I	4	2	3	2	7	4
Berlusconi II	9	1	4	0	13	1
Prodi II	3	3	1	0	4	3
Sub-total	16 (73%)	6 (27%)	8 (80%)	2 (20%)	24 (75%)	8 (25%)

This table is based on Moury and Timmermans, 2008

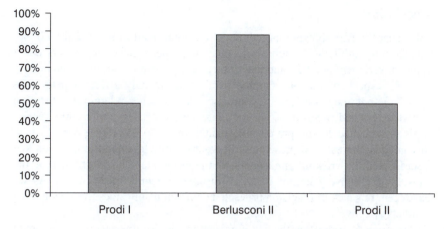

Figure 3.1 Governmental bills passed by Parliament

only had half of their bills passed. On the contrary, almost 90 per cent of the bills presented by the Berlusconi II government were passed. Obviously, we have to take the points into consideration that the two Prodi governments did not run their full course and that the executive made good use of 'decree laws', 'delegating laws',[11] and the vote of confidence (Capano and Giuliani 2001; Vassallo 2007). However, it is striking that the proportion of bills passed by the centre-left government is much lower than that of the bills passed by the Berlusconi II government (and most European governments, where it is close to 90 per cent [Moury 2005]).

There may be several explanations for this. The first concerns the Italian political system, where each government bill must be approved in an identical form by both chambers and where political coalitions are a fragmented assemblage of disparate parties. All the other explanations are specific to the centre-left governments: Prodi I was a minority coalition; Prodi II had a very tight majority in the Senate; and Prodi himself, in contrast to Berlusconi, was not backed by a political party able to coordinate intra-coalition bargaining and thus impose a minimum of discipline on allies (Paolucci and Newell 2008) (see Figure 3.1). This lack of coordination was particularly fatal, since the small parties' votes were essential to the survival of the coalition and, with their vetoes, they were able to – and actually did – exert great power over policy-making (Conti 2008).

Finally, we do *not* observe that deals included in the common manifesto are more likely to end up being settled by a decision than those not included. This means that the common programme does not have an agenda function, in contrast to what happens in various other countries (Moury and Timmermans 2008; Moury 2010). In other words, negotiators do not have the power to tie the insertion of a policy in the manifesto to an obligation to deliver.

Conclusion

This chapter has shown that common electoral platforms in Italy do not satisfactorily fulfil their double role: that of properly informing voters about future government policies, and that of facilitating coalition decision-making.

With respect to content, common manifestoes in Italy at first appear to be complete, but they are not very precise. This inverse relationship between completeness and precision – generating extensive packages of mostly general deals – is related to the pre-electoral status of the policy agreements, which discourages parties from presenting the voters with clear commitments on key issues – and thus risking punishment by the electorate. This might also be the cause of the convergence of party platforms (see Conti, this volume). As we have seen, this lack of precision prevented common manifestoes from containing conflicts effectively.

The process of drafting the coalition agreement also gives us reason to doubt the effectiveness of common manifestoes in Italy. Despite the fact that a significant proportion of ministers were negotiators (and may therefore have 'internalized' the deals included in the programme), not all party leaders participated in the drafting of the programme and some parties did not ratify the resulting manifesto.

Further analysis shows that our initial scepticism was not misplaced. We first observed that only half of the main pledges were fulfilled and, indeed, important pledges, repeatedly emphasized during the campaign, were not adopted. An even less positive picture emerges if we look more carefully at the laws claiming to fulfil the pledges, some of which are far from reaching the desired outcome, either because they do not satisfactorily address the problem or because they could not be successfully implemented. Also, if we look at the laws adopted that are not based on the coalition agreement, we have reason to believe that some of these do not address the long-term wellbeing of the country, but rather specific or short-term ministerial interests.

The record on the management of interparty policy conflict also confirms our initial scepticism. Unsurprisingly, given the negotiating process, common manifestoes do not represent an obligation for parliamentary parties to deliver the results that they imply. Conflict is quite often followed by non-decision (mostly the non-passage of a bill through Parliament) and quarrels over deals included in the coalition agreement do not appear to be different in this regard. This is particularly true for the centre-left coalition parties: in their documents, well aware of their weaknesses, they took much care in defining common policies. Regrettably, they did not dispose of a strong party structure that was able to manage intra-coalition bargaining and thus ensure the discipline of the majority around these commitments.

This is not to say that these governments were unable to adopt any important policies at all: as mentioned above, half of the pledges were fully fulfilled and translated into significant reforms. Romano Prodi's last chance would have been to invest in explaining and defending these policies before the public, an opportunity he did not take. As we saw in the recent elections, this lack of investment brought the downfall of his coalition and handed Berlusconi electoral victory.

Notes

1 It consisted of electing three-fourths of the senators and deputies by means of the first-past-the-post system in single-member districts, and the other one-quarter by means of a proportional representation (PR) system. The system for electing the two chambers differed in a number of respects: for a complete review, see Katz 2006.
2 With the exception of the 1994 election.
3 The authors demonstrate that media coverage of the campaign included a substantial amount of information on the specific pledges of the main political parties (Costello and Thomson 2008).
4 The 617 members of the Chamber of Deputies are elected by PR throughout Italy, with the exception of the Valle d'Aosta and Italians abroad. The coalition with the most votes in the 617 member-districts is guaranteed at least 340 seats (55 per cent). The same 55 per cent floor is used for the Senate but is applied region by region (Katz 2006).
5 The Ulivo had made a pre-electoral agreement with Rifondazione Comunista.
6 The new label under which the CCD and CDU were grouped together after the 1996 election; the name was changed to UDC in March 2001.
7 For more details on the codification, see Moury and Timmermans 2008.
8 For more details on the codification, see Moury 2010.
9 This table is based on Moury and Timmermans 2008.
10 A possible type of conflict resolution is, of course, coalition termination, which may or may not involve early elections. This is codified as a non-decision.
11 'Decree laws' do not require the prior authorization of Parliament, but must be approved by Parliament within 60 days; 'delegating laws' are promulgated by Parliament on the basis of prior authorization by Parliament and do not need further ratification.

References

Bartolini, S., Chiaramonte, A. and D'Alimonte, R. (2004) 'The Italian party system between parties and coalitions', *West European Politics*, 1: 1–19.

Capano, G. and Giuliani, M. (2001) 'Governing without surviving: An Italian paradox', *Journal of Legislative Studies*, 4: 7–36.

Conti, N. (2008) 'On Political fragmentation: stay in or stay out? The role of small parties in the Italian Centre-Left', *Journal of Modern Italian Studies*, 13(3): 388–404.

Costello, R. and Thomson, R. (2008) 'Election pledges and their enactment in coalition governments: a comparative analysis of Ireland', *Journal of Elections, Public Opinion and Parties*, 18(3): 239–56.

De Winter, L., Timmermans, A. and Dumont, P. (2000) 'Belgium: On Government Agreements, Evangelists, Followers and Heretics', in W.C. Müller and K. Strøm (eds.) *Coalition Governments in Western Europe*. Oxford: Oxford University Press.

Di Palma, G. (1977) *Surviving without Governing: The Italian Parties in Parliament.* Berkeley: University of California Press.

Frognier, A.P. (2000) 'The Normative Foundations of Party Government', in J. Blondel and M. Cotta (eds.) *The Nature of Party Government. A Comparative European Perspective*, London: Macmillan.

Katz, R.S. (2006) 'Electoral reforms in Italy: Expectations and Results', *Acta Politica*, 41: 285–99.

Klingemann, H.D., Hofferbert, R.I. and Budge, I. (1994) Parties, Policies and Democracy. Boulder, CO: Westview Press.

Moury, C. (2005) 'Coalition government and party mandate: Are the ministers bound by the coalition agreement?', Unpublished PhD thesis, University of Siena.

—— (2010) 'Coalition government and party mandate. How the coalition agreement constrains the ministers', *Party Politics.*

—— and Timmermans, A. (2008) 'Conflitto e accordo in governi di coalizione: come l'Italia è sempre meno un "caso differente", *Rivista Italiana di Scienza Politica,* 3.

Müller, W.C. and Strøm, K. (eds.) (2000) *Coalition Governments in Western Europe* Oxford: Oxford University Press.

—— and Strøm, K. (2008) 'Coalition Agreements and Cabinet Governance', in K. Strøm, W.C. Müller and T. Bergman (eds.) *Cabinets and Coalition Bargaining.* Oxford: Oxford University Press.

Paolucci, C. and Newell, J. L. (2008) 'The Prodi government of 2006 and 2007: A retrospective look', *Modern Italy,* 13(3): 281–89.

Royed, T. (1996) 'Testing the Mandate Model in Britain and the United States: Evidence from the Reagan and Thatcher Eras', *British Journal of Political Science,* 26: 45–80.

Strøm, K., Müller, W.C. and Bergman, T. (eds.) (2008) *Cabinets and Coalition Bargaining: The Democratic Life Cycle in Western Europe.* Oxford: Oxford University Press.

Timmermans, A. (2006) 'Standing apart and sitting together. Enforcing coalition agreements in multiparty systems', *European Journal of Political Research,* 2: 263–83.

Thomson, R. (2001) 'The programme to policy linkage: the fulfilment of election pledges on socio-economic policy in the Netherlands, 1986–1998', *European Journal of Political Research,* 40: 171–97.

Vassallo, S. (2007) 'Government under Berlusconi: the functioning of the core institutions in Italy', *West European Politics,* 30(4): 692–710.

Verzichelli, L. and M. Cotta (2000*)* 'Italy: From Constrained Coalition to Alternative', in W.C. Müller and K. Strøm (eds.) *Coalition Governments in Western Europe,* pp. 433–497. Oxford: Oxford University Press.

Virgilio Di, A. (1996) 'Le alleanze elettorali. Identita partitiche e logiche coalizionali', *Rivista Italiana di Scienza Politica,* XXVI (3): 519–85.

4 The programmatic convergence of parties and their weakness in policy making

Nicolò Conti

Summary

In the last decade, in spite of a large number of parties taking part in elections, the Italian party system has shown an increasing simplification in the programmatic supply, with two large coalitions showing a process of convergence of their policy platforms. In this chapter, I will show that on the crucial themes characterizing the confrontation between neo-liberalism vs. regulated capitalism, the distance between the two coalitions has progressively reduced. I will also discuss how, although the ability of the government to process key policies has remained low, thanks to this programmatic convergence the quality of the policy making could also improve.

Introduction[1]

For more than a decade, from the fall of the old party system and the birth of new parties in 1994 to recent times, the ideological positioning of the Italian parties has been a contentious matter. In particular, the creation of new parties with no clear ideological affiliation has created many uncertainties in the scholarly debate and in the general public as to the attribution of such parties to traditional party families. Additionally, the transformation of some old parties into new ones with fresh political views has also created uncertainty as to how complete their break is with their old, and often radical views. At the same time, in the electoral campaigns, parties have been particularly tenacious in describing their adversaries as very distant from their own programmatic positions, to the point that voting has often been presented to the electorate as a choice between radically different world views. As a consequence, the tone of electoral campaigns has often had a rather dramatic feel which may well have contributed significantly to electoral mobilization. However, in the last general elections of 2008 the leaders of the two main parties (Silvio Berlusconi and Walter Veltroni) have addressed reciprocal accusations to each other of plagiarism of their respective manifestoes. The picture seems therefore rather puzzling and the real nature of party ideology needs to be clarified.

This picture raises many questions, some related to the understanding of the new Italian party system, others related to the policy making. In particular, at first glance the Italian case does not seem to fit the normal functioning of bipolar party competition in majoritarian democracies, which usually leads to convergence toward the centre in an attempt to intercept the median voter (Downs 1957). If this were proved to be true, it would show that Italy has not overcome its exceptionalism and still remains a case of polarized politics (Sartori 1976) in spite of the change in the party system and in the electoral law since the early 1990s. Furthermore, the Italian case would very much go against the predictions of the theorists of the cartel party (Katz and Mair 1995) who have, in fact, predicted the ideological convergence of parties in contemporary democracies upon the centre of the policy spectrum.

Furthermore, polarization creates the conditions for poor policy making, as the confrontation between majority and opposition in polarized systems tends to be characterized by ideological extremism and political irresponsibility (Sartori 1976). Polarization and poor policy performance deeply characterized the First Republic (Cotta and Isernia 1996). If their persistence was also proved to be true in the Second Republic we would find clear evidence of another sickness of the Italian case that would add to the troublesome picture illustrated in *Italy Today*.

This chapter will present, first, a longitudinal analysis focused on the patterns of party competition in the policy space based on the measurement of the distance between party programmatic platforms. For this purpose, I will analyse six general elections including the last one of the First Republic with a proportional representation (PR) electoral system in 1992, three elections with a mixed (PR-plurality) system from 1994 to 2001, and the last two elections in 2006 and 2008 characterized by a return to a PR system (with some important majoritarian aspects). The time span is long enough to allow a limited longitudinal analysis. In practice, though, this limited period is disproportionately relevant due to the transformation that occurred in moving from the First to the Second Republic, through the transitional period of the mid-1990s. Second, in light of the findings of the first part of my analysis, I will discuss the influence of party ideology on policy making.

Together with the other issues addressed in this volume, the difficulties in producing a moderate multi-party system and an effective policy making process are chronic problems in the Italian system. Have they found appropriate solutions in the evolution from the First to the Second Republic? Is the Italian party system really as polarized as party leaders have made it seem to voters? Do theories of party competition in liberal democracies find in Italy a deviant case – a sick man – at least with reference to the dimension of the programmatic offer? Is the ideological distance among parties an obstacle to effective policy making in this country? This chapter will address the above questions.

Ideology *within* poles

In this first part of the analysis, I make use of data drawn from the party manifestoes issued for the general elections. In particular, attention focuses on some specific dimensions of the party programmes that are extremely relevant for party competition. To be more specific, I refer to the policy preferences on the two alternative models of socio-economic development that are often described using the labels of *neoliberalism* and *regulated capitalism*. In recent times, analyses (Hooghe *et al.* 2004, Gabel and Hix 2004) have shown that in Europe, the patterns of party competition are shaped predominantly around the confrontation between these two models. Hence, I attempt to build an index of the socio-economic preferences of the parties as they are voiced in the electoral discourse through the party manifestoes. The main point is not to describe the position of parties on the left to right scale (even if some implications can be drawn from this analysis in this respect, too). Instead, following the research problems that I identified above, I am more interested in seeing to what extent parties distance themselves from each other, regardless of their positions in the left-right continuum.

In my analysis, I apply an index for the estimation of the policy preferences of parties about alternative options of socio-economic development. This index is built using six variables, each covering a broad policy issue. Every variable indicates the percentage (salience) of quasi-sentences dedicated to a particular policy issue as a share of the total number of quasi-sentences in the manifesto.[2] Hence, the higher the value, the more a party has emphasized a given policy issue in its discourse. The following are the policy issues presented in the index:

* Market regulation positive[3]
* Social justice positive[4]
* Welfare state expansion positive[5]
* Welfare state limitation[6]
* Labour groups positive[7]
* Labour groups negative[8]

I have subtracted the total share of quasi-sentences expressing a negative orientation toward measures for regulating capitalism and a social-market economy from the total share of quasi-sentences expressing positive orientations. The result is a measure where the more positive values reflect a preference for *regulated capitalism* while the more negative values express a preference for a *neoliberal platform*.

In Figure 4.1 we see a representation of the policy preferences of the parties on issues of social economy and regulated capitalism. The parties analysed in this table are the largest ones of the Italian party system: the three mainstream parties of the centre-right, FI and AN which then merged together forming the PDL in 2008, and from 2001 the Unione di Centro (Centre Union). Three parties of the centre-left, the DS and the Margherita (Daisy) which recently merged forming the PD, and in 2008 also Italy of Values ((Italia dei Valori, IDV). Finally, three more

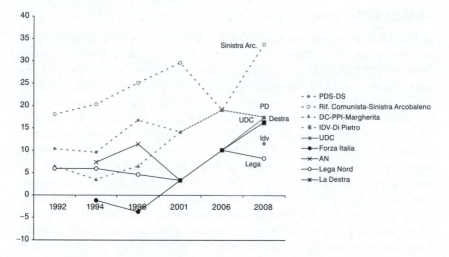

Figure 4.1 A socio-economic index of the positions of Italian parties (1992–2008) (source Conti,2008b

peripheral parties, RC, LN and La Destra (The Right). Where coalition manifestoes are present, the relevant manifestoes also represent other minor parties.

To start with, it is important to note that the parties show a number of distinctive positions until 1996, while from 2001 to 2006 the picture looks much more simple with only two to three points represented in the diagram. In 2008 there is again an increase in the number of programmatic positions available for the electoral market. The reason is that before 2001 the parties kept their individual manifestoes distinct, even when they built an electoral alliance. On the contrary, from 2001 the programmatic offer looks much simplified, as each of the two coalitions produced a unitary manifesto, and in 2001 only RC participated in the ballot as a challenger party with an alternative platform. In 2008, consequent to the crucial simplification in the format of the party system, where the main parties had merged into the PD and the PDL and sought, at the same time, to isolate the most radical parties (but see the case of the neo-fascist Alessandra Mussolini which is briefly discussed by Mammone and Veltri in their introductory chapter), these last contested the elections externally to any alliance and so they presented their manifestoes separately. These dynamics of the electoral competition produce evident implications for my analysis. They show that using this methodology it is possible to have more precise estimates of the positions of the individual parties in 1994, 1996 and 2008. In 2001 and 2006, however, we can refer only to the alliance compromises represented by the joint manifesto of each of the two poles. However, this change in the object is also part of the variation that I intend to describe. I assume that the positions of the individual parties vary from the point of compromise marked by the joint manifesto of each alliance and also that this is something that the present study cannot assess with accuracy. For example, individually, radical parties would certainly occupy positions that are more extreme than those of their respective coalition manifestoes. On the other hand, the mainstream parties of different coalitions would probably be closer than their respective coalition manifestoes. At the same time, for the problems raised in this chapter, it is probably more relevant to note that the extensive commitment of the parties to joint manifestoes in itself represents an unprecedented convergence within the two poles. Hence, it is evidence of a path toward programmatic convergence within the overcrowded Italian party system, although the scope of such convergence can only be assessed for coalitions in 2001 and 2006, but not for the individual parties. When, in 2008, a counter-tendency developed with two radical parties (Rifondazione Comunista and La Destra) marking a distance from their respective poles, their realignment did not overturn the process of unification at work within each of the two poles, which was well represented by the creation of the PD and PDL. And, in fact, the two radical parties suffered electoral ruin, resulting in their removal from Parliament.

Ideology *between* poles

I now analyze how the increasing degree of convergence *within* the two poles has also resulted in ideological convergence *between* the poles. We can see that overall, political competition on socio-economic themes shows a tendency in favour of various degrees of social protection and market regulation. Indeed, if we exclude the case of FI in 1994–1996, it seems that no other party in Italy has promoted a clear neo-liberal agenda, while pledges in favour of social protection and market regulation have become more recurrent. Overall, the Italian party system seems predominantly to express a preference for a 'social market economy', with the only partial exception of its largest party, notably FI. This shows that in this country the discourse of even a large part of the centre-right maintains an important social dimension, while at the same time it stays cautious about making strong statements in favour of the free market. In particular, in the Second Republic the Italian right has not evolved very much into neo-liberal ideological positions and instead proposes various measures of social market policy and resistance toward the free market. This constitutes a major difference compared with the neo-liberal orientation of the centre-right in other European countries, regarding which only the political discourse of FI could, at some points, be considered a vague approximation. But hints of neo-liberalism in FI never really evolve into a mature neo-liberal platform, and over the years we instead find signs of a change in direction. In fact, Figure 1 shows the centre-right's social sensitivity increasing over time to the point that, in 2008, the share of arguments in favour of a social market economy in the manifesto of the PDL is almost as large as in the one of the PD. The shift of Forza Italia leaves the neo-liberal stance rather unrepresented in the Italian system where greater inclination to regulated capitalism and social protection overall largely prevails. Hence, it should not be surprising that Italy is one among the EU countries characterized by lower economic freedom and larger state intervention in the economy (see also Hanretty in this volume on the 'media market').[9]

This certainly does not mean that in Italy socio-economic issues have always been ones of consensus. On the contrary: parties sometimes support different degrees of social protection, a different political role for the labour groups, and various degrees of market regulation, as Figure 4.1 shows. In particular, if we consider the point in time where a greater differentiation in the positions is visible (1996), we see that the parties occupy a large range of positions and, in particular, the distance between the two major parties (DS and FI, whose positions are at the two extremes, without considering the even more distant communist RC) is as large as 21 points. Finally, the picture does not show strong evidence in favour of programmatic convergence during the 1990s. At best, it seems plausible to argue that the neo-liberal orientation is clearly undermined in Italy by a diffuse preference for a social market economy and even by some protectionist options (see also Simoni, Chapter 17, this volume).[10]

We now move our attention to 2001. As mentioned above, this year saw a simplification in programmatic supply with just three alternative platforms presented: two from the competing coalitions – the centre-right House of Freedoms and the centre-left Olive Tree – and that of RC, the only challenger party of any relevance among those refusing to take part in a large coalition. The most important implication of this development for our research questions lies in the fact that the diversity of positions previously found is now much reduced. In fact, this phenomenon marks the beginning of a path toward convergence between programmatic platforms. Indeed, if we exclude the only challenger party (RC), whose position seems to diverge from the mainstream ones to an even greater extent than before, the distance between the two coalitions is 11 points, which is much less than five years before. Furthermore, 2001 seems clearly to water down the only programmatic platform showing any hint of neo-liberalism, that of Berlusconi's Forza Italia.

In 2006 this tendency was reinforced as a consequence of the realignment of a relevant party that had still contested the 2001 elections alone, Rifondazione Comunista, which now participated in the centre-left coalition. This means that for the first time since the birth of the new Italian party system, the whole political spectrum had converged on just two electoral/governmental programmes. This reduced the scope for variation in programmatic supply since only two alliance agendas were now available to voters. At the same time, the tendency to reduce the distance between programmatic platforms was also confirmed, as the distance was now exactly 9 points.

In 2006 there was a general shift in favour of the regulated capitalism option. We could argue that this represents a shift toward the left of the policy spectrum. It is interesting to note that the centre-right showed the same tendency, having a similar shift to the centre-left. Hence, we could also argue that a shift by one coalition results in a similar shift by the other coalition. One possible explanation of this could be that the centre-left was influenced by Rifondazione's entry into the coalition. But the Italian economic crisis, characterized by economic stagnation, declining international competitiveness and deteriorating purchasing power of households, could also explain a growing demand of social protection from the electorate, to which the parties responded. Either way, it is interesting to see that the shift is common to both coalitions, and that as a result, the distance between the coalitions did not increase and actually became smaller than it had been since 1994.

We have seen that since 2001 most actors of the Italian party system have structured their socio-economic policy platforms around the pattern opposing left vs. right, while the competition within either of these poles has been greater within the left where RC marked its distance from the centre-left until 2001. We should also note that the ideological distance between the two coalitions remains remarkable. The difference between the centre-left and the centre-right coalition in the socio-economic index shows that until, and including, 2006 there were still options for the voters to choose between alternative policy programmes. At the same time this difference was not that extreme. Contrary to the rhetoric of political leaders and to the dramatization of the tones in the electoral campaign, if we consider only the programmatic supply, socio-economic politics in Italy seems more about *who is better at doing things* than about radically different political projects. The ideological polarization seems to have reduced over time, and the remaining distance does not allow one to identify genuine polarization. We should also note that in 2006, the total variation between left and right is smaller than ever, the two extremes of the political spectrum (RC and Lega Nord) having converged onto more moderate programmatic platforms. The variation is surprisingly small in 2006 when we think that this reflects the policy commitments of more than twelve parties taking part in the coalitions. Finally, this evidence shows a tendency to establish a bipolar system of centripetal competition even in the presence of a large number of parties as has happened in other European countries such as Belgium and Finland (Pappalardo 2002).

This tendency reached a peak in 2008 when the socio-economic platforms of the two main party competitors became almost undistinguishable. Their manifestoes have never been so close in this important dimension of the programmatic supply. For example, they both propose a rich set of measures to increase wages and improve safety in the workplace, to fight unemployment and help young people to find jobs. Moreover, they both propose measures of social housing and benefits for mothers, as well as economic incentives of a similar nature for entrepreneurs.

At the same time, the platforms of the Unione di Centro and La Destra are close to the ones of PD and PDL. The scores of these four parties in the socio-economic index range from 16.2 to 17.4. It seems that the Italian party system has definitely evolved into one of centripetal competition that is typical of bipolar systems and most mature democracies (Downs 1957, Sartori 1976). While the other two parties taking part in the centre-left and centre-right coalition – respectively IDV of the ex-public prosecutor Antonio Di Pietro and the LN – follow with 11.6 and 8.3. Hence, these two parties assign greater emphasis to other programmatic subjects, but certainly they do not oppose an alternative, neo-liberal economic project to the PD and PDL.

In the end, it seems that the massive proliferation of parties up to 2006 was quite disproportionate compared to the relatively small variation in programmatic supply. Even if we consider the coalition manifestoes as the lowest common denominator agreements among coalition partners – a point of compromise among coalition partners whose original preferences vary from this point of compromise – there is reason to believe that the scope of total variation would not in itself justify the existence of over twelve relevant parties.[11] If, as we have seen, ideological distance cannot provide a credible justification for the number of parties, we should search elsewhere for an explanation of this phenomenon. In any case, this work can contribute to the literature that party proliferation and factionalism and their negative influence on policy making were increasingly unrelated to ideological/programmatic divisions in the party system and should therefore be explained in another way.

The party system and the policy making

In spite of the evidence of an ideological convergence of the Italian parties – a clear sign in the direction of centripetal competition that should help the development of more effective policy making through pragmatic competition over policies – the quality of Italian policy making has remained low and is particularly characterized by a recurrent decision-making deadlock. Although Moury documents in this volume an activeness of the Italian government in trying to implement its programmatic commitments, we also see that much of the legislation started by the government is, in fact, stopped by Parliament. This creates a discrepancy between the governmental output and the legislative outcome. For example, an independent study (CIRCAP, University of Siena, various issues) shows that in 2008, by the end of a twenty-month activity and just before the actual fall of the Prodi government, the parliament had passed only 32.4 per cent of the bills initiated by the executive for the implementation of its programme. The same study shows that despite its greater duration, between 2001–2006 the Berlusconi government experienced levels of conflict and factionalism within its parliamentary majority that have increased over time, affecting the policy-making capacity and the ability of the executive to implement its programme. This, in spite of the pro-activeness of the executive that has initiated legislation aiming to implement up to 80 per cent of its programme; only a part of it has actually been approved by the parliament.

As it is shown by long-lasting economic stagnation (see Iona *et al.*, Chapter 15, this volume), Italian political institutions are still largely unable to give responses to many economic problems of the country despite the ideological convergence of parties over socio-economic issues. Certainly, the Second Republic presents a moderate, although fragmented, party system that is deeply different from the one of the First Republic and it should not, therefore, constitute a structural obstacle to effective policy making. It is common wisdom that poor policy making is due to the litigious nature of the Italian government coalitions. Surely, the size of such coalitions has not helped in terms of their discipline. But what are the main causes of the extraordinary proliferation of parties in the Italian system and of their involvement in government?

As I have documented above, ideological diversity does not seem to be a credible explanation. The institutional structures (electoral law, public financing) certainly provide a better explanation of the phenomenon. The mixed (PR-plurality) electoral system in place in the period 1994–2001 and the new PR-plus-bonus system introduced in 2006 have certainly not contributed to reducing the number of parties, but they have forced them to build alliances (D'Alimonte 2006). Moreover, a generous system of public financing (Pacini 2009) has created incentives even for the smaller parties to keep their distinctiveness and take part in elections without considering merger with other parties. Other factors such as the inadequate rewards from larger parties to some individual personalities who have then created their *partito personale* ('personal party') should also been considered (Conti 2008a). But the collusive attitudes of the larger parties should be mentioned as well as, until 2008, they preferred to make all kinds of efforts to include the smaller parties in electoral alliances in order to gain even a small increase in the electoral support, rather than to isolate them, thereby encouraging their disappearance from the electoral market as finally happened in 2008.

On their side, small parties have not limited themselves to occupying office and preserving influence and resources for their leaders (on this widespread habit see also Carbone in this volume). In spite of the pay-offs paid to them in terms of public office such as ministerial posts, they have gone well beyond an office-seeking approach and they have exerted a strong veto power on policies (Conti 2008a). This has added complexity to any coalition which, in the end, resulted in a complicated alliance of many parties each with policy and office goals. Small parties were very active during the policy decision phase in order to have their preferences considered or, at least, to gain some rewards from the government. This, in the end, has put every government under a double pressure: the rapacity of small parties for public office during the phase of government formation, resulting in their disproportionate formation weight; their veto power in the agenda setting and in the policy making of the government, resulting in an equally disproportionate coalition weight (Conti 2008a). However, their ambitions of office/policy maximization have not been without costs, not only on the purposefulness of the government but also for survival of the same small parties. Especially when one considers that most of these parties do not have the monopoly of political representation of a cleavage and that other ideologically equivalent competitors could be found in the party system, it is easy to understand that their survival is linked to their strategy. The creation, in 2007–2008, of the two large parties characterized by programmatic convergence and competition for the median voter, appears to be a proper answer to the problem of party system fragmentation. They have refused alliance with most small parties condemning them to disappearance from Parliament. However, this has not only brought about the disappearance of parties whose values and beliefs can be represented in public office by other parties, but also of some radical parties (Communists, Greens) whose positions are now not represented in Parliament. It remains to be seen what kind of effect this simplification in the political landscape will produce on the institutional performance of policy making.

Conclusion

After fifteen years of existence, the party system of the Second Republic shows evidence of some interesting trends. On the one hand, there is a clear tendency toward the convergence of programmatic supply. We have seen that the positions of the parties in the policy space indeed tend to converge, in particular in the key socio-economic issues. At the beginning of the analyzed period the distance is still quite large, but then it is progressively reduced. Up to and including 2006 there is still some distinction that makes the two coalitions alternative to each other, but 2008 shows a tendency toward similarity between the main parties. In the end, the Italian party system has achieved, like most mature democracies, two important conditions for effective party competition: bipolarity and ideological convergence. This has also been accompanied recently by a reduction in the number of parties. It is the result of a slow ideological realignment that has brought Italy from party polarization, through segmented and finally to moderate multi-partism.

It remains to be seen whether this will produce more purposeful executives, greater party discipline and more effective policy making. Certainly, this has not been the case in the recent past if one considers the poor performance of the country in many socio-economic fields of which the present volume provides some clear evidence (see Iona *et al.*, Milio and Minetti in this volume). As well, one should consider the increased pro-activism of the executive in initiating legislation (see Moury, Chapter 3, this volume) to which a legislative outcome of the same magnitude has not followed due to deadlock in parliament.

In the end, there is a good potential today in Italy to move from irresponsible party government to a party government seriously engaged in the implementation of its announced programme. Obstacles related to the format (number of parties) and the mechanics (ideological distance among parties) of the system have been removed. This is, however, a recent achievement, while the picture of the recent past was much more problematic. It remains to be seen whether in the future parties will be able to maximize gains over this achievement or, instead, they will shift back to the long-lasting sicknesses of the system.

Notes

1   A previous version of this chapter has been published as Conti (2008b) in *Modern Italy* (www.informaworld.com). Given this, I also wish to thank the journal editors and Taylor & Francis Ltd.

2   The quasi-sentence is the coding unit and it refers to an argument. A sentence can contain one or more arguments, hence one or more quasi-sentences.

3   The quasi-sentences related to this policy issue make reference to: the need for regulations designed to make private enterprises work better; actions against monopolies and trusts, and in defence of consumers and small businesses; encouraging economic competition; social market economy.

4   Concept of equality; need for fair treatment of all people; special protection for the underprivileged; need for fair distribution of resources; removal of class barriers; end of discrimination such as racial or sexual discrimination, etc.

5 Favourable mentions of need to introduce, maintain or expand any social service or social security scheme; support for social services such as health service or social housing. This category excludes education.
6 Limiting expenditure on social services or social security; otherwise as welfare state expansion, but negative.
7 Favourable references to labour groups, working class, unemployed; support for trade unions; good treatment of manual and other employees.
8 Abuse of power of trade unions; otherwise as labour group positive, but negative.
9 In 2009, an index of the *Wall Street Journal* and the Heritage Foundation, also used by international organizations such as the International Monetary Fund and the World Bank, ranked Italy as 76th freest economy in the world, in a group of moderately free countries.
10 In particular, Alleanza Nazionale and the Lega Nord propose different solutions for the protection of the European market from third countries, but also for the defence of the domestic market from EU competitors.

References

Circap (various issues), *Rapporto sul governo in Italia*, Online. Available: www.gips.unisi.it/circap/rapporto-governo.

Conti, N. (2008a) 'On political "fragmentation": stay in or stay out? The role of small parties in the Italian centre-left', *Journal of Modern Italian Studies*, 13(3), 388–404.

—— (2008b) 'The Italian parties and their programmatic platforms: How alternative?', *Modern Italy*, 13(4): 451–64.

Cotta, M. and Isernia, P. (1996) *Il gigante dai piedi d'argilla*, Bologna: Il Mulino.

D'Alimonte, R. (2006) 'Una riforma elettorale come si può', *Il Mulino*, 6: 1183–88.

Downs, A. (1957) *An Economic Theory of Democracy*, New York: Harper.

Gabel, M.J. and Hix, S. (2004) 'Defining the EU Political Space: an Empirical Study of the European Election Manifestos, 1979–1999', in G. Marks and M. Steenbergen (eds.) *European Integration and Political Conflict*, Cambridge: Cambridge University Press.

Hooghe, L., Marks, G., and Wilson, C.J. (2004) 'Does Left/Right Structure Party Positions on European Integration?', in G. Marks and M. Steenbergen (eds.) *European Integration and Political Conflict*, Cambridge: Cambridge University Press.

Katz, R.S. and Mair, P. (1995) 'Changing models of party organization and party democracy. The emergence of the cartel party', *Party Politics*, 1(1): 5–28.

Pacini, M.C. (2009) 'Public Funding of Political Parties in Italy', *Modern Italy*, 14(2) 183–202.

Pappalardo, A. (2002) 'Il sistema partitico italiano fra bipolarismo e destrutturazione', in G. Pasquino (ed.) *Dall'Ulivo al governo Belusconi*, Bologna: Il Mulino.

Sartori, G. (1976) *Parties and Party Systems: A Framework for Analysis*, Cambridge: Cambridge University Press.

5 When politics matters

Federalism, Italian style

Christophe Roux

Summary

Italy's federalization is an ongoing process which is part of a broader political and institutional adaptation that has been taking place since the early 1990s. This chapter explores the goals it was supposed to reach and the paradoxes it has revealed given the gap between what was planned and what has been accomplished. It also challenges the conventional view of a popular demand for federalism, claiming that it is rather an elite-driven process. It concludes with an evaluation of the degree of decentralization the Italian state has reached, shedding light onto the direction given to Italian federalism since the victory of Silvio Berlusconi's coalition in 2008.

Introduction

The bill adopted by the Italian Council of Ministers on 3 October 2008 and approved by the lower house of the Parliament (the Camera dei Deputati) on 23 March 2009 is the latest of the discontinuous steps that have been transforming Italy from a unitary into a federal state over the course of a decade. For reasons of brevity I cannot recount here the detailed content of federal reforms (see Baldi 2006). It is more important to stress the political impact of the process that is leading to a dramatic empowerment of regions considered as federal units. In a country that is characterized by strong territorial imbalances, and in which the central government (later reinforced by European regional policies) has long had a tradition of assistance aimed at limiting the still important socio-economic gap between north and south, federalism cannot be considered as a mere technical issue. Rather, it became a salient topic during the 1990s. As has been shown by Diamanti (1995), the territorial cleavage in Italian politics was not activated by the main political parties of the First Republic, even if some parties were especially well-rooted in some regions more than in others. As we will see, this has changed under the Second Republic. As an illustration, it is worth remembering the speech delivered by former president of the Italian Republic, Carlo Azeglio Ciampi, on 31 December 2002:

The spirit of collaboration is even more necessary in this phase of our history. We are developing a democratic state, inspired by the principles of federalism with solidarity. It has roots in our communal history [...] and in the plurality of states on the basis of which unified Italy was born. To create rules for good government and relationships of fair collaboration, including in the fiscal field, between central government and communal, provincial and regional levels, is a difficult task [...]. One can be open to any innovation as long as the principle of solidarity remains firm and as long as national unity in no way is put under threat. There are intangible principles which cannot be bargained.[1]

As in any country where national unity is considered as a key constitutional value, federalism has potential consequences on the very sustainability of the polity. For this reason, federalism, a reform sometimes presented by certain actors as a vector of modernization, by others as a threat, is an important topic for scholars interested in understanding the 'shadows' that threaten Italy. While it must be said that it is too soon to assess the concrete effects of this very slow and complex process, there is little doubt that this reform represents a reverse in the way Italy has managed its territorial imbalances since 1861. Until the early 1990s, the solution to this unsolved issue was to be found in a top-down process through which central government supported deprived areas 'from above' (from the so-called 'special laws' in the liberal period to the 'regional development policies' in the Republican era). With federalism, the would-be solution is now seen as a bottom-up process by which regions (and sub-regional bodies) are empowered and, in a way, 'forced' to perform well in economic and administrative management. What is fascinating in the current phase is that even something that at first sight seems to be a dramatic change is 'filtered' by traditional political contingencies that transform a potentially strong 'great reform' – whatever its consequences might be – into an uncertain change that still relies on political bargaining (between political forces and levels of territorial governance).

This chapter does not develop a technical analysis of the legal provisions and practices of the new Italian federalism. It rather takes the federal issue to enable us to assess the extent to which this specific tool has kept its promises and has improved Italian democracy. Hence, it is a way of attempting an evaluation of Italy's transition from both an institutional and a political perspective.

It is worth remembering that, though improving Italian regionalization has been a recurrent issue until the late 1990s (Roux 2008: 326–8), only from 1999 were specific provisions adopted for the transformation of Italy's territorial organization; the main constitutional reform happened in 2001. Among its effects, it established the federal principle of distribution of powers: the state has exclusive powers in a limited number of areas (that was the case before for regions), while regions have a general competence. However, the domains in which only the State can intervene concern the main issues whereas regions had only limited competence. The same can be said about the capacity of expenditure even if Article 119 establishes the principle of fiscal federalism without entering into further details. This constitutional law, the last important one, approved by the centre-left Parliamentarian majority was confirmed, after the 2001 general election, by referendum in October 2001. Berlusconi's government attempts to go one step further with a very broad constitutional reform, approved by the Parliament in November 2005; it failed, with the rejection of the bill by referendum in June 2006. In the current phase (since 2008) it has proposed a new bill, which must still be discussed by the Italian Parliament. As we can see, federalism has a rather recent story in Italy and it has been linked to the search for an institutional solution to what was perceived as a unsatisfactory working of democracy.

The rest of this chapter will be divided into three main sections. The first will review the reasons for which federalism has been thought as a good institutional tool to improve Italian democracy. The second points out a number of discrepancies between the goals assigned to federalism and the actual situation it has produced. The final section (the conclusion) will describe the most recent developments of the federal reform under the fourth Berlusconi cabinet and the uncertainties they raise.

The expected virtues of Italian federalism

Several factors can explain the rise of federalism in Italy. Europeanization has been mentioned since 'European cohesion policies have furnished strong incentives to the formation of a regional level in unitary national territorial systems or their strengthening in decentralized unitary territorial systems', while it has also 'legitimated the tendency to regionalism, particularly in those countries (like Italy) where this tendency has been justified by the poor performance of the unitary state model' (Fabbrini and Brunazzo 2003: 113). The latter consideration introduces a second factor that has been proposed to explain support for federalism. As experts observe, 'policy makers and politicians have frequently pushed for decentralization as a panacea for the ills of poor governance' (O'Dwyer and Ziblatt 2006: 327). Federal bodies are seen as more efficient, responsive and accountable than a heavy central structure. In that sense, central governments can use decentralization as a kind of 'diet', along with privatization, and federalism is considered as a good specific policy tool to do so.

However another, and less 'technical', variable should be introduced, that is the political mobilization for federalism embodied, mainly, by the Northern League (NL). As already mentioned, this political party, born in 1991 as a gathering of several regional leagues already active in the northern part of Italy in the 1980s, has been one of the most prominent actors of the political change observed with the breakdown of the First Republic. It has activated the territorial cleavage within the Italian political system (Gomez-Reino 2000) and put the federal issue onto political agendas, even if its propaganda had sometimes mentioned – for strategic purposes (Diamanti 1998) – secessionism as a political goal. The Northern League was not the only party with territory-oriented political claims in Italy (even if the literature is relatively under-developed on this aspect, other similar parties were active, especially in Valle d'Aosta and Alto Adige), but it was the only one to be successful in putting territorial reform onto the political agenda. It was possible thanks to its electoral strength and its discourse against disappearing 'old' parties; then, even if the League's electoral performance decreased in the 1990s, it happened in a context marked by a strong party fragmentation and a polarization of political competition. As a consequence, the Northern League was weaker but it was anchored in the bipolar game, which has divided Italian politics into two equivalent, though highly fragmented, parts on the centre-left and on the centre-right. Such a configuration enables one to understand why the federalist watchword has not disappeared. The federal motto has also been echoed by Forza Italia (FI), a party rooted in the northern part of Italy and, actually, a challenger for the LN which remained a leading party only in a limited number of bastions (Diamanti 2003). Those parties, well rooted in northern regions that will prove to be sensitive to federalism, have promoted or included this issue in their policy programme to maintain or develop their electoral support in these areas.

Since then, federalism has seemed to become more and more an object of apparent consensus, beyond the policy factors and the political mobilization of the NL. The reform of territorial organization has been incorporated into a broader frame in which new institutions were described as a necessary step to renew Italian democracy. Not only has this quest for improving democracy proved to be rather unsuccessful (Bull and Rhodes 2007), but such an emphasis partly consisted of a transfer of responsibility from political actors to institutions (charging the system rather than politicians themselves) and it has become a common interpretive framework (which does not mean that it is necessarily convincing). Meanwhile, the constitutional design has been presented as the expression of a popular will: Italians wanted a better system of territorial governance.

All these elements can be found when one reads the contents of political debates in these years. For instance, during the opening session of the so-called *Bicamerale* – which gathered all political forces – its president Massimo D'Alema declared that:

> [T]he country is living a difficult transition but which [...] has generated the force and tension that are necessary for a positive evolution of the Italian society, towards a historically possible and politically shared solution to the crisis [...]. This transition [...] must complete its path obtaining an institutional system which is more efficient, modern and, above all, consistent with the changes which had already happened within the civil conscience of the country. All this implies [...] a move from the institutions to the citizens [...], a guarantee of balanced constitutional powers [...]. Hence, a set of principles [...] aimed at designing a more vivid democracy, rich of a better articulation on our territory, more complete [...] more stable because based on the responsiveness of a system of government and a global strengthening and modernization of our system of guarantees and a more rigorous control on the efficiency and the running of our public administration.[2]

This excerpt is just a short element among many discourses that have been developed to explain, justify and legitimate the reform, but it provides a meaningful illustration of this new institutional advocacy.

This is not just mere rhetoric. The conditions under which the 2001 reform was approved by Parliament offer a good illustration of this belief among those centre-left politicians who were not initially convinced by the reform and who have been constrained to put it on their political agendas. The project has been reintroduced after the severe defeat in the 2000 elections of the centre-left majority elected in 1996. This defeat was characterized by clear territorial characteristics since the gap between the two main coalitions and their leaders had been important in Piedmont, Veneto and Lombardy. Let us remember that while the Northern League won between 5 and 6.4 per cent of valid votes in regional elections at the national level between 1990 and 2005, it obtained, in the three northern regions, 12.4 in 1990, 15.8 in 1995 and 23.7 per cent in 2000 (but only 13 per cent in 2005). The centre-left majority interpreted this defeat as a clear message sent by northern voters, like the leader Piero Fassino who affirmed that this electoral choice 'expressed the difficulty in the relationship between the centre-left and the northern society. Where society is more dynamic, the centre-left had a greater difficulty to understand and represent this reality. We should pay serious attention to the North. We appointed as candidates three very strong personalities and we got a bad result. Our problem is to re-establish a proper channel of communication' (*La Repubblica*, 17 April 2000). This 'channel of communication' was represented by the federal reform that was approved by the smallest majority in the last day of the legislature. The goal was to limit the electoral support of the centre-right in northern regions (Diamanti 2003: 83).

Hence federalism has become a kind of political obligation for all political forces in the process of political transition. Federalism has been recognized as the right tool in the field of territorial organization because of its efficiency and its popular legitimacy. When the centre-left obtained again the majority in 2001, Forza Italia presented federalism as a true panacea:

> [I]ntroducing federalism (or devolution) [...] simply means that regions can make laws in a given number of fields in order to better satisfy citizens' territorial interests [...]. Federal countries have a higher level of sustainable development, a lower level of administrative expenditure, a better efficiency and are more responsive to citizens' demands. Federalism means self-government, hence getting decisions closer to citizens fitting better with territorial needs.[3]

These arguments were paradoxically sustained precisely by those who fought against the 'federal turn' of the Italian Constitution in 2001.

Three paradoxes of the Italian federalism (before 2006)

Is federalism the panacea to Italian problems? Of course, in itself, it cannot be sufficient and other reforms are still on the way and a lot of points (balance between legislative and executive powers, electoral law, party system and so on) are still very much under discussion (Ceccanti and Vassallo 2004). It is still possible to try to make an assessment, even if it is partial and will need to be updated, of the federal pattern in Italy, by looking at the extent to which the scope assigned to federalism has been reached. I propose to do it by asking three questions: (1) Has federalism brought institutions closer to the citizens? (2) Has it improved political and administrative efficiency? (3) Is it still desired by citizens?

First, the basic idea that federalism is a way of making decisional arenas closer to citizens seems to come from common sense; however it is not so obvious. The regional administrative town can be closer to citizens compared to Rome but previous research has already shown that this is not necessarily the case. The widely acclaimed study by Robert Putnam (1993), despite the severe weaknesses in his historical interpretation, has shown that not all regional governments perform well in terms of responsiveness and accountability. He clearly showed that centre-south regions (islands included) tend to underperform (for a further confirmation, see Milio in this volume). It may be reasonable to wonder to what extent the weakest regions – often described as suffering from problems such as clientelism, inefficiency, corruption and violence – will be able to fight against these difficulties more easily with more autonomy, given the fact that these challenges are often attributed to the context of those regions. Unfortunately, research on federalism from a southern perspective is lacking: in the meantime, the dominant impression is that the federal issue seems to be led by the North while it seems to be experienced rather passively by the South. Even in the 'special' regions that enjoy a larger autonomy, performances are not higher. In the Sardinian case, for example, most of the political actors are rather critical when they are asked to assess the way in which regional autonomy, obtained in a specific context, has been used (Brunazzo and Roux 2004). It is true that what has been called 'federalism' or 'devolution' (the centre-right version of the project between 2002 and 2006) is more complex and that the new territorial architecture is based on subsidiarity, with a relevant role acknowledged to municipalities and provinces as the first pillars of local bodies. Though now considered as the main level of governance, it is not obvious that the regions are so close to citizens. An illustration of such a risk is the message sent by the main associations of local bodies (*Associazione Nazionale dei Comuni Italiani, Unione delle Province d'Italia, Unione Nazionale Comuni Comunità Enti Montani*) during the 2005 regional elections. They asked candidates (and, through them, regions)

> to abandon neo-centralist [...] logics and to consider themselves as governing bodies, with essentially legislative and steering functions, going beyond the various ways of direct management that keep on existing at the regional level; to avoid exercising administrative functions that could be exercised in

a more appropriate manner by other levels of government. Local autonomies have proved to be able to face the challenge of federalism in order to implement a system able to put deciders closer to those who are concerned by their decisions and to guarantee better services, a better efficiency, more participation, more social equity and more territorial cohesion.[4]

The reasons that have been advocated for federalism are repeated by representatives of infra-regional bodies to defend the goals originally fixed by reformers.

Is federalism the right tool to provide efficiency? It is difficult to answer since, as another paradox, this reform has introduced federalist trends rather than a fully fledged federalism. When Antonio Maccanico, the former minister for Institutional Reforms in the Berlusconi cabinet, declared on 8 March 2004 in the Senate that 'we will have a Republic, one and indivisible, but with a strong federal structure', he actually described quite well the situation of federalism. The new constitutional settings are the product of political compromises. As a consequence, there are still a number of limitations to the federal form of the state, which is not defined 'federal' in the Constitution (as it is the case in truly federal states), and the powers enjoyed by central government are still very extended.

Moreover, a number of dispositions are not yet completed, and Italian federalism appears to be a slow step-by-step process. The constitutional framework remains the one established with the 2001 constitutional framework and 'it is a clear and shared view that with regard to federalism the situation must still be considered transitional and that an effort to complete and/or clarify some of the aspects introduced by the 2001 reform in the broader framework of a more comprehensive and coherent institutional rearrangement is necessary' (Cotta and Verzichelli 2007: 194). In such a phase, former prerogatives of central government and new regional powers are partly conflicting. As a notable consequence, the Constitutional Court is now in charge of a growing number of cases: from 25 in 2000 it has moved to 43 in 2001, 96 in 2002 and 98 in 2003 (Mirabelli 2006: 253). The Court has more and more territorial conflicts to deal with, which is a perhaps logical consequence of the new settings, but this tends to slow the processes down. In any case, at least, it seems clear to all actors that what is at stake is no longer the choice between centralism and federalism, but rather the structure federalism will have. Moreover, some key mechanisms are still waiting to be implemented. There have been many controversies about the cost of bringing federalism into force,[5] but fiscal federalism has not been clarified. It is an important limit since, as underlined by the commission in charge of preparing the implementation of fiscal federalism, the reform of the *Titolo V* of the Italian Constitution is like 'a motor waiting for fuel: it can be as sophisticated as possible but without it, it will not be able to start'.[6]

Last but not least, is federalism wanted by 'the people'? It would mean that Italians are at the same time interested in and favourable to federalism. Neither of these two elements are obvious and this point requires further clarification. As for interest in federalism, this is not an issue that appears in the list of the main topics that worry Italians, according to opinion polls. In some cases, federalism has not been even included in the list of items that were used in opinion polls performed in recent years in Italy. In other cases, people were asked to make a list of the most urgent problems Italy had to face (see Table 5.1). Federalism is considered the least important topic. Even in the case of social categories that are more likely to vote for the House of Freedoms, data have shown that federalism is not a key issue.[7] During the 2006 electoral campaign, federalism did not receive attention.

Table 5.1 Most urgent problems for Italy (in % 2006)

Rank	Topic	Very important	Important	Not very important	Not important at all	Don't know
1	Unemployment	80	15	3	2	1
2	Health policy	76	15	6	3	0
3	Criminality	75	16	7	1	0
4	Fiscal evasion	73	18	6	2	1
5	Justice	70	20	6	3	0
6	Education	69	20	7	2	2
7	Pollution	68	21	7	4	0
8	Taxes	66	24	7	2	1
9	Inefficiency of public administration	61	25	9	3	2
10	Immigration	59	23	12	5	1
11	Southern economic backwardness	57	26	11	4	2
12	Federal reform	29	27	23	13	9

Source: *Il Sole 24 Ore*, 2 February 2006

Table 5.2 How much do you trust the following organizations, associations, social groups, institutions? (in % 2005)

	Northwest	Northeast	Centre	Centre-south	South and islands	Italy as a whole
Municipality	59.1	51.6	51	41.4	30.5	45.5
	(+ 13.6)	(+ 6.1)	(+ 5.5)	(- 4.1)	(- 10)	
Region	48.2	40.3	54.2	40.8	29.4	41.4
	(+ 6.8)	(- 1.1)	(+ 12.8)	(- 0.6)	(- 12)	
State	31.8	35.8	37.7	40.1	40.3	37.0
	(- 5.2)	(- 1.2)	(+ 0.7)	(+ 3.1)	(+ 3.3)	
European Union	48.2	47.2	57.8	54.8	54	52.4
	(- 4.2)	(- 5.2)	(+ 5.4)	(+ 2.4)	(+ 1.6)	

Source: *Il Venerdì di Repubblica*, 16 December 2005

This lack of interest has been criticized by both fervent opponents (*L'Unità*) and supporters (*La Padania*) of the reform. Are Italians in favour of federalism then? It is possible to distinguish between political attitudes to federalism (what Italians say about it in opinion polls) and political behaviour (what they do when they vote). In terms of attitudes, if we assume that public opinion in Italy is homogeneous on this question, the answer is negative. Indeed federalism is clearly a divisive issue both in terms of territory and political affiliation (see Table 5.2).

This survey is interesting because it was performed in the month following the vote of the centre-right version of federalism (i.e. 'devolution'). It shows that the level of trust in regional and local bodies is slightly different depending on the part of Italy: while Northern Italians trust largely decentralized institutions compared to the state, it is quite the reverse for those in the South. The difference is marked by the attitude towards local bodies between the northwest part of the country and southern regions (26 per cent for municipalities and almost 19 per cent for regions). Differences are less important when considering the level of trust in the state and in the European Union. These data show that if the state is seen as less reliable than regional and local bodies for most Italians (northwest, northeast, central), it is not the case for the whole peninsula. These data confirm previous research (Vassallo 2001). How do Italians behave when they are asked to vote for or against federalism? Two referenda have been organized on this topic in 2001 and 2006. In 2001 a rather 'soft' version of federalism was approved with a very low turnout (34.1 per cent, one must keep in mind that it was organized only one month after the terrorist attacks of 11 September, and that federalism was not the most pressing issue at that time). It was approved by 64.2 per cent of the voters (valid votes) and with a majority expressed in all regions but Valle d'Aosta.

The 2006 referendum, provoked by the mobilization of the centre-left against the centre-right reform, indicates a far less enthusiastic reaction. It is difficult to tell precisely to what extent provisions that dealt with federalism were concerned, in the voters' minds, with the broad package of institutional reforms provided by the Berlusconi government. After contradictory opinion polls,[8] the results were clear enough. The turnout was 53.6 per cent, which is not very high considering the broad scope of the reform, but was much better than for other similar referenda organized under the Second Republic, especially taking into account the technical character of the reform. Eventually the reform was rejected (61.3 per cent against, 38.7 per cent in favour). The territorial distribution of the electoral participation has not brought changes to the traditional patterns of participation observed in Italy. The turnout was relatively high in northern and centre-north regions (except in Trentino Alto Adige) and relatively low, less than 50 per cent, in centre-south, southern and insular regions, even if, as noted by Bull and Pasquino (2007), there was a relative increase in the turnout in southern regions in 2006 compared to the 2001 referendum. As for the vote, Italians eventually said 'no' to federalism in the form wanted by the centre-right majority (Table 5.3). In particular, southern regions massively rejected federalism, apparently understanding it as synonymous with a withdrawal of the central government, which they considered as a source of economic and social support for less developed areas. This is the case of the

Table 5.3 Results and territorial distribution of the constitutional referendum held on 26–27 June 2006, in Italy

Regions	% 'no'	Macro-regions	% 'no'
Piemonte	56.6	North	52.6
Valle d'Aosta	64.3		
Lombardia	45.4		
Trentino Alto Adige	64.7		
Veneto	44.7		
Friuli Venezia Giulia	50.8		
Liguria	63		
Emilia Romagna	66.5		
Toscana	71	Centre	67.7
Umbria	68.7		
Marche	66.1		
Lazio	65.4		
Abruzzo	66.7	South	74.8
Molise	71.7		
Campania	75.3		
Puglia	73.5		
Basilicata	76.9		
Calabria	82.5		
Sicilia	69.9	Islands	70.6
Sardegna	72.3		
Estero	47.9	Estero	47.9

Source: Italian Ministry of Interior's website (accessed 9 July 2006)

regions that gave strong electoral support to Forza Italia, such as Sicily. Only in Lombardy and Veneto, along with foreign constituencies, have a majority of voters expressed themselves in favour of the reform. It is reasonable to think that 'the measures were widely perceived as threatening to undermine national standards of provision in key sectors' (Bull and Pasquino 2007: 688).

Conclusion: which future for Italian federalism (after 2006)?

Federalism seems to reflect all the contradictions that define the current state of Italian society. A reform depicted as necessary, positive and desired by the people has been confronted with an unachieved institutional pattern, difficulties of implementation and political instrumentalization, while creating uncertain legal conditions and divided public opinion. At this point, the assessment provided by Cotta and Verzichelli (2007: 193), who say that the notion of federalism 'has been used with excessive easiness and a great deal of ambiguity' and 'the situation must still be considered transitional', is still correct. The centre-left has had to be cautious on the topic in the cause of defence of national solidarity, while the centre-right has received a warning with the clear defeat registered at the referendum of June 2006 on 'devolution'.

What happened then? Under the Prodi cabinet between May 2006 and February 2008 the two bills designed by the government on the fiscal side of the reform – in which it is stated that 'the federal process is fiscal or it has no innovative value' – were not presented to the Italian Parliament. This is understandable – not because of the supposed internal divisions of the late centre-left coalition Unione (already mentioned in the previous chapters) – but rather because none of the components of the coalition was a supporter of federalism. Now, after the clear-cut victory of the right in 2008, federalism has come back onto the governmental policy agenda. The political configuration proposes once again the 'axis of the North' already put into evidence by Diamanti and Lello (2005). The Northern League is pivotal in securing an absolute majority in Parliament for the new main right-wing party (the PDL). In the Berlusconi IV cabinet, the federal process is managed by a proper department, the *Ministero delle Riforme per il Federalismo*, at the head of which is the historical leader of the Northern League, Umberto Bossi. After several consultations in September-October 2008, a bill was adopted on 3 October 2008. It was transmitted to the Senate on 29 October 2008.

This bill was acclaimed by the government as a major step in the federalization of Italy: 'to make fiscal federalism, given the Italian Constitution which is in force, is an obligation'; previously, it was 'not only a lacuna, but rather a *vulnus*' according to Treasury Minister Giulio Tremonti.[9] However, the text promoted by the Berlusconi IV cabinet is only *preparing a further step* in the process, which intervenes at each territorial level (regions, provinces, cities). It aims to provide the missing rules for the implementation of the principle of fiscal federalism included in Article 119 of the Italian Constitution: (i) the taxing power and revenue sharing formulas (*tributi* and *entrate*) applicable to communes, provinces, metropolitan cities and regions, (ii) coordination of the rules of public finances, (iii) institution of a fiscal equalization funds (*perequazione*) for territories with lesser fiscal capacity *per capita*.

It is too early to evaluate the impact of what is only a partial reform. First of all because it is too general: it is only a framework, which can be modified by the Parliament; furthermore, it only announces further provisions that are impossible to predict. However, some elements have already been criticized by some economists: the reform does not respect the philosophy of fiscal federalism and is too dependent on the political context that has made this bill possible.[10] Others have warned that federalism should not be considered as a panacea: though one can expect that it is likely to foster transparency, responsibility and efficiency in public decision-making, the risk is that, in an excess of confidence in [the] capacities [of the reform] to promote catching-up and development, the federal reform would be 'let alone' and overcharged by duties and expectations, while it should be added to and supported by other structural reforms for the country. In other words, the risk would be to believe too much in the shock therapy of federalism, underestimating the conditions of the context in which it is settled, and especially those regarding the basic structure of the country, the one that regions and local authorities will have to keep on dealing with

(Pammolli and Salerno 2008: 2)

Further research will certainly be required to understand the actual dynamics of federalism in the country. At least two questions can still be put on the research agenda: from a technical point of view, how will Italian federalism be concretely organized and implemented? Linked to this, but in a more political perspective, will federalism be the right tool to reduce enduring territorial imbalances in Italy?

Notes

1 Messaggio di fine anno del Presidente Carlo Azeglio Ciampi agli italiani, Rome, Palazzo del Quirinale, 31 December 2002. Online. Available: www.quirinale.it/ex_presidenti/Ciampi/Discorsi/Discorso.asp?id¼21147 (last accessed 7 July 2008).
2 Relazione introduttiva al progetto di legge costituzionale, 30 June 1997. Online. Available: www.camera.it/_dati/leg13/lavori/rifcost/docapp/rel1.htm (last accessed 17 January 2008).
3 Source: Forza Italia website: www.forza-italia.it (accessed 10 April 2006).
4 ANCI, UPI, UNCEM, *Per un Patto autonomista tra Regioni e Autonomie locali. Impegni e proposte per i candidati alle prossime elezioni regionali*, Rome, ANCI, UPI, UNCEM, 2 March 2005.
5 See on this aspect *Il Corriere della Sera*, 16 November 2005; *Il Sole 24 Ore*, 17 November 2005; *La Repubblica*, 17 November 2005; *Italia Oggi*, 28 March 2006.
6 *Relazione sull'attività svolta dall'Alta commissione per la definizione dei meccanismi strutturali del federalismo fiscale*, Rome, 2005, p. 3.
7 See the analysis of political scientist Roberto D'Alimonte in *Il Sole 24 Ore*, 22 February 2006.
8 See *Libero*, 18 November 2005 and *L'Unità*, 20 November 2005.
9 Press conference at Palazzo Chigi, Rome, 3 October 2008 (video available: http://video.palazzochigi.it/consiglio_20081003.asx (last accessed 5 November 2008).
10 In September 2008, a comment made on the bill by two economists in the online newspaper *La Voce* noted that one article organized a *de facto* financial guarantee based on a tax on oil production for Sicily (where one of the parties which supports the current Berlusconi government, the Movimento per le Autonomie, is hegemonic, reflecting the need of finding a political equilibrium in the coalition rather than the will to improve the technicalities necessary to the functioning of federalism): on this see Boieri and Bordignon 2008. A further comment of the Sicilian region (press office) by Arena (2008) and the immediate 'reply' of Boieri and Bordignon are all available online at www.lavoce.info (last accessed 12 November 2008).

References

Arena, G. (2008) 'La Regione Sicilia e la riforma Calderoli', *La Voce*, 18 September.

Baldi, B. (2006) *Regioni e Federalismo. L'Italia e l'Europa*, Bologna: Cooperativa Libraria Universitaria Editrice Bologna.

Boieri, T. and Bordignon, F. (2008) 'Federalismo ad personam', *La Voce*, 14 September.

Brunazzo, M. and Roux, C. (2004) 'La démocratie régionale en Italie: un modèle à nuancer', *Pouvoirs Locaux*, 60: 108–17.

Bull, M. and Pasquino, G. (2007) 'A long quest in vain: institutional reform in Italy', *West European Politics*, 30(4): 670–91.

—— and Rhodes, M. (2007) 'Introduction. Italy: a contested polity', *West European Politics* 30(4): 657–69.

Ceccanti, S. and Vassallo, S. (eds). (2004) *Come Chiudere la Transizione*, Bologna: Il Mulino.

Cotta, M. and Verzichelli, L. (2007) *Political Institutions of Italy*, Oxford: Oxford University Press.

Diamanti, I. (1995) 'Le territoire est-il de droite?', in I. Diamanti, A. Dieckhoff, D. Musiedlak and M. Lazar (eds). *L'Italie, une nation en suspens*, Brussels: Complexe.

—— (1998) *Il male del Nord. Lega, localismo, secessione*, Rome: Donzelli.

—— (2003) *Bianco, rosso, verde...e azzurro. Mappe e colori dell'Italia politica*, Bologna: Il Mulino.

—— and Lello, E. (2005) 'The *Casa delle Libertà*: A House of Cards?', *Modern Italy*, 10(1): 9–35.

Fabbrini, S. and Brunazzo, M. (2003) 'Federalizing Italy. the convergent effects of Europeanization and domestic mobilization', *Regional and Federal Studies*, 13(3): 100–20.

Gomez-Reino, M. (2000) 'A territorial cleavage in Italian politics? Understanding the rise of the northern question in the 1990s', *South European Society and Politics*, 5(3): 80–107.

Mirabelli, C. (2006) 'Local autonomies, regionalism and federalism in the Italian experience', in J. Fedkte and B.S. Markesinis (eds). *Patterns of Regionalism and Federalism: Lessons for the UK*, Oxford: Hart.

O'Dwyer, C. and Ziblatt, D. (2006) 'Does decentralization make government more efficient and effective?', *Commonwealth and Comparative Politic,s* 44(3): 326–43.

Pammolli, F. and Salerno, N.C. (2008) *Democrazia, Occupazione e Produttività: Il Federalismo e la Sfida della Crescita nel Mezzogiorno*, Rome: CERM.

Putnam, R. (1993) *Making Democracy Work*, Princeton: Princeton University Press.

Roux, C. (2008) 'Italy's path to federalism. Origins and paradoxes', *Journal of Modern Italian Studies*, 13(3): 325–39.

Vassallo, S. (2001) 'Regioni, "governatori" e federalismo. Come la leadership può cambiare la geografia', *Le Istituzioni del Federalismo*, 3–4: 643–74.

6   Family politics, the Catholic Church and the transformation of family life in the Second Republic

Stefania Bernini

Summary

In recent years a number of issues related to ethical and moral questions have taken central stage within the Italian political debate; the family in particular has emerged as a privileged instrument of political confrontation and propaganda. In itself, this is not a new phenomenon. The legal definition of what constitutes a family has represented a major scope of political confrontation throughout the post-war years, and any reform carried out in this area has provoked divisive reactions. In recent years, the controversies that have surrounded the regulation of medically assisted procreation and the attempt to regulate unmarried stable cohabitations have once again brought to the fore the political relevance of the family in contemporary Italy. Both debates, as well as a more recent controversy surrounding the introduction of the institute of the *testamento biologico* have showed the political use of ethical issues, as well as the role of the Catholic Church in establishing a dominant agenda on matters related to morality.

Introduction: the ambiguous role of the Italian family

During the last twenty years in Italy, the family has played a multifaceted and somewhat ambiguous role. On the one hand, when compared to other European countries, families seem to have retained a peculiarly strong social role. Families still represent the main provider of individual welfare, on the basis of strong links of support and dependency between generations (see also some discussion on welfare, job flexibility and social protections in Simoni's chapter). At the same time, Italy's dramatic fall in birth rates, and the phenomenon of the 'long thin family' show that transformations have taken place in Italians' family life and the expectations associated with it.

The ambiguities associated to the social role of the family in Italy are mirrored in the attitudes shown by Italian politicians. Throughout the years, politicians across the political spectrum have paid tribute to family values as the backbone of Italian society; however, scarce social support for families has represented a long-lasting feature of Italian social policy. Rather than being supported by the state, Italian families have long been treated as having the sole responsibility for individual care and support.

It is therefore legitimate to ask what is in the pledge of protection of the family ritually affirmed by Italian politicians. My suggestion is that such a pledge represented, primarily, an ideological and cultural standpoint supportive of traditional values. In Italy, protecting the family meant essentially resisting transformations taking place in the way in which men and women choose to manage their sexual, reproductive and emotional lives.

Discussing the relationship between politics, family and the Church helps to explain the nature of some of the shadows hanging over contemporary Italian society. In what follows I will argue three main points: first, that politicians' rhetorical investment in 'family values' (not supported by coherent pro-family policies) has generated structural inequalities in terms of citizenship entitlements, on the basis of sexuality and lifestyles; second, that the Catholic Church has used the family to create a political space for itself; third, that the exploitation of the family as a means of political confrontation has undermined the possibility of engaging with social transformations and has limited the possibility of expanding social and civil rights in Italy.

The family and the Catholic cultural project in Italy

As discussed at length in Garau's contribution to *Italy Today*, the aftermath of World War II presented the Catholic Church with the challenge of having to re-establish itself in new democratic polities. A crucial means by which the Church reasserted its power was by establishing an overall authority on ethical issues, which allowed it to gain a vital role in decision-making processes. In recent years, the legitimacy of the Church's involvement on policy making in ethically sensitive areas seems to have become a *fait accompli*, while the fields open to such involvement have multiplied.

In a recent article, Vincenzo Ferrone (2008: 33–5) has argued that the Catholic Church's missionary zeal, which aimed to establish a Catholic cultural hegemony in the public sphere, intensified during the papacy of John Paul II (1978–2005). Ferrone contrasted the uncompromising attitudes of the Wojtyla years with the post-war period, when the Church seemed more willing to recognize the sovereignty of the state. The works of the Constitutional Assembly, in which Catholics took an active part in laying the foundation of the new democratic republic, would demonstrate their endorsement of the prerogatives of the secular state. In the case of the family, however, this went hand-in-hand with the determination to insert in the Constitution notions and definitions in accordance with the teaching of the Church. Christian Democrats (DC) fought hard to include a definition of the family as an institution of natural right, based on marriage and governed by immutable principles. Articles 29, 30 and 31 of the Italian Constitution established marriage as the only recognized basis for family life, and assigned to the state the primary duty of preserving the family's unity. In the Constitution, the rights of the family as an institution superseded the rights of its individual members, and the protection of the family as a whole took priority over the guarantee of the 'legal and moral equality' of the spouses.

Outside the political sphere, a determined effort to affirm the Church's authority on family life was pursued by Pope Pius XII (1939–1958) through all available means of social communication. Pacelli asserted the centrality of the family to the creation of a Christian society and provided detailed guidance on family life, the meaning of marriage, and the relationship between the spouses. Moreover, Pacelli understood the extent to which the Church's project could be helped by secular professional organizations, including those representing doctors, nurses and lawyers, willing to act on its behalf in the social sphere. Professional organizations played a major role in the creation of the paradoxical situation (also described by Garau in this volume), according to which Catholic representatives act as influential members of supposedly neutral committees of experts advising on ethical matters of central importance to the Church.

The church and the political sphere

In the post-war years, the Church found in the DC a reliable representative on matters related to the family. However, the political transformations of the 1990s drastically changed the situation of the Church.[1] In particular, the disappearance of DC, which had been continuously in power throughout the post-war years, put an end to the so called 'political unity' of Catholics and brought about a declaration of political neutrality by the Catholic Church. Such neutrality in terms of party politics, however, did not mean a neutrality of the Church towards Italian political and social life.

In January 2006, the then-president of the CEI (the Italian Episcopal Conference), Cardinal Camillo Ruini illustrated the new horizons open to the Italian Catholic Church. Speaking of the forthcoming elections, Ruini stated that the Church intended to maintain a position of neutrality towards the competing political parties, but called Catholic electors to make their choice paying attention to statements such as 'the family is based upon marriage' and the 'respect of life from conception to its natural end'. Ruini criticized the growing tendency to introduce norms destined to undermine the social role of the family founded upon marriage, appealing to future Italian legislators to refrain from taking similar steps (Ruini 2006). Although Ruini avoided singling out specific parties, the reference to the introduction of partnership agreements in the centre-left coalition's electoral programme was not difficulty to see.

A similar line had already been taken up by the CEI in the 1996 election, shortly after the collapse of the DC. Then, the Church declared its support for candidates willing to stand for the respect of the person, the defense of human life from the moment of conception, and the promotion of the family founded upon marriage (Donovan 2003:107–9). This defined the Church's new 'cultural project oriented in a Christian direction'; not an attempt to recreate a sole party of the Catholics, but rather to provide 'guidance' to Catholic voters in a plural political system. The new horizon of the Church was the establishment of a

Catholic hegemonic culture. The transformations under way in the Italian political system supported such a project. The political fragmentation of the Catholic vote, far from depriving the Church of a referent in the political sphere, multiplied the number of parties claiming to be the most suitable representative of Catholic values. This had significant implications for the treatment of the family and more generally for any discussion concerned with morally sensitive issues.

A clear example of the tendency to exploit complex ethical questions for political reasons arose shortly before the publication of this chapter around the case of Eluana Englaro and the ensuing debate on the introduction in Italy of the so-called 'Dichiarazione Anticipata di Trattamento' (DAT). On 9 February 2009 Eluana Englaro died following the suspension of artificial feeding, which had kept her alive for the seventeen years she had spent in a persistent vegetative state. The suspension of artificial feeding was the outcome of a legal battle pursued by her father for more than a decade. In November 2008 the Corte di Cassazione (i.e. the Supreme Court of Cassation) sanctioned the legitimacy of suspending the interventions that kept Englaro alive, on the basis of a recognition of her will in this sense, orally expressed before her accident. This is not the place to discuss at length the complex legal, ethical and medical issues that surrounded the case. The political reactions that followed the ruling of the Cassazione and the position taken by the Church, however, are relevant to this analysis. Immediately after the Cassazione's ruling, the president of the CEI, Cardinal Angelo Bagnasco, accused it of constituting a potential 'first step toward euthanasia', and called for new protective legislation in this area. Besides the Church, calls for new legislation came from a range of parties throughout the political spectrum, albeit with different aims. On one hand, the government called Parliament to intervene to prevent courts from passing principles considered at odds with the respect of life. On the other hand, the centre-left coalition criticized the lack of legal instruments able to guarantee the respect of individual will in relation to medical treatment. In both coalitions, the issue tested the ability of achieving an overall consensus and gave some space to the representatives of the secular parties present in both areas. On the whole, however, the debate was dominated by the strong position taken up by the government and by Berlusconi himself, who, in line with the position of the Church, uncompromisingly condemned the suspension of artificial feeding in Englaro's case. In early February 2009, the government went so far in its attempt to stop the suspension of Englaro's care, as to promote an *ad hoc* decree, which eventually the President of the Republic refused to sign. The initiative received the strong support of the Church and resulted in a far-reaching institutional and public controversy. As in the case of artificial insemination discussed later in the article, the debate was characterized by an overall confusion and the prevailing of ideological stances.

Family politics

From the 1990s, the most open endorsement of family values has come from parties on the centre-right of the political spectrum, and both the National Alliance (AN) and Forza Italia (FI) made frequent reference to the family, starting from their programmatic documents. In AN's Charter of Values, published in 2000, the family and the 'right to life' appeared next to the nation, state sovereignty, and law and order, as the core values of the right (Tarchi 2003). The family was presented there as the embodiment of traditional values and upheld against transformations seen as a form of social and cultural decadence often defined as 'moral relativism'. This included erroneous conceptions of individual freedom likely to undermine the cohesion of the family as well as of society as a whole.

In the case of FI, the family constituted a frequent theme of political rhetoric since the creation of the party. In 1994, in the speech in which he announced his new political engagement, Berlusconi referred to the family as the 'original cell of every society', acknowledged it as one of the guiding values of his new party, and pledged to protect its dignity and its welfare through 'a new Italian miracle' (Berlusconi 1994). In FI's message, the family suggested a commitment towards solidarity and justified politics considered close to Catholic sensitivities. It also provided a theme around which the different political cultures present in the centre-right coalition could converge (Diamanti and Lello 2005). With the exception of a few dissenters, FI endorsed a conception of the family as an institution based on marriage and pursued a restrictive approach to sexual and reproductive rights. The contrast with the tribute paid by Berlusconi to individual rights and liberal values was apparent (Croci 2001: 9). The reference to the family fitted perfectly with FI's individualistic-familistic project: the family carried the responsibility for individual welfare and represented the sole sphere of individual responsibility. Rather than engaging with the reality of family life, Berlusconi's message fuelled the revival of Italy's 'familistic' culture discussed by Carboni in his contribution in this volume.

Finally, the family was used by Berlusconi as a useful metaphor to describe his own political and personal trajectory, as he presented himself alternatively as a father engaged in the rescue of his country, the offspring of a hard-working family, the devout son, and the patriarch at the head of a large family (Farrell 1995; MacCarthy 1996). Berlusconi's own reference to the family underlines the irony that strong supporters of traditional family values have themselves family lives that hardly comply with traditional models. The contradiction between a political message upholding traditional family values and Berlusconi's own lifestyle became even more glaring following his wife's accusations of inappropriate sexual conduct (including sex with under age women) in the spring of 2009. The protracted sex scandal that followed underlined the divergence between the rhetorical upholding of family values by centre-right politicians and their own family lives. The instrumental use of the family in Italian political discourse became thus obvious.

The first consequence of the political use of the family by the centre-right and the strong intervention in this area by the Catholic Church is that pursuing a liberal agenda in family politics has become a risky enterprise in Italy. This has affected the avenues open to parties on the centre-left of the political spectrum.

The position taken up by the centre-left Left Democrats (DS), in relation both to the issue of medically assisted procreation and the regulation of unmarried cohabitation seemed in the first instance to be an attempt to mediate between contrasting expectations. The necessity to pursue a difficult mediation from contrasting expectation became even stronger in the centre-left following the creation of the Democratic Party (PD) in October 2007. The stated aim of the new party was to bring together Italy's 'reformist' forces, in a continuation of the Olive Tree coalition. The new party's statement of values indicated the upholding of Constitutional values and the recognition of the secular state as the most characterizing elements of the party's identity. The family was included in the party's Charter of Values as one of the founding social structures and families 'in their concrete conditions' acknowledged as the main intended beneficiaries of social policy and public support (PD 2008: 8).

Beyond such general common inspirations, however, the political forces that formed the new party diverged profoundly on questions related to family and ethical issues. In particular, the presence in the party of a significant Catholic component openly committed to the teachings of the Church, made it necessary a multifaceted – and in some cases seemingly contradictory – approach to the family and bio-politics, as the examples discussed later in the article show.

A family for the twenty-first century: modernization or decay?

The 1960s have been widely acknowledged as the moment in which marked signs of transformation in attitudes towards family life emerged in Italy. In relation to marriage, the decade saw both a surge in rates of first marriages and the beginning of a steady growth in marital separations, suggesting that ending an unhappy marriage was becoming increasingly acceptable in Italy across the social spectrum (Saraceno 2004). This shift in attitudes was not exclusive to Italy, but belonged to a wider trans-national revolution in values that had started already by the late 1950s.

In Italy, however, transformations in values and attitudes had to confront a strong social presence of the Church and the authority this exercised over the regulation of ethical and moral issues. In the 1960s, the notion of 'permissiveness' was widely employed by catholic commentators to define what they saw as an involution in Italian customs and values, seen as the consequence of the abandonment of Christian values. From a catholic perspective, permissiveness was the most dangerous by-product of modernity and as such had to be pushed back.

The lengthy political battle fought over divorce provides a good example of the difficulty of introducing secular reforms related to the family. As it has been widely acknowledged, the issue of divorce was imposed to the Italian political agenda by the small Partito Radicale, against the open opposition of the DC, and the cautious attitude of the Italian Communist Party (PCI). Although a first law was presented to Parliament by the socialist Loris Fortuna in 1965, the first divorce law was approved only in 1970, thanks to the favorable vote of the PCI. In 1974, the DC made a final – unsuccessful – attempt to repeal the law by referendum. If the defeat of the referendum showed that Italian society had embraced a secular view of marriage, the troublesome route followed by the law proved the resistance of the main political parties to engage with a controversial issue, and the difficulty of the political sphere to catch up with social and cultural transformations.[2]

Attitudes towards separation and divorce were only part of the transformations taking place in family life. Remarkable changes were also happening in the way in which marriage was entered and managed, particularly in relation to reproduction. The post-war period saw a steady increase in the age at which Italian women married and had their first child – who, more and more often remained an only child. Such transformations were not only the consequence of practical (especially economic) constraints; they suggested that marriage and family life no longer met individuals' expectations, especially in the case of women. By the 1990s, marrying late, having fewer children, and in some cases, separating, divorcing and remarrying had become consolidated trends. Marriage, however, had not lost its social significance. In contrast to other Western European countries, divorce rates in Italy grew slowly and cohabitation remained comparatively limited (Zanatta 1997). Moreover, marriage remained the ultimate choice for the great majority of people when they decided to have children. Pre-marital and extra-marital sexual relationships had become widely accepted, but reproduction remained strongly connected to marriage.

The general – contradictory – picture was that of a country where most of the people still viewed marriage as the only suitable context for reproduction, but also where a growing number of couples no longer saw having children (particularly more than one child) as a necessary part of married life. As Italy reached one of the world's lowest fertility rates, it became clear that the resilience of marriage as an institution had not supported a strong investment in reproduction. On the contrary, since the 1950s – and more markedly since the 1960s – Italians proved remarkably successful in controlling their fertility despite a social and political context in which contraception was not only condemned by the Church but also made illegal by the state (Santini 1997).

As in the case of divorce, and also in the sphere of reproduction, only in the 1970s did legislative reforms start to catch up with changes that had already happened in social and cultural spheres. The repeal of legislation forbidding the sale of contraceptives in 1971, the establishment of family planning clinics in 1975 and the passing of the law on abortion in 1978 secularized the regulation of reproduction in the country. The defeat of the referendum called in 1981 to repeal the law on abortion confirmed that these legislative transformations were consistent with the views of the majority of Italians.[3] Despite this, abortion, and more generally the issue of women's control over reproduction, continued to re-emerge in Italy as a terrain of confrontation between different political cultures and as a major field of intervention for the Catholic Church.

Regulating sexuality and cohabitation in Italy

The issue of artificial reproduction has recently brought to the fore the tensions that surround the regulation of women's fertility, the complex relationship that exists between reproduction and notions of desirable family life, and the political significance of these issues in Italy. It has also emphasized the social significance of reproduction in Italy, highlighted, as Bonaccorso (2004) has showed, by the treatment of those couples unable to conceive who are 'denied the right to make a choice'.

In February 2004, the Italian parliament approved a new law regulating the access to so-called 'medically assisted procreation'. An area largely ignored by law became subjected to one of Europe's most restrictive regulations. Among the restrictions introduced by the law were the prohibition on using gamete donation (the type of treatment that requires the use of sperm or egg donors) for in vitro fertilization (IVF) treatments, and the exclusion from treatment of couples who sought IVF, not because they were unable to conceive, but in order to avoid the transmission of infectious or genetically transmittable diseases.[4]

The law designed by Parliament was openly endorsed by the government led by Silvio Berlusconi and was approved with a wide majority. Not only did the centre-right coalition (with only few dissenters among 'liberals') vote in favour of the law, but also part of the Daisy, the centrist Catholic-oriented component of the opposition, now part of the centre-left PD. On the other side, the law was strongly criticized by a large part of the opposition as well as by medical and scientific organizations and women's groups.

A referendum to modify the law was held in June 2005.[5] The promoters of the referendum included numerous personalities from Left Democrats, Rifondazione Comunista, the Radical Party, but also some dissenters from the centre-right coalition, and a number of independent intellectuals. The leader of AN, Gianfranco Fini, expressed himself in favour of a partial liberalization of the law, causing a strong controversy within AN and the centre-right coalition.

Moreover, the campaign for the referendum saw the mobilization of a number of associations representing IVF treatment users, as well as promoters of scientific and medical research.

In the harsh campaign that preceded the referendum, defenders of Law 40/2004 asked voters to abstain, to prevent the referendum from reaching the minimum quorum of votes. The strategy proved successful and, with only about a quarter of electors having voted on 12–13 June 2005, the referendum was declared void.

It is hard to establish to what extent the low turnout at the referendum represented an endorsement of Catholic positions and how much was the outcome of the difficulty of engaging with complex technical and scientific issues, not helped by the scarce information provided by the media throughout the campaign (Bodei 2005). From a political point of view, however, the failure of the referendum was widely read as a victory of Catholic positions.

In 2007, the front that had come together for the referendum on Law 40 mobilized again, this time to oppose the introduction of partnership agreements, proposed by the centre-left coalition, then in power. This once again highlighted the difficulty of the centre-left coalition to pursue secular reforms in relation to the family. The inclusion of the question of partnership agreements in the centre-left coalition's electoral programme in 2005 required a lengthy mediation with the Catholic components of the coalition.[6] Once in power, an even more difficult undertaking faced the Government's attempt to transform the manifesto's general principles into an actual law proposal. The task fell to the Minister for Equal Opportunities, Barbara Pollastrini (Left Democrats), and the Minister for the Family, Rosy Bindi (Daisy). In February 2007, after months of negotiations between the secular and Catholic components of the centre-left alliance, the government finally approved a law proposal. The 'Italian way' to the regulation of stable cohabitations, as Rosy Bindi called the proposed DICO (*Diritti e Doveri dei Conviventi*), tried to regulate rights and duties of cohabiting partners while avoiding the model of partnership agreements operating in other European countries and widely criticized by the Italian Catholic Church. In presenting the law, its authors and supporters insisted that the new set of rights was not comparable to those instituted by marriage. Great emphasis was put on the fact that the DICO would regulate already existing situations and should not be seen as an alternative to marriage. Particular stress was put on the fact that the new institution did not represent a substitute for marriage for same-sex couples. Indeed, the law proposal did not make explicit reference to the existence of a sexual relationship between the partners and excluded any public ceremony likely to be criticized as a 'quasi-marriage'. The overall message sent to the Italian audience seemed to be that the DICO represented little more than an administrative procedure, which did not challenge the traditional notion of marriage and the family.[7]

Ultimately, however, neither the adoption of such a cautious approach nor the fact that leading Catholic personalities (beginning with Bindi) had played a crucial role in the writing of the text, were sufficient to protect the proposed reform from a barrage of criticism. A widespread accusation was that of introducing an unnecessary and 'complex third way between cohabitation and marriage', jeopardizing the fundamental prerogatives of the family as the union in marriage of a man and a woman (Galeazzi 2006).

With few exceptions, the opposition uniformly accused the centre-left government of undermining the family and embracing a dangerous relativism for instrumental reasons. The strongest attack came from the Church itself, when the CEI declared the impossibility for Catholics to accept a law acknowledging forms of cohabitation outside marriage.

Confronted with the rigid position upheld by the Catholic hierarchy, the supporters of the reform had little success in their attempt to defend the introduction of a new legal framework for cohabitation while refusing to acknowledge the equal legitimacy of different forms of family lives. Once again, the debate over the family had represented an occasion for ideological confrontation, hardly engaging with the multiform and changing realities of family life.

Conclusions

Significant changes have taken place in family life in Italy over the last fifty years, most notably, in relation to reproductive patterns. Attitudes towards marriage have also changed, as people increasingly started to marry less and later and a growing number of them showed that they no longer considered marriage as a life-long commitment or expectation. At the same time, however, the social meaning of marriage as the basis of family life has proved more resilient than in most Western European countries. The number of divorces grows in Italy, but remains relatively low, while reproduction rarely takes place outside marriage. In other words, the shape of the family changes, but marriage and family life retain a strong cultural value. Moreover, the family remains a sensitive theme of political confrontation, as shown by recent controversies provoked by the introduction of restrictive rules for the management of medically assisted procreation and the law proposal on partnership agreements. Although pertaining to different areas, both questions were criticized as having an impact on the family's rights and attributions and both proved highly controversial and divisive across the political spectrum. Two elements emerged from these debates. The first concerned the influence exercised by the Catholic Church and the extent to which Catholic values are constructed in political discourse as a constituent part of Italian culture to be upheld in law. The question has become crucial in recent years, as the Church has shown a growing determination to assert its position on a growing range of ethical issues. The second is the tendency to treat the family as an ideal rather than as a social reality.

Political confrontations over what the family should be have often ignored what actual families have become. A uniform concept of 'the family' has been upheld by supposedly pro-family positions as a means of opposing the introduction of measures considered likely to weaken 'traditional family life'. From this perspective, the growing diversity of family life in Italy has often been considered with concern, as the consequence of an unwelcome transformation of values, while the definition of the family contained in the Constitution has been used as the definitive argument against the introduction of reforms. This has ignored the experience of a growing number of people, whose family lives diverge from that described (or prescribed) by the Constitution. Among the others, it has silenced the experiences of one-parent families and families in which parents are not married, as well as that of children born outside wedlock and of same sex parents and partners. Within public discourse, the justification presented for this has often been that such families constitute 'minorities' experiencing problems irrelevant to the majority of the Italian population. From more conservative and catholic perspectives, the point has also often been made that conferring specific rights to forms of family life other than those sanctioned in the Constitution would be tantamount to encouraging socially undesirable lifestyles. Little space has been given to the analysis of the limitation that the influence exercised by the Church is imposing to individual rights. However, the determination of the Catholic church to affirm a hegemonic role in the moral sphere and the willingness of a number of political actors to support such a project result not only in the marginalization of the expectations of those people whose family life differs from the catholic model, but in overall limitation of the attribution of citizenship in Italy.

Notes

1   On the consequences of the disintegration of the DC and the role of the Church, see Donovan 2003.
2   On the transformation of attitudes towards separation and divorce, see Barbagli 1990, and Barbagli and Saraceno 1998.
3   Law 194 approved in 1978, *Norms for the social protection of maternity and the induced interruption of pregnancy*, usually referred to as 'abortion law' had in fact wider and more ambitious aims, stating the social relevance of maternity and the need to consider the induced interruption of pregnancy on the basis of social as well as medical and psychological considerations; for a statistical analysis of the impact of the law since its inception, see Buratta and Boccuzzo 2001.
4   Such restrictions were presented as a means of preventing the use of medically assisted procreation for the 'selection' of healthy children. The anti-eugenic argument was also at the basis of the prohibition of cloning, the production of human embryos for research, and the freezing and conservation of embryos. The new legislation also limited to three the number of embryos implanted at any treatment and restricted women's possibility to refuse to continue the pregnancy once the fertilization of the egg had taken place. Single people and homosexual couples were also excluded from access to medical treatment.
5   Among the elements of the Law 40/2004 that the referendum aimed to abrogate were the obligation to produce a maximum of three embryos and to implant them in one single operation, the prohibition to select embryos to be implanted and the exclusion from IVF of fertile couples at risk of transmitting genetic or infective diseases to naturally conceived children. The referendum also asked for the repealing of the prohibition for women to revoke their consensus to the implant once the egg had been fertilized and crucially, the elimination of the reference to the 'rights of the conceived', which for the first time introduced in Italian law the principle according to which the embryo should be treated as a subject of rights.
6   The formula introduced in the electoral programme of the Unione committed the future government to introducing the legal acknowledgement of the 'rights, prerogatives and faculties' of those living in stable partnerships – commonly defined in Italy as 'coppie di fatto', *Per il bene dell'Italia. Programma di governo 2006–2011* (p. 72).
7   According to Article 1 of the proposal, DICO concerned adults of either sex living together, in the presence of links of affection and material and moral assistance and support, and in the absence of relatedness, either through marriage, blood, adoption or affiliation. The existence of a stable cohabitation had to be registered with the local council; however, the registration did not need to be a joint act, but could be done separately by the two people (art.1.1).

References

Barbagli, M. (1990) *Provando e Riprovando*, Bologna: Il Mulino.
Barbagli, M. and Saraceno, C. (eds.) (1998) *Separarsi in Italia*, Bologna: Il Mulino.
Barbero, D. (1955) *Matrimonio fondamento della famiglia*, VII Convegno Nazionale di Studio dell'Unione Giuristi Cattolici Italiani, Rome, 3–5 November.
Berlusconi, S. (1994) 'Discorso della discesa in campo', 26 January, Online. Available: www.forzaitalia.it/silvioberlusconi.
Bernini, S. (2007) *Family Life and Individual Welfare in Post-war Europe. Britain and Italy Compared*, Basingstoke: Palgrave-Macmillan.
Bodei, R. (2005) 'Un'illusione ottica ha ingannato i sostenitori del sì', *Il Sole 24 Ore,* 24 June.

Bonaccorso, M. (2004) 'Making connections: family and relatedness in clinics of assisted conception in Italy', *Modern Italy*, 9(1): 59–68.

Buratta, V. and Boccuzzo, G. (2001) 'Evolution and epidemiology of induced abortion in Italy', *Journal of Modern Italian Studies*, 6(1): 1–18.

Croci, O. (2001) 'Berlusconi's triumph. Language and politics in Italy from Moro to Berlusconi', *Journal of Modern Italian Studies*, 6(3): 348–70.

Diamanti, I. and Lello, E. (2005) 'The Casa delle Libertà: A House of Cards?', *Modern Italy*, 10(1): 9–35.

Donovan, M. (2003) 'The Italian State: no longer Catholic no longer Christian', *West European Politics*, 26(1): 95–116.

Falcucci, F. (1963) 'La famiglia società naturale fondata sul matrimonio', in *La famiglia e le trasformazioni della società Italiana,* Movimento Femminile della DC, Rome, 9–10 February: 9–14.

Farrell, J. (1995) 'Berlusconi and Forza Italia: New force for old?', *Modern Italy*, 1(1): 40–52.

Ferrone, V. (2008) 'La "sana laicità" della Chiesa bellerminiana di Benedetto XVI tra "potestas indirecta" e "parresia"', *Passato e Presente*, 73: 22–40.

Galeazzi, G. (2006) 'Le divisioni nel centro-destra', *La Stampa,* 13 December.

MacCarthy, P. (1996) 'Forza Italia: the New Politics and Old Values of a Changing Italy', in S. Gundle and S. Parker (eds.) *The New Italian Republic: From the Fall of the Berlin Wall to Berlusconi,* London: Routledge.

Martina, G. (1977) *La Chiesa in Italia negli ultimi 30 anni*, Rome: Studium.

Santini, A. (1997) 'La Fecondità', in M. Barbagli and C. Saraceno (eds.) *Lo Stato delle Famiglie in Italia*, Bologna: Il Mulino.

Saraceno, C. (2004) 'The Italian family from the 1960s to the present', *Modern Italy*, 9(1): 47–57.

Tarchi, M. (2003) 'The political culture of Allenza Nazionale: an analysis of the party's programmatic documents', *Journal of Modern Italian Studies*, 8(2): 135–81.

Zanatta, A. L. (1997) *Le Nuove Famiglie,* Bologna: Il Mulino.

7 The media between market and politics

Chris Hanretty

Summary

The Italian media has traditionally suffered from a lack of autonomy from politics. This lack of autonomy has historical roots. Owners of print and (later) broadcast media have found it difficult to profit, and have thus pursued political goals instead. This has had consequences for the types of journalists recruited. The public broadcaster RAI has thus found it difficult to resist pressure from politicians, pressure which predates Berlusconi's entry into politics, but which has been accentuated because of it. The issue of the independence of RAI and the duopoly in the television market thus remain substantial and unresolved issues for the Italian media.

Introduction

The Italian press and broadcast media do not enjoy a good reputation abroad. Sometimes this reputation is unmerited. When international commentators discuss how the Italian media *entertains* people, they typically focus on crasser elements of Italian television programming – 'bosoms falling out of skimpy dresses' (Jones 2003: 117) – instead of less accessible 'high culture' programming. (An example of the latter might be Roberto Benigni's recitation of Dante in prime-time without commercial interruptions). Broadcast executives have often insisted that Italian television, at its best, is the equal of any other European television.

More often, however, international comment focuses on how the Italian media *informs* people. Here, international and domestic opinion is typically strongly negative. One commentator said: 'In particular, it is argued that the press is not properly independent due to a number of factors: dependence on owners who use it to pursue their own political agendas; tendency to conflate opinion and information; vulnerability to business interests, especially in financial reporting; [and] the demise of the tradition of investigative journalism' (Lumley 2000: 402). These criticisms apply with even greater force to the broadcast media, where the public service broadcaster RAI[1] has, since its inception, been subject to political interference of varying intensity and where the main commercial broadcasting group, Mediaset, is owned by the leader of Italy's largest party and current Prime Minister, Silvio Berlusconi.

The situation these criticisms describe is undesirable both aesthetically and normatively: aesthetically, because politicization of the broadcast media has produced what one BBC correspondent described as 'sloppy and substandard' broadcasting with 'news footage [...] as shaky and out of focus as a holiday video [...] [and] reports [which] are thin on facts but dense on comment' (Frei 1996: 62); normatively, because political interference (from politicians or media owners) may result in a lack of alternate sources of information, a basic requirement of democracy. This risk is not just theoretical: the non-profit organization Freedom House downgraded its rating for press freedom in Italy from 'Free' to 'Partly Free' due to Berlusconi's interference in RAI in 2003, and restored it upon Berlusconi's 2006 exit from government.

It is this lack of autonomy from politics – at a time when other European countries such as Spain are moving forward – which makes Italy the sick man of Europe as far as the media is concerned. This sickness is, however, chronic, and as such precedes Berlusconi's entry into politics. In this chapter I demonstrate how the media's lack of autonomy has historical roots which considerably predate Berlusconi.

Owners

The market for newspapers during the first sixty years of the Kingdom of Italy was not promising: at the kingdom's founding in 1861, only a quarter of the Italian population could read (Castronovo *et al.* 1979: 10–1); and universal (>90 per cent) literacy would not come before 1959 (Banks and International 2007). At 1/35th the daily wage of an average industrial worker, the cost of buying a newspaper was also prohibitive for many ordinary Italians at the start of the twentieth century (Zamagni 1989: 118).

Limited potential readership meant that sales were paltry by international comparison. The *Corriere della Sera* became Italy's biggest selling newspaper when, in the first decade of the new century, it started selling more than 200,000 copies daily (Castronovo *et al.* 1979: 143). In the UK, the *Daily Mail* – then

Table 7.1 Press circulation per 1,000 population

Country	1950	1975	1990	2004
Sweden	433	572	526	481
United Kingdom	609	431	388	290
Italy	108	113	106	137

Source: Banks and International Databases (2007), UNSECO Institute for Statistics (http://stats.uis.unesco.org)

Note: The Herfindahl-Hirschman index (HHI) is a commonly used indicator of concentration. Figures of over 1000 indicate a concentrated market; figures over 1800 indicate a highly concentrated market.

the best-selling newspaper in the world – sold five times as many copies. These differences between Italy and other European countries persisted even as literacy and real incomes converged (see Table 7.1).

Limited sales meant limited profitability. Consequently, continued losses had to be compensated for by other means. During the early development of the Italian press, most revenue for most newspapers came from governmental or partisan sources; even extraordinary daily sales could never cover costs (Mazzanti 1991: 49). In the first twenty years of the twentieth century, occasional subsidies were replaced with more obvious forms of intervention. This was the period in which the first Socialist and Catholic party newspapers emerged, funded by direct subventions from the parties, income passed on from elected party officials, and traditional subsidies from sympathetic industrialists. Large industrial groups also began making their first acquisitions in the newspaper market in this period. (Emblematic of this move is FIAT's acquisition, through its president Giovanni Agnelli, of *La Stampa*). These new actors – the political parties and large industrial groups – were content to subsidize newspapers that would otherwise be loss-making because it allowed them to exercise a voice in Italian politics.

Unprofitability was consistent: even in the mid-1970s, a time of great interest in politics, only 17 of 74 newspaper chains were able to turn a profit (Murialdi and Tranfaglia 1994: 5). (The government responded by introducing a system of *ad hoc* subsidies). Ownership, however, gradually changed. Christopher Wagstaff (2001: 297; emphasis added) felt able even as late as the start of the current century to state that

> Newspapers can be owned by companies that exist for, and earn their revenue by, publishing. Alternatively, they can be owned by companies which exist for, and earn most of their revenue from, other activities, and for whom the newspaper is merely a tool for promoting those other activities [...] *Italy at the moment has almost none of the first kind of newspapers.*

In truth, this judgment was belated. In the 1970s, dedicated media groups had begun to enter what was by then a weakened marketplace. Rizzoli, a Milan-based publisher, acquired a majority stake in the *Corriere della Sera* in 1974; it was followed by the purchase, a year later, of *Repubblica,* Italy's second newspaper, by Carlo De Benedetti. These two groups are now the largest print media groups in Italy (see Table 7.2). Though these groups derived their entire revenue from publishing, they were still involved in politics: Rizzoli was only allowed to purchase the *Corriere* after a previous suitor, Eugenio Cefis, had been blocked by the Christian Democrats.

The arrival of Rizzoli and De Benedetti was welcomed. Staff believed that since both were *editori puri* (pure proprietors) they would not seek to influence the line of the newspaper or to shape its coverage. This had obviously been the case with the party newspapers, and to a lesser extent with the larger newspapers. In part, these expectations were met with the confirmation of the existing director, Piero Ottone, as editor-in-chief, a decision which upset the DC. Subsequently,

Table 7.2 Print media groups in Italy

Group	Principal publications	2008 market share
Gruppo Editoriale l'Espresso	Repubblica, l'Espresso	26.9
RCS Mediagroup	Corriere della Sera, Gazzetta dello Sport	26.8
Il Sole 24 Ore	Il Sole 24 Ore	11.5
Caltagirone Editore	Il Messaggero, Il Mattino, Leggo, Il Gazzettino	10.4
Poligrafici Editori	Resto del Carlino, La Nazione, Il Giorno	8.5
Degree of concentration	*(Herfindahl Hirschman Index)*	*1,820*

however, the group was recapitalized through Vatican-connected banks, and a new director – Franco di Bella, subsequently revealed to be a member of the influential Masonic lodge P2 – was installed (Castronovo *et al.* 1979: 10–4).

The influence of these editors, and the use they made of newspapers to speak to other elites, created journalism written for those in the know. American journalist William Porter was heavily critical of the self-referentiality of Italian journalism, particularly in its political aspects: Italian journalism is difficult to read, he argued, not because it is overwhelmingly intellectual, but because it is 'stylized and in-group': in political reporting the numerous labels attached to the various party factions meant that those who were not regular readers, and thus did not know these labels, had great difficulty in understanding even basic political reportage (Porter 1983: 15). It is therefore unsurprising that sales continued to lag even after great advances in literacy and purchasing power: Angelo Del Boca, in *Giornali in Crisi* (1963), estimated that 62 per cent of Italian had the means and education to read a newspaper but never bothered to do so (Porter 1983: 4).

Journalists

Since owners bought newspapers in order to push a political line, journalists were hired to help create that political line. This was particularly the case with the editors of the different newspapers. This tendency for editors to be primarily political characters was strengthened with the advent of fascism (which, ironically, signaled the ascent to power of a former journalist). Fascism had multiple negative effects on journalism, the most immediate of which was the systematic purge of all journalists who were not members of the Fascist party and, as a natural concomitant, the promotion of all those who declared themselves to be committed partisans. Thus, 'the fascist parenthesis finished by freezing and depriving of all sense those timorous moves towards European – in particular, Anglo-Saxon – models of journalism' (Mazzanti 1991: 84). 'Political and ideological militancy became, at the beginning of the Twenties and Thirties, a winning card as far as entering the profession was concerned' (Becchelloni, in his preface to Mazzanti 1991: 14).

Turning journalists into fascists was easier because at the time there were relatively few journalists, at least in comparison to the total population. There are still relatively few journalists: despite the over-inflated membership numbers of the Order of Journalists (see below), the number of journalists per capita is quite low. According to UNESCO figures for 2002–2003, the number of full-time journalists employed in Italy per 1,000,000 population was 153 in comparison to 203 in the United Kingdom and 627 in Sweden. It should be noted, however, that the number of daily newspaper titles in each of these countries is roughly the same, at about 100 (slightly less in Sweden and Italy, slightly more in the UK). Journalists are therefore fewer in number and less concentrated.

Conversion of the journalistic corps into cheerleaders for fascism was perhaps also made easier by the fact that many Italian journalists of the time were upwardly mobile, drawn from the middle to upper classes. 'Advocates, procurators, and notaries made up the backbone of Risorgimento-period political journalism in Piedmont. Next to the advocates and the teachers there were numerous doctors […] who, having signed on as volunteers, subsequently entered the journalistic profession definitively' (Castronovo *et al.* 1979: 62). Several years later Porter (1983: 52) reported that entrants into the journalistic profession were 'generally […] not only well educated, but well connected'.

The limited number and high social profile of journalists, together with the protection of their political patrons, meant that reputation-building measures – investment in education, and commitment to certain professional rules and values – were derided as unnecessary. One noted journalist asked,

> How does one grant a degree in journalism? It's like granting a degree to novelists, to painters. The journalist is one who creates. How on earth can you release a diploma in creativity?
>
> (quoted in Farinelli *et al.* 1997: 328)

The first courses in journalism did not begin until the 1980s (Murialdi and Tranfaglia 1994: 31): the first university degree in journalism was created only later. Consequently, Italian journalists typically have less formal education than journalists in Spain or the United Kingdom, and less education specific to journalism (Mancini 1999: 104; Canel and Piqué 1998; Henningham and Delano 1998).

Equally, the first self-regulatory codes only appeared towards the 1990s, with professional codes of ethics first appearing at two newspapers with diametrically opposed points of view (*Il Sole 24 Ore*, owned by *Confindustria*, and *Il Manifesto*, the communist daily), before a nationwide agreement on ethical codes agreed by the journalists' union in 1993 (Zaccaria 1998: 523). This development was late by comparison with other continental European countries.

Why was there underinvestment in such reputation-building measures? I suggest that there are two reasons: first, given the social profile of journalists, there was no reputation deficit to remedy. There was, and is, no Italian equivalent of the 'hack' journalist. Second, such measures are often undertaken as part of what sociologists would call a 'professionalization project': the attempt to strike a bargain with the state whereby professions agree to regulate themselves in exchange for a state-granted monopoly on the exercise of their profession, allowing the profession to pursue social closure and extract monopoly rents. Yet the fascist state had already permitted premature social closure by creating the Ordine dei Giornalisti (Order of Journalists). This Order was created in 1925 by the fascist regime to control entry into the profession. Quickly supplanted by the fascist trade unions which grew up around it, it existed in limbo for much of the post-war period until Law 69 of 3 February 1963 stated, formally, that 'no one may assume the title or exercise the profession of journalist if not registered on the list of professionals'. The constitutionality of this provision has been repeatedly tested.

The registration requirement is a mild inconvenience: the Order's full list, comprising over 80,000 names and available online includes many who are journalists in name only (including numerous politicians). [2] A more serious barrier was represented by the esame di idoneità (aptitude test), which had a failure rate of around 15 per cent (Porter 1983: 59).

The institutional apparatus of journalism – the Order of Journalists and the associated trade union the FNSI – was thus over-developed, whilst agreement on the key values of journalism was under-developed. Particular in this respect is the debate over objectivity. Italian journalism has never had much truck with the notion of objectivity, stressing the inexorably interpretative element of journalism over the relaying of brute facts. The most well-known critic of objectivity in journalism is Umberto Eco, who wrote that

> when one chooses to publish instead of throw out an item of news, one carries out an act of interpretation which derives from the importance that [one] as a journalist judges the item to have [...] the journalist does not have a duty to be objective [...] [He must] convince the reader not that he is telling the truth, but rather [...] that he is telling 'his' truth
>
> (quoted in Mazzanti 1991: 194)

Opposition to this line never formed a majority. While Eco's philosophical pedigree is not in question, the release from the demands of objectivity must have been welcome to those journalists who were, through conviction or necessity, pushing a partisan line. One should therefore be skeptical about the reasons which led to the discrediting of the notion of objectivity: as former editor of the *Corriere della Sera* Piero Ottone (1996) put it, 'never say objectivity doesn't exist. It's the alibi of those who want to tell you bullshit'.

RAI

Given the limited autonomy of the printed media from politics, the prospects for political autonomy of the broadcast media – typically subject to greater regulation in most European countries – were not good. After fascism, post-war broadcasting in Italy was not remade by the Allies as it was in Germany; indeed most books on the history of RAI – the public broadcaster established in October 1944 – demonstrate the substantial organizational continuity between the fascist EIAR and the new company (Chiarenza 2002).

Until the 1960s, RAI was largely controlled by the Christian Democratic party. It broadcast news full of parades, ministerial declarations and the positions of parties within the majority. Opposition parties were essentially ignored. There was, indeed, no pretence that the broadcaster was independent: one Minister admitted as much in a Parliamentary debate towards the end of the 1950s:

> Naturally, the board of RAI decides [shouts from the left]. Well, if you don't like that, then the DC decides. You don't like that either? Do you mind that Italians have given the DC a majority? It is the Italian people that decide to elect men inspired by the principles of the Christian Democracy [applause from the centre]. This is the fact of the matter, even if you don't like it
>
> (quoted in Veltroni 1990: 99)

The DC's grip on the broadcaster began to weaken in the 1960s as the smaller parties of the governing coalition – the Republican, Liberal, and Social Democratic parties – began to demand some influence in the broadcaster. Some steps forward were taken: Enzo Biagi, one of Italy's most respected journalists, was recruited to head the *telegiornale* (television news), and for a time obtained some measure of independence from the governing parties; but 'amongst the guarantees which Biagi had not obtained (and perhaps had not even thought to ask) was the possibility of choosing capable journalists, unconstrained by the party apparatus, and not necessarily drawn from the press offices and the youth secretariats of the political parties'. The experiment ended quickly, as Biagi 'soon realized the impossibility of setting a new course with such human resources... and, at the first occasion, resigned' (Chiarenza 2002: 103).

The model developed was one whereby RAI obtained the consent of the political parties, and thus continued access to funds from the license fee (which formed a part of RAI's income, supplemented by advertising) by granting each party an area within the broadcaster where it could impose its own vision. The system worked after a fashion, and the 1960s were a boom period for RAI. Ultimately it was the intervention of the Constitutional Court which made reform necessary. The Court had been asked to decide whether RAI's monopoly on broadcasting was constitutional: in a nuanced judgment, it held that this monopoly was legal as long as certain conditions were met – including a measure of independence from the executive (Volcansek 2000: 121).

The executive was thus forced to deliver earlier promises to reform RAI. It did so in collaboration with the PCI, which gave support to ever-weaker DC-led governments as part of its Historical Compromise. In terms of structure, the reform granted parliament greater powers over the broadcaster (including the power to appoint the board) which had previously been enjoyed by the executive. The leitmotif of the reform could not be a commitment to objectivity or impartiality as proclaimed by other European public service broadcasters: the promise was neither philosophically reputable nor credible. Rather, the key concept was pluralism, which had the advantage of being 'relatively fresh', even though 'few knew what it meant: it would therefore be discussed for quite some time' (Ufficio Stampa della Rai 1976: 248).

The idea of a plurality of voices was initially appealing but ultimately led to the abandonment of any commitment to objectivity and the division of the broadcaster into competing spheres controlled by the parties: the phenomenon of *lottizzazione*, or

> division of the most powerful or prestigious roles in an organization or institution by agreement of the parties (or party factions, or more generically, by powerful interest groups) which indirectly or directly exercise control through individuals whom they designate on the basis of essentially political characteristics, and thus not necessarily on the basis of any specific technical ability
>
> (Murialdi 1997)

This division was rigid and exacting: the channels had their associated political areas – the first channel for the DC, the second channel to the secular parties in the governing coalition, and (from 1987) the third channel to the PCI. Within each channel, political affiliations were carefully controlled so that a socialist director (i.e. belonging to the PSI) was always paired with, say, a left-leaning Christian Democrat (Padovani 2005: 110).

Lottizzazione has had critics and defenders. The latter have typically argued that extending political influence over the broadcaster to a wider range of parties caused much greater openness (Padovani 2005). I would argue that the decision to divide RAI up in this way was very much *faute de mieux* given Italian journalism's difficulty in credibly claiming to be objective. Irrespective of its defects or virtues, the system was partly dismantled when the established party system collapsed in 1992. By then, however, RAI was facing new threats from commercial competitors – in particular, the Mediaset group owned by the current Italian Prime Minister.

Private broadcasters

In the same sequence of judgments which led to reform of RAI, the Constitutional Court also discussed the idea of commercial television. Such television would be permissible, the Court argued, only on a local basis; national commercial broadcasting, lacking the safeguard of parliamentary control, could result in intolerable dominance of the political thought of the country by a commercial interest. Yet the court 'could not envision how any local broadcaster could parley a single local market into one of national scale' (Volcansek 2000: 122).

This was precisely what Silvio Berlusconi did. He competed initially with a number of publishing groups: Rizzoli, Mondadori and Rusconi. These groups, though, persisted in producing the same self-referential, overly intellectual fare which had retarded sales of newspapers: 'attached to their origins in the world of books [they] tried to create programs of cultural value but didn't fully understand either the language of television or the nature of its business' (Stille 2006: 57). Additionally, these groups seemed to have greater difficulty in finding capital to finance their television ventures than the 'parvenu builder of suburban condominiums', and Berlusconi 'drove his competitors (and himself) deeper and deeper into debt until they sold out to him': Rusconi sold Italia 1 to Berlusconi in 1983, and Mondadori followed a year later with Rete4 (Stille 2006: 63).

Berlusconi's new media venture had little political content and less news, dedicated as it was to importing American soap operas and films at low cost, and selling at a high price the ad spaces contained therein. Yet the new media venture had to be interpreted in a political key. Of all the parties present in Italian society at that time, the new venture most closely resembled Bettino Craxi's PSI, which had shed its socialist vocation in an attempt to become a catch-all party. *Craxismo* was built around modernity and a celebration of the new and individual; Berlusconi, who looked to America for his television content, and who had beaten off the bookbinders, seemed to embody that modernity. A political alliance thus formed between the two men from Milan.

Berlusconi needed the political alliance: his national network was not legal and various assets were indeed seized by prosecutors in Turin, Rome and Pescara (Volcansek 2000: 125). Craxi, Prime Minister during this period, hastily issued a government decree declaring Berlusconi's stations to be legal; this decree was subsequently turned into law after Craxi forced it on his coalition allies.

The decree not only cemented Mediaset's control over half of the spectrum, but also led other parties to scramble for increased influence over RAI. The PSI now viewed the ascent of commercial broadcasting as a better path to influence than funding or supporting the Italian public television. The Christian Democrats, in exchange for ratifying the status quo in commercial television, demanded greater influence over the public broadcast but needed to build a broader coalition in support of RAI should the PSI withhold its support entirely. In such a context, RAI director-general Biagio Agnes 'realized that he could no longer count on the parliamentary support of the socialist party to finance the company through progressive increases in the license fee [...] [and] advertising. Who then could be counted on? Only the communists remained' (Balassone and Guglielmi 1995, p. 19)

The PCI – as represented by a youthful Walter Veltroni – was thus offered the possibility of nominating the chief editor and director of the third channel, RaiTre. This signalled the incorporation of all the major parties into the system of *lottizzazione*, and the establishment of a parallelism between RAI and Mediaset, now recognized not as neutral observers but as parties within politics itself.

Problems of duopoly

The established party system collapsed in 1993, leaving only the former Communist Party – renamed as the Left Democrats – to compete in the 1994 elections. The last legislature dominated by the old parties passed a number of reforms, including a 1993 reform of RAI which:

- reduced the size of the board from sixteen to five
- gave the power to nominate board members to the Presidents of the two chambers of the Parliament (who until that point had traditionally been appointed from opposing coalitions)
- reduced the board's term in office to two years.

The reform was only ever intended to be temporary, but governed RAI for the next eleven years.

Fearful of the probable victory of the left, Silvio Berlusconi founded his own party, Forza Italia, and became prime minister in 1994. His government lasted six months and had little impact on public policy, but made the issue of Berlusconi's conflict of interests extremely salient: how could one man be Prime Minister whilst retaining ownership of half of the television market and indirect control over the remaining half?

The centre-left was forced to deal with these issues when it came to power in 1996. Whilst the generic issue of conflicts of interest was more difficult to solve than might readily be appreciated, issues relating to the media seemed more tractable. Indeed, the incoming government had a perfect alibi for imposing measures that would hurt its principal opponent: two years earlier, the Italian constitutional court had ruled that legal provisions which allowed one person to own three networks were unconstitutional. The Court, perhaps seeking to protect itself, did not give its ruling immediate effect, but rather left untouched a minor transitory provision, in effect, giving Parliament a deadline to rewrite media law.

That deadline was rapidly approaching when the centre-left was elected. Had the government done nothing, Berlusconi's television channels would have ceased to be legal, and would have fallen into a constitutional black-hole. Surprisingly, the government decided to throw Berlusconi a lifeline, and passed a decree (No. 545 of 23 October 1996) extending the deadline. In exchange, it asked parliament to pass a thorough reform by July 1997. At this point, the issue might still have been resolved, for the law that eventually passed seemed to place exacting limits. It prevented operators from gaining more than 30 per cent of the television market, or from gaining more than 20 per cent of the advertising market in print and broadcast combined – limits which Berlusconi's group exceeded. This semblance may have been illusory: one noted legal scholar (Zaccaria 1998: 32) judges that the only reason the bill was passed was because it had been sufficiently watered down. Indeed, deputies from Berlusconi's party, Forza Italia, abstained on the bill rather than voting against it.

The law entrusted a new sectoral watchdog to determine whether the television companies had breached these limits. The watchdog took one year to be set up, another year to publish rules stating how it would conduct the investigation, and a further year to conduct the investigation, at the end of which – in June of 2000 – it released a sophisticated judgment which had negligible effect. The watchdog found that both RAI and Mediaset controlled more than 30 per cent of the market (Table 7.3). However, the watchdog took advantage of an escape clause in the law, according to which market shares in excess of 30 per cent were permissible if they did not damage competition and if such shares were the result of 'natural growth' of the company.

It remains unclear why the centre-left was so generous in its dealings with Berlusconi. Certainly, harsher measures would have endangered ambitious projects for constitutional reform which needed Berlusconi's consent, and quicker action was made impossible by communist opposition to liberalizing measures in the law – in particular, privatization of the network operator Stet. More generally though, tough action against Mediaset would have required simultaneous reform of public television, according to the false parallelism between the two TV channels. 'Mediaset needs RAI to justify having three channels, resisting centre-left attempts to reduce this number to two. RAI, the argument goes, could justify its shift [...] to popular programming by pointing to Mediaset' (Hibberd 2004: 152). Similarly, since the Mediaset channels were partisans in support of the centre-right, the RAI channel must perforce be agents of the left (remember: there is no possibility of considering either group objective and for that reason independent). This parallel benefitted both broadcasters, but left unsolved the problems of oligopoly. Since the efforts to reform RAI, including the removal of one channel (legislative proposal S1138), failed in 2000, no firmer plan of action (which was also politically credible) could be taken either by Parliament or by the regulator.

Table 7.3 Market share of television companies, 1997

Group	Min. share	Max. share
RAI	44.0	48.1
Mediaset	29.6	32.3
Cecchi Gori/Telemontecarlo	0.6	0.7
Tele+	5.6	6.2
Local networks	4.7	5.1
Others	15.5	7.6
Degree of concentration (HHI)	*3106.8*	*3481.5*

Source: Agcom.

Berlusconi

Following Berlusconi's return to power in 2001, his government proposed new legislation concerning both anti-trust limits in the media and the governance of RAI. The law (Legge Gasparri) was passed in December 2004 after having initially been vetoed by President of the Republic Carlo Azeglio Ciampi. The law's premise is that the relevant market is not the television market or the newspaper market *per se*, but rather the media market as a whole (the so-called *sistema integrato delle comunicazioni*, or SIC). The law decreased the maximum permissible share of the market to 20 per cent, but since this limit is calculated on the basis of a much larger market, it has the effect of legitimating much larger holdings. Reform of the governance of RAI was less imaginative: the board increased from five to nine members, who would now be elected by the Parliament (seven members) and government (two members, of which one is the President) acting in concert. The bill also proposed privatization of the public television, but this seems now unlikely to happen now.

Berlusconi's behaviour towards the media, and RAI in particular, has been just as controversial as his government's media legislation. On a state visit to Bulgaria in 2002, Berlusconi declared that 'the use that Biagi, Santoro and Luttazzi have made of public television – paid for with public money – is criminal. The new RAI administration must see that this does not happen again'. Following this incident – widely reported in the international press – Santoro's contract was not renewed and Biagi's show was discontinued.

There is no evidence, apart from this declaration, to suggest that Berlusconi asked the public service broadcaster board members directly to dismiss Biagi or Santoro. It is possible that the statement itself was sufficient either to convince members of the board (appointed by members of Berlusconi's coalition) or the Director-General Agostino Saccà (candidate for re-appointment at the end of his mandate in 2004) that not renewing the contracts would win political favour. At the very least the fact that RAI dismissed these individuals after a statement of this nature shows the company was shockingly blasé about public perception of its independence from government.

Direct contact between Berlusconi and RAI employees has often been alleged. Former President of the RAI, Lucia Annunziata, claimed during a press conference with journalists from the international press that she 'knew for a fact' that Berlusconi called television executives behind her back. It was not until December 2007, however, that direct evidence was found, when the *Espresso* magazine published a transcript of a phone call between Berlusconi and Saccà (by this time director of fiction) in which the Prime Minister asked for two women to be given auditions for upcoming dramas. (The women were close to centre-left senators Berlusconi was allegedly trying to corrupt.) Following the publication of the transcripts Saccà was not dismissed, only transferred to a less important post; even this measure was met with opposition from the centre-right members of the board.

Whilst this evidence demonstrates that Berlusconi can ask for favours at the broadcaster, and get them, one can overstate Berlusconi's influence on public television. I have elsewhere (Hanretty 2007) demonstrated that there was no big shift in RAI's coverage, measured in terms of the screen-time given to parties of the left and right respectively, before and after Berlusconi's coalition got the chance to nominate a new board; continued political fighting over the broadcaster is thus likely to be part of a longer, positional game aimed at cementing influence in the media.

Conclusion

In sum, Italian media owners have always pursued politics, not profit. Berlusconi is no different in this respect. Journalists have always been recruited with their political affiliation in mind: those who work for Mediaset and RAI are no different. RAI has always been subject to political influence of some kind or another, and this too continues under Berlusconi. There has therefore been substantial continuity. However, other states have gone beyond continuity and reformed their media systems. The fact that Italy has not, and thus that its media continues to enjoy limited autonomy vis-à-vis politics, speaks to the sickness of the media system and also to the malady which afflicts Italy in general, namely a limited capacity for serious structural reforms.

Notes

1 RAI means 'Radio Televisione Italiana' – originally created as Radio Audizione Italiana, RAI still uses its old acronym.
2 See: http://www.annuariogiornalistiitaliani.it/home.asp

References

Balassone, S. and Guglielmi, A. (1995) *Senza rete. Politica e televisione nell'Italia che cambia*, Milan: Rizzoli.

Banks, A. and International Databases (2007) *Cross-national Time-series Data Archive*, Databases International.

Canel, M.J. and Piqué A.M. (1998) Journalists in Emerging Democracies: The Case of Spain, in D.M. Weaver (ed.) *The Global Journalist*, Cresskill, NJ: Hampton Press.

Castronovo, V., Giacheri Fossati, L. and Tranfaglia, N. (1979) *La Stampa Italiana nell'eta Liberale*, Bari: Laterza.

Chiarenza, F. (2002) *Il Cavallo Morente. Storia della RAI*, Milan: Franco Angeli.

Farinelli, G., Paccagnini, E., Santambrogio, G. and Ida Villa, A. (1997) *Storia del Giornalismo Italiano: Dalle Origini ai Giorni Nostri*. Turin: UTET.

Frei, M. (1996) *Italy: The Unfinished Revolution*. London: Sinclair-Stevenson.

Hanretty, C. (2007) 'The Gospel truths of Italian media bias', *Comunicazione Politica*, 8(1): 31–48.

Henningham, J. and Delano, A. (1998) 'British Journalists', in *The Global Journalist: News People Around the World*. Cresskill, NJ: Hampton Press.

Hibberd, M. (2004) 'RAI under the Centre Right', *Italian Politics: A Review*, (19): 150–65.

Jones, T. (2003) *The Dark Heart of Italy*, London: Faber & Faber.

Lumley, R. (2000) 'Newspapers', in G. Moliterno (ed.) *Encyclopedia of Contemporary Italian Culture*, London: Routledge.

Mancini, P. (1999) 'Giornalisti in Italia: indagine socio-demografica sui professionisti dell'informazione', *Problemi dell'informazione*, 24(1): 92–108.

Mazzanti, A. (1991) *L'obiettività Giornalistica: un Ideale Maltratto*, Naples: Liguori.

Murialdi, P. (1997) 'Per una ricerca storica sulla lottizzazione', *Problemi dell' informazione*, 22(1): 7–11.

Murialdi, P. and Tranfaglia, N. (1994) 'I quotidiani negli ultimi vent'anni: crisi, sviluppo e concentrazioni', in V. Castronovo and N. Tranfaglia (eds.), *La Stampa Italiana Nell'Età Della Tv, 1975–1994*, Rome: Laterza.

Ottone, P. (1996) 'Il decalogo del giornalista', *Repubblica*, 25 September.

Padovani, C. (2005) *A Fatal Attraction: Public Television and Politics in Italy*, Oxford: Rowman & Littlefield.

Porter, W. (1983) *The Italian Journalist*, Ann Arbor, MI: University of Michigan.

Stille, A. (2006) *The Sack of Rome: How a Beautiful European Country with a Fabled History and a Storied Culture Was Taken Over by a Man Named Silvio Berlusconi*, New York: Penguin.

Ufficio Stampa della Rai (ed.) (1976) *Pluralismo, Appunti dell'Ufficio Stampa*, Rome: Rai Radiotelevisione Italiana.

Veltroni, W. (1990) *Io e Berlusconi (e la Rai)*, Rome: Editori Riuniti.

Volcansek, M.L. (2000) *Constitutional Politics in Italy: The Constitutional Court*, Hampshire: Macmillan Press.

Wagstaff, C. (2001) 'The Media', in *Cambridge Companion to Modern Italian Culture*, Cambridge: Cambridge University Press.

Zaccaria, R. (1998) *Diritto dell'Informazione e della Comunicazione*, Padua: CEDAM.

Zamagni, V. (1989) 'An International Comparison of Real Industrial Wages, 1890–1913: Methodological Issues and Results', in P. Scholliers (ed.) *Real Wages in 19th and 20th Century Europe: Historical and Comparative Perspectives*, Oxford: Berg.

Part II
History, memory and politics

8 The legacy of the strategy of tension and the armed conflict in a context of (non)reconciliation

Anna Cento Bull

Summary

This chapter argues that Italy's apparent inability to complete successfully the transition from the First to the Second Republic and renew its political institutions is, at least in part, due to the country's failure to deal with its problematic legacy of political conflict and ideological confrontation. Italy went through a period of violent conflict in the late 1960s and 1970s which has left a legacy of bitter divisions, antagonisms and recriminations. The conflict also prevented a truth recovery process about past crimes and the achievement of full justice through the courts. Indeed, since the collapse of the First Republic, Italy has shown extremely high levels of political conflict and mistrust. The chapter argues that there are strong resistances to truth recovery from various social and political actors, and that in this situation, many appear to favour a form of 'collective amnesia'. Yet it is precisely the use of lies and amnesia that is preventing the emergence of tolerant identities and is fuelling mutually exclusionary narratives and interpretations of the conflictual past, as well as cultures of victimhood.

Introduction

This chapter raises the question of whether the Italian inability to bring its never-ending transition to a successful completion is partly due to the country's failure to deal effectively with its problematic legacy of ideological confrontation and violent political conflict. The analysis considers the growing literature on post-conflict national reconciliation, especially as regards historical memory, justice and truth-telling. While this literature is generally applied to countries, notably in Africa and Latin America, which have experienced a transition from an authoritarian regime to a liberal democracy, coupled with the occurrence, in their recent history, of a bloody and prolonged civil war, it has been recently been extended to cover democratic European countries, including the UK (Northern Ireland) and contemporary Spain.

In the Italian case, the parallels are obvious, albeit with some important caveats. While the country has gone through a traumatic political transition since the early 1990s, this has involved a move from one form of democracy to another, rather than a full-blown process of democratization. Furthermore, even though Italy also experienced a period of violent conflict in the late 1960s and 1970s, this had ended well before the crisis of the First Republic, thereby seemingly reducing the urgency of overcoming past divisions at the same time as reaching a consensus over institutional reforms and constitutional renewal. In reality, however, pacification is not the same as reconciliation. Without the latter, old enmities can persist and even rekindle. The violent conflict of previous decades has left an enduring legacy of divisions, recriminations, and 'politicization of victimhood', occasionally even spilling over into physical violence, as at the Genoa world summit of July 2001, where violent clashes between demonstrators and the police left one person dead and several wounded, amid allegations of police brutality. More recently, in October 2008, a few episodes of violence involving student demonstrators, extreme-right militants and the police, briefly marred the peaceful protests against Berlusconi's government educational reforms. In addition, recent polemics around historical revisionism, especially in relation to fascism/anti-fascism and the place of the Italian Resistance in the national memory (see Arthurs in this volume; Mammone 2006), have shown that ideological confrontation remains as strong today as it was during the First Republic. To what extent can this situation be attributed to the fact that Italy has not embarked on a process of national reconciliation? Conversely, has the country attempted such a process but failed? If so, what are the reasons for this failure?

This chapter therefore examines whether (and how) Italy has addressed its divisive past of ideological contraposition and political violence or whether it has opted instead for a 'collective amnesia' of its recent history. This raises a further issue: whether the literature on conflict resolution and national reconciliation offers tested and recognized 'best practices' in coming to terms with a divisive past, whether these practices involve remembering or forgetting the bitter divisions and violent deeds of recent decades, who should initiate such acts of remembering and/or forgetting, the role played by the judicial process in dealing with the perpetrators and victims of violence, and indeed who is included among the victims.

Ways to approach national reconciliation

There are three contrasting approaches to achieving national reconciliation after a period of deep internal divisions erupting into violent conflict (Rigby 2002). The first approach is through retributive justice, whereby the violent crimes are prosecuted through the courts and the rule of law is upheld and applied. For many scholars and experts this is the only approach that can bring both truth and justice to the victims of political violence and must precede any attempt at national reconciliation. As Boraine (2006: 19) put it: 'No society can claim to be free or democratic without strict adherence to the rule of law'.

However, critics argue that retributive justice is not appropriate for transitional processes, for both moral and practical reasons. Morally, because of its adversarial nature which puts the victims under considerable pressure while often not succeeding in redressing their grievances, and because it exacerbates conflict relations, thereby running the risk of re-opening violent confrontations. Practical reasons include the difficulty of ensuring justice through the criminal courts when the old elites retain power in the new regime or there are no clear winners emerging from the collapse of the old regime, but there is instead a relatively equal balance of power. Where the state has played a part in the political violence of the past, it is also very difficult to achieve justice through the courts, because of its determination to deny the truth and cover it up (Rolston 2000).

The second approach is based on collective amnesia, often accompanied by amnesty, which is predicated on the need to ensure a peaceful transition to democracy, build new political institutions and guarantee the respect of civil and human rights. As these are the overriding goals, they should not be put in jeopardy through any well-intentioned but misplaced pursuit of retributive justice or a public search for truth and redress in relation to past violence. As Mendeloff (2004: 372) argued, 'lies, distortions, or amnesia in the service of tolerant, non-self-glorifying, non-victimizing national identities are preferable to truths that can fuel victimization myths, scapegoating, and intolerance'.

For the advocates of this approach, Spain has provided the best example of a country where the decision not to confront and re-open its history of violence clearly paid off, allowing a stable and secure democratic system to emerge out of the old authoritarian regime. Yet Spain is also often cited as a case where collective amnesia has proved short-lived, due to increasingly vocal requests for truths about the civil war (Blakeley 2005), the persistence of political grievances and violence, and mistrust for democratic institutions (MacDonald and Bernardo 2006). Recently, amnesia in Spain was all but broken, with the Zapatero government passing a law on historical memory that honours republican victims, and the Church responding by beatifying 498 priests and nuns killed in the Spanish Civil War.

Finally, the third approach, which has become increasingly important following the end of the Cold War, relies on the idea of 'restorative justice' and focuses on achieving reconciliation through a process of truth-telling about past violent acts and violations of human rights, accompanied by reparations and apologies to the victims, and the construction of a shared narrative of the conflictual past. In 1995, South Africa led the way by establishing a Truth and Reconciliation Commission, which 'was charged with investigating gross human rights abuses that occurred between 1960 and 1994' (Graybill and Lanegran 2004: 5–6). Since the emphasis was on promoting reconciliation and healing, an amnesty was promised to those perpetrators who fully disclosed and acknowledged their past crimes, even though it was granted selectively. Inspired by the South African example, numerous 'commissions' have been set up, mainly in Latin American and Eastern Europe, with mixed results.

On the one hand, this approach is seen by many as a more effective and moral way to achieve justice, truth and a stable democracy during a transitional period than either retributive justice or amnesia (Hayner 2001). According to Barkan (2006: 7–8) 'since 1989 countries that embraced a process of redress are more likely to have a strong democracy than those which have not'. According to the critics, however, 'alternative' paths to reconciliation present notable risks, particularly in terms of securing the accountability of perpetrators through identification and/or punishment (e.g. Abrams 2001). In addition, what constitutes the 'truth' is contested: 'the history that is revealed by truth commissions can only be a partial truth. The very process of uncovering a part of the truth and granting it the status of official, public and authoritative record can serve to cover up other aspects of the past' (Rigby 2002).

In short, none of the three main approaches is devoid of risks and failings. Indeed, most commentators are at pains to point out that each nation-state must be able to work out its own path to reconciliation, taking into account its own history, local conditions, political pressures and groups dynamics. What appears to be important is that a consensus is achieved as to which path to reconciliation is followed. Such a consensus must include the political elite and also, as much as possible, civil society and grass-roots organizations, including victims' associations. The latter must at least acquiesce to the strategy agreed on by the political leaders.

The Italian case is interesting because it shows a lack of consensus on dealing with the past both among the elites and among civil society, with the result that all three main approaches to national reconciliation outlined above have been attempted and largely failed. Retributive justice has only obtained partial results, and even these have largely gone unacknowledged or have been hotly contested; amnesia is probably the preferred option of the political elite but is constantly threatened by new revelations, memoirs, conspiracy theories, and what is known as 'dietrology' (the search for the hidden truth behind an event); restorative justice has been advocated/attempted by isolated public figures but largely boycotted by the political elite.

One of the reasons for the lack of a clear strategy on dealing with the past is that there is little agreement in Italy as to what kind of political violence the country experienced in the 1960s and 1970s. For part of the political elite and the media as well as for many protagonists it is possible to talk of a 'creeping' or 'low-intensity' civil war raging in the country in those years, with escalating episodes of ideology-inspired guerrilla violence involving both extreme-left and extreme-right armed groups, often fuelled deliberately by foreign bodies in the context of the Cold War (Fasanella *et al*. 2000; Fasanella and Pellegrino 2005). For others, however, this definition represents a gross exaggeration, promoted by those who have an interest in exonerating themselves from public blame. Furthermore, on the political right there is a widespread conviction that the neo-fascist groups never seriously contemplated a 'revolutionary war' against the state, whereas this was systematically attempted by the extreme left (Ilari 2001; Scipione Rossi 2006).

As for more sinister acts of violence, known as *stragismo*, which involved bombing attacks against civilians in crowded places, starting with a bombing attack in Piazza Fontana, Milan, on 12 December 1969, these are still hotly contested. On the left, political elites, the media and the grassroots organizations continue to claim, with the support of judicial findings, that these acts were carried out by neo-fascist groups as part of a wider 'Strategy of Tension' masterminded by other forces, including state bodies, and aimed at weakening and discrediting the Italian Communist Party. On the right, political elites, the media and the grassroots dismiss such interpretations as unfounded and argue either that the Strategy of Tension is a leftist invention or that it was masterminded by state bodies to discredit the neo-fascist party, the MSI. The Italian Judiciary has been caught up in these political controversies, since on the right there appears to be a general consensus that most magistrates have been (and still are) biased in favour of the left, while on the left there is a prevailing opinion that the highest Judicial Court, the Court of Cassation, has been manipulating the outcomes of criminal trials so as to avoid incriminating rightist groups.

In this context, the trend in Italy towards public acts of remembrance in relation to the recent violent past, including political terrorism and its victims, appears to have taken on a peculiar meaning: remembering refers not to the need to remember the violent conflict with its publicly recognized, (judicially) assessed, truth(s) regarding victims and perpetrators; rather, it refers to the need to remember *what is not yet known or properly acknowledged*. It is the act of violence itself that is remembered (lest it be forgotten), while both the perpetrators and the circumstances remain unknown (and in most cases the source of endless conspiracy theories). In short, public acts of remembrance simply underline that the truth has not been ascertained either through retributive or restorative justice while amnesia is itself impossible to achieve. Let us consider the different paths to reconciliation that have been tentatively followed and assess their successes and, above all, their failures.

The limits of retributive justice in Italy

Considering episodes of political violence and terrorism involving both extreme-left and extreme-right armed groups, but excluding *stragismo*, the judicial process can be deemed to have been fairly successful, bringing many perpetrators to justice and ascertaining the full facts surrounding these events. The main exception concerns the kidnapping and assassination of Aldo Moro in 1978, for which five separate trials, established that the Red Brigades were guilty and had acted alone. As is well known, Moro was at the time President of the DC and was on his way to Parliament where a new government with the external support of the PCI was to be sworn in. The outcomes of these trials have been refuted by many commentators, part of the media and most of the left, on the basis that behind this episode lurked various obscure forces which, for political reasons linked to the logic of the Cold War, were strongly opposed to Moro's strategy of the Historic Compromise and wanted him dead. To this end they facilitated the actions of the Red Brigades, for example through the use of infiltrators, or by obstructing the investigations of the police during the 55 days in which Moro was held prisoner. Despite some experts dismissing all conspiracy theories surrounding this episode (Satta 2003 and 2006, Drake 2006), many others (Flamigni 2003, Accame 2005, Zedda 2005) give credit to the numerous puzzling circumstances and unanswered questions which have ensured that numerous books, films and documentaries on the topic have appeared since Moro's death.

Retributive justice has unveiled much of the truth behind *stragismo*, but, in the face of repeated episodes of deliberate obstruction on the part of state bodies, especially the intelligence services, it has been unable to secure clear-cut verdicts on individual perpetrators. In addition, the length of the judicial process itself, due in no small part to these episodes of obstruction, has been detrimental to the pursuit of justice. It was only in 2005 that the long and tortuous search for justice through the courts for the 1969 Piazza Fontana bombing, which left seventeen people dead and eighty-four wounded, came to an end, with an ambiguous verdict. The final sentence recognized that the extreme-right organization Ordine Nuovo (New Order – ON) had been responsible for this attack, but also acquitted, on the basis of incomplete evidence, neo-fascist defendants Carlo Maria Maggi and Delfo Zorzi, respectively ex-leader and ex-member of ON in Venice-Mestre, as well as Giancarlo Rognoni, ex-leader of the Milan-based La Fenice extreme-right group. Despite retrospectively establishing that both Franco Freda and Giovanni Ventura, of ON in Padua, had indeed been responsible for this massacre, the courts were unable to prosecute them, since they had already been acquitted in 1987. In 2004, the final verdict for a trial concerning a 1973 attack carried out at the Milan police headquarters, in which four bystanders had been killed, ended with a similar ambiguous verdict, and hence with the acquittal of Maggi, Zorzi and Francesco Neami, all of ON, who had been charged with planning and organizing this crime. As in the retrial for Piazza Fontana, however, the Court of Cassation established that ON as a group was responsible for the massacre.

Following these verdicts, the media declared the trials a failure, since after 36 years from the first bombing massacre only a handful of perpetrators had been found guilty. Of these, only Luigi Ciavardini, Giuseppe Valerio Fioravanti and Francesca Mambro, of the neo-fascist group Nuclei Armati Rivoluzionari (NAR) had been found guilty (for the 1980 Bologna station massacre, which left 85 people dead and more than 200 wounded) on the basis of the evidence amassed by the investigating magistrates. Others, such as Gianfranco Bertoli, the material perpetrator of the 1973 Milan attack, or ex-ON member Vincenzo Vinciguerra, sentenced to life in prison for an attack carried out in Peteano in 1972, in which three *Carabinieri* were killed, were self-confessed culprits. Even these guilty verdicts, however, have left a trail of suspicion and widespread feelings that justice has not been done.

With regard to the Bologna massacre, there are lingering concerns that the judicial evidence relied on the testimony of dubious witnesses. For their part, Ciavardini, Fioravanti and Mambro have always proclaimed their innocence. As for the 1973 attack in Milan, the material culprit, Bertoli, had always proclaimed himself an anarchist. With the final acquittal, in 2005, of Maggi, Neami and Zorzi, there thus appeared to be one vital missing link between this crime and neo-fascist leaders, despite the Court of Cassation ruling that the massacre was to be attributed to ON as a group. Finally, as regards Peteano, Vinciguerra had confessed to the attack in an attempt to 'put the State on trial' and force the full truth regarding the

Strategy of Tension to be revealed through the courts. By his own admission, he failed in his goal, for which he blamed the attitude of the Judiciary, which in his view connived with other bodies in covering up for the state (Vinciguerra 1989, 1993, 2000).

Retributive justice has not ended its course with these sentences: in November 2008, 34 years after the bombing of an anti-fascist demonstration in Brescia on 28 May 1974, which left eight people dead and 108 wounded, a retrial began in the city. As in the Milan trials, ON representatives were among the main defendants: Zorzi, Maggi, Maurizio Tramonte, as well as the ex-leader Pino Rauti. However, it is generally believed that this trial will not be able to achieve a sentence, as it largely relies on the same witnesses and the same evidence brought forward in the Milan trials.

Given the unsatisfactory and patchy outcomes of the judicial trials on the bombing massacres carried out between 1969 and 1980, those fragments of truth that have emerged through the courts, which in themselves are not inconsiderable, have gone largely unacknowledged by the media and the political world. As the literature on national reconciliation tends to stress, establishing the truth through the courts is one thing, acknowledging it is another: reconciliation involves precisely a public process of acceptance of the (often unpalatable) truth about the violent past. By contrast, in Italy the ambiguous nature of many verdicts has allowed different political actors to construct, and give resonance to, their own particular truth. This attitude has been at the roots of the failure of the second approach, based on restorative justice.

Restorative justice: a non-starter?

The impossibility of reaching a political consensus over the need for a process of truth-telling was especially in evidence during the works of the Parliamentary Commission on Terrorism in Italy and on the Failed Identification of the Authors of the Massacres, particularly during the period 1994–2001. Originally set up by Law 172, on 17 May 1988, the Commission was chaired first by Senator Libero Gualtieri, of the Republican Party, and later, from 1994, by Senator Giovanni Pellegrino, of the Left Democrats (DS). Its main task was investigating the reasons which had prevented the identification of those responsible for massacres and other acts of subversion since 1969. According to D'Agnelli (2003: 3), Pellegrino aimed deliberately at 'the construction of a comprehensive historical-political judgement', including a shared judgement on recent historical events. In the early years of his chairmanship, in a climate strongly conditioned by the fall of the Berlin Wall, the collapse of the Italian First Republic, and the renunciation of both Marxism and fascism by the communist and neo-fascist parties – as exemplified by their change of names – seemed to indicate that this aim would succeed.

However, following a hardening of attitudes, partly due to the appearance of Silvio Berlusconi on the political stage, which refuelled long-standing animosities, as well as to the right's bitter reaction to the Clean Hands investigation into systematic corruption during the First Republic, any hope of reaching a consensus evaporated. Despite repeated attempts by Pellegrino to convince the various political party representatives on the Commission to agree on a shared interpretation of the past, its works came to an end in 2001 with the publication of eighteen separate reports. Interpretations of the past varied dramatically. The reports by representatives of the Northern Alliance put the entire blame for terrorism, including the bombing massacres, on the left, specifically identifying Giangiacomo Feltrinelli, editor and ex-leader of the Gruppi di Azione Partigiana, as the mastermind behind the Strategy of Tension, supported by Eastern intelligence services. Conversely, the report produced by the Left Democrats put the blame for the massacres upon the neo-fascists in connivance with various state forces and Western intelligence and military organizations.

Soon after the folding of the 'Commission on the Massacres', in 2002 a new Parliamentary Commission, the 'Mitrokhin Commission' was set up by Berlusconi to investigate the links between the KGB and representatives of the left parties during the Cold War. The Commission relied on the classified material brought to the West by former KGB archivist Vasilif Mitrokhin. Widely considered by the left to be a crude political instrument based on unreliable information and used to discredit the opposition, the Commission ended by producing two reports in March 2006. One report was presented by the Chair, Forza Italia's Senator Paolo Guzzanti, and supported by the representatives of the centre-right parties, while the other was supported by the representatives of the centre-left parties. Needless to say, the former emphasized the role of Eastern intelligence services and Italian and foreign extreme-left groups in the bloody events of the Cold War period, including the 1980 Bologna massacre, for which it suggested that Palestinian terrorists had been the culprits. By contrast, the centre-left report largely dismissed these interpretations as unfounded and based mainly on hearsay.

The numerous political memoirs and autobiographies produced by the protagonists of the events of the 1960s and 1970s also failed to throw light on them. Such memoirs fall largely into two categories: those that could be defined as 'conversion stories', in which the narrators/protagonists acknowledge their responsibility for past violent deeds, and 'justification stories', in which the narrators view their past deeds either in a heroic light or as the outcome of a process of victimization, thus shifting the blame upon others, including the police, the state, the extreme left or extreme right, or indeed the *cattivi maestri*. While varying greatly in terms of their sincerity, moral viewpoint, degree of repentance and interpretations, these memoirs have not provided any new understanding of Italy's bloody terrorist acts and 'political mysteries', but have tended to address a specific audience (right-wing or left-wing). Furthermore, they have not gone far in offering redress for the victims, with a few commendable exceptions.

The only consensus for some form of restorative justice seems to be around the need to establish official Days of Remembrance for the victims of political violence and terrorism. In May 2007, a new law established that 9 May, the day when Moro was found dead, was to be dedicated to honouring the victims of terrorism and massacres. The text also made explicit reference to the need to 'construct a shared historical memory in defense of the democratic institutions'.

Given that the law was approved by the Lower Chamber almost unanimously, with 420 votes in favour, only one against, and 46 abstentions (from communist parties), the political elite were agreed on this act of reconciliation. Similarly, 27 years after the downing of a civilian plane at Ustica – which is widely believed, but has never been officially proved or acknowledged, to have been hit by American fire during a military operation against Colonel Gaddafi – a Museum of Memory was officially opened in Bologna, on 27 June 2007, with the aim of honouring the victims.

However, as mentioned in the Introduction, the consensus among the elite did not extend to a process of truth-telling. Rather, as argued below, the preferred option by the political elite in recent years seems to consist of a combined process of honouring the victims on the one hand, and promoting collective amnesia regarding the perpetrators and the circumstances surrounding the political violence of the 1960s and 1970s, on the other. This leaves just a few voices advocating the creation of some form of Truth Commission to deal with the country's violent past: Pellegrino himself, Guido Salvini (the main prosecutor in the Piazza Fontana re-trial), and representatives of the associations of the victims of terrorism, including the President of the Brescia Association, Manlio Milani. While Salvini asked for a special Commission of judicial experts and historians,[1] Milani hoped that the truth – he no longer seemed to expect justice through the courts – would emerge from the new Brescia trial:

> Nowadays I expect [from the trial] at least a wide reconstruction of the history of those years, the path that led to those tragic events, the reasons why they happened. We want to know if statesmen acted against the State rather than defending it [...] The institutional credibility of the present hangs on those events.[2]

Collective amnesia: fuelling victimization myths

During the First Republic, collective amnesia appeared to be the main preoccupation of the Italian State, concerned with concealing its own involvement in the Strategy of Tension: it is in this light that many trials have interpreted the episodes of obstruction of justice, which included withholding or destroying sensitive information, producing false information, helping defendants escape abroad, threatening potential witnesses for the prosecution and other dubious, even criminal, acts.

Following the collapse of the First Republic, and the impasse reached by the Commission of Inquiry on the Massacres, more recent indications point towards all the main parties favouring an end to the search for the culprits and to confronting the history of political violence during the Cold War. This approach can be gauged from the decision, taken in 2006, to 'securitize' the documents gathered by the Mitrokhin Commission, together with some material viewed by the Commission on the Massacres, preventing external public access for the next twenty years. As 34 Italian historians stated, in an official complaint sent to the Presidents of the two Chambers on 26 December 2006, 'This decision, if confirmed, risks to lead to a paradoxical result: the works of these two commissions, rather than bringing us nearer to the truth, could contribute to create a thicker and more lasting veil of ignorance upon some crucial nodes of our history' (www.loccidentale.it/node/327).

According to one of these historians, Fulvio Cammarano, the decision must be understood in the light of the prevailing fear among the political class, both on the left and on the right, of 'an exasperated public use of history with which, in Italy more than elsewhere, each side tries to delegitimate its opponent for the sake of a few electoral decimal points' (www.loccidentale.it/node/329). This seems a likely account of the current tacit understanding among the political elite in favour of a strategy of truth-evading. The problem with this strategy is that it appears to be more conducive to mutual antagonism and to conflicting constructions of victimhood than to reconciliation.

Recent studies of the political narratives and self-narratives produced by supporters of AN have shown the existence of a strong practice of counter-memory as regards the political history of the country and the role of neo-fascism (Catellani *et al.* 2005, Cento Bull 2007). The neo-fascists are systematically represented as a brave but persecuted 'community', used as scapegoats by sinister forces, criminalized by the state, constantly attacked by the extreme left (Baldoni 1996, Adinolfi 2005). On the left, there is a comparable tendency to subscribe to the concept of a 'civil war', with reference to the guerrilla violence of the 1960s and 1970s, in ways which absolve all protagonists of moral responsibility and 'agency', turning them into victims of a generalized climate of violence or, alternatively, of a deliberate brutal repression by the (fascistic) state (Capanna 1994, Bermani 2003, Segio 2003). In this way the condition of victimhood is being claimed by and for each of the groups responsible for the conflict. One of the effects of these reconstructions is to deprive the real victims of the political conflict and the massacres of proper recognition of their status, which the recent acts of public remembrance can only partially compensate for. Indeed, the real victims feel aggrieved and insulted, resenting the increasing status of celebrities in which the ex-terrorists appear to have been cast and claiming, by contrast, that they have had no voice (Fasanella and Grippo 2006).

Conclusion

The never-ending institutional transition discussed in the Introduction is neatly paralleled by a never-ending impasse of national reconciliation. Italy has not been able to adopt a clear and consensual strategy to achieve this end, with the result that various approaches have been attempted with only partially successful results. There are various reasons for this, and especially for the absence of a sustained and meaningful process of truth-telling and truth-acknowledgement. The main reason, as recognized in the literature on national reconciliation, is to be found in the manner in which the First Republic ended, that is to say, without a clear winner and with the survival of most of the political class of the previous regime.

Admittedly, old parties have disappeared and new ones have emerged, however, many of the 'new' parties are reincarnations of old ones or incorporate the political elite of old parties. The emergence of a delicate and unstable balance between the centre-right and the centre-left coalitions is a further factor, predicating against the disclosure of difficult truths about the past which can have damaging and unpredictable repercussions on some of the parties within each coalition. In this context, it is tempting for the political elite to opt for a policy of continuing concealment of the past, so that no one wins or loses credit with the electorate. Third, it is possible that part of the political class is genuinely concerned about the destabilizing effects of a process of truth-telling, and is therefore acting in the name of the general good. Fourth, while truth-telling is avoided, the plight of the victims is being increasingly acknowledged by both sides of the political spectrum and redressed through public acts of remembrance.

It may be possible to argue that Italy is gradually finding its own specific way of dealing with its divided past and coming to some form of national reconciliation. However, the high degree of antagonism between the different political coalitions, the conspiracy theories and victimization myths which promote mutually exclusive attitudes and beliefs among the parties, with contrasting constructions of 'heroes' and 'villains', suggest otherwise. Intolerance and sectarianism thrive upon 'politics of victimhood', and political violence is never far removed. In addition, the non-disclosure of the truth about the recent historical past creates an unhealthy situation in which the political elite can use their knowledge selectively for reciprocal 'blackmail' or, conversely, to foster deals and agreements behind closed doors, not unlike the First Republic.

Constitutional revision and institutional design are without doubt essential components of a successful transition to a new and stable democratic regime. However, redress and reconciliation after a period of violent conflict are also increasingly recognized as essential elements of a healthy democracy. If Italy is finally to end its transitional phase, it needs to take into account all three dimensions. Recent steps towards acts of remembrance indicate that this is now happening, but, as for the other two dimensions, mutual antagonism and fear of giving the opponents an unfair advantage seem to block any decisive drive along this path. In this context, moral decline and political decline go hand in hand.

Notes

1　See *Corriere della Sera* on 9 May 2009.
2　For a full reference see: www.informazione.it/a/b271a127-afc4-4afe-bc52-ba036a1b8c33/Piazza-della-Loggia-il-nono-processo-Milani-liberiamo-la-memoria?v.

References

Abrams, E. (2001) 'Truth without Justice?', *Policy Review*, 105: 73.
Accame, F. (2005) *Moro si Poteva Salvare*, Bolsena: Massari.

Adinolfi, G. (2005) *Quel Domani che ci Appartenne. Passato, Presente e Futuro in Camicia Nera*, Milan: Barbarossa.

Baldoni, A. (1996) *Il Crollo dei Miti*, Rome: Settimo Sigillo.

Barkan, E. (2006) 'Historical reconciliation: redress, rights and politics', *Journal of International Affairs*, 60(1): 1–15.

Bermani, C. (2003) *Il Nemico Interno. Guerra Civile e Lotta di Classe in Italia (1943– 1976)*, Rome: Odradek.

Blakeley, G. (2005) 'Digging up Spain's past: consequences of truth and reconciliation', *Democratization*, 12(1): 44–59.

Boraine, A. L. (2006) 'Transitional justice: a holistic interpretation', *Journal of International Affairs*, 60(1): 17–27.

Capanna, M. (1994) *Formidabili Quegli Anni*, Milan: Rizzoli.

Catellani, P., Milesi, P. and Crescentini, A. (2005) 'One Root, Different Branches', in P. Klandermans and N. Mayer (eds.) *Extreme Right Activists in Europe: Through the Magnifying Glass*, London: Routledge.

Cento Bull, A. (2007) *Italian Neofascism. The Strategy of Tension and the Politics of Nonreconciliation*, Oxford: Berghahn.

D'Agnelli, A.R. (2003) 'Conoscenza storica e giudizio politico. Il ruolo degli storici nelle Commissioni parlamentari d'inchiesta sul terrorismo', *Cantieri di storia*, Sissco, Lecce, 25–27 September, Online. Available : www.sissco.it//fileadmin/user_upload/Attivita/ Convegni/cantieriII/uso_pubblico/dagnelli.rtf.

Drake, R. (2006) 'The Aldo Moro Murder Case in Retrospect', *Journal of Cold War Studies,* 8(2): 114–25.

Fasanella, G. and Grippo, A. (2006) *I Silenzi Degli Innocenti*, Milano: Rizzoli.

——— and Pellegrino, G. (2005) *La Guerra Civile. Da Salò a Berlusconi*. Milan: Rizzoli.

——— and Sestieri, C. with Pellegrino, G. (2000) *Segreto di Stato: La Verità da Gladio al Caso Moro,* Turin: Einaudi.

Flamigni, S. (2003) *La Tela del Ragno: Il Delitto Moro*, Milan: Kaos Edizioni.

Graybill, L. and Lanegran, K. (2004) 'Truth, justice and reconciliation in Africa: Issues and cases', *African Studies Quarterly*, 8(1): 1–18.

Hayner, P.B. (2001) *Unspeakable Truths: Confronting State Terror and Atrocities*, New York: Routledge.

Ilari, V. (2001) *Guerra Civile*. Rome: Ideazione.

MacDonald, R.B. and Bernardo, M.C. (2006) 'The politics of victimhood: historical memory and peace in Spain and the Basque region', *Journal of International Affairs*, 60(1): 173–96.

Mammone, A. (2006) 'A daily revision of the past: fascism, anti-fascism, and memory in contemporary Italy', *Modern Italy*, 11(2): 211–26.

Mendeloff, D. (2004) 'Truth-seeking, truth-telling, and postconflict peacebuilding: Curb the enthusiasm?', *International Studies Review*, 6: 355–80.

Rigby, A. (2000) 'Amnesty and Amnesia in Spain', *Peace Review*, 12(1): 73–79.

——— (2002) 'Three contrasting approaches for "Dealing with the Past": collective amnesia, retributive justice and prioritizing truth', *CCTS Newsletter*, 18, Online. Available: www.c-r.org/ccts/ccts18/3apprch.htm.

Rolston, B. (with M. Gilmartin) (2000) *Unfinished Business: State Killings and the Quest for Truth*, Beyond the Pale Publications: Belfast.

Sartori, G. (2004) *Ingegneria Costituzionale Comparata. Strutture, Incentivi ed Esiti*, Bologna: Il Mulino.

Satta, V. (2003) *Odissea nel Caso Moro: Viaggio Controcorrente Attraverso la Documentazione della Commissione Stragi*, Rome: EDUP.

—— (2006) *Il Caso Moro e i Suoi Falsi Misteri*, Soveria Mannelli: Rubbettino.

Scipione Rossi, G. (2006) *La Destra e gli Anni di Piombo nella Prospettiva della Storicizzazione*, Rome: Fondazione Ugo Spirito.

Segio, S. (2003) 'Le estreme conseguenze. Radicalità, lotta armata e politica', *Una città*, 117, Online. Available: www.micciacorta.it/racconto.php?id_racconto=22.

Vannucci, A. and Cubeddu, R. (2006) *Lo Spettro della Competitivita. Le Radici Istituzionali del Declino Italiano*, Soveria Mannelli: Rubettino.

Vinciguerra, V. (1989) *Ergastolo per la Libertà, Verso la Verità sulla Strategia della Tensione*, Florence: Arnaud.

—— (1993) *La Strategia del Depistaggio*, Bologna: Il Fenicottero.

—— (2000) *Camerati, Addio. Storia di un Inganno, in Cinquant'anni di Egemonia Statunitense in Italia*, Trapani: Avanguardia.

Zedda, D. (2005) *Il Caso Moro. La Teoria Cospirativa e i Suoi Fondamenti*, La Riflessione Editore.

9 Fascism as 'heritage' in contemporary Italy

Joshua Arthurs

Summary

This contribution examines the presence of the fascist past in Italy through the lens of the built environment. Focusing on one well-known case – the Foro Italico in Rome – it considers the historical processes and debates that led to the survival of the regime's monuments after the Second World War; recent political and aesthetic controversies about their present-day function; and their significance as 'symptoms' of a more fundamental crisis afflicting contemporary Italian society. The Italian far right, which often uses these spaces as memorials to the fallen regime, has aligned itself with architectural preservationists who emphasize the monuments' importance as exemplars of interwar Rationalist architecture. In this way, the protection of fascist remains has become a vehicle for the aestheticization, heritagization and normalization of the *Ventennio Nero*, integrating Mussolini's regime into a depoliticized representation of Italian history. On one level, this chapter addresses questions about the memory and continued resonance of the fascist past in contemporary Italy; at the same time, it engages with broader and comparative analyses of the use and re-use of physical space in moments of political and social transformation; the history of vandalism, *damnatio memoriae* and ideological violence; and the politics of heritage conservation and memory.

Introduction

In his first press conference since winning Rome's mayoral election in April 2008, Gianni Alemanno laid out the goals of his new administration (*La Repubblica* 2008; Brunazzo and Gilbert 2008). In keeping with the themes of his campaign, Alemanno – the candidate of the 'post-fascist' Northern Alliance with a long history on the more extreme fringes of the Italian far-right – promised a tougher approach to crime and public safety, economic development and a crackdown on illegal Roma encampments.[1] Alongside these pledges, he added another important priority: the dismantling of the new museum housing the Ara Pacis, a monument built in 13 BCE to honour the Roman emperor Augustus. The building in question, designed by the renowned American architect Richard Meier, had been inaugurated only two years earlier under the stewardship of Alemanno's predecessor and rival, the centre-leftist Walter Veltroni. Built in glass, steel and white travertine, the structure is an aggressively modernist presence in one of Rome's oldest neighbourhoods. Since it was originally conceived, Meier's project has divided architectural critics, inflamed political passions and been derided as a 'cesspit', 'a real disgrace' and 'a genuine act of violence committed against the city' (Sassi 2006, Frischia 2006).

What elicited such vitriol? Even allowing for the tremendous importance that Italians assign to public architecture, the outrage seems hard to fathom. Why would the demolition of an archaeological pavilion be such a pressing concern for mayor-elect Alemanno only two days after his electoral victory? The answer lies not so much in concerns over design or archaeological preservation, as in the historical and political subtext that surrounds the Ara Pacis and its adjacent area. The monument was originally excavated in the late 1930s by Mussolini's fascist regime, and was installed in its present location as part of a massive Augustan *mise-en-scène* that also included the emperor's mausoleum, a large square (Piazzale Augusto Imperatore) and several new buildings (Kostof 1978). The message – driven home not only by the juxtaposition of ancient and modern construction but by inscriptions and reliefs extolling martial virtue and imperial conquest – was clear: the site demonstrated the rebirth of the Roman spirit (*romanità*) in fascism and the capacity of Mussolini's 'New' Italy to reclaim and regenerate the classical heritage of the Eternal City. The controversy surrounding the Ara Pacis Museum was therefore not only aesthetic but political, an expression of profound and longstanding debates over the significance of the fascist past. As much as its jarring modernism, the building's offense was that it challenged and disturbed a cityscape that for decades had been intimately tied to the memory of Mussolini's regime. This association was reinforced at the museum's public unveiling in April 2006, which was disrupted by skinheads from the neo-fascist Movimento Sociale-Fiamma Tricolore (*La Repubblica* 2006). To date, opposition to the project has come overwhelmingly from the right, from Alemanno to the flamboyant art critic Vittorio Sgarbi to Prime Minister Silvio Berlusconi.

The Ara Pacis episode – which, at present, remains unresolved – powerfully demonstrates the long and disquieting shadow that the *Ventennio Nero* still casts over contemporary Italy. More than six decades after its demise, Mussolini's regime remains a source of intense controversy, a frame in which enduring conflicts are played out. In part, this is due to the persistent presence of the far right in political life. Italy was the first European country after World War II to witness the emergence of a major neo-fascist party (the MSI), and its successor – the 'post-fascist' Northern Alliance – has been an important partner in Silvio Berlusconi's recent coalition governments. Scholars have also pointed to the post-war Republic's failure to undertake a significant de-fascistization of Italian society, from the judiciary and civil service to basic 'mentalities' (Pavone 1995, Dondi 1999, Domenico 1991).

Reminders of Mussolini's regime are not confined to the realms of party politics or state bureaucracy, but are inscribed in the quotidian landscape of towns and cities across the peninsula. Even more than in many other European countries, daily life in Italy tends to take place in the public sphere. The *piazza*, more than the private home, is the central venue for social interaction, political participation, commerce and religious community (Isnenghi 1994). Mussolini's regime was fully cognizant of the power of the *piazza*, and sought to overcome the liberal distinction between public and private; its goal was a 'totalitarian' society that subjugated the individual to the collective (Berezin 1997). The public square therefore became a venue for mass ritual and political spectacle, as well as a space in which to collect, discipline and observe crowds. The built environment was also an important showcase for the achievements of fascism. Through an aggressive programme of urban renewal, new construction and archaeological excavation, it sought to negate old stereotypes of Italian backwardness and indolence, and present a dynamic and youthful nation to the rest of the world (Gentile 2007, Horn 1994).

The physical remains of this 'anthropological revolution' remain ubiquitous today, from the 'New Towns' of Pontine Marshes to the gleaming neo-classical structures of Rome's EUR district. In the present contribution, I reflect on the significance of these sites. What does it mean that so much of contemporary life – from morning commutes and football matches to the postal service and government bureaucracy – takes place against a backdrop designed during the fascist *Ventennio*? Should we concur with Robert Musil's famous dictum that 'there is nothing in the world as invisible as monuments [...] they are erected in order to be seen [...] but at the same time they are somehow impregnated against attention [...]' (Musil 1986: 320)? Or do these architectural remnants embody an unresolved past and enduring tensions? Iconoclasm and the refashioning of public space have long been crucial instruments of political and social transformation (Bevan 2006, Levinson 1998, Gamboni 1997); why does this process not seem to have taken place – at least not in a concerted, coherent and consistent manner – in Italy, and what problems does this failure pose?

In answering these questions, I focus upon one well-known case – Rome's Foro Italico – as a lens through which to consider contemporary attitudes towards interwar architecture and, by extension, the fascist past itself. I provide a brief overview of the site's history and development, and then explore more recent debates over its current position in Italian life. The chapter concludes by looking at how responses to the Foro Italico connect to larger debates over the meaning of fascism in present-day Italy, and by suggesting a possible way of negotiating its architectural legacy in the future.

Mosaics, marbles and memories: the Foro Italico

Of all the monuments built during the fascist *Ventennio*, arguably the most emblematic and evocative is the Foro Italico (formerly the Foro Mussolini) in Rome. Situated just north of the Vatican, west of the Tiber and at the foot of Monte Mario, it was built between 1928 and 1938 as the main athletics centre for Rome and, by extension, for the entire nation (Masia *et al.* 2007, Caporilli 1990, Comitato dei Monumenti Moderni 1990). In keeping with this sporting function, it also housed the headquarters for the Opera Nazionale Balilla, the regime's main youth organization, as well as those of the Italian Olympic Committee (a function it still performs today). The complex consists of several major elements (Figure 9.1).

The largest and most prominent is the Piazza dell'Impero, a long square stretching from the Tiber to the main stadium. It is decorated with mosaics depicting scenes from Roman mythology and the history of fascism from the exploits of the early *squadristi* to the conquest of Ethiopia. Towards the Tiber, it is framed on one side by a large marble obelisk inscribed with the words 'Mussolini' and 'DUX', and on the other by a series of marble blocks commemorating important dates on the fascist calendar, like the anniversary of the March on Rome, the 'Battle for Grain' and the proclamation of Empire (Figure 9.2).

Close by is the Stadio dei Marmi, an oval athletics field with a racing track, surrounded by marble neo-classical statues of nude male athletes (Figure 9.3).

The Foro is framed by a series of buildings that include an Academy of Physical Education, an aquatic centre, a tennis stadium, a fencing academy and a youth hostel. Whereas most of the site is cast in strongly classical tones with gleaming white marble, these structures are built in an angular, Rationalist style that was meant to demonstrate the regime's commitment to modernist aesthetics. As its iconography and designated purpose suggest, the Foro was envisioned as a space in which to train, strengthen and discipline young bodies and build a new generation of muscular, dynamic Italians – and therefore one of the most vivid and complete expressions of fascist ideology and its aspirations for future generations.

ROMA - FORO MUSSOLINI - LO STADIO DEI MARMI

Figure 9.1 The Foro Mussolini

118   *Joshua Arthurs*

Figure 9.2 The Mussolini Obelisk

Figure 9.3 The Stadio dei Marmi

Until quite recently, the Foro Italico has remained precisely as its designers intended, with little disruption to the slogans and iconography on display. To account for its longevity, one must first consider the immediate circumstances surrounding the demise of Mussolini's regime. In the days following the Duce's removal from power on 25 July 1943, Italians took to the streets to celebrate the end of a regime that had led them into a disastrous war abroad and economic hardship at home (Aga Rossi 2000). Across the peninsula, crowds tore down posters and chiselled the *fascio littorio* from public buildings; significantly, the target of such activities was most frequently representations of Mussolini himself, as opposed to the regime in general or aesthetic representations of fascism (Luzzatto 2005: 35–9). Rather than direct their ire against an entire system – one closely entwined in the daily lives of most Italians – they staged a symbolic ritual murder of the man whose very person had come to embody the experience of the past twenty years, foreshadowing the very real desecration of the Duce's corpse two years later at Piazzale Loreto. Still, the initial popular reaction to 25 July should be seen primarily as a spontaneous emotional release, a venting of frustrations and resentments rather than a coordinated political response (Gallerano 1988: 316–321).

However, this early flurry of iconoclasm was brief and limited. The military administration soon repressed anti-fascist demonstrations with brutal force, out of the concern that they would become increasingly revolutionary in nature (Gallerano *et al.* 1969: 15–37). With the armistice of 8 September 1943, Italy became a battleground for the occupying Allied and German armies as well as for a civil war between partisans and the fascist loyalists of the Repubblica Sociale Italiana (Italian Social Republic – RSI; also known as the Republic of Salò). Given the void in legitimate civil authority and the fracturing of the peninsula (Pavone 1988), there seems to have been little opportunity or political will for a comprehensive and coordinated campaign of *damnatio memoriae*. Significantly, the Foro Italico escaped these early upheavals unscathed, and its survival was assured in June 1944 when it was used as a rest centre for the Fifth Army following the Allied liberation of Rome. The symbolism of this designation was not lost on the site's new occupants, and soldiers were encouraged to tour the remains of Mussolini's vainglorious fantasies (US Army Rest Center 1944). Allied troops ceded the site, now renamed the Foro Italico, to local authorities in 1948.

Years of military occupation had damaged the Foro, but it remained in use throughout the 1940s and 1950s as a sporting venue and the headquarters of the Italian Olympic Committee (CONI). Given the infrastructural and economic damage inflicted during the war, it is unsurprising that recovery efforts focused more on using available resources than on demolishing the traces of the previous regime. Certainly, the early post-war period did see a steady condemnation of fascist architecture by critics and commentators. The monumental aesthetic favoured by the regime was roundly dismissed as little more than 'a pseudo-modern mask for classical megalomania' (Zevi 1993: 164); a popular refrain was 'basta con i balconi!' ('enough with the balconies'), suggesting that buildings themselves were in some way to blame for the demagogy of the past twenty years. To the architectural theorist Bruno Zevi, the symmetry and modularity of classicism made it inherently totalitarian, stultifying and rhetorical (Zevi 1994). To overcome this burden, post-war planners had to think democratically and on a human scale; vernacular forms began to replace classical monumentality (Doordan 1989: 64).

Despite such criticism, the Foro Italico escaped significant controversy until the late 1950s when it was designated as one of the main venues for the Rome Olympics of 1960 (Caporilli 1990: 136). To accommodate the Games, the organizers renovated some of the crumbling infrastructure and built a new Olympic Stadium adjacent to the Piazza dell'Impero. CONI also restored the fascist-era mosaics, murals and inscriptions, and even employed the same company that had originally designed these decorations (Pirani and Tozzi 1998). Unsurprisingly, this move provoked an outcry from the Left. The restoration of the Foro Italico was a 'lost opportunity', wrote the communist magazine *Vie Nuove* (Natoli 1960: 30). Instead of using the Olympics as the occasion to remake and revitalize the area, the authorities had spent millions only to 'realize the "imperial" projects of twenty years ago' (ibid.). To hold the Olympics against a fascist backdrop would be an embarrassment to Italy, a troubling message to foreign visitors and an insult to the memory of the Resistance. Provoked by this initial incident, *Vie Nuove* undertook a campaign, 'L'Italia da Cancellare' ('The Italy to Erase'), in which it catalogued the physical remnants of the regime across the peninsula (*Vie Nuove* 1960). In the view of the communists, the prominence of fascist monuments and inscriptions materially demonstrated the failures of the post-war Republic, its abandonment of anti-fascist values, and the reluctance of the Christian Democratic government to confront an uncomfortable past. In the end, they argued, there was little to differentiate between the Olympic triumphalism of 1960 and the imperial posturing of the 1930s.

Curiously, the Christian Democrats did make some minor modifications to the iconography of the Foro Italico. To assuage traditional sensibilities, or possibly to avoid scandalizing tourists, bronze fig-leaves were placed over the genitals of the statues at the Stadio dei Marmi (Marbles Stadium) (Benton 1999); evidently full-frontal nudity was more offensive than slogans like *Molti nemici, molto onore* ('Many enemies, much honour') and *Duce, vi dedichiamo la nostra giovinezza* ('Duce, we dedicate our youth to you'), which remained in public view. In addition, the government added three new dates to the marble blocks in the Piazza dell'Impero, marking the end of the regime in 1943, the proclamation of the Italian Republic in 1946, and the new Italian Constitution in 1948. Instead of purging the site of its fascist associations, the goal seems to have been to superimpose new layers of symbolism that supplemented, rather than replaced, its original iconography. In this way, the post-war Republic could lay claim to the Foro without engaging in a controversial and potentially revolutionary act of iconoclasm. This was reinforced in the Games' promotional materials, which often celebrated the classical tenor of the complex without touching upon its original significance. According to the official Olympic bulletin, the Stadio dei Marmi had 'a classic touch [...] it was indeed an excellent idea to have these enormous white statues standing out in the sun against the dark green of the Monte Mario cypress trees' (CONI 1957: 11); however, the publication studiously avoided mentioning whose idea this had been in the first place.

Since the 1960 Olympics, the Foro Italico has continued to serve as one of Italy's main sporting and entertainment venues. It hosts the Italian Open tennis competition, is home to both of Rome's professional football teams, and was the venue for the 1990 World Cup final. Yet in recent years, it has once again become an object of social, cultural and political controversy. The smooth surfaces of the Piazza dell'Impero have made it the focal point of Rome's skateboarding scene, and its marble blocks and walls are frequently covered with graffiti (Figure 9.4). For the most part, these should probably be understood as generic vandalism – random acts of defacement, without expressly political content – rather than purposeful iconoclasm (Gamboni 1997). They suggest that, at least for some young Romans, the Foro's monumental aura has been extinguished and that the site has simply been incorporated into the quotidian cityscape. At the same time, however, the declining condition of the site has also reinvigorated its symbolic significance. In recent years, neo-fascists have begun to use the Mussolini obelisk as a shrine to the Duce and the 'Martyrs' of Salò, and see the Foro Italico as a testament to the achievements of the regime. One impromptu far-right group has even published a website on which it tracks acts of vandalism and exposes skateboarders and taggers who 'violate' this sacred space.[2]

Figure 9.4 Neo-Fascist memorials at the Mussolini Obelisk

Figure 9.5   Neo-Fascist memorials at the Mussolini Obelisk

In an interesting turn of events, neo-fascists have made common cause with historical preservationists in agitating for the site's upkeep (Figure 9.5). Since the 1980s, critics have begun to reappraise the architectural legacy of the *Ventennio*. In the words of one organization, enough time has passed for the Foro Italico to be recognized as a testament 'to the richness of ideas and inventiveness of our twentieth century' and 'an exceptional monument [...] for the clarity and breadth of its urban design' (Comitato dei Monumenti Moderni 1990: 7, 24). Even Giorgio Armani has praised the statues of the Stadio dei Marmi as 'proud and magnificent, radiating glory, honed and powerful, every muscle in clear relief even when inactive', and in 1985 modelled his homoerotic Emporio Armani advertising campaign on these nude figures (Mott 2003). The entire complex was eventually recognized as a protected artistic and historical property by the national government, 'notwithstanding its ideological orientation' (report by the Ministero per i Beni Culturali e Ambientali, reprinted in Marchetti 2004: 142). Despite these measures, in 2000 the state proposed that the complex be privatized to help reduce the national debt and CONI's budget deficit (Stanley 2000). The announcement prompted massive outrage from right-wing parties and architecture lovers alike, who likened the sale of the Foro to privatizing the Colosseum or Piazza Navona. Figure 9.6 shows a poster calling for the preservation of the Foro Italico.

Although the government eventually scaled back its plans, portions of the venue have been turned into a private recreational facility, and for most of the past five years much of the Foro has been covered with scaffolding for repairs and cleaning. Even these restorations have met with disapproval: in recent months, the heritage group Italia Nostra has expressed concerns that sandblasting would permanently damage the marble surfaces, and that the advertising posted over the Mussolini obelisk detracts from the dignity of the monument. Even worse, with privatization, a site built 'to celebrate physical and athletic education is now a spot for sweaty dancing, fatty hamburgers, beer and Coke, and blaring music' (Bari 2008). At last reporting, renovations had ground to a halt under the orders of Rome's new mayor. As with Richard Meier's Ara Pacis Museum, Gianni

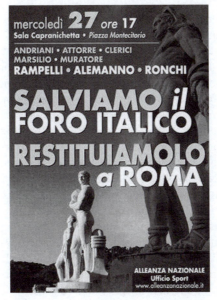

Figure 9.6 Alleanza Nazionale poster calling for the preservation of the Foro Italico

Alemanno has signalled his commitment to blocking any major re-workings of fascism's architectural legacy.

Just a monument? heritagizing the fascist past

If contemporary Italy is indeed the sick man of Europe, then the Foro Italico and other fascist-era monuments can usefully be understood as symptoms, as indicators of a more profound crisis afflicting the body politic. This diagnosis follows several interlocking lines of interpretation. First, as the story of the Foro Italico suggests, contemporary controversies about the fascist past are intimately tied to the chaotic and divisive experience of the Second World War. Italy's particular war experience – as Axis power, occupied territory and divided nation – meant that there was no possibility of a comprehensive agenda of *damnatio memoriae*. The lingering social and ideological conflicts originating in this era have made it all the more difficult to find the necessary political will, as has the reluctance of post-war Italian society to confront its fascist past. As seen in the debates surrounding the 1960 Olympics, the problem of fascist architectural heritage was used as a political weapon between Left and Right, rather than being approached as a mature process of national introspection and reconciliation (for a related debate, see Cento Bull in this volume).

The continued use of the Foro Italico in the decades after World War Two also demonstrates the extent to which post-war society remained dependent on infrastructure built during the fascist era. The *Ventennio Nero* was a period of dramatic transformation for the peninsula, and in many ways signalled the arrival of the twentieth century in Italy. However, this last point also has a more troubling corollary – namely that the fascist vision of modernism and modernity retains a powerful grip over the Italian imagination. For better or worse, Mussolini's was the only regime to impose a modernist aesthetic on Rome and attempt a dramatic remaking of its urban fabric; since 1945, successive governments have been careful to act as preservationists rather than interventionists. The disciplined, muscular and aggressive symbolism on display at the Foro Italico represents one of the only viable counterpoints to the historical panorama of the Eternal City. Because of this enduring appeal, the idea of a 'modernizationist' regime is frequently invoked by apologists on the far right. In a recent interview, Alemanno insisted that fascism's 'historically positive' aspect lay in its development of the country's infrastructure, land reclamation and innovative construction (Follain 2008). Nor has praise for the regime's architecture been limited to neo-fascists: against prevailing orthodoxies that deny the merit of interwar design, the left-wing architecture critic Giorgio Muratore has repeatedly insisted that the *Ventennio* was 'among the richest periods of our architectonic culture' and that, for the sake of 'history, documentary value, and objective urban and aesthetic qualities', it should be conserved (Comitato dei Monumenti Moderni 1990: 23–24).

Muratore's argument that fascist architecture forms an integral part of Italy's architectural heritage presents both promises and challenges. The possibility of assessing interwar architecture without the burden of ideological judgment is certainly encouraging. There is no denial that Mussolini's regime favoured aesthetic diversity and gave opportunities to innovative architects of every stripe. At the same time, however, the notion that the Foro Italico should be accepted as just another layer in Rome's architectonic strata, as much as the Roman Forum or Saint Peter's, could also be viewed as a dangerous form of passive acceptance. It is somewhat disingenuous to aestheticize or depoliticize what was a profoundly political project; the exemplary Rationalist architecture manifested in the Foro Italico was not built despite fascism, but because of it. It is no accident that the voices most eager to 'remove politics' from the discussion tend to belong to Mussolini's ideological heirs. A similar 'normalizing' or relativizing tendency has been evident in other aspects of Italian cultural life over the past decade. The recent popularity of historical newsreels has resulted in a representation of the fascist era under the rubric of 'come eravamo' – innocent nostalgia for 'the way we were' that avoids mention of the daily violence, corruption and coercion perpetrated by the regime (Fogu 2006: 159). Such a 'colour-blind' presentation of the past offers ample opportunities for distortion and misrepresentation (Mammone and Veltri 2007). One of the most egregious expressions of this tendency is the Right's current attempts to draw an equivalency between anti-fascist partisans and the Nazi-backed fighters of the RSI in the 'civil war' of 1943–1945 (Pezzino 2005; Miller 1999). The Resistance has increasingly been undermined as the moral basis of post-war Italian democracy, though Berlusconi and his allies have yet to offer a legitimate alternative. In the same way, 'heritagizing' fascism's monumental remains offers uncritical legitimation and the valorization of a deeply troubling past. More profoundly, it creates a space – both discursive, and, as we have seen, physical – for the re-emergence of illiberal, xenophobic and nihilistic currents in Italian society. While historical and aesthetic revisionism can usefully foster the critical re-examination of outdated orthodoxies, it also runs the risk of debilitating moral relativism and muddying the waters of public perception (Mammone 2006).

Conclusion

What, then, should be done? How should contemporary Italians negotiate the presence of the fascist past? As the controversies surrounding the Ara Pacis and the Foro Italico suggest, interventions that substantially recast the regime's architectural legacy seem fated only to intensify conflict and provide a platform for Mussolini's apologists. The window of opportunity for a campaign of *damnatio memoriae* has long since closed. Conversely, the inaction of recent decades suggests that mere passivity will do little to dispel the shadows cast by the *Ventennio*. While considerably more work needs to be done to resolve this problem, I would like to advance one possible avenue for negotiation. Many other societies have had to reckon with the material remains of a problematic past. Germans today wrestle not only with reminders of the Nazi era but those that recall decades of national division and communist rule (Rosenfeld 2000, Ladd 1997); the monuments and symbols of the Confederacy remain controversial in the United States, generations after the Civil Rights movement (Levinson 1998). While debates persist in both these countries, there has nevertheless been a more thoughtful and deliberate reckoning with architectural remains. An instructive example can be found at the Nazi Party rally grounds in Nuremberg (Macdonald 2006). Concerned about the implications of 'heritagizing' or 'mythologizing' this site, local authorities decided on an intriguing policy of 'calculated neglect'. By deliberately allowing the stadium to crumble under the weight of time, they hoped to demonstrate the absurdity of Hitler's 'Thousand Year Reich'. At the same time, planners erected a Documentation Centre, encouraging visitors to approach the site with the critical lens of history rather than the admiring gaze of heritage.

Might such 'critical preservation' (Bevan 2006: 175–201) work at the Foro Italico or other reminders of the *Ventennio Nero*? At the very least, inserting some form of explanation – as through labelling, panels or museum display – might have the salutary effect of mediating between fascist iconography and its contemporary audience. It might also strengthen the didactic value of these sites in both historical and aesthetic terms, and provide a meaningful justification for their preservation. As long as these sites are devoid of deliberate and reasoned commentary, and are allowed to speak for themselves, they will continue to debilitate a nation that has become the 'Sick Man of Europe'.

Notes

1 While Alemanno positioned himself as a 'mainstream' conservative during the campaign, he is one of the leading exponents of the radical stream Destra Sociale (Social Right), as well as a protégé (and son-in-law) of Pino Rauti, the neo-fascist

126   *Joshua Arthurs*

leader who rejected the moderate turn of AN in the mid-1990s. During the election, he
also caused a stir by openly wearing the Celtic cross, a symbol commonly associated
with neo-Nazi and white supremacist groups.
2 See www.foroitalico.altervista.org.

References

Aga Rossi, E. (2000) *A Nation Collapses: the Italian Surrender of September 1943*,
Cambridge: Cambridge University Press.
Bari, S. (2008) 'Foro Italico: continua la sabbiatura dei marmi nell'indifferenza dei mass-
media', *vignaclarablog.it*. Online. Available: www.vignaclarablog.it/200807092648/
foro-italico-continua-la-sabbiatura-dei-marmi-nellindifferenza-dei-mass-media.
Benton, T. (1999) From the Arengario to the Lictor's Axe: Memories of Italian Fascism,
in M. Kwint, C. Breward, and J. Aynsley (eds.) *Material Memories*, New York: Berg.
Berezin, M. (1997) *Making the Fascist Self: The Political Culture of Interwar Italy*, Ithaca,
NY: Cornell University Press.
Bevan, R. (2006) *The Destruction of Memory: Architecture at War*, London: Reaktion.
Brunazzo, M. and Gilbert, M. (2008) The Right Sweeps the Board, *Journal of Modern
Italian Studies*, 13(3): 422–30.
Caporilli, M. (1990) *Il Foro Italico e lo Stadio Olimpico: Immagini dalla Storia*, Rome:
Tomo.
Comitato dei Monumenti Moderni (1990) *Il Foro Italico*, Rome: Clear.
CONI (Comitato Olimpico Nazionale Italiano) (1957) 'Foro Italico Olympic Center',
Bulletin Officiel, (1): 10–1.
Domenico, R.P. (1991) *Italian Fascists on Trial, 1943–1948*, Chapel Hill, NC: University
of North Carolina Press.
Dondi, M. (1999) 'The Fascist Mentality after Fascism', in R.J.B. Bosworth and P. Dogliani
(eds.) *Italian Fascism: History, Memory, Representation*, New York: St. Martin's Press.
Doordan, D.P. (1989) 'Changing agendas: Architecture and politics in contemporary Italy'
Assemblage, (8): 60–77.
Fogu, C. (2006) 'Italiani brava gente: the Legacy of Fascist Historical Culture on Italian
Politics of Memory', in R.N. Lebow, W. Kansteiner, and C. Fogu (eds.) *The Politics of
Memory in Postwar Europe*, Durham, NC: Duke University Press.
Follain, J. (2008) Italy needed Fascism, says the New Duce. *The Sunday Times (London)*.
Online. Available: www.lexisnexis.com/us/lnacademic/frame.do?tokenKey=rsh-
20.152930.30946612862&target=results_listview_resultsNav&reloadEntirePage=true
&rand=1228246301738&returnToKey=20_T5283891392&parent=docview.
Frischia, F. (2006) 'An e l'Ara Pacis senza pace: Alemanno, visita con Sgarbi', *Corriere
della Sera*, 20 May.
Gallerano, N. (1988) 'Gli italiani in guerra 1940–1943: appunti per una ricerca', in F.
Ferratini Tosi, G. Grassi and M. Legnani (eds.) *L'Italia nella Seconda Guerra Mondiale
e nella Resistenza*. Milan: Franco Angeli.
—— Ganapini, L. and Legnani, M. (1969) *L'Italia dei Quarantacinque Giorni: Studio
e Documenti*, Milan: Instituto Nazionale per la Storia del Movimento di Liberazione.
Gamboni, D. (1997) *The Destruction of Art: Iconoclasm and Vandalism since the French
Revolution*, London: Reaktion.
Gentile, E. (2007) *Fascismo di Pietra*, Bari: Laterza.
Horn, D. (1994) *Social Bodies: Science, Reproduction and Italian Modernity*, Princeton:
Princeton University Press.

Isnenghi, M. (1994) *L'Italia in Piazza: i Luoghi della vita Pubblica dal 1848 ai Giorni Nostri*, Milan: A. Mondadori.

Kostof, S. (1978) 'The Emperor and the Duce: the Planning of Piazzale Augusto Imperatore in Rome', in H.A. Millon and L. Nochlin (eds.) *Art and Architecture in the Service of Politics*, Cambridge, MA: MIT Press.

Ladd, B. (1997) *The Ghosts of Berlin: Confronting German History in the Urban Landscape*, Chicago, IL: University of Chicago Press.

Levinson, S. (1998) *Written in Stone: Public Monuments in Changing Societies*, Durham, NC: Duke University Press.

Luzzatto, S. (2005) *The Body of Il Duce: Mussolini's Corpse and the Fortunes of Italy*, New York: Metropolitan Books.

Macdonald, S. (2006) 'Undesirable heritage: Fascist material culture and historical consciousness in Nuremberg', *International Journal of Heritage Studies*, 12(1): 9–28.

Mammone, A. (2006) 'A daily revision of the past: Fascism, anti-fascism, and memory in contemporary Italy', *Modern Italy*, 11(2): 211–26.

—— and Veltri, G.A. (2007) 'La memoria daltonica del fascismo', *Il Ponte*, 62(3): 89–97.

Marchetti, P. (2004) 'Il vincolo del Foro Italico nel cinquantesimo anno dal termine dei lavori', *MdiR/Monumenti di Roma*, 2(1/2): 133–47.

Masia, L., Matteoni, D. and Mei, P. (2007) *Il parco del Foro Italico: la Storia, lo Sport, i Progetti*, Cinisello Balsamo (Milan): Silvana.

Miller, J.E. (1999) 'Who Chopped Down That Cherry Tree? The Italian Resistance in History and Politics, 1945–1998', *Journal of Modern Italian Studies*, 4(1): 37–53.

Mott, G. (2003) *Foro Italico*, New York: PowerHouse Books.

Musil, R. (1986) *Selected Writings* (B. Pike, ed.), New York: Continuum.

Natoli, A. (1960) Vecchi vizi e occasioni perdute, *Vie Nuove*, 30.

Pavone, C. (1988) 'Tre Governi e due Occupazioni', in F. Ferratini Tosi and G. Grassi (eds) *L'Italia nella Seconda Guerra Mondiale e nella Resistenza*, Milan: Franco Angeli.

—— (1995) *Alle Origini della Pepubblica: Scritti su Fascismo, Antifascismo e Continuità dello Stato*, Turin: Bollati Boringhieri.

Pezzino, P. (2005) 'The Italian Resistance Between History and Memory', *Journal of Modern Italian Studies*, 10(4): 396–412.

Pirani, F. and Tozzi, S. (eds) (1998) *Severini al Foro Italico*, Rome: Fratelli Palombi.

La Repubblica (2006) 'L'Ara Pacis riapre dopo sette anni', Online. Available: www.repubblica.it/2006/04/sezioni/cronaca/apertura-ara-pacis/apertura-ara-pacis/apertura-ara-pacis.html.

La Repubblica (2008) 'Alemanno, sicurezza e sviluppo "E via la teca dell'Ara Pacis"', Online. Available: www.repubblica.it/2008/04/sezioni/politica/roma-alemanno-sindaco/roma-alemanno-sindaco/roma-alemanno-sindaco.html.

Rosenfeld, G.D. (2000) *Munich and Memory: Architecture, Monuments, and the Legacy of the Third Reich*, Berkeley, CA: University of California Press.

Sassi, E. (2006) 'L'Ara Pacis inaugurata tra le polemiche', *Corriere della Sera*, 22 April.

Stanley, A. (2000) 'Rome Journal: Italy's Fascist Buildings in Style, and for Sale, *The New York Times*. Online. Available: http://query.nytimes.com/gst/fullpage.html?res=9E05E7 DC1138F931A25754C0A9669C8B63&sec=&spon=&pagewanted=all.

US Army Rest Center (1944) *Forum of Italy*, Rome: US Army Rest Center.

Vie Nuove (20 August 1960), 14, 'Togliere all'Italia la truccatura fascista'.

Zevi, B. (1993) *Architecture as Space: How to Look at Architecture*, New York: Da Capo.

—— (1994) *The Modern Language of Architecture*, New York: Da Capo.

Part III

Institutional(ized) Exclusion?

Translocation and secretion?

10   The Northern League and its 'innocuous' xenophobia

Martina Avanza

Summary

Umberto Bossi's Northern League has become a significant political and social actor in contemporary Italy. Indeed, it plays a major role in Berlusconi's government and in shaping its programme, especially when it comes to immigration or security. The Northern League – especially if compared with neo-fascist groups or parties – is often portrayed as a tolerable democratic and popular force, a harmless and mostly 'folkloric' phenomenon. Even if the xenophobic approach is a strong marker of the party's ideology, of the activists' identity, as well as of the local and national policies it formulates, Italian parties, voters, journalists and even scholars still do not classify the League as a xenophobic right-wing movement. This chapter instead shows that Bossi's party has skilfully built an apparently inoffensive racism, which is actually a true 'strength' in its strategy of legitimization.

Introduction

Born in the 1980s as a peripheral phenomenon, the Northern League has become a significant political and social actor in contemporary Italy, playing a major role in Berlusconi's government and in shaping its programme. While only a minority at a national level, the League has influence in northern regions (without the League, neither the Right nor the Left are able to win elections in the most prosperous regions, those of the north) and uses this position to gain power within Berlusconi's coalition. The party almost pursues two goals: to transform Italy into a federation (on this topic, see Roux's contribution in this volume) and to promote a very restrictive immigration policy.

The Northern League – especially if compared with neo-fascist groups or parties – is often portrayed as a tolerable democratic and popular force, a harmless and mostly 'folkloric' phenomenon. Its key references are the 'northern territory' (renamed Padania) and an allegedly 'unclassifiable (ideological/ political) nature'. This chapter shows – through ethnographic observation – that the League has skilfully built an apparently inoffensive racism, which is actually the true 'force' for its strategy of legitimization. In fact, even if the xenophobic approach is a strong marker of the party's ideology, of the activists' identity, as well as of the local and national policies it formulates, Italian parties, voters, journalists and even scholars still do not classify the League as a xenophobic right-wing movement.

An unclassifiable party?

The Northern League, considered by the Italian press as the real winning party in the April 2008 legislative elections,[1] does not fit in any obvious classification. If one meets its activists, reads its literature, attends its meetings (Avanza 2007), one finds extreme violence against migrants as the striking feature dominating all discourse. In fact, the verbal and symbolic violence (such as making pigs urinate on plots of land allocated to the construction of mosques, or spraying perfume on Nigerian prostitutes on a train which they had 'polluted') is not only recognized but asserted and professed as legitimate by its perpetrators. Yet physical violence, which the Italian extreme right of fascist descent classically advocates, is strictly prohibited by the League's activists, who prefer to refer 'Gandhi's passive resistance'. Similarly, while it is common for activists and official representatives of the League to deliver xenophobic and Islamophobic lectures, they will not tolerate another historical trait of the Italian right: anti-Semitism. Likewise, the Leaguists' physical appearance does not match the stereotypes generally ascribed to the extreme right. For instance, the participants of the nocturnal patrols which the Green Volunteers[2] (green being the party's colour) organize in the 'quarters infested by extra-communitarian immigration' all seem perfectly harmless: some are women (two women were in charge of organizing such patrols in Milan and Bergamo), some are obese, some unimpressive skinny young men, or retired senior citizens. I even saw a handicapped woman in a wheelchair participating in a march.

Whether this apparent harmlessness is an intentional construct or only fortuitous would be difficult to ascertain. But the Green Volunteers as a group offer an image which is a far cry from the extreme-right ideal-type parade featuring an angry mob of skinheads ready to fight. While observing (in Brescia, April 2003) a rabble of young activists from the neo-fascist group Forza Nuova (New Force), I was impressed by the extent to which the impression they generate could differ. The extreme-right activists, all men, young, dressed in black, very short hair, bearing flags and wearing T-shirts showing symbols inspired with Nazism, were standing in a train station, looking mean, legs slightly apart and arms crossed. They were only a handful in number, they were not shouting any slogans, but they were demonstrating an aggressiveness, if not a menace, which I had never seen among the Green Volunteers. Their homogeneity (in terms of sex, age, dress code, hair style and body language), coupled with the military trousers and high boots they were wearing, gave them a distinctly martial identity. On the contrary, the Green Volunteers make up a heterogeneous group only distinguishable through the green colour clothes (shirt, scarf and armband) they wear, and not displaying anything reminiscent of the military dress code. Armed with mobile phones to 'alert the police in case of hurdles', and lighted torches to signal their presence, their intervention is often nothing more than posting pamphlet warnings stating that the area is 'controlled by the Green Volunteers'. In fact, outbursts seldom occur during these rounds and are severely disapproved of if they do.[3] Even through the way they walk, the Green Volunteers more resemble a group of strolling pedestrians talking in small groups than a paramilitary-type gang. Hence, the walks do not comprise, as with the extreme-right groups described by Virchow (2007), a real-time apprenticeship of discipline, synchronized walking and slogan chanting, and any other similar behaviour typical of virile military squads. In that sense, the Leaguist patrols offer to external observers a somewhat unlikely sight, as if the individuals were not fit for the type of action they had set out to conduct. The Green Volunteers thus personify the unlikely, almost disturbing, figure of organized and xenophobic but (apparently) innocuous activists.

This apparently harmless racism, which one could easily associate with 'pub talk' xenophobia, is a major strength for the League. Indeed, despite its policies and the discourse of its representatives, the League has always managed – in Italy, but less so abroad – to present itself as siding along neither left nor right wing politics, claiming instead to be territorial (representing the north of the peninsula, but not a specific ideology), and defender of the working class. This grassroots support, which has been confirmed through elections, is an important factor of legitimacy for the League, even from the point of view of the Italian Left. In 1996, Massimo d'Alema, the ex-communist leader of the PD, qualified the League as a 'left limb' due to its support from the working-class. Pierluigi Bersani, of the same party, in 2006 proclaimed the League to be a 'popular force'. Antonio Di Pietro, party head of Italy of Values and twice minister under a centre-left government, declared that: 'the League is a party of the people and its leaders are sincere' (*La Repubblica,* 27 November 2008). The classification strategy (to present itself as a territorial and working-class party), which has been adopted by the League since its inception, has an obvious effect and can partly explain its success among the voters of the extreme left, who have been the most noticeable losers of the 2008 legislative elections. These voters do not have to assume that they 'have sold their soul to the right'. Indeed, even scholars seem to assume that the League is not a far-right party (Ignazi 2000). Most of them consider the League to be a populist party (Tarchi 2002, Albertazzi and McDonnel 2007) even if this label, as Mudde (1996) has shown, is far from being neutral. As Mammone points out, people such as the European MP Mario Borghezio are genuine right-wing extremists. In a recent meeting with French neo-fascists, he 'advised activists to infiltrate into civil society and local/regional assemblies by using a "regionalist" or "Catholic" camouflage ("this is a good way not to be classified as nostalgic fascists") but maintaining a concealed fascist spirit' (Mammone 2009: 179).

A differentialist *Weltanschauung*

The innocuous aspect of the League activists is not only due to their pro-working-class and harmless appearance; it is also linked to their feeling (which I have felt sincere) that they are not racist and which provides them with an evidently clear conscience. In fact, they still assert not to be racist while patrolling the streets at night with torches (rather reminiscent of the Ku Klux Klan practices), shouting 'stop the invasion', 'no stealing gypsies in our quarters', 'build your terrorist mosques elsewhere', and distributing pamphlets which claim 'we don't want the Koran in Milan' or 'Allah is great and the Kalashnikov is his Prophet'. It would be fair to say that, unlike what has been described in the *Journal of Contemporary Ethnography*'s special issue on the extreme right, the activists do not entertain a racialist vision of the world (Blee 2007). The Green Volunteers do not claim White or Aryan superiority nor associate themselves to the White Power ideology, even if the most politicized ones are familiar with the classic extreme right authors, such as Julius Evola. The following speech made by one of the participants in the nocturnal patrols offers a typical example of the Green Volunteer's rhetoric by which they avoid being classified as xenophobic:

> The leftists say we are racists. But what does it mean to ask people to come and then ask them to live under a bridge? They are not animals, are they? And what about the women who end up as prostitutes, being the victims of organized crime, is that to be considered leftist generosity? No, I am sorry to say, but I agree with Mao: it is better to give them a fishing rod and for them to learn how to fish. In my view, if we allow them in, we have to provide them with decent living conditions, with dignity, because they are also human beings. But if we say that, we are racists!! On the other hand, the leftist who sleeps nicely at home and lets it all happen, he is not racist!

Similarly, during a conference on globalization, one the Green Volunteer in charge told activists: 'they want us to believe that what we say is unjust. We could be sentenced to jail, or at least accused of immorality. But we also say that they should be helped in their own country. Isn't this solidarity? That, nobody will say!' This type of justification, by which the activists accepting it are freed of any sense of guilt, has been meticulously constructed by the League which advocates a differentialist vision of the world.

To justify radical antagonism with a multicultural society while avoiding being accused of racism, the League resorts to the politically correct principle of 'respecting cultural diversity'. According to that, the 'massive' presence of migrants is a threat to the 'identity' of both the host indigenous populations and those uprooted from their motherland. To respect the culture of the people hosting as well as that of the migrants, it would be necessary for all to remain in their own homes. In 1990, a poster from the League was already proclaiming that: 'To bring blacks here is slavery'. According to this logic, mixing cultures is tantamount to destructing them and thus multiculturalism is simply unthinkable. To illustrate this point, ideologists from the League often use a metaphor by which the world is composed of different colour dots (representing the different peoples on Earth) explaining that, by mixing these dots, the colours will end up disappearing and only grey will remain ('the identity-less amalgamated man'). The same idea is more violently expressed in an electoral poster dating back to 1990, which has often been reused since: a woman, who personifies the 'centralist State', is cooking heads, legs and arms of different colours (black, yellow or white) in a huge cauldron, symbolizing the 'multicultural society'.

The Leaguist culturalist invective is mostly centred on Islam, which is considered both as a religion and as a way to envisage the world. The 'Islamic culture', considered to be homogeneous and immune to historical change, is supposed to be incompatible with secularism and more generally with the 'European Christian civilization'. Gilberto Oneto, one of the party's main ideologists, sustained that 'Europe and the Islamic world have been undergoing a lethal war for two thousand two hundred years'. If the 'Sarasin' came with scimitars in the past, they now present themselves as 'poor immigrants', nothing has changed: 'it is the same intolerant, arrogant and blood-thirsty culture wanting to destroy the European Civilization'. He concludes: 'they are not immigrants;

Figure 10.1 Now or never again. Stop the Islamic invasion (a pamphlet of the Lega Nord youth movement)

Figure 10.2 Now it is enough. Just get out (an anti-Islamic pamphlet of the Lega Nord)

they are invaders' (*La Padania*, 24 January 1999). This is how Umberto Bossi is able to claim 'cultural self-defence' to be a 'natural reaction' to the migration phenomena (Bossi and Vimercati 1998).

This philosophy is well summarized by the two posters shown here (Figures 10.1 and 10.2): one displays a woman wearing a burqa, symbol of Islam's supposed backwardness; the other portrays an isolated man among praying Muslims.

In a legal document, the League claims a 'differentialist vision of the world', a concept borrowed, as many xenophobic and neo-fascist European parties have done, from Alain de Benoist's Nouvelle Droite (New Right) (Spektorowski 2000, 2003), and maintains that real racism is to be found in 'the destructive action and thoughts peddled by globalization, which aims at constructing an Anglophone and totalitarian Global Village through the promotion of a planetary liberal sub-culture, based on the ruins of the peoples' (Mussa 1998). In order to put this vision into practice, the League created the Padania Cooperation, constituted as a small non-governmental organization with the official motto: 'Let's help them in their homeland'. In a similar way, Bossi has repeatedly supported the abolition of the poor countries' foreign debts, as well as the intensification of development and cooperation policies.

An actor of an increasingly restrictive immigration policy

Listening to Umberto Bossi's speeches, one would almost believe that it is really for the benefit of migrants that he devised, in 2002 together with Gianfranco Fini (as already mentioned in this volume, leader of the rightist heir to Italian 'historical neo-fascism', namely the National Alliance), one of the most restrictive migration laws in Europe. It calls for: digital fingerprints to be taken by the police of all 'extra-communitarians' (even those legally entitled to stay on Italian soil);[4] restricted family reunion; preference to be given to descendants of Italian emigrants during recruitment (thus favouring blood descent); facilitation of the expulsion of illegal immigrants; impeding the issuance of the political refugee status. The law was so harshly repressive against illegal immigrants that some sections, especially those linked to the modalities of expulsions, were withdrawn in July 2004 by the Constitutional Court for violating the fundamental rights of some individuals. Yet, this law is still considered too lenient by the League who has been actively lobbying, since its return to power in 2008, to make it harsher.

Since the beginning of Berlusconi's fourth government (April 2008), the League, which holds the Ministry of Internal Affairs, has been attempting – and achieved in July 2009 – to ascribe illegal entry onto Italian soil as a criminal offence, thereby punishable with up to four years imprisonment or, at least (owing to the fact that the already overcrowded Italian jails would not have the capacity to bear the consequences of such a measure) with a fine (ranging from €5,000 to €10,000). Nonetheless, according to the security bill proposed by the League, any migrant who remains in Italy after receiving an expulsion warning, is liable to up to four years imprisonment. Moreover, the League is currently trying to pass a law which will disallow free medical care for illegal immigrants and will authorize doctors to report such patients to the police (security bill approved in the Senate on 5 February 2009). The party wanted to go further and oblige doctors to denounce their illegal patients, but the majority refused to impose such a constraint on the medical community. Such has not been the case for the money transfer operators who face the risk of having their businesses closed down unless they report these 'aliens'. Still not satisfied, the League also achieved the project of forbidding illegal immigrants to marry or to legally register their newborn children.

The League justifies such a stern stance against unregistered foreign migrants by its will to fight against 'illegal immigration' which is considered to bring criminality to the host population, and despair and exploitation to the migrants. This is not racism, the League argues, since the party fully accepts foreigners in a 'legal situation', working and 'respecting the law'. This alleged acceptance is, however, questionable. Not only has the League always barely tolerated the physical presence of such foreigners in public spaces (the party opposes the construction of mosques and some Leaguist mayors have removed public benches to avoid them being used by extra-EU immigrants), but in 2008 the party started to promote legislative initiatives against these 'legal' migrants. It has already managed to create a tax (between €80 and €200) on the issuance of resident permits (security bill approved in the Senate on 5 February 2009).

The income thus collected is meant to be transformed into a 'migration influx prevention fund' which would finance development projects in countries that have underwritten a bilateral agreement with Italy (in other words, countries accepting back their expulsed nationals and ensuring tight control of their migrants' departure). 'This is real people solidarity' commented one of the measure's promoters, Senator Lorenzo Bodega, 'to help' them believe in their own country, and not to make them believe that the long-gone El Dorado still exists' (*La Padania*, 6 February 2009). Once again, it is for their 'own good' that the League wants to tax migrants.

Once the tax is paid, and the ever-increasing acceptance criteria fulfilled, these migrants should obtain a resident permit functioning along the same line as the Italian driving license: the 'bad immigrant', as would be the case with a 'bad driver', will 'lose points' (the specific criteria still need to be clearly defined); the loss of all the points will lead to the migrant's expulsion. According to Senator Bodega, far from being hostile to the migrants, this system will promote a better integration by rewarding 'positive and honest immigration, the one that works, produces and which is perfectly integrated'.

At the same time, this 'ideal immigrant' described by Bodega is still not safe from further legislative initiatives promoted by the League. For example, the party has proposed that any non-EU immigrant should deposit €10,000 upon applying for a VAT number (which is compulsory in Italy to start any commercial or professional activity or to set up a small business). On this matter again, Bossi's movement exhibits seemingly good faith: this measure will prevent the exploitation of undeclared employees by foreign entrepreneurs, especially Chinese: 'it is slavery. If to denounce this and to try to guarantee the workers' rights is racism...' (*La Padania*, 13 January 2009).

In this ebb and flow of measures against migrants, the League has not spared their children. It has designed, established and legalized 'integration classes' which these children will be compelled to attend if they are not sufficiently proficient in the Italian language. These classes will also teach the 'respect of territorial and regional traditions', as well as 'the moral and religious diversity of the host country'. While the Church and the political opposition point out the inherent risk of creating ghetto classes, the League retorts that this is, of course, to help better integration.

This policy of harassment, if not persecution, has aroused vehement resistance among Catholics, the medical profession (given the role of informant), the opposition, but also some of the rightist coalition parties. Fini, despite his long attachment and close links with neo-fascist parties, defined the League's measures as 'openly discriminatory'. Yet, the League managed to impose them, and this reveals the real influence of Bossi's party.

From a xenophobic policy to a racist one

If legal harassment against 'extra-communitarians' was not enough, the League of 2008, unlike that of 2001, proceeds to latch on 'neo-communitarians', a new Italian category referring to migrants originating from countries newly integrated in the European Union. More specifically, the term implicitly refers to Romanians, especially the Roma who, after Moroccans and Albanians, personify the repulsive image of the 'bad immigrant', thief and sometimes rapist. As Nando Sigona shows in his contribution to this volume, it is Romano Prodi's centre-left government which initiated reactions against 'neo-communitarians' following a bloody incident provoked by a Romanian in 2007 in what is called a 'nomads' camp' but which is actually nothing more than a slum. Berlusconi's government, especially through its Leaguist Interior Minister Roberto Maroni, capitalized on this initiative, despite the fact that their projects are limited by European norms, for which no distinction should be made between old and new Europeans. In January 2009, Maroni had to abandon a legislative statutory order planning to expel EU citizens likely to 'threaten law and order' (targeting Romanians without naming them), after the EU's expressed doubts about its compatibility with the Schengen Treaty and threatened to launch a lawsuit against Italy.

Previously the EU had been reluctant to confront the Italian government, despite the fact that some of the laws it promoted were evidently racial measures. In May 2008, Maroni declared a 'state of emergency' against the presence of gypsy communities in the Lombardia, Lazio and Campania regions, and declared the police commissioners of Rome, Milan and Naples, 'Special Commissioners for the influx of Roma'. In order to tackle this emergency, Minister Maroni ordered a massive census of all Roma living in nomadic camps in their region, whether adults or under-age, EU nationals, Italians or from other countries.[5] This measure therefore addresses an ethnic category, not a national one: thereby this is not a xenophobic but a racial measure. Once again, a taboo has been lifted by the League and its allies who are able to apply racial discrimination policies. As Nando Sigona shows in his chapter, this census is nothing less than a racial record: not only are the counted individuals named, but it is carried out by the police forces employing investigation techniques, such as taking digital fingerprints.

This security build-up, using methods which are rather reminiscent of one of the most dreadful times of Italian history (i.e. the census of Jews which preceded the racial laws and deportation) is led by the League through the interior Minister Roberto Maroni, with the same proclaimed good faith and the same conviction of not being racist as that of the Green Volunteers patrolling at night to chase away the non-EU migrants assaulting 'our' quarters. Conducting a 'census' of Roma children, which has been heavily criticized, even by the Church, allegedly aims to protect them from exploitation by their families. The Minister explains with conviction that the aim is to grant these children their rights. However, these measures do not emanate from the Family Planning Minister, but from the Interior Minister, and they are not part of social or family policies; they are instead part of a proposed new security policy ('pacchetto sicurezza'). If the need was to highlight their security dimension, all it requires is to recollect the Minister's own words when, at the end of October 2008, he declared that since 'the first phase is now over' (the census), the second phase could then be initiated, which was the 'evacuation of the abusive camps' – 124 out of 167 registered – and the eviction of illegal immigrants. Here as well, the improvement of the Roma's wellbeing (those entitled to a resident permit) is meant to be at stake, since 'equipped villages' in which they will be able to live with dignity, he assures, will replace the demolished squalid camps.

Yet none of the Leaguist mayors would ever let such a village be constructed in their municipality. Indeed, the League is very active locally (in regional, provincial and city councils of Northern Italy) to prevent any initiative favouring migrants in general and Roma in particular, such as: awarding low-wage housing, or constructing reception centres, or parking areas for nomads and mosques. If its elected members lack the means to significantly influence municipal decisions, the League organizes demonstrations, such as the ones repeatedly held in Milan against the opening of an Islamic primary school. One of the most controversial initiatives of this kind has certainly been the 14 October 2000 demonstration in Lodi (Lombardia) against the construction of a mosque on a granted municipal plot, where demonstrators spread pig excrement on the ground. These types of actions have been repeated several times. Minister Roberto Calderoli, one of the most important leaguist representatives, suggested creating a 'pig (maiale) day' in order to label this method of opposing the construction of mosque.

Numerous other demonstrations have been organized by the League to condemn immigration as a root-cause to criminality, prostitution, drug trafficking, smuggling and sexual violence. Such demonstrations often occur following particularly shocking crimes allegedly committed by a foreigner (theft with violence, kidnapping, rape). This particular atmosphere enabled the League to present 'immigrants' on the whole as the source of all social evils. Although these demonstrations have not led, so far, to aggressive outbursts, the party officials usually deliver particularly violent speeches. During my field research I have heard, with scepticism, mayors – above all Giancarlo Gentilini, nicknamed 'the sheriff', who has held two mandates in Trevisio – Parliamentarians and even future Ministers such as Roberto Calderoli, say things like: 'we don't want these Taliban, they should go home to beat up their women and leave our daughters alone'; or: 'the immigrants are poor buggers? My ass! These bastards want to invade us, we have to stop them'; and also: 'they want to come to Venice? Let them come, but beware, they'd better not burst our balls or we'll sink them in the canals'.

Xenophobia: a place to take in the Italian political market?

Xenophobia is thus central to the Northern League's political programme, but this has not always been the case. During its first electoral rise in the 1990s, the party was the main federalist movement. However, it is only later that the League saw all the other main parties following in its steps to become similarly 'federalist'. (see Roux's contribution in this volume). Initially Berlusconi's ally for the 1994 legislative elections, the League saw its electorate flee towards Forza Italia, and thereafter became an internal opponent, to the extent of causing government's downfall less than one year later. Raising the stakes in order to survive, the League started to demand independence. In 1996, it became the biggest political movement of the North. But the 'dream' of an independent Padania took too long to materialize and prevented the League from forming alliances, thus excluding it from the political scene. Compelled to forgo its independence project in order to ally once again with Berlusconi during the 2001 elections, Umberto Bossi had to find a new 'grand cause' with which to ostensibly distinguish the League from other right-wing parties. He therefore invested in a still-unexplored political terrain in Italy and promoted the League to be the only entrepreneur of xenophobia. Needless to say, the National Alliance also demanded a restrictive migration policy, but this party has been (even if controversially) engaged in a process of 'democratic normalization'. The League instead proudly maintained a 'protest party' profile and anti-migration campaign.

Encouraged by this particularism within the political market, by the media hype over the 'immigration problem' in Italy, and by Jörg Haider's victory 1999 in Austria (the latter has been publicly invited to a League's meeting), the League has progressively toughened its stance on immigration which has occupied a central place in its arguments and field of action since the end of the 1990s. The fact that it claims no direct link with fascism, and does not accept anti-Semitism, has eased the task: it was not encircled by any 'cordon sanitaire' (as was the case with the National Front in France), thus enabling its third participation with a coalition government; and it did not suffer any sanction from Brussels (as Haider did when elected in Austria). The grassroots basis of its activists, generally seen as harmless folklorists, has also contributed to shaping the League's image as a working-class party which dares say what all think but keep themselves to themselves. This is one of the League's major strengths: a de-complexed, (physically) non-violent xenophobia, belligerent but which cannot be assimilated to its more usual manifestations (Nazi, fascist and anti-Semitic), militant but (apparently) 'innocuous'. The analysis of the League offers a chance to ponder what new shapes xenophobic parties can take and what their strategies of legitimization can be. Successful strategies in this case, if the party can still, in Italy, pretend to be something else other than what it really is: a party championing a policy which is xenophobic against migrants and racist against some national minorities, such as the Roma.

Notes

1 With more than 8 per cent of the votes nationally (almost twice the amount obtained during the legislative elections of 2006), the Northern League has once again become a major political force in the northern regions (the only area in which it contested elections), especially in its historical stronghold of Veneto and Lombardia – where, since the end of the 1990s, it had been losing support.

2 Founded in 1998 and lead by one of the most xenophobic leaders of the League, the member of the European Parliament Mario Borghezio, the Green Volunteers (see www.volontariverdi.org) are responsible for organizing the 'patrols'. After several police investigations, about the legality of its 'patrols', the group should now be free from any lawsuit. Indeed, the League has succeeded in legalizing the patrols (see the security bill approved in the Senate on 2009).

3 The most serious slip-up happened in October 2000 in Turin. A young militant from Borghezio's group set fire, unintentionally it seems, to shelters of Romanian migrants

located under a bridge (with no casualties). Ten people were arrested for this and Borghezio was sentenced in 2005 to a five-month prison sentence with parole. The youngster was then expelled from the party.

4 The term 'extra-communitarian' (extra comunitario), lately meaning belonging to a country outside the European Union and seemingly technical and neutral, has in fact a strong negative connotation in Italy. Indeed, the term is never applied to migrants from Western countries (USA, Canada, Australia, Japan), but only to those from poor countries. In Italy, it is often associated with the problems these migrants are supposed to cause ('extra-communitarian crime', 'raped by three extra-communitarians'). The term is in fact never used in a positive sense.

5 On the EU's attitude about the census of the Roma population see Sigona's chapter in this volume

References

Albertazzi, D. and McDonnel, D. (2007) *Twenty-First Century Populism. The Spectre of Western European Democracy,* London: Palgrave.

Avanza, M. (2007) 'Les "purs et durs de Padanie". Ethnographie du militantisme nationaliste à la Ligue du Nord, Italie (1999–2002)', unpublished thesis, Ecole des Hautes Etudes en Sciences Sociales de Paris.

Benford, R. and Snow, D. (2000) 'Framing Processes and Social Movements: an Overview and Assessment', *Annual Review of Sociology*, 26: 611–39.

Blee, K. (2007) 'Ethnography of the Far Right', *Journal of Contemporary Ethnography*, 2: 119–28.

Bossi, U. and Vimercati, D. (1998) *Processo alla Lega*, Milan: Sperling & Kupfer.

Ignazi, P. (2000) *L'estrema destra in Europa*, Bologna: Il Mulino.

Mammone, A. (2009), 'The eternal return? Faux populism and contemporarization of neo-fascism across Britain, France and Italy', *Journal of Contemporary European Studies*, 17(2), pp. 171–192.

Mudde, C. (1996) 'The War of Words : Defining the extreme-right party family', *West European Politics*, 19(2): 225–48.

Mussa, G. (1998) 'Padania, Identitá e Societá Multirazziale', *Enti Locali Padani Federali*, 2.

Spektorowski, A. (2000) 'The French New Right: Differentialism and the idea of ethnophilian exclusionism', *Polity*, 33 (2).

Spektorowski, A. (2003) 'Ethnoregionalism: The intellectual New Right and the Lega Nord', *The Global Review of Ethnopolitics*, 2(3).

Tarchi, M. (2002), 'Populism Italian Style', in Y. Mény and Y. Surel (eds.) *Democracies and the Populist Challenge,* London: Palgrave.

Virchow, F. (2007) 'Performance, emotion, and ideology : On the creation of 'Collectives of Emotion' and Worldview in the contemporary German Far Right', *Journal of Contemporary Ethnography*, 2: 147–64.

11 'Gypsies out of Italy!'

Social exclusion and racial discrimination of Roma and Sinti in Italy

Nando Sigona

Summary

A recent national survey has revealed how widespread and deeply rooted anti-Romani sentiments are among Italians from all social backgrounds. The aim of this chapter is to investigate the political and institutional side of this dark shadow of contemporary Italy by reviewing the key policy initiatives on Roma and Sinti taken since November 2007, when the Italian government issued decree No. 181 (1 November 2007), declaring 'a nomad emergency' for the first time in Italian recent history. The chapter will also highlight continuities and discontinuities in public discourse and policy between the current government led by Silvio Berlusconi and the previous one led by Romano Prodi.

Introduction[1]

> Fellow members of the Northern League, my word is revolution! This is the gospel according to Gentilini: the decalogue of the first sheriff major. I want a revolution against illegal migrants. I want a revolution against nomad camps and the Gypsies. I destroyed two [nomad camps] in Treviso. And now there is not even one left. I want to eliminate [Gypsy] kids who steal from elder people. If Maroni [the Northern League Minister for Internal Affairs] says zero tolerance, I want double zero tolerance.
>
> (Gentilini, 14 September 2008)[2]

At the *Festa dei Popoli Padani*, a meeting organized in Venice by the rightist Northern League, Giancarlo Gentilini, senior member of the party and deputy major of Treviso addressed the crowd with these words. The intervention provoked numerous protests and the Public Prosecutor's Office of Venice opened an inquiry against Gentilini on the grounds of instigation to racial hatred. At the time of writing, the investigation is underway but the accused does not appear to be concerned. In a statement to the press, he stated: 'What I said reflects the will of my citizens. It is not racism, but order, discipline and respect for the law'.[3]

Appealing to the *vox populi* to justify racist declarations is not rare in the Italian political panorama (see Avanza's chapter in *Italy Today*). This phenomenon is even more alarming when it directly involves government representatives, demonstrating how certain types of discourses are entrenched in institutions, with evident risks for institutional discrimination on ethnic grounds. An episode which, in 2005, involved the then Minister of Justice, Roberto Castelli, is illustrative of this reality. Commenting on a decision taken by a magistrate on a specific legal case, Castelli condemned the release of two Roma women accused of an attempted kidnapping in Lecco as unacceptable, stating that:

> The verdict of Lecco is the last one of many; it is the final straw and demonstrates that at least a part of the judiciary is out of touch with what the ordinary people feel [...] The magistrate has to judge according to the common opinion of the people
>
> (quoted in Fazzo 2005: 10)

Statements like this are neither isolated nor unique, nor do they only exclusively concern the current right-wing coalition government. In 1999, the UN Committee on the Elimination of Racial Discrimination (CERD 1999) expressed concern 'at the situation of many Roma who, ineligible for public housing, live in camps outside major Italian cities', and stated that 'in addition to a frequent lack of basic facilities, the housing of Roma in such camps leads not only to a physical segregation of the Roma community from Italian society, but a political, economic and cultural isolation as well'. This assessment was confirmed in the following years by national and international organizations involved in the monitoring of racism and xenophobia (see ECRI 2002, 2006, Sigona and Monasta 2006).[4] On the contrary, statements like those of Gentilini and Castelli capture the *zeitgeist* of contemporary Italy and translate a widespread sentiment that unites representatives on various levels of the main political parties, a large proportion of the media and the majority of public opinion (Monasta 2008). Research carried out by the Institute for the Study of Public Opinion (ISPO) shows how the Italians' image of Roma and Sinti is based on lack of knowledge, both with regards to their numbers, their origin and their legal status. The image of the Roma and Sinti is extremely negative in comparison to other nationalities/ethnic groups and can be grouped into two main subcategories: 47 per cent see Roma and Sinti as thieves, delinquents and criminals, and 35 per cent associate them with marginalization, degradation, poverty and homelessness (ISPO 2008, Arrigoni and Vitale 2008).

It is estimated that there are approximately 140,000–160,000 Roma and Sinti in Italy (Scalia 2006). They represent approximately 0.25 per cent of the population in Italy and they place the country in fourteenth place among European countries regarding the presence of this group (Piasere 2004). A little under half of these people have Italian citizenship. The remaining half is made up of European Union citizens and migrants and refugees from non-EU countries.[5] Despite being a numerically limited presence, they are extremely visible in the public arena as a result of the stigma attached to them by the main population and the mass media. The stereotypical image of the 'Gypsy' associated with the Roma and Sinti has an age-old history. It is a cultural construction whose 'effects of truths' (Foucault 1980) have had repercussions on the life experiences and opportunities of thousands of Roma and Sinti. This widespread and deeply rooted construction associates the Roma and Sinti 'by nature' as being nomadic, intrinsically other, different, asocial and kidnappers of children (Tosi Cambini 2008, Todesco 2004, Monasta 2008).

According to Simoni (2008a: 84):

> While hostile statements towards other minorities generally cause some public or private reaction, anti-Roma hate language usually carries few consequences even in contexts otherwise used to guarded language.

In this chapter I aim to investigate the political and institutional side of this dark shadow of contemporary Italy by reviewing the key policy initiatives on Roma and Sinti taken since November 2007, when the centre-left government led by Romano Prodi issued decree No. 181 (1 November 2007), declaring 'a nomad emergency' for the first time in recent Italian history. It will discuss the context in which these measures were adopted and their implementation. The recent developments which followed the electoral victory of Silvio Berlusconi and his right-wing partners, and led several parties to accuse the government of institutional racism, will also be explored.

The *discovery* of the 'nomad emergency'

Since the last round of the EU enlargement in January 2007, there has been a growing alarm in Italy over the risk of what some commentators have termed a 'tidal wave' of migrants coming from Romania and Bulgaria to 'invade' Italy. In particular, public and media attention focused on the migration of Romanian Roma. Old prejudices, widespread antiziganism (see ERRC 2000, Sigona and Monasta 2006, Sigona 2008) and the specific characteristics of Romani migration and livelihood strategies, which make them a visible presence in most Italian cities, have all contributed to creating a growing alarm towards the Roma (see also Mai 2009).

'Before Romania entered the European Union, Rome was the safest capital in the world [...] It is necessary to resume repatriations' (quoted in Belpietro 2007: 23): it was the beginning of November and the then Mayor of Rome, Walter Veltroni, without any hesitation, named the Romanian migrants responsible for the wave of criminality which was alarming the citizens of the Italian capital.

On the contrary, until the beginning of November, the central government had not paid much attention to the issue and any initiatives had been scarcely coordinated between different government units. As a senior civil servant noted: 'Until not long ago the situation seemed to be under control and beyond the competence of the central government [...] we probably underestimated the dimension of the phenomenon.[6]

Similarly, in an interview with the *Financial Times* (quoted in Dinmore 2007), Romano Prodi said: '[…] nobody could expect that scale of influx. Nobody was expecting the outflow from Romania across Europe'.

The turning point was the murder of Giovanna Reggiani allegedly committed by a Romanian citizen in Rome. At that point, Prodi's centre-left government, which was preparing to pass the 'security packet' – a set of measures to combat crime and terrorism – decided to extract some of the proceedings to make them immediately effective through decree-law No. 181/2007, the main aim of which was to facilitate the expulsion of communitarian citizens whenever the authorities identified them as a threat to public and state security.

During the days immediately after the decree came into being, police forces carried out a systematic survey of authorized and unauthorized Romani settlements. The raids, which were often nocturnal or in the early hours of the morning, put great pressure on residents, many of whom left the country 'voluntarily'.

In the first hours following its approval, the decree-law had gained the almost unanimous support of Italian political parties – dissent only emerged after a few days, particularly in parliamentary debate. In contrast, it raised a chorus of protest from NGOs and the voluntary sector, as well as from important international observers who showed concern for a decree which was formally ethnic-blind, yet in reality seemed to be directed at a specific group of people: the Romanian Roma.

This statement of the President of the Council of the European Parliamentary Assembly echoes the widespread concern:

> The arrest of a Romanian suspect in this murder should not, however, lead to a witch-hunt of Romanians. The Italian government may have the right to expel a number of people on public safety grounds, but all decisions must be subject to judicial review and taken on an individual basis rather than collectively.[7]

On 19 December 2007, two weeks before the deadline for the conversion of the decree into law, the Minister for Parliamentary Affairs informed the assembly of the government's decision to renounce the conversion.[8] However, ten days later, on 29 December, a new decree (No. 249/2007) was sent to the President of the Republic for the required signature. The new decree expanded on the substance of the preceding decree to include measures to combat 'international terrorism', reinforcing the idea of the link between migration and terrorism in public opinion.

The public debate: a contemporary witch-hunt?

Giovanna Reggiani's murder in Rome inflamed the political debate. Politicians from different orientations battled for position in the crucial political terrain of security. A brief examination of the 'emergency' debate helps trace the boundaries of the issue at stake. Following the incident in Rome, there was a large parliamentary consensus on the need for intervention on the 'Romanian Roma emergency'. However, immediately after the publication of the decree, unanimity disappeared, giving room to partisan political interest. In the early hours following the incident, the then leader of the new Democratic Party (PD) and mayor of Rome, Veltroni, expressed deep sympathy for Reggiani's family and argued for a tough reaction by the government and labelled the emergency decree: 'the first official initiative' of the PD. The aim is to challenge the 'old dichotomy' which sees 'security' as a prerogative of the right-wing and 'solidarity' of the left-wing (Veltroni quoted in Colombo 2007: 16).

In the leftist side of the government coalition the decree caused tensions. The then Minister of Welfare, Paolo Ferrero, played a key role mediating between the different positions emerging in his party, Rifondazione Comunista (RC). According to RC Senator Milziade Caprili, 'the left must emotionally reconnect to the grassroots [...] Nomad camps are not located in wealthy neighbourhoods but in the periphery' (quoted in Rosso 2007: 2). Similarly, the founder of RC, Fausto Bertinotti, argued that it is time for the left to acknowledge the importance of security rather than denying the influx of Roma from Romania can be a problem. But, he stressed,

> We need to avoid scapegoating [the Roma]; instead we should find the root causes of the problem. [...] there is a well-founded concern which could lead to a xenophobic outburst. It is not enough for the left to be tolerant and any initiative of repression has to go alongside others of integration.
>
> (quoted in Preziosi 2007: 5)

On the right side of the political spectrum, Gianfranco Fini, the leader of the right-wing party National Alliance, former deputy Prime Minister and current Speaker of the *Camera dei Deputati*, led the way for 'a flood of vitriolic anti-immigrant rhetoric' (Hooper 2007) against the Roma who, he stated in an interview to the *Corriere della Sera* (Di Caro 2007: 5), 'have no scruples about kidnapping children or using their own children for begging', who 'consider theft to be virtually legitimate and not immoral', and feel the same way about 'not working because it is up to the women to work, even through prostitution'. He concluded with 'to talk of integration with people with a "culture" of that sort is pointless'. Fini accused the decree of being too bland and argued that in Rome alone, 20,000 people should be expelled and between 200,000–250,000 in Italy.

Franco Frattini, the then vice-president of the European Commission and current Italian Foreign Minister also raised his voice: 'the decree is not enough as it limits its scope to the removal of dangerous individuals and not also to those without adequate resources' (quoted in Terracina 2007: 5).

Interestingly, the leader of the right-wing 'separatist' (see Roux's chapter as well as Avanza's contribution) party Northern League, Umberto Bossi, attempted to reframe the problem by including migration in general. In his terms:

> Nowadays everyone speaks of Roma and Romanians and forgets that there are many other immigrants, which bring many other problems. It is not only the Roma who cause trouble in this country
>
> (quoted in Garavaglia 2007: 1)

To conclude, this outline has shown a widespread use of inflammatory statements and a general agreement on where to put the blame for the 'emergency' among the main political actors. This is confirmed in the following quote from a representative of the National Office Against Racial discrimination (UNAR): 'We are witnessing a deterioration of political debate. What was once considered racism has now become acceptable and it is often supported and legitimized by the instrumental and inaccurate use of statistical data'.[9]

The direct and indirect effects of the decree-law

What impact did the decree have? Did it produce the mass expulsion of Romanian Roma as some had feared and others had hoped? By 18 December 2007, the decree had produced 408 expulsion orders, of which 262 were for reasons of 'public security', 124 for 'imperative motives of public security' and 22 for 'non-compliance with residence requirements'. Ten days later, on 27 December, a few hours before the decree expiry deadline, the total had risen to 510 expulsion orders, of which 181 were for 'imperative motives'. It is therefore possible to say that, quantitatively, the decree did not produce a mass expulsion of EU citizens.

Nevertheless, it must be noted that while it proved impossible to get hold of official data on the country of origin of the expelled – despite several requests to the Ministry of the Interior – from the information gathered in various Italian cities (Rome, Milan, Naples and Bologna) through associations, prefectures and newspapers, it seems that the Romanian citizens, particularly Romanian Roma, were by far the main 'beneficiaries' of the decree. While some supporters of the measure have explained the result with the existence of an objective threat among Romanians more than in other groups, we are more inclined to see this result as the outcome of the selective and discretionary implementation of the decree. This is also confirmed by the fact that as soon as the decree came into force, authorized and unauthorized nomad camps all over Italy were subjected to systematic police searches (Sigona 2008).

However, beyond its direct effect, the decree has also had side effects, though not unwanted, both in symbolic and material terms.

In fact, by officially sanctioning the existence of a security emergency, the decree has not only legitimized those extreme right groups who have traditionally appealed to the fear of the 'other' as a political tool, but also those local authorities, who for several years now, have opposed the presence of Roma on their territory by adopting eviction measures. In 2007, before the 'emergency' was declared, in one year the Municipality of Rome evicted more than 6,000 people, many of whom were Roma.[10]

Figure 11.1 Poster by the extreme right organization Forza Nuova (Trieste, 2009).

Figure 11.2 Poster by the ruling centre-left coalition, celebrating its security credentials, (Rome, 2007).

Changing government, changing policy? Elections and the political use of the 'Gypsy issue'

The electoral campaign for the 2008 national elections was probably the first in Italian history to include the 'Gypsy issue' as part of one of the running party's official programmes. In contrast, as a recent study has shown (Sigona 2006), on a local level the presence of the 'Gypsy problem' has been playing an important role in administrative elections for years.

The electoral manifesto of Silvio Berlusconi's People of Freedom states its 'opposition to unauthorized nomad camps and the removal of all those without any legal standing and without legal residence', which in the executive summary becomes 'the removal of illegal camps and the eviction of nomads without residence and means of support'. Confirming approaches and tones witnessed in the previous months, also in the centre-left government, Berlusconi's manifesto chose to deal with the Roma and Sinti exclusively within the discourse of security and repression.[11]

According to Simoni (2008a: 84–86), the problem is rooted in the incapacity of a significant part of the Italian population to live, even if only temporarily, next to people who, due to their behaviour or even simply their way of dressing, correspond to the image of the 'gypsy':

> Once a person is perceived as a 'gypsy', the repulsion felt towards him/her is such that it persists regardless of whether the person lives in the most sordid 'nomad camp', in a well equipped caravan or in a council house.

Institutions are extremely influenced by public opinion and politicians' constant pressure towards the evictions of Roma and Sinti. In some cases the political language is particularly direct, as the following statement by a Northern League MEP shows: 'After having carried out accurate calculations and having listened to the local residents [...] we have arrived at our proposed number of nomad presences: zero' (Matteo Salvini quoted in Simoni 2008a: 84).

In mainstream public discourse, the eviction is presented as of value in itself. Few people feel like challenging this assumption. While the tone of right-wing politicians tends to be more explicit and inflammatory, most centre-left politicians structure their argument around the concepts of 'legality' and 'certainty of sanctions', hinting at or explicitly referring to the illicit attributes of the 'nomads', stating that the simple application of the existing laws for all citizens can act as a push factor against the Roma community. This mechanism is far from new. Rather it has characterized the relationship between modern states and the Roma, following (at least in continental Europe), the abolishment of specifically anti-gypsy penal laws, which had been in existence in many states (Simoni 2005).

Up until not long ago, the practical effects of the disappearance of ethnic-specific regulations were limited by the possibility of drawing on another source of repressive instruments, this being the legislation on immigration. This allowed a whole range of coercive treatments (e.g. administrative custody, expulsion orders) which were far more efficient than penal proceedings for minor crimes. In many urban contexts, a Romani presence regarded as excessive or too visible could therefore easily be limited by the extensive application of existing formally ethnic-blind legislation against undocumented immigration, which had previously been 'dormant' in other cases. Of course, the enlargement of the EU has made these instruments inapplicable to Romanian citizens, including the Roma.

It is clear that given this background, the declarations made in the electoral manifesto of Berlusconi's party, when all is considered, represent a logical continuation of an institutional culture already in place under the previous government.[12]

Governing the 'state of emergency'

In this section, I will review the policy measures put forward by the Berlusconi's government following up to the electoral promise. To confirm the significance of the 'Gypsy issue' in Italian current political debate, it took the government less than two weeks from when it assumed office (8 May 2008) to issue the first act on the subject.

This was the Prime Minister's decree No. 122/2008 which declared 'the state of emergency in relation to the "nomad settlements" in the territories of Campania, Lombardia and Lazio'. As a justification for the decision the text mentions the 'extremely critical situations', created by the presence of nomads as well as other 'non-EU illegal residents' living in cities and towns in conditions of extreme marginality and, therefore states, it is 'the extreme precariousness of these settlements' that is causing 'serious social alarm which could lead to severe repercussions in terms of public order and safety of the local population'.

With three successive implementation orders (Ordinanza del Presidente del Consiglio dei Ministri, Nos. 3676, 3677, 3678 of 30 May 2008), one for each region, Berlusconi appointed three Special Commissioners with the task to set up the 'necessary interventions' needed to solve the emergency. Among these is the:

> Development of action plans for overcoming the emergency including, in case the existing camps are unable to satisfy the housing needs of residents, the identification of other suitable sites for authorized camps; measures capable to provide [the residents] with the *minimum* levels of social and health services; interventions capable of facilitating the social integration of those transferred to the authorized camps.
>
> (Ordinanza del Presidente del Consiglio dei Ministri, No. 3678/2008; emphasis added)[13]

Alongside these medium-term actions, the decrees foresee a series of preventive policing measures, including the 'monitoring of authorized nomad camps and the identification of illegal settlements', the 'identification and the census of people present in camps, including minors, through fingerprinting and biometric data collection', and, whenever a violation of legal and administrative laws is identified, the 'adoption of all the necessary measures needed for enforcing removal and expulsion' of the individuals concerned (ibid.).

An unusual census

The mapping of 'nomad camps' and the collection of biometric data of their residents started in June 2008. Roberto Maroni, the Minister of the Interior, assured that 'it will certainly not be an ethnic data collection but rather a real and proper census to guarantee that those who have a right to stay can live in decent conditions and to send those who do not back home' (Maroni 2008). However, if it was a 'real and proper' census, why did they not send researchers from the National Statistics Institute instead of police officers to collect the data? And if it was a 'real and proper' census, why was the right to anonymity not respected? Finally, on what legal grounds were Italian Roma and Sinti included in the census? These are just some of the questions which were raised by human rights activists in Italy and abroad bringing international attention to Italy,[14] with delegations of several international agencies and NGOs visiting Italian nomad camps – just to mention a few: Amnesty International, Human Rights Watch, European Parliament, Council of Europe Human Rights Commissioner, Organization for Security and Cooperation in Europe. Among the several expressions of concern and condemnation, one positive evaluation in early September 2008 gained an extensive coverage in Italian media.

> The evaluation by the European Commission, with its complete appreciation of the measures adopted by the Italian government towards the nomad camps does not need commenting on: it is clear and explicit. However, what is still missing is a public apology by all those Italians, who as part of the opposition both inside and outside Parliament, did not hesitate to throw mud on Italy in order to contest the Government action.
>
> (Alfredo Mantovano, press statement, 4 September 2008)

The above is the Undersecretary of State for the Home Affairs' commentary on the statement of the European Commissioner Jacques Barrot asking for apologies from all those who had found the politics and attitude of the Italian government towards the Roma and Sinti racist and discriminatory.

But what exactly did Commissioner Jacques Barrot say? According to Mantovano, Barrot expressed a 'total appreciation of the measures adopted by the Italian government towards the nomad camps'. In reality the positive evaluation was far more limited and hesitant. Barrot (Jacques Barrot, press statement, 4 September 2008) writes: 'This report [referring to a Ministry of the Interior's report sent on 1 August 2008] indicates that neither the decrees, nor the guidelines, or the methods of carrying out the actions, authorize the collection of data on the ethnic origin and religion of the people in the census' and that 'according to the report', the actions by the Italian government 'are compatible with communitarian law'. However, the form used in Naples for the collection of data included the ethnicity

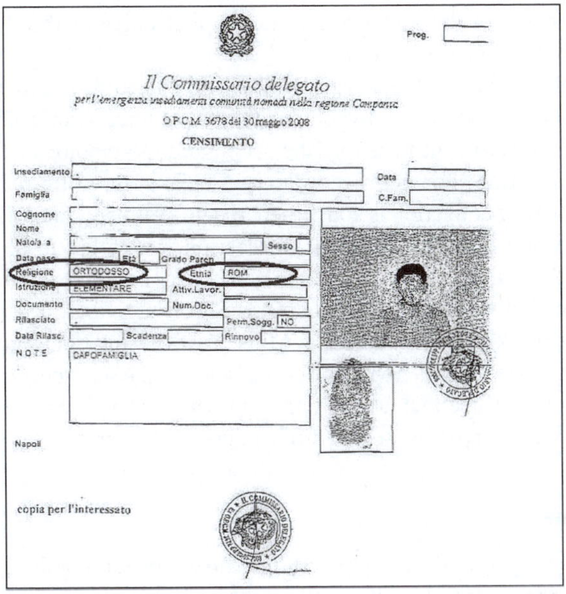
Prog.
Il Commissario delegato
per l'emergenza insediamenti comunità nomadi nella regione Campania
OPCM 3678 del 30 maggio 2008
CENSIMENTO
Insediamento
Data
Famiglia
C.Fam.
Cognome
Nome
Nato/a a
Sesso
Data nasc.
Età
Grado Paren.
Religione ORTODOSSO
Etnia ROM
Istruzione ELEMENTARE
Attiv.Lavor.
Documento
Num.Doc.
Rilasciato
Perm.Sogg. NO
Data Rilasc.
Scadenza
Rinnovo
NOTE CAPOFAMIGLIA
Napoli
copia per l'interessato

Figure 11.3 Form for the collection of personal data and fingerprints (Naples, 2008).

and religion of the person taking part in the census, as well as the biometric data (see Figure 11.3).

Therefore Barrot's press statement only refers to the issue of the collection of personal data, which Maroni and his undersecretary euphemistically call 'census' (Roberto Maroni, press statement, June 2008); furthermore in the brief statement, the commissioner repeats (four times) that the evaluation is based on what the government has affirmed in its report sent on 1 August 2008. Unfortunately, the report has not been made public and cannot be found on either the Ministry of the Interior's website, or on European Commission's. Given this, it would be useful to recapitulate on the chronology of the events in search of some hints.

As mentioned earlier, the collection of biometric data and the screening of nomad camps started in June 2008, a few days after the appointment of the three Special Commissioners. On 23 July, well into the 'census', the government issued a circular containing the guidelines for its implementation. In an attempt to dispel the doubts regarding the discriminatory nature of the initiative, this document emphasized the 'humanitarian' nature of the census, specifying that: 'First and foremost, they are measures aimed to put an end to the current situation of degradation and to promote legally acceptable living conditions for the communities in question' (Ministero degli Interni 2008: 1).

However, in the following paragraph, the government reiterates what until a few days earlier had appeared to everyone as the unequivocal main aim of the measures: 'This is *also* to safeguard public security and the same people living in such settlements, recently targeted by episodes of intolerance and xenophobia which took place in the territories of the capital cities of the three regions in question' (ibid., emphasis added).[15]

Specifically regarding the census, in the guidelines it is clarified that this 'has to be considered instrumental to achieve the social integration [of the Roma], by enabling the Government to define the scope and the typology of the necessary interventions and develop them accordingly'. As far as the criticized fingerprinting and biometric data collection is concerned, the government states that these would be employed only 'in cases where identification, which has to be proved, is not possible with available personal documents and credible circumstances [...] respecting the individual and the conditions of privacy' (ibid.: 2).

Only one week passed before the Minster of the Interior sent the European Commissioner the 'secret' report. Another month passed and, on 5 September 2008, Barrot confirmed that, solely based on what was stated by the government, the 'census' was compatible with European law.

Conclusions

Through an analysis of the main policy initiatives concerning the Roma and Sinti carried out since November 2007, this chapter has not only shown how deeply seated anti-Romani feelings are in contemporary Italy, but more importantly, how these feelings have become an important component of the political battle around the issue of security, in which all main parties engage with the aim of proving their credentials (see Carboni's chapter in this volume).[16]

While the current Italian government cannot be deemed the initiator of such an approach, it has gone a long way in exacerbating anti-Romani feelings for electoral purposes. As some commentators have noted (Colacicchi 2008, Simoni 2008a), anti-Romani racism has changed and has slowly acquired a new dimension with the old stereotypes being skilfully manipulated to become useful political tools.

Prodi's government has certainly contributed to fuelling a weak culture of civil rights by not taking sufficient distance from the wave of hysteria towards Roma, and Romanian Roma in particular, which has risen in recent years.[17]

The analysis of the enforcement of the first decree from November 2007 has shown how formally ethnic-blind legislation can be applied selectively and with discretion. Moreover, it has also revealed the need to focus not only on the direct effects of policy measures – in this case the number of expulsions – but also on its indirect (but not unwanted) consequences, which, I would argue, represent *de facto* examples of the institutionalization of anti-Romani racism.

Finally, examining decree No. 122/2008 and the following implementation orders which detail the tasks and guidelines for the Special Commissioners, while the positive impact of international lobbying is clear having it forced the government to tone down the exasperated tones of the election campaign through some formal alterations *en route* to its policy (i.e. the guidelines issued on 23 July 2008), the impact they have on the ground remains unclear.[18] In this regard, it is important to point out that by the time the guidelines were issued, the government had already achieved its primary goal of showing Italian voters that the 'zero tolerance' approach was not a mere electoral promise.[17]

Notes

1 I wish to thank Kristin Sian Jenkins for her assistance in the preparation of the final manuscript and the Oxford Department for International Development for a research support grant.

2 Gentilini's speech is available online at www.osservazione.org

3 This statement is available online at www.oggitreviso.it/node/9563 and published by *Oggi Treviso* (October 2008).

4 On May 2008, following an alleged kidnapping attempt of a newborn baby by an underage Roma girl in Naples, local residents reacted by setting fire to several Roma encampments. The Neapolitan branch of the Democratic Party, instead of condemning the indiscriminate violence against the Roma, put up posters all over the neighborhood which, stated: 'No more Roma camps in Ponticelli!'. For a detailed analysis of the event see COSPE 2008; Saudino 2008.

5 Data on the numbers of Roma and Sinti living in Italy are based on estimates produced over time by academics, activists and local administrators. They have an indicative value and are subject to significant alterations, often in relation to the political value that they can have in any given political situation, see Brunello 1996; Piasere 2005.

6 Department for Equal Opportunities, Rome. Interview carried out on 13 December 2007.

7 Statement by René van der Linen, president of the Assembly of the Council of Europe, 7 November 2007. Online. Available online at http://assembly.coe.int/ASP/ NewsManager/EMB_NewsManagerView.asp?ID=3325.

8 Article 77 of the Italian Constitution establishes that in case of necessity and urgency, 'the government may issue provisional measures with the force of law [...]'. However, the Constitution also states that 'legal decrees lose effect at the date of issue if they are not confirmed within sixty days of their publication'.

9 Interview carried out in Rome in December 2007.

10 Please see the official website of Rome City Council at www.comune.roma.it Accessed on 20 November 2007.

11 In the text the term 'nomads' is used as a synonym for the Roma and Sinti and the 'nomad camps' are designated as places specifically suited for them (for a critique of Italian housing policy for Roma and Sinti see Piasere 1991, 2005, Brunello 1996, Sigona 2005).

12 It is worth noticing that not all the components of the former centre-left coalition shared the 'securitarian' approach to the Roma. On the contrary, in the current government this approach is endorsed by all its member parties.

13 One may wonder why one of the aims of the measures is to restore only *minimal* social and health services given that most residents of the authorized areas are Italian and/or EU-citizens.

14 For a critical review of the legislation see Simoni 2008b.

15 It is worth mentioning the use of *also* to introduce what, until the day before, was the main aim of the government.

16 The exclusion of Rifondazione Comunista from the current Parliamentary Assembly has made combating discrimination and advocacy for minority and migrants' rights more difficult as the two main parties in the Parliament – the PDL and the PD – are both after the same electorate and have shown no intention to leave aside the security discourse, which proved very effective in the last electoral round.

17 For a discussion of data on criminality in Italy see Ministero degli Interni 2007.

18 Another example of the degree of institutional antiziganism and xenophobia which pervades current Italy is decree No. 11 issued on 23 February 2009 to crack down on sexual violence and illegal immigration. Once again, the 'necessity and urgency' required for issuing a decree rather than being based on hard data – Berlusconi himself admitted that the number of sexual assaults fell last year and data also show these crimes are mainly committed by Italian citizens against family members (Ministero

degli Interni 2007) – is legitimized instead on the *vox populi* or public hysteria. However, there is more in this episode which, I would argue, reveals the spread of institutional racism and antiziganism in Italy. On 17 February, just three days after the incident in Rome which triggered the government to issue decree No. 11/2009, the police, showing remarkable efficiency, arrested and imprisoned two Romanian Roma. On 12 March 2009, the results of the DNA tests on the two alleged perpetuators revealed that they were not responsible for the assault. However, and this is another alarming aspect of this story, the Italian investigators rather than admitting the mistake, are still keeping the two Roma in jail on the pretext of a range of minor offences. This could be explained as a form of retaliation against one of the two Romanians who has accused the Italian police officers and their Romanian colleagues of having forced him to confess; an accusation that the police *obviously* deny.

References

Arrigoni, P. and Vitale, T. (2008) 'Quale legalità? Rom e gagi a confronto', *Aggiornamenti Sociali*, 3: 183–94.

Belpietro, M. (2007) 'Veltroni leader del paese dei furbi', *Panorama*, 15 November.

Brunello, P. (1996) (ed.) *L'urbanistica del Disprezzo*, Rome: Manifestolibri.

CERD (1999) *Concluding Observations of the Committee on the Elimination of Racial Discrimination: Italy*. 07/04/99 (CERD/C/304/Add.68), Geneva: United Nations.

Colacicchi, P. (2008) 'Ethnic profiling and discrimination against Roma in Italy: New developments in a deep-rooted tradition', *Roma Rights*, 2: 35–44. Online. Available: www.errc.org/db/03/B8/m000003B8.pdf.

Colombo, D. (2007) 'Sicurezza, Veltroni impone il decreto', *Il Sole 24 ore*, 1 November.

Di Caro, P. (2007) 'Fini: impossibile integrarsi con chi ruba', *Corriere della Sera*, 4 November.

Dinmore, G. (2007) 'Romanian influx a shock, says Prodi', *Financial Times*, 7 November. Online. Available: www.ft.com/cms/s/0/4b963c18-8cd7-11dc-aa10-0000779fd2ac.html ?nclick_check=1.

COSPE (2008) *Incident Report – Violent Attacks Against Roma in the Ponticelli district of Naples (Italy)*, Brussels: European Union Fundamental Rights Agency

ECRI (2002) *2nd Report on Italy adopted on the 22 June 2001*, Strasbourg: ECRI.

ECRI (2006) *3rd Report on Italy adopted on the 16 December 2005*, Strasbourg: ECRI.

ERRC (2000) *Campland: Racial segregation of Roma in Italy,* Budapest: ERRC.

Fazzo, L. (2005) 'Castelli: giudici lontani dal popolo', *La Repubblica*, 9 February.

Foucault, M. (1980) *Power/Knowledge*, Brighton: Harvester.

Garavaglia, M. (2007) 'Sveglia Padania, tocca a noi', *La Padania*, 4 November.

Hooper, J. (2007) 'Italian right calls for repatriation of Roma', *The Guardian*, 5 November 2008, Online. Available: www.guardian.co.uk/world/2007/nov/05/italy.international.

ISPO (2008) 'Italiani, rom e sinti a confronto. Una ricerca quali-quantitativa'. Paper presented at the *European Conference on the Roma population,* Rome, 22–23 January (organized by the Italian Ministry of the Interior).

Mai, N. (2009) 'The politicisation of migrant minors: Italo-Romanian geopolitics and EU integration', unpublished article (submitted to the journal *AREA*)

Maroni, R. (2008) *Camera dei Deputati. Svolgimento di interrogazioni a risposta immediata*, 2 July 2008. Online. Available: www.interno.it/mininterno/export/sites/default/it/ sezioni/sala_stampa/interview/Interventi/2100_500_ministro/0997x2008_07_02_ question_time.html.

Ministero degli Interni (2007) *Rapporto sulla criminalità in Italia. Analisi, prevenzione, contrasto*, Rome. Online. Available: www.interno.it/mininterno/export/sites/default/it/ sezioni/sala_stampa/notizie/sicurezza/0993_20_06_2007_Rapporto_Sicurezza_2006. html.

—— (2008) *Linee guida per l'attuazione delle ordinanze del presidente del Consiglio dei Ministri del 30 maggio 2008*, Rome. Online. Available: www.interno.it/mininterno/ export/sites/default/it/assets/files/15/0095_censimento_campi_nomadi_le_linee_ guida.pdf.

Monasta, L. (2008) *I pregiudizi contro gli zingari spiegati al mio cane*, Pisa: BFS.

Piasere, L. (1991) *Popoli delle Discariche. Saggi di antropologia zingara*, Rome: CISU

—— (1999) *Un mondo di mondi. Antropologia delle culture rom*, Naples: l'Ancora.

—— (2004) *I rom d'Europa. Una storia moderna*. Rome: Laterza.

—— (2005) 'Qu'est-ce qu'un campo nomadi?', conference paper: *Les Tsiganes en Europe: questions sur la représentation et action politque*, the British Academy/CNRS, Paris, 24–25 October.

Preziosi, D. (2007) 'Ferrero il mediatore ricuce, si correge la linea Veltroni', *Il Manifesto*, 6 November.

Rosso, U. (2007) 'La gente è stanca dei rom, parola di comunista', *La Repubblica*, 5 November.

Saudino, F. (2008) *Ordinarie emergenze partenopee*, OsservAzione. Online. Available: www.osservazione.org/saudino_napoli.htm.

Scalia, M. (2006) *Le comunità sprovviste di territorio, i Rom, i Sinti e i Caminanti in Italia*. Rome: Dipartimento delle Libertà Civili e l'Immigrazione del Ministero degli Interni.

Sigona, N. (2005) 'Locating the "Gypsy" problem', *Journal of Ethnic and Migration Studies*, 31(4): 741–56.

—— (2006) (ed.) *Political participation and media representation of Roma and Sinti in Italy*. Report commissioned by OSCE/ODIHR, Warsaw: OSCE. Online. Available: www.osservazione.org/documenti/osce_italy.pdf.

—— and Monasta, L. (2006) *Cittadinanze Imperfette. Rapporto sulla discriminazione razziale di rom e sinti in Italia*. Caserta: Spartaco.

—— (2008) 'Sono il nemico pubblico n.1?', *Reset*, 107: 87–88

Simoni, A. (2005) *Stato di diritto e identità rom*. Turin: L'Harmattan Italia.

—— (2008a) 'Sicurezza, legalità e lo spettro degli "zingari"', *Reset*, 107, 84–6.

—— (2008b) 'I decreti "emergenza nomadi": il nuovo volto di un vecchio problema', *Diritto, Immigrazione e Cittadinanza*, 10(3–4): 44–56.

Terracina, C. (2007) 'Il decreto non basta, via anche i senza-lavoro', *Il Messagero*, 4 November.

Todesco, D. (2004) *Le maschere dei pregiudizi. L'innocenza perduta dei pregiudizi positivi, una categoria esemplare: gli zingari* [*Quaderni di Servizio Migranti*], No. 47.

Tosi Cambini, S. (2008) *La zingara rapitrice. Racconti, denunce, sentenze (1986–2007)*, Rome: CISU.

12 The Catholic Church, universal truth and the debate on national identity and immigration

A new model of 'selective solidarity'

Eva Garau

Summary

This chapter analyzes the role of the Catholic Church in the debate on immigration and Italian national identity. While remaining the most authoritative voice raised against the often racist policies put forward by right-wing parties to deal with the phenomenon, since 2000 the Church has moved towards a new position on immigration, mostly unknown to the public and often neglected by the media. This chapter will try to show how this debate has been exploited by the Catholic hierarchy, to remark on the Church's need for a stronger feeling of national belonging strictly linked with Italy's 'Catholic origins' as well as to reassert the superiority of Christian values vis-à-vis alternative ideas of the 'good life' and a much-feared growing relativism. It will argue that the Church is putting forward an original model of identity and citizenship based on a 'selective solidarity', while seeming to aspire to the construction of a quasi-theocratic state where the concepts of religious and national belonging coincide.

Introduction

Since the late 1980s, religion has returned to centre stage in the debate on democracy, political participation and the construction of identity: scholars have started analyzing its role from different perspectives and within the framework of several disciplines, ranging from religious and cultural studies to international relations, from social and welfare studies to trans-national migration studies. Religion has emerged as an important factor in explaining not only the nature of conflict in contemporary societies but also the construction of national, multiple and collective identities, the behaviour of political parties and social movements, the process of inclusion and exclusion, and attitudes towards European citizenship.

This chapter aims to consider the case of the Italian Catholic Church and more precisely its role in the debate on immigration and Italian national identity. I will try to show how this debate has been exploited by the Church to remark on the need for a stronger feeling of national belonging strictly linked with Italy's 'Catholic origins' as well as to reassert the superiority of Christian values vis-à-vis alternative ideas of the 'good life' and a much-feared growing relativism.

It will argue that the Church is putting forward an original model of identity and citizenship based on a 'selective solidarity', while seeming to aspire to the construction of a quasi-theocratic state where the concepts of religious and national belonging coincide.

Despite the fact that the Church's main interest is not the arrival of foreigners with different cultures and religions, its contribution to the debate on immigration is of central importance. In filling the gaps left in the public sphere by the lack of participation by Italian intellectuals and by the still-confused position of the political class, the Church emerged as a leading voice in the public discussion on the theme, as can be proved by the analysis of its interventions – particularly during the autumn of 2000, year of the Jubilee, and summer of 2002, which preceded the anniversary of the 9/11 terroristic attacks. While remaining the most authoritative voice raised against the often racist policies put forward by right-wing parties to deal with phenomenon, since 2000 the Church has moved towards a new position on immigration, mostly unknown to the public and often neglected by the media.

This chapter will give account of this dramatic shift in the Church's approach to the issue through a comparative analysis of two documents published in 2000: the (then Cardinal) Joseph Ratzinger's (since 2003 Pope Benedict XVI) *Dominus Jesus* and the pastoral note 'Le città di San Petronio nel terzo millennio' written by Cardinal Giacomo Biffi, archbishop of Bologna. Both documents are particularly relevant in light of the heated debates which followed their publication.

Religion in post-modern societies

The revival of interest on the part of scholars in the dilemmas revolving around morality and beliefs was triggered, in the late 1980s, by a general acknowledgment of the historical role religion has played in the emergence and differentiation of modern nation states and their capacity for citizenship, representation and political participation. The academic debate on the issue focuses on the process through which traditional religions have redefined themselves in the post-modern era, shaping a new (political) message to maintain, increase or regain support, and the extent of their influence on local, national and supra-national politics. The central question of these studies – 'how does religion react to modernity?' (Seidler 1986) – implies a broader investigation on themes related to group identity (Leege and Kellsted 1993) and to religion as an interest group (Wilcox *et al.* 1993, Warner, 2000) capable of mobilizing people at a local level (Greenberg, 2000) and of enabling citizens to sustain multiple identities (Voye 1999).

These recent investigations revolve around a fundamental issue: 'Are there distinctive contributions that religion can make to political discourse?' and 'Are there special reasons for limiting religion's role in political discourse?' (Segers and Jelen 1998: 8). As Warner argues by quoting Antonio Gramsci, religion, similar to other ideologies, 'provides an interpretative map of the world, a system for evaluating the justice and distributive schemes as well as ethical and behavioural codes to follow' (Warner 2000: 17).

To understand better the power of the Church in national and international politics, researchers have started applying theories used to analyze group identity and interest groups to religious organizations. According to them, group consciousness requires an awareness of membership and psychological attachment to the group (Tajfel 1981, Conover 1986). Moreover, group identification is characterized by three different factors: power discontent, system blaming and orientation toward collective action (Wilcox *et al.* 1993: 72, Miller *et al.* 1980, Gurin 1985, Klein 1984, Cook 1989). The study of 'polarized group affect', the affinity towards members of one's own group and hostility towards members of different groups, shows how both attitudes determine a more active political participation on the part of members (Wilcox *et al.* 1993: 72). As a result, competition between religions has a positive effect on participation and, conversely, religious monopolies inhibit personal religiosity (Jelen and Wilcox 2002). This is why Catholics in Protestant countries exhibit higher levels of religious observance than where they are the majority. Applying this interpretative model would also imply an acknowledgment of the deeper internal cohesion and orthodoxy of minority religions – such as Islam – in Italy. This logic acquires particular relevance in light of social psychologist Serge Moscovici's studies on minority influence, according to which minorities can create a social conflict such that the majority will be forced to move towards a compromise in order to release the tension. In this sense, minority groups can modify the mainstream trends and beliefs in society as long as they follow a set of fixed rules, such as consistency and cohesion, to name few (Moscovici 1976).

After World War II, the Catholic Church, forced to give up temporal powers and having lost its control on political affairs, reshaped its own role within national boundaries and in international affairs, while gaining more freedom to assert its views on controversial issues and ethical problems (Vallier 1971: 18). Through this process, it managed to reinforce its power rather than surrender to its evident decline, while gaining increasingly stronger support from citizens whose trust in the institutions was being weakened by religion itself (Putnam 1993, La Porta *et al.* 1997: 333–338).

Scholars such as Voye (1999), Warner (2000), Cochran (1981), and Segers and Jelen (1998) agree on the interpretation of religions and particularly Catholicism as new experts in practical ethical issues, which allows them to have a great impact on decision making, especially vis-à-vis unequipped political actors and governments. With the shift from a codified and institutionalized public morality to a more individualistic attitude according to which choice is relegated to the private sphere, Catholicism presented itself as a 'neutral consultant' in the field of ethics in post-modern societies. Following this process, representatives of the Church in Europe became opinion-makers and points of reference for states unable to make decisions on controversial matters (Warner 2000, Vallier 1971, Segers and Jelen 1998). To achieve this new status the Church had to change substantially: it presented itself as de-dogmatized and more careful about the language it employed to put forward solutions to controversial questions, as for instance referring more often to human rights rather than to the 'laws of God'

(Warner 2000: 278). As a result, contemporary societies have to deal with the paradox of Catholic representatives acting as influential members of consultative committees on ethical dilemmas which are supposed to offer disinterested and neutral opinions on questions of central importance for the Church. The presence of Catholic representatives in the round table set by the Italian government to open dialogue with Muslim communities represents a clear example of the new position occupied by religion in the public sphere. Warner insists on the impossibility of the Church to play such a role, since it implies distancing itself from its own set of values and its particular idea of the world (ibid.).

The description of religious groups as new neutral experts on ethical matters, capable of influencing the political debate and the state's decision making on 'ethical issues', applies perfectly to the Italian Catholic Church.[1] The Christian Democrats have always been a key factor in explaining the Church's influence within the political sphere well beyond the 1992 scandal of Clean Hands. If, until then, the Church had always been represented in Parliament,[2] the so-called 'Catholic question' has far from died out with the DC, as Bernini explains in her contribution to this volume. One of the many proofs of both this close relationship and the new role of the Church as the state's neutral consultant on ethical issues is the so-called *vademecum* written by Ratzinger in 2003 to give Italian MPs instructions on which laws and measures discussed by Parliament are ethical and which ones are not (Provenza 2003). Policies linked to subjects such as divorce, abortion, artificial insemination, research on stem cells and euthanasia have always been considered ethical questions and therefore, despite having a clear position on them, the Church has offered its views to the state as a neutral expert; more recently immigration has also been constructed as an ethical issue.

The principle of truth and the Church's 'rational' approach to 'the other'

The Church's involvement in the debate on immigration does not seem to coincide with growing political awareness of the phenomenon, which began in the early 1990s, following the fall of the Berlin Wall and the war in former Yugoslavia. Until recently the Church spoke on matters related to the foreign presence within the country from a sociological perspective derived from the doctrine according to which immigrants have to be considered as brothers to be welcomed and supported in name of an unconditional love and Christian charity. This official position of the hierarchy towards those traditionally defined by it as *gli ultimi* changed dramatically at the turn of this century. The Church started engaging in the debate on specific laws and measures to the extent that it became one of the strongest voices in the public discussion on the theme. The two documents mentioned earlier, Ratzinger's *Dominus Jesus* and Biffi's pastoral note, represent a clear turn in the Church's attitude towards immigration, from a general good-will based on the traditional Christian charity towards a much more political and utilitarian attitude, which I will refer to as a 'rational selection' (versus a 'natural selection').[3]

The incipit of the *Dominus Jesus*, extracted from Mark's Gospel (16: 15–6), opens with a reminder of the Church's universal mission of bringing the Gospel to every single human being in the world and of differentiating between 'who will believe and will be saved and who will not believe and will be condemned'. This pure doctrinal statement acquires in the following paragraph a political meaning, in an attempt to establish which attitude the Church should have towards those who do not believe. The Church, Ratzinger writes, looks with sincere respect at those 'ways of behaving and living', that, however different from the Church's, reflect a ray of that truth which enlighten all men (Ratzinger 2000a: 1). In less than a page, Razinger establishes a double premise, defining other religions firstly as arbitrary choices among different lifestyles, and secondly as a sort of partial derivation from a superior truth – a ray descending from the only origin – and later on simply as 'contemporary cultural demands' (ibid.). According to him, the most appropriate means to deal with these ways of life is dialogue, considered as the only possibility of communication in a world threatened by relativistic theories, aimed at 'justifying religious pluralism not only *de facto* but also *de iure*' (ibid.: 2). To correct this growing relativism according to which no revelation can be the only one, 'it is necessary to reassert the definitive and complete character of the Catholic universal revelation' (ibid.). Here the Cardinal introduces for the first time that concept of rationality destined to be so controversial in his Regensburg lecture 'Faith, Reason and the University – Memories and Reflection'.[4] Indeed, he goes so far as to say that Catholicism allows people to penetrate the truth through the use of 'coherent intelligence', whereas other religions consist of a mixture of experience and common sense on which men's wisdom is based (ibid.: 7). As a result, 'it is not possible to neglect the fact that their faith comes from different mistakes, when not from superstition' (ibid: 8). In this respect, the dialogue can be seen as an attempt to bring salvation to those who are excluded from it. The dialogue has to be based on an equal dignity of the different interlocutors, even though this equality refers to individuals, the subjects who carry the beliefs and not to the specific contents of those beliefs. The document specifies that only after a sincere conversion, which represents a necessary and sufficient condition, only then 'You are not foreigners nor guests, but rather co-citizens of the saints and relatives of God' (ibid.: 8–9)

The choice of terms such as 'foreigner' as opposite to 'citizen' is not a random one. It expresses a precise political concern on the part of the Church, rather than simply the need for a doctrinal specification. Moreover, an analysis of the interventions on the issue by the Church's representatives shows that they often seem to identify belonging to a different religion with a state of immigration, thus using the two terms as interchangeable. In this way, they mix the concepts of national identity and religion and assume, for instance, that all Muslims are foreigners.

Ratzinger argues that as long as relativism will be seen as a 'philosophy of humanity' capable of guaranteeing tolerance and democracy to our societies, it will have as its first result that of 'marginalising even more those who insist in defending Christian identity and its mission to spread the universal truth'

(Ratzinger 2000b: 2).This statement represents a fundamental first step in the strategy developed by the Church to reassert its own role in the country: a strategy based on the presumption that the Catholic Church has today become a victim, a minority without freedom of expression and therefore has to be protected and supported by the state which is today promoting a false model of tolerance.

Moreover, Ratzinger claims Catholic paternity over the idea of 'tolerance as an expression of freedom of conscience' (ibid.). According to him, this principle of respect for freedom has been manipulated into including the contents of what is tolerated, assuming that different religions and views of the world have equal dignity and therefore neglecting the existence of a universal and objective truth. In this respect, 'tolerance means a renunciation to truth, which is indeed today perceived as a secondary and irrelevant issue'. As a consequence, the Cardinal glosses, faith and superstition, experience and illusion cannot be differentiated from the truth (ibid.). Without a search for truth, the recognition of other religions itself becomes contradictory, as there is no clear criterion of discernment between what is positive and what is negative or resulting from a superstition, as opposed to a religion (ibid.). One might question how such a criterion could be formulated, since it seems clear that a hypothetical one suggested by the Church would be certainly based on a particular idea of the truth and therefore probably unacceptable and arbitrary for those who do not share the same faith. Here, Ratzinger does not engage openly with a definition which is already implicit in the document and seemingly based on rationality.

Selective solidarity: the Church's utilitarian criterion to interpret immigration

The *Dominus Jesus* can be considered as a general theological speculation, addressing the whole Catholic community but referring to non-Catholics in explaining the Church's attitude towards the other religions and is written in a formal technical language which leaves its polemical and practical implications at an implicit level. On the contrary, Cardinal Biffi's pastoral note, written a week after Ratzinger's document, begins by addressing a limited audience (the people of Bologna and more precisely 'the believers') and a precise issue (the roots of these citizens' Christian identity) and its polemical intent becomes quite clear from the beginning.

The document opens with a call to the people of Bologna for a stronger awareness of the privilege of belonging to this great city and the pride this belonging requires. Despite this glorious past and world fame, Biffi proceeds to reflect on the 'undeniable drop of tension' intended as spiritual and ethical relaxation, occurring not only in Bologna but in the rest of the world as well (Biffi 2000: 20). The city, he states, seems to have lost its traditional attachment to those ancient values on which its civilization was built, an issue which leads to the need for identifying what he calls 'the difficult challenges of our time' (ibid.: 21). To these challenges, Biffi states, the city should react not with panic or alarm, but rather ask itself how to preserve its own identity. 'The challenges which already dominate us are mainly two: the growing flow of people coming to us from countries which are far and different from us and the spreading of a non-Christian culture among Christian populations' (ibid.).

This last statement opens the way to a section of the pastoral note entitled *The issue of immigration*. In the first paragraph (*A surprise*) Biffi states that first it is necessary to acknowledge that the massive arrival of immigrants to the country has been a surprise for 'all of us', where 'us' means both the Church and the state. According to him, the latter seems still unable to deal with the situation rationally; nonetheless the Church too has been caught unprepared and despite its efforts to alleviate the discomfort of the newly arrived, it has proved incapable of developing a shared and less abstract position on the matter. Nevertheless, the Cardinal argues that solving social issues such as that of immigration is not a duty of the Catholic Church. Charging the Church with such a responsibility and expecting it to confront these 'problems' would be a sign of an intolerable 'integralism', since its mission rather consists in spreading the Gospel and Christian love. From Biffi's perspective, this evangelical mission has to be universal and therefore 'it cannot tolerate any deliberate exclusion of addresses'. Catholics are called to answer this 'undeclinable responsibility' which they have towards all the newly arrived ('Muslim included'), a responsibility alleviated by the awareness of possessing a truth which is 'absolutely not comparable with the (even though valuable) faint ideas offered by other religions and particularly Islam'. Moreover, Biffi remarks on the duty already discussed in the *Dominus Jesus*, of 'helping them [the immigrants] to reach the knowledge of the truth according to their concrete means' (ibid.: 23).

Having established these general premises based on Christian values and duties and an explicit call for a differentiation in the state's and the Church's respective responsibility in relation to immigration, in the section entitled *A realistic approach,* Biffi begins to tackle the issue at a more practical level. This paragraph opens with the claim that in dealing with the diverse scenarios of immigration, Christian communities cannot avoid to 'consider and judge differently the diverse individuals and groups in order to realistically react towards them in the most appropriate way' (ibid.). The Cardinal engages in an analysis of the different cases, starting with 'Catholic immigrants': they – regardless of the language they speak and the colour of their skin – have to be treated in a way that makes them feel that 'within the Church nobody is foreigner'(ibid.).

The Cardinal goes as far as to set out a sort of regulatory plan on practical issues in order to clear the way from possible misunderstandings and avoid contradictory responses on the part of the Church. In particular, as he clarifies, the attitude towards non-Christians, who have to be 'loved and supported in their needs as much as possible', has to follow what was established by the guidelines published by the Italian Episcopal Conference in 1993, which is that to avoid a dangerous confusion, they cannot be granted churches, or indeed places used for activities linked with the Catholic cult (Biffi 2000: 42, Nota CEI 'Ero foresterio e mi avete visitato' 1993).

The following section of the pastoral note, entitled *General remark*, addresses 'the desirable behaviour of the state' and of its representatives towards immigration. It contains the most direct statement on what the Cardinal sees as the most adequate means to deal with the issue, which later became the cause of a heated debate. 'The criteria to allow immigrants in the country cannot be merely determined by the economy or welfare [...] It is necessary to become concerned about preserving the identity of the nation, since Italy is not a deserted land with no history and living traditions, clear cultural and spiritual features, to be populated indiscriminately as if it did not have a patrimony of civilization which needs to be saved' (Biffi 2000: 23–24). According to Biffi, in order to build a peaceful coexistence, if not an even more desirable integration, the state cannot consider immigrants without realizing that, at the starting point of the process of integration, they are not equal (ibid.).

Paragraph 44 can be seen as the most controversial in the whole document. Here the Church's representative embarks on the analysis of the case of Muslim immigrants, arguing that: 'the case of Muslims has to be dealt with using a particular attention. They have a different diet, a different non-working day, a way of conceiving the role of women very distant from ours. But above all, they have a strictly integralist view of public life so that the perfect identification of religion and politics is part of their faith, even though they wait until they prevail before imposing it' (ibid.).[5]

Before bringing the focus back to the city of Bologna, Biffi concludes this more polemical part of the document with a short section concerning Catholicism as the historical national religion, to remind his addressees that, even though Catholicism is no longer the official state religion, it is nevertheless the traditional religion of the Italian nation as well as the source of its identity and the premise to all its past greatness. Therefore, according to him, it is 'absolutely inadequate' to compare it to other religions or cultural views. Moreover, he argues that a democracy that grants minorities a freedom of expression which damages the majority or does not imply respect for what today represents the foundation of Italian society, is a very peculiar democracy. He goes further in mentioning as an example of 'substantial intolerance' the case of those Italian schools where the crucifixes have been removed following the request of students and families who have faiths different from the Catholic one (ibid.: 24–25).[6]

This central part of the pastoral note, a sort of separate document in the document, ends precisely with the above definition of the intolerance of our democracies. Biffi specifies that not everything linked with modernity has to be considered as evil: in his view it is just necessary to distinguish between 'what can be accepted and what must not'. The criterion for this distinction should never be political as politics aims to find a compromise and stipulate agreements, but should rather answer 'a call for faithfulness to an immutable truth based on our identity as believers' (ibid.: 25–26).

Biffi's main point becomes clear when he states that Italian contemporary society seems to be led by mere 'opinions', often antagonistic to a Catholic view of the good life, which prove aggressive towards the country's own traditions and history since they look at Catholicism with hatred. According to him, the outcome of such a trend in the relatively short term will be that 'Europe is either to go back to Christianity or it will become Muslim': no matter what direction it is going to take, the 'culture of nothing' has no chance to prevail. Indeed, 'this culture indifferent to values will not resist the ideological assault of Islam': the latter can only be defeated by a return to the origins and therefore necessarily to traditional Christian foundations (ibid.: 27). Despite the general rhetoric of disengagement used by the Catholic hierarchy to remark upon the need to distinguish between the role of the state and that of the Church in dealing with immigration, Biffi does put forward practical solutions that the Italian state should enforce to deal with this phenomenon, as indeed the idea that the state should give preference to Catholic immigrants, who are easier to assimilate.

Conclusion

Although written in different styles and aiming to achieve different objectives, the core of ideas expressed in the *Dominus Jesus* and Biffi's pastoral note overlap and often coincide. Both documents consider different religions as ways of life resulting from empirical experience and erroneous thoughts whereas Catholicism is seen as the only religion capable of reaching the truth through a rational process, using intelligence rather than superstition or common sense. Regarding the criteria the two authors consider adequate to judge other beliefs, Ratzinger advocates that only the principle of truth – rationality – represents a means to defeat contemporary relativism, while Biffi, even though agreeing on the principle of truth, focuses more on a practical, utilitarian criterion to regulate the relations with people who have different ideas of the good life: the common characteristic which can promote and facilitate integration on the part of immigrants and the prerequisite to welcome them can only be Catholicism. The choice of Catholicism as the only solution to matters related to immigration is based on a common syllogism which both Ratzinger and Biffi construct, which starts from the non-demonstrable and non-self-evident premise that 'every man provided with logic and rationality sees the truth and therefore is Catholic' and ends with the seemingly logical conclusion that 'every Italian is Catholic'. The battle carried on by the Church becomes then a common battle which has to be supported by the whole nation, since, according to the Cardinals, it is not only the Church but Italian identity as well which is threatened. Moreover, they agree on the fact that the Church has the right to accomplish its mission through proselytising: only after a sincere conversion it is possible to become a member of the Church and – this is a recurrent message in the Cardinals' documents – 'within the Church nobody is foreigner'. Recognising the superiority of Catholicism and becoming part of the Church seems to be the only way immigrants can shift from being others, foreigners, to becoming citizens, part of the Catholic family. The concept of the Catholic family interestingly enough seems to coincide with that of the nation since not being a foreigner and therefore Italian coincides with being Catholic, following a transitive property of the above-mentioned syllogism which 'proves' that every Italian is Catholic and is aimed at granting Italian citizenship to every Catholic.

Both Ratzinger and Biffi argue that the only duty of the Church is evangelism: this process of enlightenment, the Catholic representatives claim, is made today particularly difficult, if not impossible, by the false tolerance typical of our societies. The idea that different interpretations of the good life can be attributed equal dignity results in an aggressive attitude on the part of non-Catholic individuals and groups towards a Church which becomes a victim and the only subject to whom the right of freedom of speech is denied or whose freedom of expression is seen as integralist and intolerant. Having redefined itself against the other, the Muslim threat, and defined its role as a victim, the Church appropriates the strategy typical of traditional minorities, which consists of a dual demand to the state for a positive freedom (being given more space in the public sphere) and a negative one (denying other groups the same right). According to the classical literature on identity and otherness, minorities claim for protection on the part of a state in name of the past discrimination. The Church, in a diametrically opposite way, carries on these requests in name of its glorious role in the past of the country. At a time when it seems to be struggling against an openly recognized decline in popularity, Islam is invoked to gain visibility and confirm a privileged role within the country. The constant call on the part of the Church for the defence of what is now a minority is aimed at triggering a strong response on the part of the public opinion, following the mechanism described above according to which attachment to the group is directly proportional to the perceived threat as well as to the struggle to (re)gain visibility.

Despite its remarking on the need to distinguish between the responsibilities of the state and its own, the Church presents itself as a 'neutral consultant' on the 'ethical issue' of immigration, capable of putting forward practical solutions to deal with the situation and often proving very influential in the state's decision making in this field. While enabling a rhetoric of disengagement, it seemingly aims to replace the state by granting immigrants citizenship, following a principle of 'selective solidarity' according to which all immigrants have to be loved but only those who are ready to abandon their own identity to embrace Catholicism can become Italian. More than integration, this solution seems to be a call for the need to assimilate different cultures and religions and to reduce them to a state where religion and nationality coincide. Such a system could only work in a theocratic state, where the Church would have the power to allocate rights such as that of citizenship and whose realization probably represents what the Church aspires to in the future. This hypothetical theocratic state, where being Catholic would coincide with being Italian and vice versa, would not be much different from what the Catholic hierarchy defines as the integralist Muslim idea of the identification of religion and state.

Finally, by taking such a position on immigration, the Church builds bridges with political parties such as the Northern League and National Alliance, which for different reasons and with different aims have similar attitudes towards the phenomenon and, to a certain extent, it contributes to legitimize the same stereotypes and prejudices that it publicly claims to fight.

Notes

1 As for the relationship between the Italian state and the Catholic Church, their reciprocal independence has been formalized with the Lateran Pacts signed in 1929 by Cardinal Pietro Gasparri and Benito Mussolini and later included in Article 7 of the Italian Constitution. A long process of consultation between the Italian state and the Vatican for a revision of the Pacts started in 1969, resulting in 1985 in a new 'Concordato', which affirmed the citizens' right to freedom of religion. Moreover, with the 'Protocollo addizionale', Catholicism ceased to be the official state religion (Law 121, 25 March 1985). Discussion of a possible further revision of the Lateran Pacts is still ongoing today and causing tension between the political system and the Conferenza Episcopale Italiana (*Corriere della Sera*, 16 November 2005, *La Repubblica*, 10 March 2008).

2 On the DC as 'a party born from the direct will of religious institutions' see Panebianco (1992: 229).

3 There appears to be a link between the status of the Church's representatives and their position on the issue. The Catholic hierarchy presents a fairly united front, with the only exception of Cardinal Carlo Maria Martini, archbishop of Milan, whereas some opposition from within the Church comes from individual parish priests, who have first-hand contact with immigrants through Catholic associations that work to provide relief to them.

4 The lecture delivered on 12 September 2006 raised heated reactions on the part of Muslim communities around the world. The protests arose from the ambiguity of the following passage: 'Show me just what Muhammad brought that was new and there you will find things only evil and inhuman, such as his command to spread by the sword the faith he preached'. The passage was a quotation from Manuel II Peleologus' 'Dialogue Held with a Certain Persian, the Worthy Mouterizes, in Ankara of Galatia', written in 1391.

5 Biffi shares this interpretation of Muslims as plotters waiting until they are powerful enough to impose their beliefs and turn their religion into the state's law with many representatives of the Northern League. This is the common ground on which they stand united against Islam as, for instance, in the celebrations for the anniversary of the victory of Christianity over Islam in the battle of Poitiers in 732 (Guolo 2004).

6 This is the case of Muslim Italian citizen Adel Smith, who demanded the removal of the crucifix from his children's classroom in a primary school in Ofena. In October 2003 the court of L'Aquila ruled the request had to be accepted. Despite the fact that Smith's case was given international exposure by the media, this was not the first case on which the Supreme Court had deliberated that the crucifix had to be removed from a public space. On 1 March 2000, with deliberation 2925 it closed a controversy that began in 1994 from the refusal on the part of school teacher Marcello Montagnana to vote in a classroom used as a polling station where a crucifix was displayed.

References

Biffi, G. (2000) *Nota Pastorale 'La città di San Petronio nel terzo millennio'*, Bologna: EDB.

CEI (1993) *Nota Pastorale 'Ero forestiero e mi avete ospitato'*.

Cochran, C.E. (1981) 'Introduction', in M.C. Segers, and T.G. Jelen (eds) *A wall of Separation? Debating the Public Role of Religion*, Lanham: Rowman and Littlefield.

Cook, E. (1989) 'Measuring Femminist Consciousness', *Women and Politics*, 9: 71–88.

Greenberg, A. (2000) 'The Church and the Revitalization of Politics and Community', *Political Science Quarterly,* 115 (3) (Autumn): 377–94.

Guolo, R. (2004) 'Chi brandisce la croce', *La Repubblica*, 6 January.

Gurin, P. (1985) 'Women's Geneder Consciousness', *Public Opinion Quarterly*, 49 (2): 143–63.

Jelen, T.G., and Leege, D. (1993) 'Religious Group Identifications: Toward a Cognitive Theory of Religious Mobilization', in D. Leege and L. Kellstedt (eds) *Rediscovering the Impact of Religion on Political Behavior*, Armonk, NY: M.E. Sharpe.

Jelen, T.G., and Wilcox, C. (2002) *Religon and Politics in Comparative Perspective: The One, The Few and The Many*, Cambridge: Cambridge University Press.

Klein, E. (1984) *Gender Politics*, Cambridge: Harvard University Press.

La Porta, R. and Lopez-De-Silanes, F. (1997) 'Trust in Large Organizations', American Economic Review, American Economic Association, 87(2): 333–38.

Leege, D.C. and Kellstedt, L.A. (ed) (1993) *Rediscovering the Religious Factor in American Politics*, New York: M.E. Sharpe.

Miller, A.H., Gurin, P. and Gurin, G. (1980) 'Stratum Identification and Consciousness', *Social Psychology Quarterly*, 43(1): 30–47.

Moscovici, S. (1976) *Social Influence and Social Change*, London: Academic Press.

Panebianco, A. (1992) *Le relazioni internazionali*, Milan: Jaka Book.

Provenza, M., (2003) 'Chiesa, stato e politica: un rapporto complesso', *Ateneonline*. Online. Available HTTP: <http://www.ateneonline-aol.it/030117promAP.html> (accessed 18/06/07)

Putnam, R. (1993) *Making democracy work: Civic traditions in modern Italy*, Princeton: Princeton University Press.

Ratzinger, J. (2000a) *Dominus Jesus*. Online. Available HTTP: <http://www.ildialogo.org/Ratzinger/index.htm> (accessed 21/06/07)

—— (2000b) *Presentazione 'Dominus Jesus'*. Online. Available HTTP: <http://www.vatican.edu/roman_curia/congregations/cfaith/documents/rc_con_cfaith_doc_20000905_dominus-iesus-ratzinger_it.html> (accessed15/06/2007)

Segers, M.C. and Jelen, T.G. (1998) *A wall of Separation? Debating the Public Role of Religion*, Lanham: Rowman and Littlefield.

Seidler, J. (1986) 'Contested Accomodation: the Catholic Church as a Special Case of Social Change', *Social Forces*, 64(4): 847–74.

Tajfel, H. (1981) *Human Groups and Social Categories: Studies in Social Psychology*, Cambridge: Cambridge University Press.

Vallier, I. (1971) *The Roman Catholic Church: a Transnational Actor*, Madison: University of Wisconsin Press.

Voye, L. (1999) 'Secularization in a Context of Advanced Modernity', *Sociology of Religion*, 60(3): 275–88.

Warner, C.M. (2000) *Confessions of an Interest Group: the Catholic Church and Political Parties in Europe*, Princeton: Princeton University Press.

Part IV

Mezzogiorno

A never-ending problem

13 The strongest mafia: *'Ndrangheta* made in Calabria

Ercole Giap Parini

Summary

The *'Ndrangheta* is the mafia originally developed in Calabria and represents one of the oldest and most diffuse criminal organizations in Southern Italy. It has long been underestimated by judges, police forces and political institutions – and only with the killings in Duisburg (Germany) many have realized the growing importance, and menace, of the phenomenon. The *'Ndrangheta* has spread its illegal activities well beyond the Italian borders. Moreover, it has reached a European leading position in many criminal activities including the drug trafficking (due to its strong links with similar groups in Colombia and elsewhere). This chapter analyzes the internal, rigid and 'traditionalist' organization of the *'Ndrangheta* and its control over Calabria's territory; the changing nature of its illegal activities over recent decades; and its ability to consolidate strategic alliances with mainstream politics, the 'legal' economy, professions, and part of the public administration.

Introduction

On August 2007, Duisburg, a German town of 495,000 inhabitants in the North Rhine-Westphalia, was the scene of a showdown between two *'Ndrangheta* families originally coming from San Luca, a village on the Ionian coast of Calabria (near Reggio Calabria): six people were killed at the end of a party in a restaurant owned by the family of the victims. On that occasion, German people had evidence that *mafiosi* coming from the 'profound South' of Italy carried out an apparently backward bloody feud in their territory. Internationally, there was evidence that the *'Ndrangheta* had spread its illegal activities well beyond the Italian borders.

Actually, the *'Ndrangheta* is the mafia organization originally developed in Calabria; in the Italian *mafioso* scenery it represents one of the oldest and most diffuse criminal organizations of this type. Despite its power and its deeply rooted traditions in the original territories, and despite the ability to extend its activities all over the world for half a century, the *'Ndrangheta* has long been underestimated by judges, police forces and political institutions, since it has been considered a marginal criminal phenomenon if compared to the *Cosa Nostra* or the *Camorra*.[1] For a long time in the Italian public understanding, it had the flavour of a pastoral declining world, rather than of an organization rooted in criminal affairs. Probably, this estimation is partially due to the marginal role played by Calabria in the Italian political and economic system. And, probably, it is just this underestimation that has allowed this mafia organization to become one of the world's most dangerous.

Regarding the undervaluation of the *'Ndrangheta*, Nicola Gratteri and Antonio Nicaso state (2007: 13):

> For decades the *'Ndrangheta* has been considered a raggedy and homely version of the Sicilian mafia, a typical phenomenon of a backward society, only interested in kidnappings. And this long-lasting and dangerous undervaluation has helped it become a truly transnational holding, able to influence not only politics, but also social models, lifestyle and consumption.

In fact, the *'Ndrangheta*, together with part of the regional political and administrative sector, has created an underground network of power particularly able to subjugate the most important economic resources that in Calabria are widely dependant on the public sector (see Chapter 16 by Milio concerning the damage to the EU funding allocation caused by the patronage system of power in the southern regions), owing to a long-lasting condition of marginality of the local entrepreneurial class.

Consequently, it has been a surprise for many that in Calabria there are more than 150 *cosche* (clans), comprising about 15,000 people (a significant number, since this territory is a little bigger than 15,000 km^2, with a population of nearly 2 million) whose activities, at the international and local levels, produce revenues of about €35–40 billion. What is the secret for the criminal success of such a mafia organization? The answer should be found by investigating the mixture of what is 'ancient' and what is 'modern', where an apparently backward organization is consistent with the newest forms of illicit trafficking and where the local and international strategies are functionally linked together.

This chapter starts by describing the inner organization of the *'Ndrangheta*. It then focuses on the local level of its power, which is a kind of authority exercised through a mixture of menace and people's consensus. Finally, it takes into account the relevance of the international traffic of the *'Ndrangheta*, also giving evidence of the functional links with the local level of power.

A rigid and 'traditionalist' organization guarded by secrecy and rites

The *'Ndrangheta* maintains a more traditional internal structure than the other mafia organizations. What makes it unique in the general mafia phenomenon is the reciprocal independence of the different cells constituting the *'Ndrangheta*. These cells, known as *'ndrine*, are based on blood families. This represents an element of stability, since the turnover is largely inside family-based relationships. For instance, there is a kind of 'marriage strategy' by which the bosses of the *'Ndrangheta* create blood ties with individuals capable of criminal activity. (Ciconte 1992, 1996, Paoli 2000, Gratteri and Nicaso 2007).

The fact that the word *'ndrina*, which defines a single cell of the organization, represents the root of the word *'Ndrangheta*, defining the whole organization, testifies the importance of the units to the organization. The only exception to the federative nature of the *'Ndrangheta* is represented by the peculiar role attributed to the *'ndrina* of San Luca, symbolically considered the mother of all the *'ndrine*, due to the fact that it is the most ancient in Calabria.

It is worth mentioning that the organization is strengthened by secrecy and by a formal and ritualistic entering of the new adepts into the 'honoured society'. In the report that a former Minister of the Interior, Nicola Mancino, presented to Parliament in the 1990s, rites to access the organization are described as crucial in the Calabrian mafia:

> The 'Ndrangheta, differently from Cosa Nostra, has always relied heavily on written codes, rites and symbols. Still now, during inspections and raids by the police in Calabria 'secret codes' are often found, and these are the copies – mainly written in dialect, with clumsy handwriting, by semi-literate people – of the rite and the esoteric formula through which it is possible to enter the 'honoured society'. In these 'codes' internal hierarchies were outlined; tasks and characteristics of the affiliated were predicated, together with the rules of behaviour and sanctions to the adepts
>
> (Mancino, quoted in Minuti and Nicaso 1994: 215)

The 'codes' represent the *summa* of all these aspects, and characterize the entire history of the Calabrian mafia.[2]

Enzo Ciconte (1996) asked how it was possible for an organization based on an apparently primitive structure to succeed in becoming a chief player in major illicit worldwide trafficking, and, locally, in the functioning of democratic institutions. The answer has to be found precisely in the characteristics of that structure. The significance of those rites, myths and legends defines the secret character of the organization. This plays a twofold role: (1) it strengths the faithfulness to the organizations among the adepts (see Paoli 2000, 2004); and (2) it gives a fashionable aura to the *cosche*, so crucial to attracting new adepts to the organization.

It is worth mentioning that in the last few years something is changing in the inner structure of the organization. Due to the growing dimension of the affairs and the necessity to diminish internal conflicts, coordination among *'ndrine* has been introduced. To satisfy this condition a new structure called *provincia* has been introduced and it is supposedly very similar to the Cosa Nostra's 'commission' (Gratteri and Nicaso 2007: 16).[3]

The present day power of the *'Ndrangheta*: the local level

In Calabria, the *'Ndrangheta* is particularly able to penetrate the whole economic, social and political fabric, not unlike the Camorra, whose strategies have been described in this volume by Felia and Percy Allum.

This is particularly true for many of the Calabrian territories traditionally settled by the *'ndrine*. In order to carry out this type of control over the territory, the *cosche* are engaged in an arrogant practice aimed at subduing entrepreneurs and shopkeepers, by imposing on them the '*pizzo*', that is the squeeze[4]. In 2006, more than 400 cases of squeezes were denounced in Calabria. Since these account for only a small part of the phenomenon (the victims are very often reluctant to denounce them), in order to understand the level of violence and menace over entrepreneurs, investigators monitor the acts of intimidation against them, such as damage and arson. In 2007, incidents of damage against firms or shops accounted for more than 12,000 in Calabria; the number of acts of arson were almost 1500 (DIA 2008).

Many experts and judges affirm that the control over the commercial and entrepreneurial fabric is so widespread that in many areas no one can avoid paying the *pizzo* to the local *cosca*. Many Calabrian entrepreneurs have internalized the fear brought by the continuous menace and even institutionalized it in their daily activities. Sometimes the *pizzo* is taken into account as a balance sheet item by many enterprises, even among the most important ones.

In its last report, the Antimafia Parliamentary Commission stated:

> where organized crime is deeply rooted, a parallel economic system is created; this attracts human and financial resources while subtracting them from the legal economy; as a consequence, illegality is generally known as the sole resource to make money; from this, a vicious circle stems in which 'the low economic growth produces low employment or unemployment that pushes human capital towards the illegal economy'
>
> (Antimafia Parliamentary Commission 2008: 15)

Unfair competition, collusion of public servants with the *'Ndrangheta*, and control over the economic fabric represent the perfect scenario for the so-called *Tamburo* and *Arca* judicial inquiries. These gave an impressive evidence of the *cosche*'s interests in controlling the public contracts for the modernization of the A3 highway, the principal highway branch in Southern Italy. This investigation was initiated by the DIA (the Italian Antimafia Agency) in 1999 and lasted until 2002. It revealed that a number of *cosche*, in particular the ones operating between the Gioia Tauro and the Lamezia Terme territories: Perna, Ruà, Di Dieco and Presta (from the last names of the bosses), used to exact 3 per cent of the contract from the legitimate companies, and forced them to hand over the subcontracts to firms belonging to the *cosche*. At the end of the investigation not only were *'Ndrangheta* men arrested but also functionaries of the ANAS (i.e. personnel working for the highway trust).

These inquiries suggest, the control over the economic fabric is only part of the local mafia power. The other is represented by *'Ndrangheta*'s ability to consolidate strategic alliances with mainstream politics, 'legal' economy, professionals and with part of the public administration.[5]

In the last decades, due to the mafia infiltration, thirty-eight municipal councils have been dismantled by decree of the President of the Italian Republic. The strength of this system is evidenced by the fact that for three of them the dismantle decree was applied twice. This testifies to the high level of penetration of the *'ndrine* in the Calabrian political sector, which jeopardizes the possibility of the citizens to fully exert democratic rights.[6]

Such pervasive control is of capital importance for the general strategy of a mafia organization.[7] In the 1970s, in order to consolidate strategic alliances, the *'Ndrangheta* started to connect with some of the Masonic lodges, particularly strong in Calabria's professional and political fabric. Through this alliance the local mafia seeks full social legitimacy and a stronger integration in the economy and politics (see Forgione 2008: 25).

In their traditional territories *'Ndrangheta*'s power is represented as a network of interests and complicities: at the very centre of it there are the strongest and most colluded meshes, for instance the alliance between a mafioso and a politician. The former, in fact, exerts influence on the voters (a mixture of violence and respect) which is useful for the politician to be elected. The politician, once elected, will be a loyal servant of the boss's interests. Starting from this, one encounters the so-called 'gray area'. This is constituted by colluding professionals (such as lawyers, physicians, financial consultants, and so on) for whom providing professional services to the *cosche* is imperative, and this is of crucial importance to reproduce the mafia's power. In exchange, they have the possibility of managing part of the huge revenues of the *'Ndrangheta*, and getting more power in their affairs by 'spending' some of the 'mafia aura', which is so significant in a context where the *'Ndrangheta* plays such an important role. A more exterior area of the network is populated by people who receive only minor advantages from the *'Ndrangheta*, such as a job or a council house and so on; it would be impossible to give all the examples of a marginal economy based on and controlled through the exploitation of the people's basic needs. At the most external areas of that net there are people not colluded in the mafia affairs at all; nevertheless, they are fond of a quiet life and are resigned to living in a place controlled by the *cosche*. The role of this part of the population is so crucial because they are tolerant to the *mafiosi* and provide them with a kind of social protection by repelling any attempt at social change, for instance by hindering social or political opposition to that system.

The alliance with politicians at different levels assures political and social protection to the *cosche* that overcomes the Calabria borders: from a local town councillor the *mafiosi* are able to get meet with Italian or EU deputies or public authorities. This strategy is crucial for providing a kind of political protection that men of the *'Ndrangheta* can use to influence the administration of justice, for instance in the *aggiustamento* (i.e. arrangement) of a trial.

Generally, the alliance between the *'Ndrangheta* and the politicians is carried out without conflict. Nevertheless, due to the crucial role that the group's control has over politics – and consequently over the public administration – local politicians and public administrations are often under menace. In Calabria, every year a number of violent attacks (including bombings, firebombs, and so on) are perpetrated against local administrators and civil servants and this is a true and continuous menace for democracy in many areas of the region.

Sometimes the *cosche* exceed all boundaries. On 16 December 2005 the Vice-President of the Regional Calabria Council, Francesco Fortugno, was killed in Locri, a town of 5,000 inhabitants in the Ionian coast of Calabria, traditionally controlled by the *'Ndrangheta*. After sixteen years, it was the first murder of such a high-level politician and the shock was great in Calabria and in Italy (in September 1990 Ludovico Ligato, the former chief of the Italian Railways, and an important representative of the Christian Democrat party, had been killed by a man belonging to the 'family of Condello', nearby Reggio Calabria area). The sensation linked to this bloody event testified that something was going wrong in Calabria's social peace between the mafia and politics.

The investigations following the murder were geared towards the affairs of the local ASL (Azienda Sanitaria Locale – Local Health Office) in Locri, where Francesco Fortugno had been a top manager. What emerged through this inquiry was a network of interests and complicity,[8] where the local *cosche* wanted to access the huge economic resources connected to the management of the health system in that area. This murder testifies that the *'ndrine* are easily inclined to violence whenever the core of their power is seriously compromised.

The global contemporary power of the *'Ndrangheta*

The *'Ndrangheta* is becoming one of the most important and aggressive crime organizations both at the national and the international level.

In Italy, *'Ndrangheta*'s activities are indeed diffused far from Calabria. This could be a deliberate strategic expansion of its activities or the result of 'unintentional' factors, such as the escape of the bosses from their lands of origin due to internal conflicts within the *cosche* (see Sciarrone 1998, Varese 2006). For instance, Piemonte, Veneto, Valle d'Aosta and Lombardia (especially around Milan) have been invaded by Calabrian *mafiosi* since the 1970s, in particular for the control of the local drug traffic. In the Milan area there are neighbourhoods where the *cosche* control the commercial structure in ways similar to Calabria. This is the case of the Quarto Oggiaro neighbourhood, considered completely in *'Ndrangheta*'s hands. The former president of the Antimafia Parliamentary Commission, Francesco Forgione, by emphasizing the importance of Milan in *'Ndrangheta*'s strategies, has stated that it is the 'real *'Ndrangheta* capital'.[9] In that territory this 'mafia made in Calabria' is able to make affairs and form alliances with local politicians, and the judges suspect that the *cosche* are trying to become involved in the businesses of the 2015 Milan Expo.

Nevertheless, the international level reached by this criminal organization's affairs is impressive. Even in the 2002 report, the members of the Parliamentary Commission highlighted that the Calabrian mafia had gained primacy among the other mafia organizations and was central to global illicit trafficking.

In Europe the presence of the *cosche* is very pervasive. The above-mentioned incident in Duisburg shows that Calabrian *mafiosi* are leading an expansion of their interests and some change in their strategies; in particular, they are spreading their control over financial activities and spreading conflicts traditionally managed in Calabria at a European level. It is worth mentioning that in Germany at least 300 commercial activities, particularly restaurants, are directly owned by men of the *cosche*. According to the German Intelligence Service (BND) another and more lucrative way to launder money is through stock exchange investments (Gratteri and Nicaso 2007: 213). Other European areas of diffusions are the ex-Soviet countries, Spain, Switzerland and the UK.

One of the reports presented by the DIA (2007) states that:

> In the global scene, the drug traffic management still remains the prominent and most profitable criminal activity for the Calabrian mafia organizations. These have strengthened the ability to maintain relationship with the South American 'narcos' organizations and they managed to put themselves among the most prominent in the control of cocaine import flows (Bolivia and Colombia over all) and routes from the production places to Europe
>
> (DIA 2007)

By observing the *'Ndrangheta*'s activities all over the world, the evidence emerges that we are facing a global strategy.

The *'Ndrangheta*'s criminal effectiveness in international trade is due to the *cosche*'s brokerage abilities. In September 2008, the representative in Italy of the DEA (Drug Enforcement Administration), Mr. Richard Bendekovich, pointed out the centrality of the *'Ndrangheta* in the control of the US drug market, in relation to its close connection with Colombian narcos and Mexican gangs who control the traffic across the border between Mexico and the US.

It is worth mentioning that *'Ndrangheta*'s growing importance in this kind of trafficking is connected to a change inside the Italian *mafioso* scenery. In the last decade, many of the activities in which other Italian mafia organizations were involved are now under the control of the Calabrian mafia. To understand that, it is necessary to recall the Cosa Nostra crisis following the state and civil society reaction to the 1992 slaughters in which judges Giovanni Falcone and Paolo Borsellino were killed. In a period characterized by a strong reaction by the state's institutions against mafia power in Italy, the *'Ndrangheta* showed a stronger ability to resist to this attack if compared to Cosa Nostra. In fact, a synchronous action from different sectors of the state – politics, judges, investigators and civil society – seriously challenged the Sicilian mafia that simultaneously experienced a lack of protection and of wide social consensus. Furthermore, the presence of a huge number of 'super pentiti', 'supergrasses' (inside informers), compromised the Cosa Nostra inner structure and its abilities to deal with illicit international trafficking. A greater stability of the *'Ndrangheta* has been ascribed first of all to the negligible presence of the supergrasses. In fact, the structure of this mafia, based on blood ties, became an extraordinary defence against their emergence. While stigmatizing its oppressive influence upon the territory, the drafters of the 2003 Antimafia Commission report quoted the words of Antonio Zagari, a former *picciotto* of the Gioia Tauro area, on the Calabrian coast:

> For the people born in such surroundings and trained to silence, it is not easy to denounce their friends and be considered dangerous enemies. To cause the arrest and the imprisonment of relatives brings to moral and psychological problems that are worse than the fear of revenges and retorts.
>
> (Parliamentary Antimafia Commission 2003: 30)

Starting in 2000, the *'Ndrangheta* obtained the monopoly of the European cocaine market. A number of men of the *cosche* live permanently in Colombia in order to maintain stable relationships with narcos and paramilitary armies. That *'Ndrangheta* members have a high regard for that country is testified by the strong ties between the *cosche* of the Reggio Calabria area and Antonio Mancuso, the chief of the AUC (Autodefensas Unidas Colombia) paramilitary army who managed to obtain, jointly with the *'Ndrangheta*, huge cocaine shipments to finance his paramilitary and political activities. The AUC is a paramilitary organization engaged in a long-term conflict with the insurrection forces, especially the Marxists, such as the FARC and the ELN, for the control of many Colombian areas and defence of the richest sector of Colombia's people (land owners and middle bourgeoisie).

The international affairs of the *'Ndrangheta* are still linked to drug traffic management that accounts for about 70 per cent of its international revenues. Nevertheless, other illicit trades are becoming more relevant. For instance, by illicitly organizing the disposal of dangerous waste coming from industrial production, the *cosche* offer a much requested service to the legal economy. In a competitive global economic system, many companies are eager to take the opportunity to keep the costs connected to this activity low, even at the risk of being involved in criminal activities.[10] Concerning this, investigations are in progress in Italy on nuclear waste traffic coming from a very important Italian institute of research and directed to Somalia.[11]

In conclusion, these facts confirm that the *'Ndrangheta* is becoming a true financial holding of crime, able to move organizational and financial resources towards all profitable opportunities and through the newest technical apparatuses. Besides this, it is clear that this mafia, originally from Calabria, rather than being a mere disturbing element, is playing a crucial role in the shaping of the global economy.

A 'deeply and traditionally rooted' international attitude

The *cosche*'s bent for international affairs shows that the local and the international levels are not separate in the mafia's strategies. The local level benefits from an international money flow that needs to be laundered; through this huge amount of money the Calabrian *cosche* can fund local criminal activities as well as legal economic enterprises. By doing this, the local bosses consolidate their power upon a territory whose economy is particularly weak. In turn, the men of the *'Ndrangheta* who carry on offshore activities need the social and political protection provided by the network of consensus built up by the local *cosche*. For instance, when they are escaping from international police they can go to Calabria for a place to hide. Besides that, the *mafiosi* playing at the local level exert a deep control over the workforce; in fact, they are able to provide trusty men devoted to the mafia's causes to the bosses working at the international level. This reconfirms an attitude to maintain strong control over human resources even in the international arena, where the risk of being too exposed to external forces is great.

Despite widespread opinion, the relevance of the international traffic is not something new for the *'Ndrangheta*. This is testified by the facts connected to the so-called 'Siderno Group' activities. The town of Siderno is considered one of the most important for the mafia's strategy on the Ionian coast of Calabria. Starting from the 1950s to the mid-1970s, the undisputed boss of that village was don Antonio Macrì, whose influence overwhelmed the town's area (Antimafia Parliamentary Commission 2000) even reaching Messina in Sicily. While living in Siderno, Macrì created a thick network of power and consensus that allowed him to control the local politicians who, in exchange for electoral backing, gave him easy access to public works. His influence was so strong that even high prelates took part in his power gathering. He was a true authority in Siderno, Macrì was more concerned to maintain peace and order than the police itself.

Moreover, Macrì's strategy aimed to extend his power to an international level by controlling a number of criminal activities abroad and by relying on trustworthy Calabrian emigrant families (Minuti and Nicaso 1994: 84–87). In the early 1950s Michele (Mike) Racco, a poor baker endowed with enough ability and ambition, had been initiated to the local *'ndrina* of Siderno and then sent by Macrì to Canada. In Toronto he started an important pasta factory to give himself an honest 'front', while secretly working to build up a criminal organization that in a short time became the centre of a big criminal business, relying on a trusty workforce of about fifty people, all from Siderno. Group activities were smuggling, extortion and gambling. Though the organization managed to gain a very high level of income from these activities, the *mafiosi* maintained tight links with the poor southern Italian village of Siderno.

The case of the Siderno Group is particularly relevant since it shows, even in the vocabulary used to name a mafia phenomenon abroad, the contiguity with an apparently insignificant town belonging to Southern Italy.

Besides that, in the territories of their original settlements, such as in Siderno, *mafiosi* had for a long time been engaged in minute criminal activities (cattle stealing and extortion mainly) (Ciconte 1992, Sergi 1991), therefore, this example explains how these criminals were able, through a stable organization and bold expansion strategies, to create an extended international criminal network. In other words, there are the roots of a phenomenon that has become the 'strongest mafia'.

Conclusions

In this book, while describing the Italian elite, Carboni focuses on the 'public life as a mere function of private and individual interests'. In Southern Italy, and in Calabria in particular, parts of the elites are strictly connected to the mafia's interests and constitute, together, a hidden and underground power system in which what is public is growingly appropriated inside the private sphere. Far from being a process regarding only political and social elites and the mafia, humiliation of public life becomes a widespread custom, where common people are involved as well, in a big network of connivance. The result of this process is a deterioration of public life and the compromise of social and economical innovation.

This fact also highlights that the *'Ndrangheta*, like other mafia organizations, is not merely criminal phenomenon, since it permeates social, economic and political spheres. Consequently, it has to be fought not only through judicial inquiries and police strategies: as a social system of power it has to be fought by truly democratic opposition forces that can be found in the civic society and in the political sector; as an economic phenomenon it has to be fought by giving better conditions to entrepreneurs to freely compete; as a criminal phenomenon it has to be fought by empowering police forces and prosecutors. Nevertheless, to produce this synchronous action, a true and consistent will is necessary to break a social and political equilibrium, and this appears to be still lacking in the whole Italian political agenda.

Notes

1   In reference to the Camorra, Felia and Percy Allum's chapter in *Italy Today* provides evidence of its peculiarities among the mafia organizations. From a general perspective, it focuses on the need for us to distinguish among the different organizations which are too often taken as a homogenous totality.

2   According to Malafarina (1978), the first 'code' was found in the 1930s in the village of San Luca by the legendary *carabinieri* marshal Giuseppe Delfino.

3   The Cosa Nostra's cupola is composed of the representatives of the different Sicilian mafia *mandamenti* (a *mandamento* represents a territorial-based cell). It has the function of resolving conflicts inside the organization and giving direction in the managing of criminal affairs among the different mafia families.

4   This is a classical example of the so-called 'industry of protection' (Gambetta 1993).

5   This strategy has something to do with the dynamics of a deviant subculture (see Cohen 1955, Cloward and Ohlin 1960).

6   Among many contributions to that issue, it is worth mentioning Siebert's monograph *Mafia e quotidianità* (Siebert 1996b); here the author focuses on the erosion of democracy in the territories where the mafia has settled (see also Siebert 1996a). The

menace to democratic institutions is not specific of the Italian mafia. In his study on the community of Cape Flats, Standing (2006) points out the 'threat to democracy' coming from criminal governance.

7 See in particular Santino 2001. The author evidences the crucial role played by the relationship between politicians and *mafiosi*, in order to define the characters of the mafioso power. Links between OC and politics are a steady element in order to define criminal strategies all over the world.

8 On 2 February 2009 four people were condemned to life imprisonment for the Fortugno murder. The first stage verdict strengthens the inquiring hypotheses that, at that time, the politician tried to stop the situation of corruption and mafia connivance at Locri's ASL.

9 On this see *Il Sole24ore*, 'Le rotte della *'ndrangheta* un anno dopo', 13 August 2008.

10 In September 2008, in the Milan suburbs, a 65,000 m^2 piece of land turned out to be a big dump for industrial dangerous waste. In this area, 178,000 m^3 of toxic waste were deposited from different firms of the Bergamo and Brescia areas which were in service to *'Ndrangheta* men, namely Fortunato Stellitano and Ivan Tenca.

11 These facts have emerged from the investigation on the homicide of Ilaria Alpi, an Italian journalist investigating weapons and toxic waste traffic in Somalia.

References

Allum, F. and Siebert, R. (eds.) (2003) *Organized Crime and the Challenge to Democracy*, London: Routledge.

Antimafia Parliamentary Commission (2000) *Relazione sullo stato della lotta alla criminalità organizzata in Calabria,* Rome: Parlamento italiano.

—— (2003) *Relazione annuale*, Rome: Parlamento italiano.

—— (2008) *Relazione annuale, Rome*: Parlamento italiano.

Armao, F. (2000), *Il sistema mafia: Dall'economia-mondo al dominio locale*, Turin: Bollati Borighieri.

Ciconte, E. (1992) *'Ndrangheta: Dall'Unità ad oggi*, Bari: Laterza.

—— (1996) *Processo alla 'Ndrangheta*, Bari: Laterza.

Cloward, R.A. and Ohlin, L.E. (1960) *Delinquency and opportunity: A Theory of Delinquent Gangs*, Glencoe: The Free Press.

Cohen, A.K. (1955) *Delinquent Boys: The Culture of the Gang*, Glencoe: The Free Press.

DIA (Direzione investigativa antimafia) (2007) Relazione semestrale II, Rome: Ministero dell'Interno.

—— (2008) Relazione semestrale I, Rome: Ministero dell'Interno.

Forgione, F. (2008) *Relazione annuale della Commissione parlamentare d'inchiesta sul fenomeno della criminalità organizzata mafiosa o similare'ndrangheta*, Italian Parliament: 2008.

Gambetta, D. (1993) *The Sicilian Mafia*. London: Harvard University Press.

Gratteri, N. and Nicaso, A. (2007) *Fratelli di sangue. La storia, la struttura, i codici, le ramificazioni*, Cosenza: Pellegrini.

Malafarina, L. (1978) *Il codice della 'ndrangheta*, Reggio Calabria: Parallelo 38.

Minuti, D. and Nicaso, A. (1994) *'Ndranghete: Le filiali della mafia calabrese*, Vibo Valentia: Monteleone.

Paoli, L. (2000) *Fratelli di mafia: Cosa Nostra e 'Ndrangheta*, Bologna: il Mulino.

—— (2004) 'Italian organised crime: Mafia associations and criminal enterprises', *Global Crime*, 6(1): 19–31.

Parini, E. G. (1997) 'Su alcune recenti interpretazioni del fenomeno mafioso', *Quaderni di Sociologia*, 13: 167–75.

—— (1999) *Mafia, politica e società civile: Due casi in Calabria*, Soveria Mannelli: Rubbettino.

—— (2003) 'Civil Resistance: Society fights back...', in F. Allum and R. Siebert (eds.) *Organized Crime and the Challenge to Democracy*, London: Routledge.

Santino, U. (2001) 'Mafia and Mafia-type Organizations in Italy', in J. Albanese *et al.* (eds.) *Organized Crime – World Perspectives*, Upper Saddle River, NJ: Prentice Hall.

Sciarrone, R. (1998) *Mafie vecchie, mafie nuove*, Rome: Donzelli.

Sergi, P. (1991) *La santa violenta*, Periferia: Cosenza.

Siebert, R. (1996a) *Secrets of Life and Death. Woman and the Mafia*, London: Verso.

—— (1996b) *Mafia e quotidianità*, Milan: Il Saggiatore.

Standing, A. (2006) *Organised crime. A Study from the Cape Flats*, Cape Town: Institute for Security Studies.

Varese, F. (2006) 'How Mafias Migrate: The Case of the 'Ndrangheta in Northern Italy', *Law and Society Review*, 40(2): 411–44.

14 Revisiting Naples

Clientelism and organized crime

Felia Allum and Percy Allum

Summary

Naples and the Campania region have always been labelled one of the heartlands of corruption, clientelism and organized crime; all of which polluted the local economy, civil society and politics. The Tangentopoli crisis of 1993–1994 was believed to mark an important turning point: the direct election of Antonio Bassolino as mayor of Naples was intended to introduce a new form of leadership as the premise for the rebirth of the city. Fifteen years on, despite some modest successes, little has really changed. This chapter examines the reasons for this failure: the success of clientelism and organized crime.

> 'S'il y a bien un lieu, une ville où les vautours peuvent être repus c'est bien Naples.'
> Tahar Ben Jelloun, 1992

> 'Le clientele, le avevano tutte, comunisti compresi.'
> Geronimo [P. Cirino Pomicino], 2000

Introduction

In his first public speech as President of the Republic, in June 2006, the Neapolitan Giorgio Napolitano, declared that Naples was experiencing 'the worst days of its history'. However, despite the *Camorra* war of 2004–2006, the situation was no worse, in terms of homicides, than it had been in the 1980s, even if the 'refuse crisis' is responsible for a potentially dramatic public health situation.

This said, the President's *cri du coeur* poses the question: what, if anything, changed during the much-vaunted 'Renaissance of Naples' of the 1990s? This can be analyzed in two, arguably contiguous, areas of activity: political and criminal. In these, the city can be seen to exhibit, perhaps in a more extreme form, processes and activities endemic to other parts of Southern Italy and, indeed, the country as a whole.

In this sense, the Neapolitan situation mirrors aspects, not only of southern politics, but also to some extent, of national politics in the decade of the Second Republic and hence is a major element in understanding the country's recent history. The political dimension examined is *clientelismo*; the criminal is organized crime.

The Neapolitan *Camorra* as a criminal subsystem

The Neapolitan *Camorra* is the organized crime group which originates and is based in the Campania region. Sales (1998) has explained that there is not just one, but many *Camorras* across the region; each clan reflecting the geographical, social, economic and political contexts within which it operates.

Unlike the Sicilian Mafia, the Neapolitan *Camorras* are individual clans seeking survival through alliances. They lack collective coordination, have great flexibility, are extremely violent and have extensive political contacts. In theoretical terms, they form part of the Neapolitan social system and work within it as a criminal subsystem which has changing characteristics depending on the local context (Allum 2006). This is the case with Calabria's *'Ndrangheta* analyzed by Parini, this volume. The *Camorra* therefore represents another dark shadow over Italy.

Clientelism in post-war Naples

The term 'clientelism' has known a multitude of uses and abuses. By clientelism, we understand a form of political participation in which politician–citizen linkages are based on a general exchange of non-specified but personalized services rendered in return for electoral support. It was known before the Great Reform Bill in England as 'treating' and in Italy today as *voto di scambio* (barter vote).

We hypothesize that the Christian Democratic (DC) party in Naples, and the Italian south in general, was largely organized in the immediate post-war period around a series of notables and their clientele networks and transformed as a result of Amintore Fanfani's period as National Party Secretary (1954–1959) into a 'syndicate of political machines' controlled by a political class of provincial bosses, never becoming a true mass party. This transformation was promoted, *inter alia*, by the growth of the welfare state, in which the 1950s 'Southern policy' played a major role. In fact, the partisan use of public agencies enabled young party officials to create clientele networks with the objective of organizing the middle classes and peasants into an army of DC voters. Indeed, in representative regimes, as Pizzorno (1991: 307) has also observed, there are two basic methods for winning elections: to implement political projects or to grant favours. The former is the more difficult because projects are rarely implemented in their proposed form, while the latter poses, in the long run, resource problems (causing public expenditure crises), often leading to a debasement of the political class, as occurred in Italy in the 1980s and 1990s.

However, to understand the operation of the system and the ease with which it became a constituent part of the DC in the 1960s and 1970s, we must first understand the party's informal structure as it developed in the area in the previous decade. Local party organization was a pyramid with a hierarchy at several levels. At the top were the faction leaders (*capicorrente*), often the main national leaders or influential cabinet ministers; immediately below them were the principal 'lieutenants', i.e. other professional politicians, almost always MPs or heads of important public agencies and provincial party secretaries. Further down the pyramid were the *grandi elettori*, i.e. the people who controlled local clientele networks: small town mayors and councillors, communal party secretaries, but also members of the liberal professions. Lower down still were the *capielettori* who were often difficult to distinguish from the *grandi elettori*. They were usually activists who were part of a social network, whether familial, territorial or occupational. Brancaccio (1999: 525) has described the role of a DC *capoelettore* in the Bagnoli district of Naples from 1960 until his death in 1985 in these terms:

> The DC in Bagnoli was organized round the person of Pasquale Sansone, local party secretary. [...] Loyal member of the '*Doroteo*' faction, he was the undisputed leader of the DC in Bagnoli. If we reason in terms of social networks, we see that all the party's relations converge on him at election times, give rise to an 'action set' that ensures that the candidate(s) he supports, receive a significant number of preference votes. He is not only the '*Doroteo*'s man in Bagnoli', but also the intermediary between the local *clienteles'* demands and the party leadership: he has also an active role of 'broker' in which he manages the demands that come from below, addressing them to the appropriate power centre. All in all, he manipulates social relations, to make a personal profit.

Even *camorristi* exercised this role, as became clear from the *Camorra* trials of the 1990s. In the judgment in the '*Maglio* trial', in which one DC and two PSI MPs were found guilty, the judges wrote:

> There is no doubt that local politicians of the '*Doroteo*' faction have [...] entertained collusive links with the criminal structure in question [i.e. the *Camorra*], as there is no doubt that the latter controlled and conditioned entire local councils [...] From the trial evidence it emerged that, after the constitution of the association, the collection of votes was always performed by local politicians linked to the *Doroteo* faction
>
> (*Corte di Assise di Napoli* 2000: 2981–2)

Finally, the persons furthest from the notables and political bosses were the *gallopini* (canvassers) and the ordinary voters, many of whom had become clients because they had received material help (or the promise of it) at some time. Thus, if the clientele networks were the basis of the DC bosses' power in Naples and the South, with ordinary voters tied not only to a government party, but directly to a faction or a political boss, the latter had strong control over them. Put simply, in an economic situation in which unemployment and poverty were endemic, to be given a job and integrated into a *clientele* network could make the family's fortune. Moreover, between 1946 and 1992, it was a closed political system: the

DC and minor parties were permanent government parties, as if by divine right. By the end of the 1960s, a patronage system based on political machines had been created, almost province by province, but it remained a hotchpotch system tied to the personality of the provincial boss.

At this point, we suggest the hypothesis that this system underwent modification in the course of the 1980s. What actually changed was the emergence of a new race of politicians, the 'business politician' – represented in Naples by Cirino Pomicino, Giulio De Donato, Alfredo Vito and Francesco De Lorenzo – who founded his power on 'personal networks' in civil society and no longer on the mechanisms previously in vogue (i.e. party membership). A Neapolitan administrator has outlined the strategy of this new race of politicians:

> The method used by Pomicino to gain power, which ha[d] progressively led him to hold posts of ever greater importance and deal with matters of ever greater significance, had as point of departure the alliance with people inside local institutions and bodies active in all moments of collective life that could be translated into support. The successive passage was the translation of this support into electoral strength. From here he derived a power within the party: employed by him so as to increase those alliances, that support and so that power, to be used decisively every time there was the possibility of obtaining a return in political terms and of votes
>
> (Brancaccio 2002: 98)

The key to the system was political patronage. For example, ministerial office allowed Antonio Gava (son of former DC minister Silvio Gava) to enlarge his *clientela*: during his time at the Post Office Ministry (1983–1987), 3,808 people from the Province of Naples (almost 20 per cent of all jobs) were added to the Post Office staff in the province, which represents only about 10 per cent of the national population. In addition, his political secretary's influence also grew, as the latter was able to appoint forty disabled persons from his small hometown. Finally, what has been called 'the institutionalized bribe system' (Marino, 1993: 129) operated, in which all parties were involved, as a Neapolitan building contractor admitted under judicial interrogation:

> The first meeting took place in Rome with the Hons. A. and B. The discussion was vague and the two DC MPs asked me if I was interested in public works for the World Cup and to my affirmative reply, they assured me of their support. Afterwards B told me that our initial discussion could materialize and directed me to the party city secretary C. I met him and he asked me for 300 million lire; then it was the turn of the PSI with whom we agreed a sum of 400 million; for the Liberal Party (PLI) I went personally to D.'s house and he sent me to the party city secretary E. for a payment of 70 million; then I spoke with F for the Republican Party (PRI) and we discussed 50 million. And finally with G for the Social Democrat Party (PSDI): 70 million. All

these sums were asked for in return for speedy approval of the City Council resolutions

(*L'Espresso*, 2 May 1993: 65)

So the real change in Naples and the South in the 1980s and early 1990s was the rejection of a collective partisan logic by the new political generation. Politics became a business, losing its ideological and programmatic dimension. Indeed, it increasingly became a means for members of the new professional petty bourgeoisie to impose themselves individually and get rich quickly. Political careers depended less on party organization (which had, moreover, virtually lost its basis in civil society; professional politicians set up their own personal secretariats) and were more determined by one's ability to insert oneself in 'business circuits'. Money had replaced ideological and cultural identity in candidate–voter relations. What counted was the power to reinvest locally the resources that the politician was able to acquire thanks to his mediation with national political and administrative authorities.

It is our conclusion that what started as an 'artisan' form of activity in the 1950s had become a veritable 'industrial' type activity by the 1990s: a patronage system based on mass bribery, whose motto was the cynical 'every man has his price'.

The Neapolitan *Camorra* in post-war Naples (1946–1993)

The *Camorra* underwent an important transformation in the post-war period: in the 1950s, it started out as a basic form of crime undertaken as a survival strategy, but by the 1990s it had become a sophisticated economic and political system.

What type of *Camorra* was predominant and present when Antonio Bassolino came to power in December 1993? It was just the moment the *Camorra* was entering a difficult phase and the state, conversely, was enjoying a moment of strength (Jamieson 2000). The *Camorra*'s power base was being eroded by the number of *camorristi* who turned state's witnesses, in-fighting among members for leadership roles and the loss of political sponsors with the collapse of the DC.

Nonetheless, the *Camorra* gradually became a major reference point in the local community, providing jobs, assistance and protection. In 1982, it was estimated that there were 12 clans in Campania; by 1992, it was claimed that there were 102 clans with some 5,000 members and a year later, this had become 111 clans with some 6,700 members (*Commissione Antimafia* 1993: 2). There were two *Camorra*s living side by side and representing two different structures: the political *Camorra* of the Alfieri Confederation (also called *Nuova Mafia Campana*), which had been dominant in the decade between 1983–1993, but then lost its power and predominance in the hinterland; and the city gangs, the economic *Camorra* in the form of the Secondigliano Alliance. This latter was becoming the predominant *Camorra* and would be dominant for the next five years.

The 1970s and 1980s represented a turning point for the *Camorra*: thanks to the help of the Sicilian Mafia, it used its smuggling routes to become an important player in the drugs trade. In fact, the drugs' trade transformed the social *Camorra* into an economic *Camorra* or 'capitalist enterprise' to quote McIntosh (1973). While the majority of the *Camorra* clans thrived, thanks to the drugs trade, some clans were becoming more and more intimate with local government parties and this would transform them into political *Camorra*s.

The structure of the clans remained stable throughout the post-war period: *Camorra* families exist, cooperate when necessary, but retain their flexibility and independence. There have been attempts at integrating these clans into a hierarchical organization, such as Raffaele Cutolo's *Nuova Camorra Organizzata* (NCO) project in 1979. This ended in a bloody war between the NCO and its Sicilian-sponsored rivals the *Nuova Famiglia,* with many deaths and weakened clans as a result.

In the 1980s and 1990s, the Alfieri Confederation sought to impose some kind of chain of command and rules while the Secondigliano Alliance sought to do the same in the city. Both proved successful for a short period until their leaders were arrested, murdered or rivals no longer accepted subordination.

Looking at the kind of activities in which the *Camorra*s have been involved in the post-war period, two very different pictures emerge due to the 'structures' in which these *Camorra*s were operating. On the one hand, there were the city clans, which specialized mainly in extortion, smuggled cigarettes, drugs, illegal lotteries (economic *Camorra*). On the other, there were the hinterland clans, which moved out of the drugs trade to specializing in winning public works subcontracts: this was the case of the clans in the provinces of Naples and Caserta (political *Camorra*).

Again, looking at the structure can help to explain why some clans were able to develop a relationship with the local political elite and others were not. The city clans were only really able to influence politics at election time, as a propaganda vehicle. The 'big city' government structure in Naples made it harder to develop a relationship with a city councillor or even seek to corrupt him. The relationship with politics in Naples remained sporadic.

This was not the case in the provinces of Naples and Caserta. The 1980s proved to be a period of a close and intimate relationship between politicians and the *Camorra* which explains why, for example, Antonio Gava was prosecuted for his links with Alfieri's *Camorra* in 1996. The organization of local government allowed the *Camorra* to have an active role in politics; it did so by either seeking to influence already established politicians or in some cases, it ensured the election of its own representatives: such was the case, for example, in San Cipriano d'Aversa in 1981, in Casal di Principe in 1985 or in Marano in 1990 (Allum 2006: 165–166). The strengths and weaknesses of the local structure allowed them to do this.

Thus when the Bassolino City administrations came to power, the *Camorra* was not at its strongest. They hoped that they would contribute to eliminating it. To this end, many new projects were introduced with the object of relaunching the city of Naples.

Clientelism in second millennium Naples

The reforms of the electoral system, both at local (direct election of the mayor) and national (mixed single-member-regional PR list system for both Houses of Parliament) levels, introduced in the wake of the 'Bribesville' scandals, were intended to cure the Italian political system of its vices by securing stable government built on alternating (left-right) parliamentary and communal majorities. It was believed that a major cause of the country's ills resulted from a static electoral system, which fragmented partisan representation (and so a lack of solid government majorities) and placed a premium on the personalization of politics at the expense of policy choices. With these reforms, patronage politics would be replaced by issue politics.

Did they succeed? The picture a decade and a half later is very mixed. A greater, if fragile and uncertain, government stability was achieved at the national level (average life: 23 months) and certainly a more robust political stability at the local level, at least in so far as the City of Naples is concerned, which has had three mayors in almost fifteen years as against ten in the preceding thirteen. The post-Bribesville period opened with the euphoria of Bassolino's election as mayor and the promise of Naples' 'renaissance', but what is the result fifteen years later?

Despite the reform of the parliamentary electoral system, the Italian *anomalia* remains, but it is no longer lack of alternation in government, but rather the effects of the proliferation of small parties necessary to form ruling majorities – hence with strong blackmail potential.

The result is a Second Republic of 'unstable stability' (see Conti's chapter in this volume) as opposed to the 'stable instability' of the First Republic. However, the abolition of the preference vote and the introduction of a proportion of single-member constituencies has modified the national political scene; according to some, for the worse. Thus, the former DC Minister, Paolo Cirino Pomicino (2002: 37), claims that 'many candidatures in safe seats are bought' and quotes, with regard to Naples, the name of Sergio Iannuccilli, *Forza Italia* candidate in Naples' Senatorial constituency of S. Carlo all'Arena: Iannuccilli funded the Martusciello brothers who control the local party on Berlusconi's delegation.

Moreover, Pomicino is not the only witness to note that the old traditional methods are still current in Naples. For example, in the 2001 general and local elections, candidates were seen going around 'paying domestic bills and rents in entire wards and donating Easter eggs, Easter cakes, pasta, oil and doughnuts', not to mention the return of *portavoti* (flunkeys), who promised 'thousands of preferences to this or that candidate' (Lucarelli 2001: IV), as seen in other southern regions (Mammone 2008). They were active to such an extent that a journalist wrote of a 'Naples which in this campaign has returned at a stroke to the Lauro era and the eighties' (Rumiz 2001: 10). Moreover, Ciro Provitera – also known as *'O Brillantina* – played a similar role for Berlusconi's party in the Sanità district to that of Pasquale Sansone in ensuring votes for DC candidates in Bagnoli, in an earlier era: 'here the votes do not descend from big brother [Berlusconi]. It is something that ascends from the foundations of the *Bassi* [slums]; it is guaranteed by the "friends" (*amici*)' (ibid.). In such a situation, unsurprisingly, polling day ended in violence.

It was little different five years later: the infiltration of *Camorra* candidates in party lists (both at communal and ward levels); the buying and selling of votes (€30–70 a preference vote and €1,500 for packets of 100–150 votes); threats of extortion and intimidation of those who refused *Camorra* deals. More recently, three further incidents have confirmed, once again, the region's political praxis with serious political and social consequences. The first was the 'house arrest' of the President of the Campania Regional Assembly, Sandra Lonardo Mastella, wife of the leader of the UDEUR party and Minister of Justice in the Prodi government. There were charges of attempted corruption by bringing 'coercive' pressure on the manager of a local hospital trust (ASL Sant'Anna and Sabastiano of Caserta) to procure 'favours' for her party (Del Porto 2008: III); this led directly to her husband's ministerial resignation with withdrawal of UDEUR support for the governing centre-left coalition, so the fall of the government led by Romano Prodi, premature dissolution of parliament and, subsequent new general elections (Mastella and his party recently joined Berlusconi's centre-right coalition at the EU elections).

The second is potentially more serious for its possible public health consequences: the so-called *emergenza rifiuti*, as a result of which domestic refuse was piling up in the city streets. It is a complicated affair, even if the initial idea was simple, but ambitious: use the refuse to produce energy, reducing costs, while liberating its disposal from *Camorra* clans' control: cooperation between a big company (IMPREGILO-Fibe), the national government and the specially-created Emergency Commission was initiated in 1994 specifically to that end, but exactly the opposite occurred. It was due to a combination of circumstances: *Camorra* control of landfill sites, equipment and personnel; and public protests against the sites chosen for the clean, green, energy-generating incinerators to be built, causing delay to their completion. This was all to the reciprocal convenience of those concerned (Gomez 2008: 67–70), which naturally led to rapid saturation of existing landfill sites and so appeasement with *Camorra* clans was considered inevitable. Bassolino is claimed to have declared: 'Here you need a General, a soldier or a policeman. Because, if we continue to do something, we shall end up either in jail or bankrupt' (Bonini 2008: 17). On 2 February 2008, the preliminary hearing against Bassolino and 26 defendants on charges of fraud and deception, which they vigorously denied, started, and quickly adjourned, while refuse continued to pile up in the streets and the population began to raise barricades in a number of districts. Many groups took advantage of Prime Minister Berlusconi's decision to hold a Cabinet meeting in the city to address the question, to protest and visit 'mob justice' on gypsies, burning down a camp on the outskirts, after the police had moved the inhabitants for their protection. Finally, on 17 December 2008, after a local administrator had committed suicide, thirteen politicians (including two deputies), civil servants, a senior policeman and a previously convicted businessman (Alfredo Romeo), were arrested on charges of corruption and criminal association of what has been called the 'Romeo system'. The investigating magistrates claim that he created a 'business committee', in which a network of politicians and civil servants, both national and local, supplied him with advance confidential information enabling him to win public maintenance and property management contracts, not only in Naples, but also in Rome, Milan, Venice and Florence. Indeed, as an observer has explained:

> The Neapolitan scene demonstrates that it is no longer politics which imposes the price of corruption on the firm. It is the businessman who engages the politician; creates him from nothing, flatters him, directs him and fixes his goals and programmes, corrupts and appropriates him as though he was his thing. Politicians appear as poor little figures in the businessman's hands. He supports all the politician's ambitions and desires: the latter elbow each other, 'as in every self-respecting harem' […].
>
> The 'Sultan' [Alfredo Romeo] […] is generous. He gives work to friends, wives, sons, close relatives; he opens his purse with a consultancy or an insurance contract. He indicates a firm to which to give a subcontract. Sometimes ready money appears, but the real stakes are something else: make a District Councillor a City Councillor. A City Councillor an MP. An MP an Under-Secretary of State to be manipulated like a puppet
>
> (D'Avanzo 2008: 6)

The scandal has been likened to a 'new Bribesville' (*Il Giornale*, 18 December 2008: 1). It reopened the moral question in the new centre-left Democratic Party. Not surprisingly, moreover, an exasperated Mayor of Naples, Rosa Russo Jervellino, has now lost patience with the deteriorating political situation, announcing: 'either this tarantella ends or spring elections' (*RAI News*, 5 February 2008). However, we should not forget that such scandals in the 'Second Republic' are by no means confined to Naples and the South (in general, on the 'problems' of political and social ruling elites see the opening chapter by Carboni).

The Neapolitan *Camorra* today

When Bassolino left the Mayoralty in 2001 to become President of the Region (Campania), the question remained: had the *Camorra* changed? Had it been eliminated or, if not, weakened? Looking more closely at its organizational structure, activities and relationship with politics, it is clear that much has remained the same; there is more continuity than change. What change there has been, is due not to the state's anti-*Camorra* strategy, but rather the result of the *Camorra*'s own modernization project.

In 2006, it was estimated that in the city and province of Naples, 234 clans were active (Iannuzzo 2006: 14), an increase of more than double since 1992. A dichotomy between the city clans and those in the hinterland still exists. The balance of power has now shifted towards the city clans which are more visible and powerful whereas the remnants of the Alfieri Confederation and the *Casalesi* clan have been rather quiet but this does not mean that they are not active. Indeed, 2008 represented a difficult year for the *Casalesi* clan when the state systematically targeted it in order to dismantle it. The arrest of Giuseppe Setola, an important member of the clan, on 15 January 2009, marked another victory for the state and it appeared as though the clan was being brought to its knees, but one has to ask whether it is only a question of time before it reorganizes with new leaders and new economic activities.

The decade between 1993 and 2003 and beyond was a period of great violence in Naples. There were many wars (for example, the *faide di Scampia* in 2004–2005, and the *faide della Sanità* in 2005–2006) for territorial control and economic dominance. The clans of Naples fought very hard to control the latest drug routes and markets. Although the media highlighted the excessive violence and murders (with Naples often described as a 'Wild West' by the national media) they were nothing new and, indeed, this was a continuation with the past. In fact, Naples was more violent between 1983–1992 (1,749 murders) than between 1993–2002 (1,227). In 2007, there were 85 *Camorra* murders in the province of Naples compared to 59 in 2008 (whereas in the province of Caserta, there was 1 in 2007 and 17 in 2008). What might be new was that there have been many more innocent victims caught in the cross-fire and also the use of minors in drugs' transactions and murders.

The structure of the *Camorra* is still as flexible and loose as it was before. Every time there is an attempt to impose a hierarchy, it is dismantled by rivals. Clans and cartels are constantly regrouping, each time lasting as long as the drug deal, and then on to the next one. There is no new fragility; there are just families, clans, groupings and alliances all seeking to survive.

The role of women in *Camorra* clans has changed slightly. They have always been there but they are now more visible. Between 1993–2008, they became strikingly more visible and more violent (Roberti 2008). This is something new. This may be due to the fact that an important part of the male leadership of the *Camorra* has been in prison since 1995 and therefore, the wives, sisters and daughters came to the fore, taking over the reins of the clan in order to guarantee its survival (Allum 2007). This demonstrated that women can be criminal bosses in their own right.

In terms of economic activities, new and less risky ones are being undertaken. All *Camorra* clans are still involved in extortion and drugs trafficking, but they have also become involved in making and selling counterfeit goods which are less visible but which use extensive legal and illegal business networks.

Three other changes have taken place which are worth noting in terms of activity: first, the *Camorra* has developed a clear anti-state's witness (*pentito* in Italian) strategy to protect itself against the state, either by intimidating or murdering relatives of *pentiti* or by planting false *pentiti* who invent information. Second, the *Camorra* is exporting itself to Europe whereas previously this had been in the direction of Latin America. Third, we have had the rapid development of the *ecomafia* phenomenon since 1993. *Camorra* clans are, as noted above, now involved in environmental crimes, for example, the management of recycled toxic waste (Legambiente 2007: 103). Particularly active in this sector have been the *Casalesi* clan in Caserta as recently confirmed by the *pentito* Gaetano Vassallo.

In terms of the *Camorra*'s relationship with politics, it can be argued that nothing has changed despite some important trials involving politicians of the First Republic: the Maglio trial saw the conviction of Francesco Patriarca and Vincenzo Meo among others but the acquittal of Antonio Gava and the Spartacus II trial which investigated the *Casalesi* clan's relationship with local politicians. This relationship may not be visible today, but the Camorra is still very active in local government in the hinterland of Naples. Since 1991, more than 75 councils in Campania and more than 45 in the province of Naples (14 twice) have been dissolved for Camorra infiltration as well as a local health authority and, although it may have slowed down, there is still clearly a symbiotic relationship based on clientelism, as has always been the case (Roberti 2006: 11). The parties might have changed, but the *Camorra* is still managing to push its political agenda locally. Between 2000–2007, thirty local councils alone in Campania were dissolved for Camorra infiltration.

Conclusion

It is clear that the 'Renaissance of Naples' proclaimed by former mayor Antonio Bassolino, appears to have had little effect on political praxis. Clientelism and organized crime have continued to flourish with highs and lows, according to the seasons, as the scandals break, despite intervention by the national political authorities, but even these have been intermittent. The reasons appear to be as much national as local. The latter turn largely on the inability of Bassolino's second administration and the subsequent ones of Riccardo Marone and Jervolino to bring to fruition important medium-term territorial projects (e.g. Bagnoli, S. Giovanni, NE zones) or resolve the personal security situation and refuse problems of Naples.

The national reasons concern the political rupture provoked by the initial Bribesville scandal. As Briquet (2007) has argued persuasively, what was seen at the time of the scandal as the heroic struggle of magistrates and others against the 'criminal deficiencies' of the political class of the First Republic turned out to have been, on analysis, the opportunity, in the new political climate created by the end of the Cold War, for what he calls 'a re-composition of the field of partisan representation' (Briquet 2007: 334). The magistracy's fight against endemic corruption in the name of a higher civic and democratic virtue enabled a younger, and largely excluded, group of politicians to replace the old one in office. However, there was no intrinsic reason why the new group of politicians should be any more virtuous than its predecessors. Indeed, there were structural reasons, and not just personal, ethical ones, which explain why this was unlikely to be the case. The most significant among these was the further degeneration of the 'catch-all' type of party.

In short, since the Clean Hands operations of the 1990s, the structure of Italian political parties has been replaced with personal 'machines', what Calise (2000:

5) has called 'the personal party', such that the corps of permanent salaried officials (the so-called *quadri*) have disappeared. This development is part of an European-wide trend of declining party membership and activism; hence the new parties are increasingly dependent on public funding, which has been exacerbated in Italy's case, first by the ending of foreign funding and subsequently by the scandals (see also the specific question of accessibility and management of the EU Structural Funds which are here analyzed by Milio). It made legitimate business reticent to contribute to party funding. The result is that the party activists and the propaganda have been taken over by elected local councillors (communal, provincial and regional), strengthening the link with the 'personalization' of politics and clientelism.

In the past, the would-be professional politician in the main parties started life as a salaried party official, who made his career by being elected to local office and, if successful, eventually to national office. If unsuccessful, he returned to his job (and salary) of party official. This *cursus* is no longer available because the parties lack funds to support a full-scale organizational apparatus, so today the defeated or retiring professional politician needs to be rewarded for his political commitment with appointment to the salaried presidencies or executive posts of local public agencies, where he is expected to use his power to advance his party's interests, or with well-paid consultancies, which can be, and are, used for the same ends.

This system of power and rewards (e.g. *Doroteismo*) existed previously, but more as an inducement; today it has become a necessity. Indeed, it has become generalized – what Calise (2000: 5) has named 'partyless partyocracy' – because alternative resources are much less readily available, if at all, than in the not so distant past. Not only a party's power and prestige, but crucially its funding, depends on electoral success. Politicians and aspiring politicians require funds and if the 'new' parties often lack them, businessmen and *Camorra* bosses do not. This simple economic fact is fundamental in explaining the survival of patronage politics and 'clientelist' practices as well as the continued interface between organized crime and politics that we first encountered in the First Republic and still see today in Second Millennium Naples.

References

Allum, F. (2006) *Camorristi, Politicians and Businessmen*, Leeds: Northern Universities Press.
—— (2007) 'Women Doing it for Themselves or Standing in for Men in the Neapolitan Camorra', in G. Findaci (ed.) *Women and the Mafia*, Amsterdam: Springer.
Allum, P. (2005) *La Repubblica in bilico*, Naples: L'Ancora.
Bonini, C. (2008) 'Prezzi di favore e appalti di facciata', *La Repubblica*, 6 February.
Brancaccio, L. (1999) 'Strategie di consenso politico a Bagnoli (1980–1992)', in C. Merletti (ed.) (a cura di) *Politica e società in Italia*, Milan: F. Angeli.
—— (2002) 'Potere personale e clientelismo a Napoli', *Meridione, Sud e Nord nel mondo*, 1(2), March–April.

Briquet, J.L. (2007) *Mafia, Justice et Politique en Italie. L'Affaire Andreotti dans la crise de la République (1992–2004)*, Paris : Editions Karthala.

Buonanno, P. and Leonida, L. (2009) 'Non-market effects of education on crime: Evidence from Italian regions', *Education of Economics Review*, 28(1), pp. 11–17.

Calise, M. (2000) *Il partito personale*, Bari: Laterza.

Commissione Antimafia (1993) *Rapporto sulla Camorra*, Rome: Camera dei Deputati.

Corte di Assise di Napoli (2000) 'Processo 11/95 nei confronti di Archetti Biagi + 77', *Sentenza del 28 Novembre.* 2000.

Del Porto, D. (2008) 'Ma il GIP: "indizi granitici". Caso Mastella rilancia le accuse dei PM sammaritani', *La Repubblica* (Naples local section), 5 February.

D'Avanzo, G. (2008) 'L'inchiesta: Il sistema Romeo padrone della città', *La Repubblica*, 18 December.

Geronimo [Paolo Cirino Pomicino] (2002) *Dietro le quinte. La crisi della politica della Seconda Repubblica*, Milan: Mondadori.

Gomez, P. (2008) 'Quanti politici finiti nella spazzatura', *L'Espresso*, 31 January.

Iannuzzo, A. (2006) *Napoli in Guerra. Analisi del fenomeno camorristico napoletano*, Naples: Cuzzolin Editore.

Jamieson, A. (2000) *The Antimafia: Italy's Fight Against Organized Crime*, Basingstoke: Palgrave.

Legambiente (2007) *Rapporto Ecomafia. I numeri e le Storie della criminalità ambiente*, Florence: Edizione Ambiente.

Luccarelli, O. (2001) 'La syndrome dei portavoti', *La Repubblica* (Naples local section), 24 April.

Mammone, A. (2008) 'Il "malessere" del Sud e la Calabria dimenticata', *Il Ponte,* LXIV(10): 35–8.

McIntosh, C. (1973) 'The Growth of Racketeering', *Economy and Society*, 2(1): 33–69.

Marino, G. (1993) *Bella e mala di Napoli*, Bari: Laterza.

Pizzorno, A. (1991) *Le radici della politica assoluta e altri saggi*, Milan: Feltrinelli.

Roberti F. (2006) 'Liste inquinate come in tutte le elezioni', *Il corriere del Mezzogiorno.* 24 May.

—— (2008) 'La ferocia delle donne di camorra', *Il Messaggero*, 4 February.

Rumiz, P. (2001) 'Napoli, Rosa la dama di ferro sfida l'armata di Martiusciello', *La Repubblica*, 7 May.

Sales, I. (1998) *La camorra, le camorre*, Rome: Editori Riuniti.

—— (2006), *Le strade della violenza. Malviventi e bande di camorra a Napoli*, Naples: L'Ancora.

Part V

Economy and political economy

15 Industrialization, convergence and governance

Alfonsina Iona, Leone Leonida and Giuseppe Sobbrio

Summary

This chapter analyzes the relationship between industrialization, convergence and governance in Italy and discusses a number of interesting facts. First, we show that the Italian economy has two long-run equilibria, which are essentially due to the different level of industrialization of the northern regions with respect to the southern regions. Second, we show that these equilibria converge over the period 1960–1971 and diverge afterwards. We argue that the convergence process of southern and northern Italian regions ended because of the slowing down in the industrialization process in the southern regions and because of the presence of inadequate political and economic institutions, especially at regional level. In our opinion, in order to address effectively the lack of industrialization in the southern regions, more adequate governance is needed at the regional level. However, we are sceptical about the possibility that such governance may be put in place because of the presence of a number of obstacles, such as the scarcity of resources, the short-run nature of the political cycle and, more importantly, the fragile situation of southern regions.

Introduction

Italy is considered a dualistic economy with a divergence pattern between the north and the south of the country. The 2008 report by SVIMEZ shows that southern Italy has been growing at a lower rate than central and northern Italy over the previous six years. According to the report, it is the southern economy that shows signs of major difficulty, made all the more visible because of the upward trends of employment and industrialization in the central and northern regions. It is well known that the economy of the southern regions represents a case of missing industrialization, in the sense that it is an economy substantially based on the agricultural and service sectors. This is a fact of the Italian economic dualism, and it is also very likely to drive the increasing industrialization gap, registered over the last six years, between Italy and its main European competitors, such as Germany, France and Spain. From this picture it seems that the Italian economy is finding it quite hard to keep pace not only with the rapid development of the global economy but also with the relatively modest dynamics of European countries.

The problems that Italy faces indicate that industry remains the only potential engine of development and growth, especially for the southern regions, and therefore it is necessary to analyze the conditions so that Italian industry can overcome its current difficulties and reach adequate levels of competitiveness. It is worth noting that, despite the importance of the industrialization process in catching up with the more-developed economies, its theoretical and empirical role has been largely ignored in studies of growth and convergence (De la Fuente 1997, 2000, Durlauf and Quah 1999, Islam 2003), and in particular by the 'growth accounting approach' studies (e.g. Temple 1999).

This is essentially due to the use of the neoclassical growth approach in the study of growth and convergence dynamics. On the one hand, such a framework is certainly useful in the analysis of developed economies; on the other hand, it may be misleading when both developed and under-developed regions are analyzed, as in the case of Italy. In the former case, the question is whether the neoclassical approach should be rejected in order to move to more refined theories of endogenous growth. In the latter case, instead, different questions should be addressed. For example: is the growth path of the economy characterized by multiple equilibria? And if so, are the different regions converging to the same equilibrium? What is the impact of industrialization on the convergence and growth process? In addressing these questions Italy appears to be a particularly interesting case study for three reasons: first, Italy can be regarded as a developed economy as its production level is classified among that of the top ten world economies; second, in spite of some industrialized regions, others represent a case of *missing industrialization*; third, all industrialized regions are geographically located in the centre-north, whereas the less industrialized regions are geographically located in the south of Italy. The latter experienced a slowing down of the industrialization process during the late 1960s and, since then, its ability to create new employment has been poor. At first glance, it seems that the differential gross domestic product per capita across Italian regions cannot be imputed to coordination failures among political institutions, as suggested by Peters (2004) for the case of world economies, because Italian regions share the same central government and all other economic and political institutions. However, this might be no longer true if we consider that since 1971 the governance was shared with a new institution – the region – and the majority of southern regions were seen as fragile institutions with weak and inefficient governance, often even connected with criminal organizations. Why a different level of development persists between the two areas of Italy is one of the main questions we want to answer in this study. To this aim, we study the patterns of growth and convergence of Italian regions over the period 1960–2005, and their relationship with the governance and the industrialization process.

Our study shows a number of interesting facts. First, we show that the Italian economy is characterized by multiple steady states. This is an important issue because in this case the policy makers should first identify the reasons for the presence of multipla equilibria and then try to address this problem with adequate policies. Indeed, in such a case, it may be not enough for the poorest economies to converge with the richest ones.

Second, we show that the convergence process across Italian regions ended before 1975. This is important because the bulk of the literature places the end of the convergence process at this year as a consequence of an external shock to the Italian economy, i.e. the 1973 oil crisis. If the convergence process slowed down before 1975, we can say that the oil crisis did contribute to the slowing down of the convergence process, but it was not its main driver. Moreover, we discuss whether industrialization is at the root of all the dynamics above by analysing the different channels through which it affects the economic growth path. For example, we discuss whether the degree of industrialization matters and whether innovation, enforced mainly in the industrial sector, spreads across regions. If this is the case, indeed, the Italian government should propose an appropriate industrial policy able to boost the industrial sector of the southern regions through, for example, investment in infrastructure rather than focusing on alternative strategies such as moving resources to the service sector. Finally, we discuss the presence of *fragile states* in the south of Italy that hinders the implementation of an effective economic policy.

In particular, regarding one result – that Italian regions seem to converge over the period 1960–1971 and diverge afterwards – we argue that in the case of Italy the standard framework of 'growth accounting' is encompassed by growth models augmented with factors accounting for the industrialization process, which plays a key role in explaining the patterns of growth and convergence. We argue that the convergence process between the south and north of Italy has ended not only because of the slowing down in the industrialization process in the southern regions but also because of the presence of an inadequate economic policy due to the region's political instability, especially since 1972 and even more after 1984 because of the closure of the Cassa per il Mezzogiorno (Fund for the South) which started a progressive ending of the central governmental intervention and a shift back to regional and local governments.

Political stability is, in fact, crucial for the economic development of a country. It affects the administrative efficiency and the successful implementation of long-term policies. Indeed, as shown by Carboni, this volume, a high level of government stability appears in some Italian regions, having encouraged politicians to plan and implement long-term rather than short-term policies. Similarly, Milio (also in this volume) points out that the worst performing Italian regions were those experiencing extreme government instability with presidents, cabinet members and executive managers only lasting short periods. The consequences of this have been the lack of coherence and continuity in management and programming, the absence of monitoring and a discretional allocation of the expenditure by politicians caring only about their personal achievements over their short terms (see Allum's chapter on Naples) and disregarding long-term policies.

We believe that our findings provide clear policy insights. In particular, on the one hand, they raise the necessity of having political classes which are more efficient, disadvantaged by the link – tacit or not – with Mafia organizations (see

Parini, this volumen, on the case of Mafia in Calabria and beyond) and focusing on long-term policies. On the other hand, they call for a portfolio of more effective long-run economic policies that may increase the total productivity and help the regions to converge.

However, such policies are highly unlikely for two main reasons. First, the Italian economy is experiencing a period of low growth and scarcity of resources. Second, the political cycle is too short to allow such policies to display their long-run effects: politicians need results within a time period that is too short to allow a strategy of development to properly take place. Also, this is even more true in the south of Italy where the efficiency of regional governments is traditionally inferior to those in the north.

The remainder of the chapter proceeds as follows. Section two analyses the convergence process across Italian regions; shows the extent of sector imbalance between the two main areas of the country and reviews some evidence in favour of the hypothesis that regional growth is driven by industrialization. Section three discusses the need for a long-run strategy of growth. Section four provides some concluding remarks.

Convergence, sector imbalance and industrialization in Italy

The issue of convergence – that is whether low per capita income economies tend to catch up with high per capita income economies – has been largely debated in economics. As in past research, in our study we use the per capita GDP (at constant 2000 prices) as a measure of the (average) welfare of the Italian regions. Our data involve a first series (1980–2005) provided by ISTAT (Istituto Nazionale di Statistica) and a second series (1960–1993) provided by the Centre for North–South Economic Research (CRENOS).

Panel A in Figure 15.1 reports the path of per capita GDP for each region.[1] The picture shows that, in terms of per capita GDP, at the beginning of the period, Umbria and Abruzzi belonged to southern Italy; whereas over time they converged with the richer regions. All other southern regions register a per capita GDP considerably smaller than the richer ones and none of them displays a clear tendency to take off. This is more evident when studying relative positions. Panel B, in fact, shows that in 2005 regions are closer than they were in 1960. Moreover, while regions experienced a strong convergence process until early 1970s, this process seems to slow down thereafter and the difference between the per capita GDP of the south and the north seems to increase. In fact, the ANOVA analysis indicates that the variance decreases until 1971 and has a positive trend afterwards (see panels C and D).[2] This trend is that the northern regions decrease, while the variance of the southern regions is rather stable.

The convergence between the north and south of Italy until 1971 is highlighted in the second column of Table 15.1, which reports their relative per capita GDP, averaged across seven intervals of five years each. From this column it is evident that the distance between the north and south decreases until 1975 and increases afterwards. The same table shows that both parts of Italy experienced a decline in

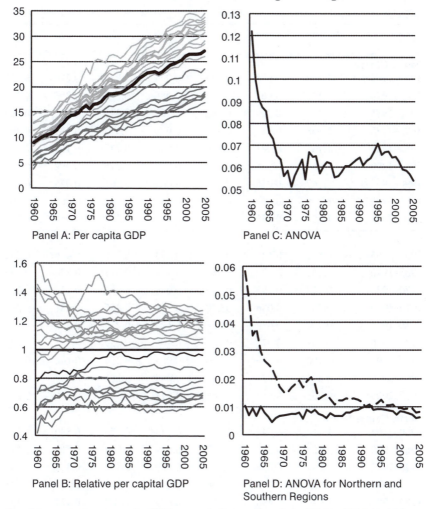

Panel A: Per capita GDP

Panel C: ANOVA

Panel B: Relative per capital GDP

Panel D: ANOVA for Northern and Southern Regions

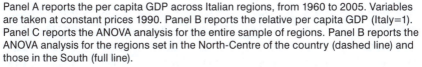

Panel A reports the per capita GDP across Italian regions, from 1960 to 2005. Variables are taken at constant prices 1990. Panel B reports the relative per capita GDP (Italy=1). Panel C reports the ANOVA analysis for the entire sample of regions. Panel B reports the ANOVA analysis for the regions set in the North-Centre of the country (dashed line) and those in the South (full line).

Figure 15.1 Per capita GDP distribution across Italian regions and ANOVA analalysis

the fraction of the value-added produced by the agricultural sector; moreover, the two regions show an increase in the value-added produced by the manufacturing sector over the period 1970–1975. These fractions decline in subsequent periods and this decline, mainly caused by the 1973 oil crisis, seems to be at the root of the reversal in the convergence path (Paci and Saba 1998, Terrasi 1999).

The gap between the north and south of Italy is also supported by the evidence that, over the period 1960–1965, the south registers a greater value-added in the

Table 15.1 Sectoral imbalances and relative per capita GDP across Italian regions

Period	Relative Y/N	VA_A/VA	VA_I/VA	I_A/I	I_I/I	L_A/L	L_I/L
North-Centre							
1960–1965	1.154	0.078	0.345	0.099	0.239	0.270	0.353
1965–1970	1.128	0.061	0.355	0.086	0.223	0.206	0.372
1970–1975	1.131	0.048	0.362	0.060	0.241	0.149	0.380
1975–1980	1.158	0.043	0.350	0.071	0.273	0.121	0.366
1980–1985	1.155	0.041	0.336	0.078	0.277	0.106	0.335
1985–1990	1.155	0.038	0.330	0.072	0.275	0.092	0.303
1990–1995	1.167	0.036	0.329	0.060	0.261	0.075	0.290
1995–2000	1.169	0.036	0.327	0.061	0.249	0.062	0.281
2000–2005	1.157	0.033	0.315	0.056	0.238	0.050	0.267
South							
1960–1965	0.637	0.143	0.239	0.133	0.246	0.466	0.232
1965–1970	0.680	0.122	0.262	0.105	0.211	0.398	0.250
1970–1975	0.710	0.103	0.273	0.088	0.284	0.332	0.260
1975–1980	0.708	0.086	0.270	0.116	0.255	0.281	0.260
1980–1985	0.704	0.082	0.258	0.129	0.235	0.223	0.251
1985–1990	0.705	0.072	0.251	0.106	0.239	0.188	0.229
1990–1995	0.700	0.069	0.250	0.085	0.269	0.166	0.228
1995–2000	0.692	0.071	0.248	0.088	0.251	0.142	0.227
2000–2005	0.705	0.065	0.248	0.078	0.238	0.116	0.230
North-Centre/South							
1960–1965	1.813	0.542	1.446	0.745	0.973	0.580	1.524
1965–1970	1.658	0.500	1.357	0.814	1.054	0.519	1.490
1970–1975	1.594	0.464	1.326	0.680	0.847	0.448	1.461
1975–1980	1.636	0.495	1.296	0.608	1.069	0.429	1.408
1980–1985	1.640	0.498	1.300	0.609	1.180	0.477	1.333
1985–1990	1.638	0.526	1.315	0.685	1.148	0.487	1.322
1990–1995	1.668	0.529	1.319	0.709	0.968	0.453	1.270
1995–2000	1.689	0.504	1.318	0.690	0.990	0.432	1.237
2000–2005	1.640	0.509	1.272	0.721	0.999	0.433	1.162

Relative Y/N is the relative per capita GDP (Italy=1). VA_A/VA and VA_I/VA are the fractions of Value Added in agriculture and in manufacturing respectively; I_A/I and I_I/I are the fractions of investments in agriculture and manufactoring respectively. All variables are measured at constant prices 1990. L_A/L and L_I/L are the fractions of employment in agriculture and manufacturing respectively.

agriculture sector and lower production in the manufacturing sector with respect to the north. Also, the investment in agriculture tends to decline over time from 1960 onwards in the northern regions, while in the southern regions it starts to decrease only in the second half of the 1980s. Moreover, manufacturing employment in northern regions is always higher than in the south; employment in agriculture is higher in the south than in the north.

Accordingly, investment in the industrial sector in the southern regions is always lower than across northern regions; except from its peak in the early 1970s, as a result of a policy of massive public transfers to firms located in the south. In summary, northern regions seem to have experienced a stronger industrialization process with respect to the southern regions.

Williamson (1965), by looking optimistically at the sector and geographical imbalances as growth-boosting devices, suggests that southern regions would catch up in a second stage of an Italian development process. Williamson explicitly links the level of national development with the process of absolute convergence across regional economies, introducing the hypothesis that the lower the degree of development of a nation, the faster some of its regions will grow and diverge from each other. The laggards would catch up in a second stage, by taking advantage of the progress of the fast-growing regions: 'the evidence on Italian regional dualism suggests optimistic projections regarding the future size of the north–south problem as Italy passes into mature stages of growth and rapidly ascends into high-income classes' (Williamson 1965: 28). In his analysis, therefore, sector imbalance will cause convergence.

This has not been the case for Italy. Nowadays, although Italy is considered a developed country, southern regions have not caught up with northern ones, and it seems unrealistic to suppose that a convergence process will take place in the near future. Del Monte and Giannola (1997) suggest that the Williamson (1965) model may also provide theoretical grounds for a dualistic economy to induce divergence, rather than convergence, across regions. They suggest that, if the process of capital accumulation has some particular features (for example, non-decreasing returns to scale) or if the production function differs across regional economies, economic activities may concentrate instead of spread across regions. This, in turn, may lead to the observed divergence pattern between the north and the south of the country.

The observation that the economic systems of the regions located in the south of Italy are unbalanced towards the agricultural sector is another well-known fact of Italian economic dualism. However, even though it is acknowledged that 'virtually every country that experienced rapid growth of productivity and living standards over the last 200 years has done so by industrializing' (Murphy *et al.* 1989: 1003), to our knowledge there are no studies that quantify the effects of such imbalances on the growth rate and the convergence path of Italian regions.

In a different study we analysed the role of industrialization in the growth process of Italian regions by investigating whether the standard model of growth is empirically superior to a model accounting for the industrialization process in explaining regional growth.[3] To perform our empirical study we compared two alternative models of growth: the well-known 'growth accounting model' as, for example, in Bairam and McRae (1999), and a variant of the 'Dowrick and Gemmell model' (1991).

Results of this study are in favour of the *non-linear conditional convergence*: regions tend to converge to their equilibrium at a decreasing rate with a speed of convergence that depends on the initial position of the region, that is, on its distance from the equilibrium. Moreover, we find that industrialization matters as it affects regional growth through several channels. First, the greater the distance from a leading region, the higher the growth rate: this evidence is in favour of the hypothesis that industrialization of poor regions follows from technological progress of rich regions. However, there is no evidence of spillovers between agriculture and industry in the same regions. Second, the higher the level of industrialization of a region and the better its ability to shift resources to the manufacturing sector, the higher the growth rate of the per capita GDP. In sum, industrialization and sector imbalances matter: growth across Italian regions is not explained by factor accumulation only. Finally, when growth processes are analyzed over 1960–1975 and 1975–2005, the analysis shows that the earlier period is characterized by strong positive effects of sector imbalances and industrialization when compared with the second period and with the whole period.

The need for a long-run growth strategy

It is worth mentioning that, in the standard analysis of convergence (see Solow 1956), one of the reasons why regional economies may not tend, in the long run, to the same equilibrium level of per capita GDP is that the market for goods and services do not work properly and therefore cannot transmit appropriate incentives to economic agents. In this situation, the intervention of the government should be directed to remove such obstacles through adequate policies, which would allow the market to transmit incentives properly.

In the case of Italian regions, we have found that there is a natural and structural tendency to diverge and this is due to the different level of industrialization across regions. For this reason, the Italian government should pursue a policy directed to increase the total factor of productivity per worker. Needless to say, we do not have much to add to the (long) list of existing problems in Italy. On the one hand, it is known that there exists a positive correlation between growth and civic tradition and, since Putnam (1993), it is thought that civic tradition is inferior to that of northern Italy. This feature also reinforces the effects of the presence of criminal organizations in southern Italy, which is another obstacle to effective entrepreneurship (Buonanno and Leonida 2008; see also other chapters in this volume for analyses on the impact of local Mafias). On the other hand, in Southern Italy the infrastructure endowment is still very poor and this, in turn, implies that firms located in the south of the country have higher costs (see, for example, Ferri and Mattesini 1997), and the list is much longer than this (see, for example, De Cecco 2007). Among others, North (1991) points out that laws can be similar in the two areas; however, informal rules can still be different. Following this approach it is easy to note that in southern Italy habits and civic sense are different from in the north.

Moreover, since 1972 Italy has been divided into autonomous regions, each one with a Parliament and a power to spend regional taxes and grants from the central government. Clearly, efficiency at the local and regional levels in southern Italy has been generally lower than in other regions and in many cases their governance has been 'fragile'. This would reflect some views that giving more resources can be a 'mistake' (Easterly 2007) or may worsen the governance itself (Rajan and Subramanian 2007). Moreover, it is not clear whether the above are causes or consequences of the absence of development.

In our opinion, what our results suggest is that southern regions need a proper economic development policy and better governance (and this appears clear also in other contributions in this volume). Indeed, the convergence process ended while the central government intervention in the south was slowing down, at the end of 1970, and many resources where instead managed by the regions. In that period, in order to speed up the long-run convergence process, the Italian government set up the already mentioned Cassa Del Mezzogiorno, a public institution that spreads massive investment in the south of Italy, not only in terms of infrastructure but also as grants to firms who decide to invest there.

The intervention itself has not been free of criticism. According to many authors, this type of intervention has created firms not really linked to the economic characteristics of the areas and considered 'cathedrals in the desert' or financed 'marginal' firms. The former were firms operating in capital intensive sectors and located in regions with relatively cheap labour costs; the latter were entrepreneurs whose activities were marginal and dependent on subsidies. Both types of firms were not able to sustain the effects of the oil crisis. There is also a general consensus about the idea that in many cases investments were only financed by grants. In other cases, firms got money and then closed soon afterwards. Scandals and corruption were involved. But all seemed worse after the decentralization of the power to regions: the industrialization policy failed after that decentralization. In 2007, the per capita expenditure in the southern regions was higher than their tax revenues, due to a large number of grants. Also, the southern regions doubled the current capital expenditure with respect to the north. This means that in the south the expenditure crowded out the investment due to the disastrous governance. Instead, with the centralized system this intervention could contribute to reducing the gap across the regions. Put differently, the observation that industrialization had positive and negative effects should not be used to discard the industrialization policy, but should suggest that we need to think carefully about governance models.

The question therefore is: is such a policy possible? It has already been shown that the current economic policy is dysfunctional (De Cecco 2007). We want to add that an industrial policy differently managed might contribute to industrialization but it must be certainly a long-run policy. In a word, Italy needs a development strategy. However, the effects of such a policy are likely to take place in more than five years, and the government needs results in a shorter time span. In other words, the political cycle is shorter than the time this policy requires to produce its effects. This, obviously, reduces the likelihood of ever seeing such a policy.

Conclusions

This chapter studies the link between industrialization, convergence and governance in Italy. Our study contributes to the extant literature in many respects. First, it shows that the Italian economy has two long-run equilibria essentially due to the different levels of industrialization of the regions located in the centre-north with respect to those located in the south of the country. We argue that a 'standard growth accounting framework' is encompassed, at least in the Italian case, by a model that accounts for the effects of resource reallocation between manufacturing and agriculture. Industrialization plays a key role in explaining patterns of growth and convergence in Italy. It impacts the growth rate of Italian regions in a relevant way through the industrial sector, spillover effects across industrial sectors and the shift of resources from agriculture to manufacturing so that regions having a relatively large agricultural sector tend to grow at a lower rate.

Second, these equilibria converge over the period 1960–1971 but diverge afterwards. We argue that industrialization plays a key role in this divergence process, as it creates a two-speed economic system, though external shocks may have reinforced such a process, because economic systems with different growth potential may respond differently to the same external shock. However, this is only one part of the story: the convergence process between the south and north of Italy has ended not only because of the slowing down in the industrialization process in the southern regions but also because of the presence of an inadequate economic policy due to regional political instability. To address effectively the problem of the missing industrialization of the southern regions, more adequate governance of the economic policy is overall needed. In particular, on the one hand, it is necessary to have political classes more efficient, free by any link with the Mafia's organizations (see Parini in this volume) and focusing on long-term policies. On the other hand, Italy needs more effective long-run economic policies. An effective development policy calls for a prolonged implementation, in line with the medium- to long-term objective of development of a competitive economy. It should involve a range of interventions as for example, policies to develop the services sector – tourism or similar – that might be seen as a complementary strategy of an effective industrial policy aimed at increasing the total factor of productivity and helping regions to converge; basic infrastructure policies, tax benefit policies, selective industrial policies, research and innovation policies and strategies in favour of human capital that could best contribute to bridge the productivity gap with the northern regions.

Nevertheless, we are sceptical with regard to the implementation of such governance of the economic policy because of many reasons like the scarcity of resources, the short-run nature of the political cycle and the fragile states of many southern regions.

Our final conclusion is that it is quite unlikely that the economic policy the Italian regions require will be put in place. This is because of a number of reasons, including the lower efficiency in the spending power of many 'fragile' southern regions and, most importantly, the difference between the times needed to implement such a policy and the time needed for the politicians to be re-elected.

Notes

1 The North of Italy consists of twelve regions, namely Piemonte, Valle D'Aosta, Lombardia, Trentino Alto-Adige, Friuli Venezia-Giulia, Veneto, Emilia Romagna, Liguria, Toscana, Umbria, Marche and Lazio. The South is usually obtained by averaging across the remaining eight regions: Abruzzo, Molise, Campania, Puglia, Basilicata, Calabria, Sicilia and Sardegna.
2 Ben-David (1994), Bernard and Durlauf (1995), Quah (1997) and Barro and Sala-i Martin (1991) suggest that the ANOVA analysis (Analysis of Variance) is quite informative. The variance is a measure of the dispersion of the group of economies under observation; therefore, the analysis of its trend series properties provides information about the convergence process. For example, a negative trend is taken as evidence in favour of the convergence hypothesis, since the dispersion of the sample is reducing; conversely, a positive trend is taken as evidence against this hypothesis. Economists refer to such analysis as the 's-convergence' analysis.
3 See our article in the special edition ('Italy in Chiaroscuro') edited by Mammone and Veltri and published by the *Journal of Modern Italian Studies* (2008)

References

Bairam, E.I. and McRae, S.D. (1999) 'Testing the convergence hypothesis: a new approach', *Economic Letters*, 64: 351–5.

Barro, R.J. and Sala-i-Martin, X. (1991) 'Convergence across states and regions', *Brookings Papers on Economics Activity*, 1: 1107–82.

Ben-David, D. (1994) 'Converging club and diverging economies', CEPR Discussion Papers 922.

Bernard, A. and Durlauf, S.N. (1995) 'Convergence in international output', *Journal of Applied Econometrics*, 10: 97–108.

Buonanno, P. and Leonida, L. (2008) 'Non market effects of education on crime: Evidence from Italian regions' *Economics of Education Review* 28(1), 11–17.

De Cecco, M. (2007) 'Italy's dysfunctional political economy', *West European Politics*, 30(4): 763–83.

De la Fuente, A. (1997) 'The empirics of growth and convergence: a selective review', *Journal of Economic Dynamic and Control*, 21: 23–73.

—— (2000) 'Convergence across countries and regions: theory and empirics', EIB Papers 2: 25–43.

Del Monte, A. and Giannola, A. (1997) *Istituzioni Economiche e Mezzogiorno*, Bologna: NIS.

Dowrick, S. and Gemmell, N. (1991) 'Industrialisation, catching up and economic growth: a comparative study across the world's capitalist economies', *The Economic Journal*, 101: 263–75.

Durlauf, S.N. and Quah, D.T. (1999) 'The new empirics of economic growth', in J. Taylor and M. Woodford (eds.) *Handbook of Macroeconomics*, Vol. 1A, Amsterdam: North-Holland.

Easterly, W. (2007) 'Was development assistance a mistake? *American Economic Review*, 97 (2): 328–32.

Ferri, G. and Mattesini, F. (1997) 'Finance, human capital and infrastructure. An empirical investigation on post-war Italian growth', Banca d'Italia Working Paper Series.

Graziani, A. (1979) 'Il Mezzogiorno nel quadro dell'economia Italiana', in A. Graziani and E. Pugliese (eds.) *Investimenti e Disoccupazione nel Mezzogiorno*, Bologna: Il Mulino.

Murphy, K., Shleifer, A. and Vishny, R. (1989) 'Industrialization and the Big Push', *Journal of Political Economy*, 97: 1003–26.

North, D.C. (1991) *Institutions, Institutional Change and Economic Performance*, Cambridge: Cambridge University Press.

Paci, R. and Saba, A. (1998) 'The empirics of regional economic growth in Italy, 1951–1993', *Rivista Internazionale di Scienze Economiche e Commerciali*, 5: 513–42.

Peters, B.G. (2004) 'Managing horizontal government. The politics of coordination', Research Paper 21, Canadian Centre for Management Development.

Putnam, R.D. (1993) *Making Democracy Work: Civic Traditions in Modern Italy*, Princeton: Princeton University Press.

Quah, D. (1997) 'Empirics for growth and distribution: stratification, polarization and convergence clubs', *Journal of Economic Growth*, 2: 27–59.

Rajan R.G. and Subramanian, A. (2007) 'Does Aid Affect Governance?', *American Economic Review, Papers and Proceedings,* 2: 322–327.

SVIMEZ (2008) 'Rapporto SVIMEZ 2008 sull'Economia del Mezzogiorno'.

Solow, R.M. (1956) 'A contribution to the theory of economic growth', *Quarterly Journal of Economics,* 70: 65–94.

Temple, J. (1999) 'The new growth evidence', *Journal of Economic Literature*, 37: 112–56.

Terrasi, M. (1999) 'Convergence and divergence across Italian regions', *The Annals of Regional Science,* 33: 491–510.

Williamson, J.G. (1965) 'Regional inequality and the process of national development: a description of the patterns', *Economic Development and Cultural Change,* 13: 3–84.

16 Twenty years of European funding

Italy is still struggling with implementation

Simona Milio

Summary

The Structural Funds (SFs) as the instrument for the European Union's cohesion policy were redefined in terms of their rules and regulations in 1988 and began financing the Regional Operational Programmes (ROP) in 1989. The SF's main target is Objective 1 regions, defined as those whose development is lagging behind, i.e. where the Gross Domestic Product per capita is at or below 75 per cent of the European Community average. From the beginning there have been significant differences between regions in implementing their Funds allocation and in respecting the principles that regulate cohesion policy. During the last decade in many EU countries it has emerged that states with weak administrative capacity are more likely to have serious problems with the mismanagement of SFs, or even with accessing them. This chapter aims to explore conditions under which SFs have been successful in other EU member states and what has failed in the Italian case. In order to identify the best practises which allow some member states and regions to perform better I will analyse four main dimensions which appear fundamental for SFs successful implementation, namely: (i) the actors that are involved in the SFs process; (ii) the context in which the implementation is performed; (iii) the rules and procedures that underpin SFs implementation; (iv) the political context.

Introduction

European Union cohesion policy has been implemented over a number of challenging years and has been the instrument enabling the delivery of the Lisbon and Gothenburg Agendas.[1] Three cycles have been completed – 1989–1993; 1994–1999; 2000–2006 – and recently a fourth period 2007–2013 has commenced.

The main target of the Structural Funds (SFs) is Objective 1 regions, defined as those whose development is lagging behind, i.e. where the Gross Domestic Product per capita is at or below 75 per cent of the Community average. The main goal is to support these disadvantaged regions to achieve sustainable development and full employment.

In the past, it has emerged in many EU countries that weak administrative capacity leads to significant problems with accessibility and management. This has led some member states (MS), such as Italy, to embark on a programme of institutional and administrative reform to increase their administrative capacity. Interestingly, along with administrative requirements it appears necessary to have certain political conditions to enable the continuity and coherence in administrative actions.

To investigate the Italian capacity to implement cohesion policy and the features required by both the administrative and political components, this chapter is divided into four sections. The first section introduces the principles and regulations of cohesion policy in order to understand the logic behind fund implementation. The second section investigates the main discrepancies that exist with the national approach to regional development. Section three examines the administrative and political bottlenecks that exist in Italy, describing the conditions which have lead to failures in EU fund expenditure and contrasting this with other successful EU MS. The concluding section proposes recommendations for improvements to the Italian scenario. Due to ongoing budgetary reviews, the issue of structural funding is becoming increasingly important. Evidence suggests that Italy is the second largest recipient of structural funding, however, Italy's failure to spend its allocation creates a weakened bargaining position for future funds. This is undoubtably a missed opportunity for a country which very much needs further investment in areas such as infrastructure.

Cohesion policy principles and regulations

The four SFs as the instruments of the EU cohesion policy were created in different periods. First, the European Regional Development Fund (ERDF) aims to reduce imbalances between regions of the Community by financing development projects in the poorer regions. Second, the European Social Fund (ESF) provides financial assistance to prevent and combat unemployment, as well as develop human resources and promote integration into the labour market. Third, the European Agricultural Guidance and Guarantee Fund (EAGGF) finances the EU's Common Agricultural Policy providing market support and promoting structural adjustments.[2] Finally, the Financial Instrument for Fisheries Guidance (FIFG) has grouped together the Community instruments for fisheries in order to support the adaptation and modernization of the sector's facilities. Along with SFs, a further instrument was created in 1994 (Council Regulation 1994), the Cohesion Fund (CF), to assist those countries whose Gross National Income (GNI) was below 90 per cent of the EU average – i.e. Spain, Ireland, Greece and Portugal. More specifically this fund was aimed at financing environmental and transport projects, as infrastructure in these two areas remains inadequate.

The major reform adopted in 1988 radically changed the largely isolated way in which the SFs had previously operated in favour of a global system of integration of their respective roles, working together towards the goal enunciated in Article 130a of the Single European Act (1986): 'reduce disparities between the various regions and the backwardness of the least-favoured regions'.[3] Since 1988, two other reforms, in 1993 and 1999, have strengthened the SFs regulation and principles and provided for greater allocation of funds. Indeed, the SFs contribution has grown from €8 billion per year in 1989 to €32 billion per year in 1999, to remain at about €28 billion per year until 2006 (EC 2001).

Despite this financial effort, the literature battles over the question whether Cohesion Policy is an instrument of distributive politics, side-payments to poorer member states, or a development tool – i.e. promoting or not economic convergence between regions. Controversial arguments suggest a very limited, and at times negligible, economic impact and little progression in terms of overcoming regional inequalities among regions (Keating 1995, Rodriguez-Pose 1998).

It has to be said that some progress has been made over the past 20 years, as suggested by the economic development in the largest beneficiaries of Cohesion Policy – Spain, Portugal, Greece and Ireland. These four MS have significantly reduced the gap with the rest of the EU.[4] Yet many authors remain sceptical of the direct relationship between SFs and GDP growth (Beutel 2002, Basile *et al.* 2001).

Clearly, the attempt to coordinate the various funding instruments was not easily achieved, and it required a long period of experimentation and socialization of administrative personnel on the benefits of coordination before the goal could be achieved. Monitoring SF investment and evaluation proved to be the most challenging aspects.

From the beginning there have been significant differences between regions in implementing their SF allocation and generally respecting the principles that regulate cohesion policy. For the purpose of understanding cohesion policy logic, I will present a brief analysis of all the regulations and dynamics that rule EU funding. In the section discussing the implementation gap, I will look at the implementation differences.

The European Council, on the basis of a proposal from the European Commission (EC) negotiated with the European Parliament, decides both the budget and rules governing the use of SFs. Consequently, each state or region formulates and gathers its proposals into a development plan to support the areas in difficulty and disadvantaged social groups. The plan is presented to and discussed with the EC for approval. After approval, the MS can draw two different typologies of programme: the Community Support Framework[5] (CSF) followed by an Operational Programme[6] (OP) or the Single Programming Document (SPD). The former, is the planning document used by the Objective 1 regions, whereas the latter comprises a single document containing the same information to be found in a CSF and OP, and is typically used by the Objective 2 areas or for Objective 1 programmes where the allocation is lower than, or does not substantially exceed, €1 billion (EC 1999).

Each programme is administered by a managing authority (MA)[7] which supervises its progress. The MA is supported by the recommended monitoring system to certify the expenditure, and by appointing an external evaluator. The

MAs inform the EC of this progress and provide it with evidence that the money is being used under the best possible conditions (certification of expenditure). The Commission examines the control systems that have been established and disburses the remainder of the contribution from the SFs accordingly.

This setting reinforces the decentralization process of SF implementation and implies that each level involved – i.e. national, regional and local – has an adequate institutional and administrative capacity to act accordingly to the system of SF regulations (Alphametrics Ltd 2003, Dimitrova 2002).

Based on the process described above and on recent research (Milio 2007, Boijmans 2003), administrative capacity is defined by four determinant actions: management, programming, monitoring and evaluation. These actions create a loop, which, if performed properly, leads to the correct implementation of the funds.

In light of the above, the major challenge for the MS is to reorganize national institutions and personnel[8] according to the multilevel approach focusing on the role played by institutions at the local level, in order to be able to:

1   Set up the Managing Authority responsible for the coordination of the overall programme;
2   Programme a multi-annual development plan based on a SWOT (strength, weakness, threat, opportunity) analysis to implement a coherent development strategy;
3   Comply with the specific monitoring indicators required to ensure that projects are implemented in line with agreed strategic priorities towards the achievement of the desired outcomes;
4   Meet the terms of the evaluation requirements, in particular as regards the ex-ante evaluation of the development plan, which is deemed necessary to identify the strategic area of interventions; the intermediate evaluation which identifies critical problems halfway through the implementation period, which may be adjusted; the ex-post evaluation that allows for lessons to be drawn in order to improve the subsequent planning period.

The Italian adaptation of cohesion policy

From rejection to adaptation

It seems clear that the success of EU cohesion policy is heavily dependent on both national and regional administrative bodies conforming to the Community's framework conditions if they want to benefit from the available financial aid.

To understand the Italian reaction to EU regulations we need to investigate the past 20 years and single out relevant discrepancies that have impeded successful implementation. There is evidence to suggest that the Mafia significantly hinders resource allocation. This chapter will not detail the Mafia's influence since this is extensively discussed both by Parini, and Allum and Allum, this volune.

In Italy the evolution of regional and cohesion policies has been deeply influenced by the presence of continuing macro-territorial differences between the north and south. The national authorities have always treated southern Italian regions – the Mezzogiorno – as a single territory with the same difficulties, cultural problems and political obstacles.

In 1950, a special fund, the Intervento Straordinario per il Mezzogiorno (Extraordinary Interventions for the Mezzogiorno), was created to provide a massive intervention of public support in those regions which were lagging behind (Cafiero 2000). The fund's management was assigned to a newly created and highly centralized state agency, the Cassa per il Mezzogiorno (Fund for the South; see also Iona *et al.* in this volume). This acted as an autonomous entity, having complete independence to implement the country's regional policy from 1950 to 1992. During this period various reforms gave the regions broad legal powers in territorial planning and economic intervention, but as Smyrl (1997: 293) notes: 'the means to carry out these policies were generally lacking'.

Therefore, until 1992 the southern regions were the beneficiaries of a national regional policy that was basically a sectorial development policy. It did not contain many features that had been built into the EU's cohesion policy approach: there was no long-term planning; a lack of individual regional knowledge led to a generalized distribution of expenditures over southern Italy rather than in target areas; monitoring or evaluation procedures were deficient (Trigilia 1992).

This highlights a clear overlap between the first cycle of SFs 1988–1993 and the end of the *Intervento Straordinario*. This transitional phase began with the closing of the Cassa in 1984, and was characterized by the progressive ending of central governmental intervention and a shift back to ordinary regional and local government procedure.

The changes took time to produce results. As shown by the SFs ex-post evaluation 1994–1999 (Ismeri 2002: 220):

> these instruments faced a series of obstacles in their implementation mostly due to the ongoing inadequacy of their administrative management […] the increasing efficiency required by the new structural policies, the breakup of the traditional relationship between national and local government, and progressive devolution highlighted the necessity in some regions of re-designing and building new capacities.

Therefore, with the beginning of the CSF 2000–2006, the Department for Cohesion Policy, set up in 1998, has launched a campaign to promote regional administrative capacity. Indeed, the success of the SFs implementation requires a general upgrading of public administration. Complex programming requires a deep modernization of the regions' administrative structure. To guarantee the actual implementation of funds at the regional level, it is necessary to set the conditions for the use of resources and to build the required capacity (Ministero del Tesoro 2003: 207).

This excursus shows how the Italian government has moved form a total closure to comply with the EU regulations to a more constructive approach. But what has happened in the other EU MS while Italy was adjusting to the EU funding procedures?

The implementation gap between north and south

Empirical evidence on SFs expenditure rate in EU Objective 1 regions show that although Italy is the second highest recipient of SFs (Table 16.1), it is the country that spends the least. Indeed, the overall performance of Italian regions has consistently lagged behind other countries. Table 16.2 shows that in the first period (1989–1993) of EU cohesion policy, Italian regions had the lowest implementation rate (73 per cent) in terms of how much they spent (payments) compared with total allocations. In the second period, 1994–1999, Italy still remained last, and it appears there has been no improvement in the last period.

How can we explain such a low performance vis-à-vis the other EU MS? It is worth looking at the breakdown of the overall expenditure percentage, given that Italian regions are responsible for the majority of funding (Table 16.3).

Although the focus of this chapter is Objective 1 regions, it is worth looking at the capacity of expenditure of Objective 2 and 3 regions, all located in the centre and north of the country (Table 16.4). Objective 2 regions are areas facing structural difficulties, whether industrial, rural, urban or dependent on fisheries. Though

Table 16.1 Allocation of Structural Funds 2000–2006 for the EU15 Member States (in € millions at 1999 prices)

Member States	Objective 1	Objective 2	Objective 3	Fisheries	Community Initiatives	Cohesion Fund	Total
Austria	261	680	528	4	358	0	1.831
Belgium	625	433	737	34	209	0	2.038
Denmark	0	183	365	197	83	0	828
Finland	913	489	403	31	254	0	2.090
France	3.805	6.050	4.540	225	1.046	0	15.666
Germany	19.958	3.510	4.581	107	1.608	0	29.764
Greece	20.961	0	0	0	862	3.060	24.883
Ireland	3.088	0	0	0	166	720	3.974
Italy	22.122	2.522	3.744	96	1.172	0	29.656
Luxemburg	0	40	38	0	13	0	91
Netherlands	123	795	1.686	31	651	0	3.286
Portugal	19.029	0	0	0	671	3.300	23.000
United Kingdom	6.251	4.695	4.568	121	961	0	16.596
Spain	38.096	2.651	2.140	200	1.958	11.160	56.205
Sweden	722	406	720	60	278	0	2.186
Total EU15	135.954	22.454	24.050	1.106	10.442	18.000	212.246

Source: Working for the Region, 2001

Table 16.2 Percentage of Structural Funds expenditure* – EU Objective 1

a. Period 1989–1993		b. Period 1994–1999		c. Period 2000–2006**	
	%		%		%
Ireland	95	Portugal	89	Ireland	82
Portugal	91	Ireland	87	Sweden	79
Ireland	87	Ireland	82	Germany	77
Greece	84	Denmark	81	Spain	75
France	84	Austria	77	Portugal	75
Netherlands	83	Greece	73	Austria	74
Italy	73	Belgium	72	Finland	72
		France	67	Netherlands	72
		Netherlands	67	Belgium	66
		UK	67	UK	66
		Italy	67	France	64
				Italy	60
				Greece	53

Source: European Commission - Annual report on Structural Funds
* % of expenditure is calculated as expenditure/total allocation
** The expenditure is calculated until December 2006

Table 16.3 Percentage of Structural Funds expenditure – Italian Objective 1 regions

a. Period 1989–1993		b. Period 1994–1999		c. Period 2000–2006**	
	%		%		%
Basilicata	92	Basilicata	100	Basilicata	64
Abruzzo	80	Abruzzo*	100	Sardegna	63
Molise	77	Molise	99	Calabria	64
Sardegna	77	Sardegna	92	Molise***	73
Calabria	80	Calabria	84	Puglia	55
Campania	62	Campania	80	Campania	51
Puglia	64	Puglia	77	Sicily	46
Sicily	57	Sicily	75		

Source: Author elaboration on data of Italian Ministry of the Treasury
*Abruzzo is 'phasing-out', i.e. it left Objective 1 status at the end of 1996
** The data in this period are up to December 2006
*** Molise is 'phasing-out', i.e. it left objective 1 status at the end of 2003

Table 16.4 Percentage of Structural Funds expenditure – Objective 2 and 3 Regions, 2000–2006

Dimension 3: rules and procedures	Degree of impact	Order of relevance
Management	95%	2
Programming	96%	1
Control system	86%	4
Monitoring system	80%	6
Evaluation system	79%	7
Project selection	77%	8
Financial procedure	86%	4
Partnership	80%	6
Coordination	77%	8
Information and publicity	82%	5
Relation between managing authorities and implimenting bodies	82%	5
Technical support	73%	9
Average – rules and procedures	80%	6

Source: Author's elaboration based on data from ÖIR (2003)

situated in regions whose development level is close to the Community average, such areas are faced with different types of socio-economic difficulties that are often the source of high unemployment. Objective 3 regions are those whose GDP per capita is higher than 75 per cent, but receive support for the adaptation and modernization of education, training and employment policies and systems.

The data shown in Tables 16.2, 16.3 and 16.4 suggest that although Italy at the national level has had a lower-than-EU average ability to implement allocated funds, some regions have interestingly demonstrated a higher than average ability to spend resources. What has been happening in some regions as opposed to others to bring about these differences in regional performance is an important question.

The arguments are different for the three blocks of regions. Objective 2 and 3 regions appear to spend a greater proportion of funds because of the following factors: (i) less radical centralization than southern regions has allowed the development of planning capacity which appears missing in southern regions; (ii) the areas affected by intervention are smaller than the whole regional territory which is covered by Objective 1 regions, allowing for an easier, dynamic development plan in terms of drafting, overseeing, coordinating and adjusting to territorial needs; (iii) consequently they have a smaller amount of resource to spend compared to those allocated to the objective 1 regions.

Given that these reasons may justify intra-state differences, what is it that creates the significant gap between Italy and other more successful MS performances, such as those registered in Spain, Ireland or Portugal?

Administrative and political bottlenecks

To identify practises that optimize the performances of MS and regions, this section analyzes four main dimensions which appear fundamental to successful SF implementation, namely: (1) the actors involved in the SF process; (2) the context in which implementation is performed; (3) the rules and procedures that underpin SF implementation; (3) the political context.

In the next four subsections I will identify the most relevant components of each dimension.[9] To better understand the Italian case, we will largely refer to regional practises given that in the planning period 2000–2006, 80 per cent of EU funding was directly managed regionally. This decentralized trend also characterizes the current period 2007–2013. Furthermore, to simplify the understanding of regional dynamics and their impact on implementation performance two regional cases have been selected with opposite results – i.e. low performing Sicily and very high performing Basilicata.

Actors

The actors involved in the process of EU funding implementation are numerous (Table 16.5). Of the eight actors listed, managing authorities (MA) and implementing bodies (IB) demonstrate the highest impact on implementation performance.

Interestingly, MAs have a 95 per cent impact on EU funding implementation. In countries where SFs have been implemented successfully, such as Ireland and Spain, MAs have the following features: (i) they are highly respected in the ministerial and departmental hierarchy; (ii) they are adequately structured and internally organized both financially and in terms of human resources; (iii) the degree of competence and knowledge of staff is adequate to the standard of

Table 16.5 Degree of impact of actors on the implementation of EU funding

Dimension 1: Actors	*Degree of impact*	*Order of relevance*
European Commission	86%	3
National governments	80%	5
Regional governments	82%	4
Monitoring committees	73%	6
Managing authorities	95%	1
Paying authorities	86%	3
Implementing bodies	93%	2
Beneficiaries	73%	6
Social partners	59%	8
External experts	70%	7
Average	80%	

Source: Author's elaboration based on data from ÖIR (2003)

role and duties undertaken; (iv) they receive competent support when necessary from a network of external experts; (v) they have developed a great capacity of coordination with other departments of the national and regional government, in order to avoid workload duplication and favour integration of actions.

IBs have a 93 per cent impact on EU funding implementation. Countries such as Spain and Portugal have achieved high levels of fund implementation thanks to efficient use of IBs. These countries have selected IBs capable of identifying, evaluating and selecting projects based on objective criteria of efficiency and effectiveness. Conversely, selection of inadequate IBs significantly contributes to failure of EU funding implementation. For example, Greece and Italy demonstrate IBs selection processes that are biased by political interference. Such a lack of transparency has lead to poor project implementation. Indeed, if the IB selected is incapable of carrying out an allocated project, this creates delays in the entire spending process.

Context

The context in which EU funds are implemented is also extremely relevant. Table 16.6 demonstrates that administrative structure and typology of interventions within a national or regional context has the highest impact on implementation.

The administrative structure in which SFs are managed is the most difficult component of the process to modify. Indeed, this has undergone significant revision in almost every MS in order to deal with the rules and procedures which underpin SFs.

Typically three scenarios can take place:

a   Rejection: In some MS the national and/or regional administrative structures fail to comply with European rules and procedure, leading to a failure in SFs implementation.
b   Adaptation: In other MS the national and/or regional administrative structures formally adopt some European rules and procedure. However, resistance still exists in other aspects, such as monitoring and evaluation procedures, which results in reasonable SF implementation.

Table 16.6 Degree of impact of context on the implementation of EU funding

Dimension 2: Context	Degree of impact	Order of relevance
Political	64%	5
Socio-economic	71%	4
Administrative structure	84%	1
Institutional structures	75%	3
Typology of interventions	77%	2
Average	71%	4

Source: Author's elaboration based on data from ÖIR (2003)

c   Learning: In this case national and/or regional administrative structures fully adopt European rules and procedure and use them also in most routine areas of administration, creating a spill-over effect. In these, MS implementation is highly successful.

The first scenario discussed above characterized the Italian case from 1994–1999 (Gualini 2004, Milio 2007). Indeed, Italy only started to spend allocated funds following a two-year delay and many EU regulations such as monitoring and evaluation were not fully implemented. Only in 1999 at the beginning of the planning period 2000–2006 did both the Italian national and regional governments start to adapt and eventually learn the EU rules and procedures (Anselmo and Raimondo 2000). The transposition of EU directives into the Italian context was impaired by the complexity of bureaucracy, particularly at regional levels.

The typology of intervention is the second most relevant component of the context. Indeed, too many measures of intervention which are not integrated slow the implementation process and dilute the effectiveness. Furthermore, they create a laxity of funds and lack of concentration on intervention central for development. Successful cases are those where the MA selected a few relevant priorities and concentrated the funds intervention on key development aspects. Italy's main problem has always been the presence of the so-called *interventi a pioggia* (scattered intervention), an attempt to satisfy numerous clientelism requests, which has resulted in inefficient short-term rewards rather than long-term development (Trigilia 1992). The main weaknesses identified were principally related to the tendency for the deployment of SFs to be driven by the availability of resources rather than policy. This approach has reduced SFs merely to financial transfers rather than development tools.

Rules and procedures

The list of rules and procedures found in Table 16.7 is not exhaustive but highlights the main requirements of the EU regulations. Among all the aspects required, management and programming appear to be the most relevant. Indeed, the EU expects each national and regional government to undertake the management and programming of SFs in order to ensure the implementation of a multi-annual programme in a sustainable manner.

Programming has a 96 per cent impact on EU fund implementation. In countries such as Ireland, where there has been the best practice related to the planning of SFs, the following characteristics have emerged: (i) guidelines for structuring the planning process are created and circulated among all the departments involved; (ii) the timings for the preparation and approval of planning documents are in line with EU requirements; (iii) the content of planning documents is thoroughly supported by 'SWOT' analysis (strength, weaknesses, opportunity and threats) and 'PEST' analysis (political, economic, social and technology) in order to respond efficiently to socio-economic contexts and favour necessary developments; (iv) experiences and outcomes of previous evaluations are integrated into subsequent

Table 16.7 Degree of impact of rules and procedure on the implementation of EU funding

Dimension 3: rules and procedures	Degree of impact	Order of relevance
Management	95%	2
Programming	96%	1
Control system	86%	4
Monitoring system	80%	6
Evaluation system	79%	7
Project selection	77%	8
Financial procedure	86%	4
Partnership	80%	6
Coordination	77%	8
Information and publicity	82%	5
Relation between managing authorities and implementing bodies	82%	5
Technical support	73%	9
Average	80%	6

Source: Author's elaboration based on data from ÖIR (2003)

planning periods; (v) monitoring inputs are taken into account to eventually readjust some interventions during the planning period; (vi) SFs planning is strictly integrated into both national and regional development plans.

Clearly the regulations and procedures associated with SF interventions had capacity-building effects. However, empirical evidence from the Italian scenario suggests that some regions are still trying to achieve the above standards of practice. For example, in Sicily, there has been a significant delay in the approval of programme planning periods 1989–1993 and 1994–1999, sometimes commencing two years after the recommended cycle onset. If we consider other regions, a strong correspondence between the time of approval and expenditure, delays are evident. For example, Molise and Sardinia had their Plurifon Operative Programmes approved by the end of 1994 with less than a year delay. These regions spent 99 per cent and 84 per cent respectively of their total allocation by 2001. In contrast, Campania and Puglia suffered a two-year delay before approval of their programmes and this affected their subsequent expenditure.

Although these programmes have been extremely fragmented, some progress is evident. SWOT analysis has been introduced to ensure consistency of development strategy, and there has been some recent improvement in monitoring and evaluation (Ernst and Young 2003).

Besides programming activities, management approaches also have a relevant impact on SFs implementation (82 per cent). Spain has demonstrated the best of such practice and this has been related to a strong coordination of actions both horizontally and vertically. Unfortunately, Italian regions such as Sicily have only shown improvements in management over recent years. This is due to administrative personnel having poorly defined roles, which lead to duplication of workloads. Also, regional administrative departments have not coordinated their activities with each other, but rather maintained inefficient, autonomous existences, avoiding a perceived 'interference' from their colleagues. In contrast, Basilicata has demonstrated superior SFs implementation through the introduction of a central coordinating body, responsible for optimizing interdepartmental collaboration and clarifying individual personnel roles.

The political dimension

Evaluations managed by internal or external authorities tend to avoid the questions which have a political dimension. However, previous Italian empirical studies stress the relevance of the political dimension in determining the effectiveness of SFs implementation (Milio 2008). Sicily, as the lowest performing Italian region, has experienced extreme government instability with presidents, cabinet members and executive managers only lasting short periods with a fractionalized political spectrum. These circumstances have lead to a negative impact on four key administrative actions: management and programming have lacked coherence and continuity, while monitoring and evaluation have not been carried out. The result has been a slowdown in SFs expenditure and a discretional allocation of whatever is spent by politicians regardless of the long-term planning period. The awareness of instability creates a situation which encourages politicians to focus only on achieving personal interests during their short terms.

However, the opposite situation is evident in Basilicata. Political stability has dominated the region since its creation in 1970 and presidents and cabinet members have always served their entire legislative term. Furthermore, during government changes politicians have tried to maintain as much continuity as possible in the roles covered by key executives. This has enabled the region to develop and capitalize on past experiences and avoid major changes in strategy or resource allocation unless absolutely necessary. Finally, the leading political party's hold on government has been cohesive, with minimal fractionalization of seats within the cabinet.

Indeed, this high level of government stability appears to have encouraged politicians to plan and implement long-term policies, with the knowledge that their endeavours would be demonstrated at the end of their term. This is in direct contrast to the short-term, personal interests of Sicilian politics. These issues are discussed further in Carlo Carboni's opening chapter of this book, which discusses political elites and their correlated disease.

In summary, these findings, in line with what has clearly emerged in Iona *et al.*'s chapter, emphasize that successful policy implementation is heavily influenced by administrative efficiency, which in turn is dependent on the political context. Political stability enables the sustainability, coherence and ultimate success of long-term development programmes by potentiating administrative credibility and efficient implementation systems, as well as by creating the 'glue' that unites civil servants in their pursuit of common goals. Conversely, political instability encourages negative outputs such as imprecise management, incoherent programming, and poor monitoring and evaluation.

Open challenges

As discussed in this chapter, MS share similar experiences and challenges – management, programming, monitoring and evaluation. Italy is struggling to spend its allocated structural funds, although there appears to be some regional variation. This is attributable to two main factors: insufficiency of regional administrative capacity and a lack of political will to maintain a cooperative and coherent context to enable programme continuity over a multi-annual period. This has been the consequence of a short-term, clientelistic approach to resource implementation, which focuses on individual achievement as opposed to community benefit (see also the case of 'clientelism' in Chapter 14 on Naples).

This loss of resources has weakened the Italian position in two main ways. First, future funding at the European level may become more difficult to attain if Italian regions continue to ineffectively spend their allocations. Second, 'lost' funds represent a missed opportunity for regional development, particularly in southern Italy, where economic indicators lag behind the standards typical of a key European nation and G8 member.

To summarize, Italy faces two fundamental challenges. One relates to administration, in terms of simplifying bureaucracy and choosing better qualified staff. The second relates to the political-institutional setting, which need reform to ensure a political class that focuses on long-term regional/national goals rather than short rewards.

Notes

1   In March 2000 the Lisbon European Council set out a strategy designed to make Europe the most competitive and dynamic knowledge-based economy in the world by 2010. At the Gothenburg European Council in 2001, the strategy was widened by adding a new emphasis on protecting the environment and achieving a more sustainable pattern of development.

2   The EAGGF is divided into two sections. The Guarantee Section finances, in particular, expenditure on the agricultural market organizations, the rural development measures that accompany market support and rural measures outside of Objective 1 regions, certain veterinary expenditures and information measures relating to the CAP. The Guidance Section finances other rural development expenditure (not financed by the EAGGF Guarantee Section).

3   The reform was achieved through five council regulations: the framework regulation (2052/88) and the implementations Regulations (4253/88, 4254/88, 4255/88, 4256/88). It became effective on 1 January 1989.

4   Between 1995 and 2005, Greece reduced the gap with the rest of the EU27, moving from 74 per cent to reach 88 per cent of the EU's average gross domestic product per head. By the same year, Spain had moved from 91 per cent to 102 per cent, and Ireland reached 145 per cent of the EU's average starting from 102 per cent.

5   The CSF should contain: Quantified descriptions of the current situation with regard to disparities in terms of income and employment, infrastructure gaps, etc. and

potential for development; a description of an appropriate strategy and the priorities selected to attain the objective concerned; account taken of indicative Commission guidance; an integrated ex-ante evaluation; appropriate indicators and targets; consistency demonstrated with other Community polices (environment, competition, public procurement, etc.); an indicative financial table with the financial contribution from the Funds, the EIB and the other financial instruments; a description of the management and control arrangements that have been set up for the implementation of the interventions forming part of the CSF; an account of the steps taken to consult the partners and the arrangements and provisions for their involvement in the Monitoring Committee; an outline of the arrangements for monitoring and evaluation; publicity actions for the CSF.

6 The CSF is implemented through OPs, which are elaborated by each region and are approved by the EC. The OP describes in detail the priorities set by the CSF and it is composed by operational interventions implemented through pluri-annual measures.

7 Usually the MA for the CSF is a national authority, whereas the MA for the OP and the SPD is a regional authority.

8 The main concern regarded the lack of expertise on the part of the administrative staff and the procedures adopted for the monitoring and evaluation of the programmes.

9 The content of sections entitled Actors, Context, and Rules and procedures is based on the report ÖIR (2003).

References

Alphametrics Ltd (2003) 'Needs of Objective 1 regions in the EU15 and accession countries in areas eligible for Structural Funds', Final Report Contract No. 2002 CE 16 0 AT 174.

Anselmo, I. and Raimondo, L. (2000) 'The objective 1 Italian performance reserve: a tool to enhance the effectiveness of programmes and the quality of evaluation', Rome: Unità di Valutazione degli Investimenti Pubblici - Ministero del Tesoro.

Basile, R., De Nardis, S. and Girardi, A. (2001) *Regional Inequalities and Cohesion Policies in the European Union*, Rome: ISAE (Istituto di Studi e Analisi Economica).

Beutel, J. (2002) *The Economic Impact of Objective 1 Interventions for the Period 2000–2006,* Final report to the Regional Policy Directorate-General, European Commission, Konstanz, Germany.

Boijmans, P. (2003) 'Building institutional capacity', Paper presented at the Annual Meeting of ISPA Partners, Brussels, Belgium.

Bueno De Mesquita, B. (2000) *Political Instability as a Source of Growth*, Stanford, CA: Hoover.

Cafiero, S. (2000) *Storia dell'intervento straordinario nel Mezzogiorno, 1950–1993*, Taranto: P. Lacaita.

Cerbo, P. (2002) 'Ragioni e problemi dello spoils system', *La Voce*, 12 November.

Dimitrova, A. (2002) 'Enlargement, institution-building and the EU's administrative capacity requirement', *West European Politics* 25: 171–90.

European Commission (1999) 'Vademecum: Plans and programming documents for the Structural Funds 2000–2006'.

—— (2001) '*Working for the Region*', Luxembourg: Office for Official Publications of the European Communities.

Ernst & Young (2003) 'Rapporto di Valutazione Intermedia POR Sicilia 2000–2006', Palermo: Regione Sicilia.

Gualini, E. (2004) *Multilevel Governance and Institutional Change*, Farnham: Ashgate.

Ismeri (2002) 'Ex-post Evaluation of the Objective 1, 1994–99', National Report – Italy, Office of Official Publications of European Communities, Luxembourg.

Jacobsen, D.I. (2006) 'The relationship between politics and administration: The importance of contingency factors, formal structure, demography, and time', *Governance: An International Journal of Policy, Administration, and Institutions*, 19(2), 303–23.

Keating, M. (1995) 'A comment on Robert Leonardi, "Cohesion in the European Community: illusion or reality?', *West European Politics,* 18(2): 408–12.

Milio, S. (2007) 'Can Administrative Capacity explain differences in regional performances? Evidence from Structural Funds implementation in southern Italy', *Regional Studies*, 41(4): 429–42.

—— (2008) 'How political stability shapes administrative performance: the Italian case', *West European Politics*, 31(5): 915–28.

Ministero Del Tesoro (2003) *Rapporto annuale del dipartimento per le politiche di Sviluppo*, Istituto Poligrafico e zecca dello Stato.

ÖIR (2003), A Study on the Efficiency of the Implementation Methods for Structural Funds; Final Report, ÖIR in association with LRDP and IDOM, commissioned by the European Union DG Regional Policy.

Olson, M. (1965) *The Logic of Collective Action: Public Goods and the Theory of Groups*, Oxford: Harvard University Press.

—— (1982) *The Rise and Decline of Nations: Economic Growth, Stagflation, and Social Rigidities*, New Haven, CT: Yale University Press.

Regulation (1988) No 4253/88 of 19 December 1988.Official Journal L 374, 31/12/1988 P. 0001 - 0014 CONSLEG - 88R4253 - 24/12/1994 - 33 P.

—— (1988) No 4254/88 of 19 December 1988. Official Journal L 374, 31/12/1988 p. 0015 - 0020 CONSLEG - 88R4254 - 31/07/1993 - 13 p.

—— (1988) No 4255/88 of 19 December 1988.   Official Journal L 374, 31/12/1988 p. 0021 – 0024.

—— (1988) No 4256/88 of 19 December 1988. Official Journal L 374, 31/12/1988 P. 0025 – 0028.

Rodrìguez-Pose, A. (1998) *Dynamics of Regional Growth in Europe: Social and Political Factors*, New York: Clarendon.

Smyrl, M.E. (1997) 'Does European Community regional policy empower the regions?', *Governance*, 10: 287–309.

Trigilia C. (1992) *Sviluppo senza autonomia: effetti perversi delle politiche nel Mezzogiorno*, Bologna: Il Mulino.

17 Labour and welfare reforms

The short life of labour unity

Marco Simoni

Summary

Contemporary trends of the Italian welfare state and labour market have been determined through concertation between the state and social partners – most notably trade unions – in the 1990s. This chapter analyses the development of concertation and conceptualizes it as a policy alliance between the centre-left and organized labour. Starting with income policies, trade unions acquired a pivotal role in economic restructuring, which later included the reform of the pension system and the labour market. By granting participatory policy making and key concessions to union members, the centre-left gained popular consensus on hard-to-swallow economic reforms. However, *concertazione* increased the segmentation of the Italian labour market which, in turn, played against its main protagonists.

Introduction[1]

Contemporary trends of the Italian welfare state and labour market have been determined by a series of crucial reforms negotiated with trade unions during the 1990s. Concertation (or *concertazione*) was initiated by technocratic governments, which lacked a clear parliamentary majority, and presided over the economic crisis of the early 1990s. However, *concertazione* rapidly assumed the longer-term characteristics of a policy alliance between the centre-left and organized labour, which was sustained throughout the decade. While greeted by wide scholarly surprise, this alliance shaped the response to international pressures coming from globalization and the run-up to the European Monetary Union: wage demands were tamed; the pension system was reformed, and its scope considerably reduced; heavy doses of flexibility were injected into the labour market. Further reforms introduced in the 2000s by governments of different partisan orientations did not alter the previously determined policy course, they merely deepened it and widened it.

The results of this policy mix are not single-faceted. During the 1990s, the Italian economy marginally improved, and employment levels started to increase again. The country joined the European Monetary Union with the first group of countries, and thereby enjoyed monetary stability and a lower premium on the service of its high public debt. However, economic reforms also had the effect of increasing the segmentation of the labour market, widening the gap between insiders and marginal workers which, in the case of Italy, largely overlapped with a gap between older and younger cohorts of citizens.

Based on the analysis of primary and secondary sources, and on interviews with key informants,[2] this chapter argues that the political alliance between the centre-left and organized labour is key to understanding the emergence of social pacts in Italy, as well as the policy content of economic reforms. Wage moderation by unions was a complement to a devaluation strategy pursued by the governments in the early 1990s. Starting with this early agreement, the trade union leadership secured for itself a pivotal place in Italian politics, and was able to shelter its membership from most of the consequences of welfare state restructuring.

During the 1990s, social pacts emerged in many different countries, with unions and employers joining the state with purposes of economic policy making. In other words, in the 1990s, Italy was only one case among others such as Portugal, Ireland, the Netherlands, Finland, Norway and others (Fajertag and Pochet 1997, 2000). A rich literature developed on this topic, which put forward five main explanations for this phenomenon. First, in some political systems trade unions might be veto players (Bonoli 2001); second, trade unions might be a repository of important information for the purpose of economic reform (Culpepper 2002); third, involving trade unions might smooth the sharpest social effects associated with liberalizations (Crouch 2000); fourth, the specific contingency of the 1990s, i.e. the run-up to European Monetary Union and the associated economic criteria, forced states to negotiate complex bundles of reforms with labour to achieve results against pressing schedules (Hancké and Rhodes 2004).

This last explanation appears particularly convincing for the Italian case. The argument contends that in Italy, peak-level concertation substituted for the absence of micro-level institutions for economic coordination. In countries such as Germany, endowed with networks of coordination at the firm and industry levels, explicit peak-level social pacts were redundant. In very flexible growing economies such as the United Kingdom, such pacts were similarly not needed because market mechanisms provided swift adjustment.[3] In intermediate cases such as Italy, under pressing economic (and political) conditions, coordination needed to be imposed top-down in order to achieve the desired results. The main problem with this explanation, however, is that it does not take into consideration the partisan aspect of the rise and development of Italian concertation.

This leaves us with the final hypothesis which explains social partnership as the policy option sought by weak governments in need of additional sources of popular consensus (Baccaro and Lim 2007, Baccaro and Simoni 2008). However, the Italian case adds a key partisan component, which is empirically and theoretically important. Indeed, an influential stream of the political economic literature contends that globalization brought about the decoupling of the political left and organized labour, as a consequence of changes both in the scope for economic management, and in the features of party competition (Kitschelt 1994: 33, Boix

1998). Instead, in Italy, a major economic crisis, coupled with the need to respond to pressures from globalization, fostered a distinctive policy alliance between the newly formed centre-left coalition and the three main union confederations.

No country for old unionism

The involvement of Italian trade unions in socio-economic policy making was welcomed with considerable surprise by international observers (Schmitter and Grote 1997: 8–9). Indeed, the Italian labour movement was known to be insufficiently cohesive, from a political and organizational viewpoint, to sustain institutionalized 'political exchange' (Regini 1984). In the post-war decades, relations between the trade unions and the state reflected cleavages in the policy arena, and in particular the communist/anti-communist divide. While the CGIL, organizing roughly half of unionized workers, was dominated by its large communist faction affiliated to the PCI, the trade union confederations, CISL and UIL, held strong informal links with the governmental parties DC and PSI (Weitz 1975, Golden 1988).

Between 1989 and 1994 this scenario changed completely. First the PCI, accounting for roughly a third of the electorate, dissolved, and its larger heir, first called PDS (Democratic Party of the Left) then DS, positioned its policies within mainstream European social democracy (Ladrech and Marlière 1999). As a consequence, the CGIL dissolved the traditional internal factions based on party affiliation.[4] In the same period, the most important governmental parties, including the DC and PSI, dissolved under the pressures of judicial investigations so that after the 1994 elections, the names (and most members) of the six most numerous party groups in the lower chamber of parliament had changed (Newell 2000). In response to a new electoral law, parties clustered around two competing coalitions: a centre-left coalition, built around the PDS-DS, and a centre-right coalition built around the leadership of Silvio Berlusconi (see Chapter 3 in this volume) .

These political changes had deep consequences on the political ties of organized labour. The trade union leaderships, and various political cliques maintaining links to the unions, previously aligned to the DC or the PSI, realigned with the centre-left coalition. Therefore, while until the 1990s the three union confederations and their factions were associated with parties that pursued different policy agendas, after that period they found themselves coupled with parties forming a single coalition. The party/union links remained, for the most part, informal. However, open support for the centre-left coalition became the rule rather than the exception.[5]

The outset of concertation: income policies

While political restructuring was ongoing, in the early 1990s Italy faced a serious economic crisis. Between 1992 and 1993, GDP contracted for the first time since 1975, consumption and investment decreased, outstanding public debt approached

110 per cent of GDP, and at the end of 1992 speculative attacks motivated by the increase of real interest rates forced the lira out of the European Monetary System. The currency crisis came close to threatening the liquidity of the central bank. Debt default, however, was avoided through unprecedented austerity measures (Signorini and Visco 2002: 78–87). These austerity measures were sustained by two tripartite income agreements, signed by the main trade union confederations in July 1992 and July 1993. The first one included the abolishment of the wage indexation system and a one-year pay freeze, and it was followed by a cut in the official interest rate by the central bank. The second one included new rules on anti-inflationary wage increases and a new system of wage bargaining.

According to most economic observers, and the two prime ministers who brokered the deals, these agreements were key to avoiding the collapse of the Italian economy (Regini 1997).[6] They favoured the process of fiscal consolidation and contributed significantly to controlling inflation. In doing so, they contributed to turn the two subsequent nominal devaluations of the currency (in 1992 and 1994–1995) into real devaluations. This was mainly due to the 1993 agreement, which created a strongly coordinated system of wage setting while leaving some room for decentralized adjustments.[7] Under its framework, social partners would bargain at the national sector level, based on the (governmentally determined) expected rate of inflation (Biagioli 2003: 116–7). Figure 17.1 displays a measure of wage militancy. While wage push appears cyclical around a stable mean between 1960 and the early 1990s, it took a clear downward trend since 1992, which lasted until 2001.

'It is worth underlining the paradox whereby the labour unions […] were called to cooperate with the governments precisely when political parties, under attack from many fronts, were indeed expelled from it' (Ginsborg 1998: 520). This paradox can be easily explained by recalling that a political realignment of organized labour was also ongoing. Arguably, during 1992 and 1993, unions were able to coordinate with the governments precisely because political parties

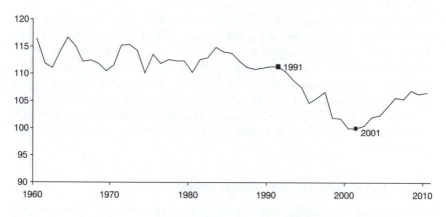

Figure 17.1 Real labour costs in Italy 1960–2010 (estimated)

Source: Ameco database, series 'Real unit labour costs: total economy'

had ceased to have a divisive influence on unions' policies, and instead allowed the emergence of political agreement among the leadership of organized labour. However, the potential for political agreement needed an important institutional innovation to be realized: the introduction of referenda on social pacts.

Classic neo-corporatist studies have explained that negotiations and compromises with employers or the state open a gap between union leadership and rank-and-file members (Pizzorno 1978, Lehmbruch 1979). This gap, motivated both by different sets of incentives and by asymmetry of information, might lead to grassroots protests and the emergence of competing unions. Indeed, the 1992 agreement met both with intra-union dissent in the CGIL and with grassroots protests. The militant faction within the CGIL denounced the agreement as illegitimate using an argument traditionally present in the toolbox of radical unionism: it contended that it was not democratically determined (Baccaro *et al.* 2001: 45–47).

In the autumn of 1992, union confederation leaders were violently opposed by competing unions that were surging at the local level. In the midst of what appeared to be a union legitimacy crisis, CGIL, CISL and UIL signed the 1993 agreement. This, however, was to be endorsed by a binding referendum among all the workers. Roughly 1.5 million workers voted in the referendum, which got an approval rate of 68 per cent. 'The referendum proved to be a powerful legitimising device for the union confederal leadership. In fact, no grassroots uprising took place this time' (ibid.: 48). A *de facto* divided labour movement was unified through democratic means. Even though 32 per cent of workers, one in three, rejected the accord, this dissent was not expressed in open protests and the minority eventually accepted the will expressed by the majority.

These events can be understood in the light of a seminal paper by Marino Regini (1984). Previous studies had underlined that representational monopoly of labour (concentration) and centralization of decision making in unions were 'institutional prerequisites' for policy concertation (Golden *et al.* 1999). Regini argued that concentration and centralization could be substituted by functional equivalents, e.g. labour political unity. However, unless the rank-and-file members have a clear sense of the benefits to be gained from concertation, the latter will be hard to endure. Indeed, under the harsh economic conditions of 1992, political unity of union leadership did not prevent grassroots uprisings. An institutional change, i.e. the adoption of referenda among workers to endorse peak-level agreements, was devised to overcome internal and external opposition.[8]

The 1992 and 1993 governments were technocratic cabinets, i.e. lacking a predetermined parliamentary majority. They were appointed to offset the legitimacy crisis of governmental parties (more than 200 out of roughly 1000 MPs were under judicial investigation, see Ginsborg 1998: 525). However, key Cabinet positions were held by socialist politicians who later became members of the centre-left coalition, including Prime Minister Giuliano Amato in 1992, and the Minister for Labour, Gino Giugni, in 1993. By supporting the devaluation strategy set by these governments through wage restraint, the unions gained a pivotal role in the making of economic policy. This role was first exerted through opposition to the centre-right in 1994, and then in the role of stable partner for economic reforms during the 1996–2001 centre-left governance period.

Reforming the pension system with the unions

In 1994, the three Italian union confederations vehemently opposed a pension reform proposed by the centre-right government led by Berlusconi. The Italian pension system, in common with that of many European countries, had been in considerable financial distress since the late 1980s. An ageing population, and the predominance of a pay-as-you-go type of benefit plan financed from payroll taxes, wherein pensions were computed according to the final salary rather than actual capitalization, combined to increase the financial stress. The deadline set by the Maastricht agreements for the European single currency put further pressure on Italy to reform, in order to enter the euro with the first group. Compared with Austria, Germany, France and Sweden – which are traditionally considered to provide generous social insurances – the Italian pension system was imposing the highest (actual and perspective) stress to public finances, including the highest proportion of pension expenditures to GDP (Schludi 2001: 7).Virtually all political actors, including the governor of the central bank, most political parties and economic commentators, agreed that there was a need to reform, but all attempts up until this point had proved either unsuccessful or ineffective (Ferrera and Gualmini 1999).

The centre-right coalition won elections in 1994. During the electoral campaign, trade union confederations – after having paid lip service to the principle of autonomy from party politics – put forward candidates for public office on the electoral lists of many different parties, but not on the centre-right ones.[9] Unsurprisingly, once in office, Berlusconi attempted to reform the pension system unilaterally, sparking the strongest wave of protests since the Hot Autumn of 1969. The trade unions called a general strike, which was suspended when, on the day before, the government withdrew its proposals. A few days later, the government resigned. The strategy towards the general strike was discussed by the leaders of the three union confederations with the leaders of the opposition.[10] The issue was not confined to the realm of industrial disputes: opposing Berlusconi's pension reform was a highly political decision, primarily motivated by the opposition to unilateral economic restructuring by the government under very harsh economic conditions.[11]

After the collapse of the centre-right coalition in January 1995, a technocratic government supported by the previous centre-left opposition engaged in negotiations on pension reform with the unions and the main employers' association.[12] Employers withdrew from negotiations at an early stage, arguing that the proposed reform was not far-reaching enough. The unions and the government eventually agreed on a reformed pension system that contained several innovations, including a 'defined contribution' method for pension determination (in lieu of the previous 'defined benefit' system) and the gradual phasing out of seniority pensions, which were among the primary causes of the financial troubles. According to a cross-country analysis on the political economy of pension reforms, the Italian reform one was one of the most far-reaching in terms of expected savings for public finances (Myles and Pierson 2001: 322–334). The reform affected virtually all sectors, including the heavily unionized ones.

The proposed reform met with protests from radical unions (particularly metalworkers' unions) and small leftist parties. The method used to ensure the viability of the accord was the same as in 1993: voting. Union confederations organized over 40,000 assemblies across firms and sectors to explain the content and the rationale of the agreement. Unlike in 1993, the net losses for workers were evident: they had to be persuaded that it was in their own interest to improve the financial sustainability of the pension system, and that a reduction of entitlements was necessary to this objective. As a consequence, 4.4 million workers voted for the referendum and the accord was approved with a 64 per cent majority (Baccaro and Locke 1996: 18–24).

The pact on pension reform reinforced the partisan nature of Italian policy concertation and, indeed, the parliamentary majority that finally approved it included the PDS. Political motivation from the side of unions becomes even more apparent when comparing the pension reform proposed by the centre-right government – which was strongly opposed by unions – with the reform eventually approved. In terms of total savings, the differences were minimal: the centre-left cooperating with the unions saved roughly 10 per cent less than the centre-right would have done. The major difference between the two reforms was attributable to the composition of savings. The centre-right reform was concentrated in the abolition of seniority pensions. These pensions allowed workers to retire after a certain number of years in employment (in particular, this was 35 years for metalworkers) irrespective of their age. On the contrary, the centre-left with the unions distributed the costs of retrenchment over a larger social base, gradually phasing out seniority pensions (ibid.: 16).

Through their protests against the centre-right reform, and their cooperation with the centre-left, the trade unions consolidated their role in the policy arena in general, and in the centre-left policy camp in particular. From the viewpoint of centre-left politicians, the protests were instrumental in the collapse of the centre-right coalition government, and unions' agreement was key to successfully passing a pension reform. To reach these aims the centre-left had only to secure minimal concessions to unions (in particular on seniority pensions, which affected disproportionately the powerful metalworkers' union) so to win their consensus on an outright retrenchment of the welfare state.

The Olive Tree Coalition and the flexibilization of the labour market

When in 1996 the centre-left Olive Tree coalition, dominated by the DS, eventually won a general election, it was clear to everyone that the trade unions would continue to play an active role in socio-economic steering. Concertation with the social partners became enshrined as the key method to address socio-economic issues.[13] The 1993 agreement on income policy was confirmed in 1996 and 1998 within wide-ranging tripartite understandings (Presidenza del Consiglio dei Ministri 1996).[14] In 1997, the 1995 pension reform was amended through bipartite talks to strengthen savings and introduce anti-poverty measures. This time, the referendum among workers passed with a majority of 84 per cent (Baccaro 2002: footnote 16). The most important policy innovation during the 1996–2001 legislature, however, related to the fields of labour law and employment regulation.

According to OECD (1999) metrics, in the mid-1990s the Italian labour market suffered from the most rigid regulation after Turkey, Greece and Portugal. According to a very influential view, the high level of unemployment that Italy shared with other large European economies was a consequence of such rigidities (OECD 1994, Siebert 1997).[15] Implicitly buying into this argument, the centre-left government embarked on tripartite negotiations aimed at increasing labour market flexibility.

In 1997, a major reform was passed, and the Italian labour market changed significantly. Agency work was introduced; procedures for employing part-time personnel were simplified; fixed-term contracts and apprenticeship contracts were made easier to adopt. In brief, the range of cheaper non-standard flexi-jobs, characterized by lower employment protections and fewer welfare entitlements, was sensibly increased alongside the 'old' full-time, permanent employment (Baccaro and Simoni 2004). The layers of labour law increased, including flexible and non-flexible occupational regimes. The centre-left reforms, as such, are often referred to as re-regulations rather than de-regulations (Lodovici 2000). Flexible workers were essentially the newly employed, while those already in occupation, that is, the entire body of unionized workers, were not affected by the reform.

As in the case of pension reform, the trade unions contributed to the design of the new rules, and also secured a regulatory function for themselves. Special clauses gave to the social partners the role to determine, in bipartite agreements, all the details not specified by law. These included, for example, the quota of specific flexi-jobs that each industry could employ as a proportion of total workers. The employers' peak association, Confindustria, openly contested these restrictive measures and continued to campaign for outright labour market liberalization, including the relaxation of employment protection in large industries. The opposition of trade unions to any further liberalization eventually pushed employers to endorse the centre-right coalition in the run-up to the 2001 elections (CESOS 2000).

Understanding concertation and its consequences

In 2002 and 2009, the centre-right government promoted two social pacts on labour market and wage bargaining issues that were signed by CISL and UIL, but met the opposition of the CGIL. However, these agreements did not carry significant policy results (Baccaro and Pulignano 2009). In 2003, another reform of the labour market, that further increased flexibility for the newly employed, was approved unilaterally by the centre-right (Baccaro and Simoni 2004). In 2007, instead, the centre-left successfully negotiated with all the unions a minor adjustment to the pension system, which was then passed through a binding referendum among workers. In other words, in the 2000s, while economic reforms on welfare and labour issues stalled, political unity of labour strongly decreased, and it became dependent on the existence of a centre-left cabinet.

The determination with which the Italian centre-left governments sought policy cooperation with labour, both in the 1990s and in the 2000s, is surprising in the light of the literature on contemporary electoral left. Given the changed electoral scenario of post-industrial globalized societies, a clear independence from unions was considered a pre-condition to victorious electoral coalitions at the left-of-centre (Kitschelt 1994). This is because traditional unionism was considered detrimental in the quest for a new programmatic identity, much needed since the end of the Keynesian consensus (Hall 1989). However, in Italy, rather than subscribing to a traditional policy platform based on broad-brushed Keynesian economics, the trade unions accepted to endorse a policy platform based on wage moderation, welfare state retrenchment and labour market flexibility. Hence, rather than being a programmatic liability for a modernizing centre-left, Italian unions were a programmatic asset, thus able to secure for themselves key policy concessions. In other words, while moving towards the centre to win the median voter – just like most of its European colleagues were doing (Glyn 2001) – the Italian centre-left used concertation as a yardstick: it would move right in the political space as much as the unions would allow. Under this logic, votes can be won from the growing pool of workers in the more dynamic sectors while minimizing the losses from the traditional left. This logic was indeed dominant among the European centre-left, which, despite many predictions, largely continued to sustain its policy alliance with organized labour (Simoni 2007).

From the union side of the bargain, if compared with previous periods of 'political exchange', the gains for labour were negative rather than positive gains, i.e. they did not entail increased advantages for workers, but reduced loss for their members. The distinction between members and non-members remains crucial to understand the implications of the economic reforms of the 1990s. Stylized evidence fifteen years after the beginning of *concertazione* highlights a growing segmentation between insider (older) workers, and marginal (younger) workers.

According to the main Italian Institute for Statistics (ISTAT), after the 1997 reform more than half of the newly created jobs were non-standard, i.e. part-time contracts, fixed-term appointments, agency jobs, and so on, totalling 2.2 million, or 23 per cent of total private employees, in 2002 (ISTAT 2002: 178). A more recent study estimates that in 2007 roughly four million people were involved in different forms of flexi-jobs (Mandrone 2008). The majority of these workers are enjoying fewer welfare entitlements than people employed on a standard full-time contract, including little – if any – income protection in case of dismissal, and no employment protection. They are *de facto* likened to first-time job seekers which have no entitlement for support (Lynch 2004).

The largest group of non-standard employees are those on a fixed-term contract which, between 1993 and 2007, grew three times as much as total employment growth. However, this increase simply put Italian numbers in line with the EU15 average in terms of the proportion of fixed-term employees on total employment. Similarly close to EU15 average, in fact a mere 0.5 per cent short of it, is the share of employees in the 15–24 age cohort that are on a fixed-term appointment: 42.3 per cent.[16] These data, comparatively not surprising, turn into an indicator of segmentation of the labour market when combined with other two factors: first, younger generations in Italy are out of work much more than in other Western European countries. Second, the Italian welfare state tends to primarily benefit the elderly.

In 2006, the employment rate in the 15–24 age cohort was a mere 25.5 per cent, versus over 40 per cent in the EU15. The unemployment rate in the same age group was 21.6 per cent compared to 15.7 per cent in the EU15: these data are particularly significant because total unemployment was instead higher in the EU15 (7.7 per cent) than in Italy (6.8 per cent).[17] In other words, the flexibility of the labour market had the effect of further pushing to the margins, in terms of reduced welfare entitlements and reduced job protection, a cohort of citizens already comparatively disadvantaged. Furthermore, this did not have a visible effect on the overall employment levels of young people: the activity rate of the population aged 15–24 has indeed decreased from 38.8 per cent in 1995 to 32.5 per cent in 2006, when the EU15 average stood at 47.9 per cent.

The cleavage between young and old cohorts is even clearer if one takes into account the redistributive effects of the welfare state. When considering a vector of spending policies, including pensions, services for the elderly, unemployment benefits, active labour market policy, family allowances and family services, and controlling for the age distribution of the population, Italy is the EU15 country with the highest ratio of per capita spending on the elderly to per capita spending on the non-elderly. This rank pre-dates the 1990s reforms, and it can be explained by how the features of social policy programmes combine with party competition (Lynch 2004). However, data from an assessment exercise on the 1995 pension reform show that the latter has exacerbated the intra-generational inequality of the Italian welfare state. By virtue of a complicated and lengthy phasing-in of the new system used to calculate individual pension entitlements, workers who entered the labour market between 1978 and 1995 (the year in which the reform was signed) will receive much higher entitlements than workers who entered the labour market after 1995 (Brambilla *et al.* 2001: 52). Similar conclusions are drawn by a study considering the trajectory of pension reform processes over time (Brugiavini and Galasso 2004). By definition, future workers were not union members at the time in which the agreement was signed.

Conclusions: A self-defeating strategy?

From many perspectives the alliance between the centre-left and organized labour in Italy was a success. Starting with 1992, public budget deficit turned into surplus (before debt servicing); since 1993, a strong export performance helped the economy to recover; in 1996, employment started increasing again after a long stagnation. Against all odds, Italy joined the European Monetary Union with the first group of countries in 1998. However, despite these positive records, Italian GDP per capita relative to the rest of the EU15 countries has been constantly decreasing since 1991, falling below the average since 2002.[18] A very slow dynamic of productivity, and adverse incentives caused by wage moderation seem to be the main suspects accountable for this relatively long economic decline (Saltari and Travaglini 2006).

While economic restructuring was important to achieve fiscal consolidation and improve the dire conditions of public finances, pension reforms and labour market flexibility have widened the cleavage between insiders and marginal workers, which in Italy overlaps to a large extent with a cleavage between younger and older cohorts. This cleavage is now mirrored also by data on unionization. Between the early 1990s and 2008, overall union density has decreased from slightly below 40 per cent to 29 per cent. If one considers only workers younger than 34, density shrinks to 19 per cent. The same figure corresponds to overall union density in the private sector, i.e. excluding public employees (Baccaro and Pulignano 2009). These data combined are suggesting, and forecasting, a continuing decrease of salience for organized labour. At the same time, in the 2008 elections, the centre-left suffered a massive electoral defeat. After that, new rifts opened between union confederations which, at the time of writing, appear hard to overcome. In other words, there are robust hints suggesting that the political alliance between the electoral left and organized labour in the 1990s sow the seeds of subsequent losses for its protagonists. Arguably, the increased segmentation of the labour market makes both union recruiting policy and social democratic electoral strategy harder to accomplish. Paradoxically, the unity of Italian organized labour in the 1990s paved the way to a socially and politically divided labour in the 2000s, and possibly beyond.

Notes

1 The author wishes to thank Lucio Baccaro, Jonathan Hopkin, Christa Van-Wijnbergen and the editors of this volume for helpful comments. Financial support from the British Academy is gratefully acknowledged.

2 A complete list of interviewees, whose kind availability is gratefully acknowledged, is available from the author upon request.

3 See Hall and Soskice (2001) for the theoretical foundations of this argument.

4 Available online at: www.rassegna.it/2002/speciali/congresso-cgil/storia/1991.htm. Last accessed March 2009.

5 See for example *Il Sole 24 Ore* 10 March 1994; 15 and 16 March 1996.

6 See also *La Repubblica*, 8 May 1994; and 'Social partners start discussions on reform of the July 1993 agreement', which is available online at: www.eiro.eurofound. eu.int/1997/02/inbrief/it9702102n.html. Last accessed March 2009.

7 The rationale for having a two-tier bargaining system is rooted in the territorial differences that characterize the Italian economy (Dell'Aringa and Lucifora 2000).

8 See Baccaro and Simoni (2007) for a cross-country analysis of the impact of internal democracy on union strategies.

9 *Il Sole 24 Ore,* same issues as above.

10 This information was obtained through interviews with party and union officials.

11 See note above.

12 Interviews have revealed that the pension reform was not simply negotiated, but actually co-written by officers of the treasury and trade unions' experts.
13 See *Il Sole 24 Ore*, 23 April 1996.
14 See 'National social pact for development and employment signed', available online at: www.eiro.eurofound.eu.int/1999/01/feature/it9901335f.html. Last accessed March 2009.
15 For a different view see Baker *et al.* (2005).
16 Ministero del Lavoro (2008)
17 Commission of the European Communities (2007).
18 AMECO database, European Commission.

References

Baccaro, L. (2002) 'Negotiating the Italian pension reform with the unions: lessons for corporatist theory', *Industrial and Labor Relations Review*, 55(3): 413–31.

—— and Lim, S.-H. (2007) 'Social pacts as coalitions of the weak and moderate: Ireland, Italy and South Korea in comparative perspective', *European Journal of Industrial Relations,* 13(1): 27–46.

—— and Locke, R.M. (1996) 'Public Sector Reform and Union Participation: The Case of the Italian Pension Reform', Paper presented at the 1996 Annual Meeting of the American Political Science Association, San Francisco, 29 August–1 September.

—— and Pulignano, V. (2009) 'Employment Relations in Italy', in G. Bamber *et al.* (eds.) *International and Comparative Employment Relations* (fifth edition), London: Sage.

—— and Simoni, M. (2004) 'The Referendum on Article 18 and Labour Market Flexibility', in S. Fabbrini and V. Della Sala (eds.) *Italian Politics,* New York: Berghahn Books.

—— and Simoni, M. (2007) 'Organizational Determinants of Wage Moderation." Unpublished Manuscript: 4th General Conference of the European Consortium for Political Research, Pisa 8 September.

—— and Simoni, M. (2008) 'Policy concertation in Europe: Explaining government's choice', *Comparative Political Studies*, 41(10): 1323–48.

——, Carrieri, M. and Damiano, C.. (2001) 'The resurgence of the Italian confederal unions: will it last?', *European Journal of Industrial Relations*, 9(1): 43–59.

Baker, D., Glyn, A., Howell, D.A. and Schmitt, J.   (2005) 'Labor Market Institutions and Unemployment : A Critical Assessment of the Cross-Country Evidence', in D.R. Howell (ed.) *Fighting Unemployment: The Limits of Free Market Orthodoxy*. Oxford: Oxford University Press.

Biagioli, M. (2003). 'Conflitto distributivo, contrattazione sindacale, concertazione e politiche economiche. Alcune riflessioni sull'esperienza italiana', *Economia e Lavoro*, XXXVI(1): 105–21.

Boix, C. (1998) *Political Parties, Growth and Equality: Conservative and Social Democratic Economic Strategies in the World Economy*. Cambridge: Cambridge University Press.

Bonoli, G. (2001) 'Political Institutions, Veto Points, and the Process of Welfare State Adaptation', in P. Pierson (ed.) *The New Politics of the Welfare State*, Oxford: Oxford University Press.

Brambilla, A. *et al.* (2001) 'Relazione finale', *Commissione per la valutazione degli effetti della legge n° 335/95 e successivi provvedimenti*.

Brugiavini, A. and Galasso, V. (2004) 'The social security reform process in Italy: where do we stand?', *Journal of Pension Economics and Finance*, 3(2): 165–95.

CESOS (2000) 'Confindustria approves new programme and management team', *European Industrial Relations Observatory*. Online. Available: www.eiro.eurofound. eu.int/2000/05/inbrief/it0005152n.html.

Commission of the European Communities (2007) *Employment in Europe*, Bruxelles: Directorate-General for Employment, Industrial Relations and Social Affairs.

Crouch, C. (2000) 'The Snakes and Ladders of twenty-first-century trade unionism', *Oxford Review of Economic Policy*, 16(1): 70–83.

Culpepper, P. (2002) 'Powering, puzzling and "pacting": The informational logic of negotiated reforms', *Journal of European Public Policy*, 9(5): 774–90.

Dell'Aringa, C. and Lucifora, C. (2000) 'La "scatola nera" dell'economia italiana: mercato del lavoro, istituzioni, formazione dei salari e disoccupazione', *Rivista di Politica Economica*, XC(X-XI): 21–69.

Fajertag, G. and Pochet, P. (eds.) (1997) *Social Pacts in Europe*, Bruxelles: ETUI.

—— (2000) *Social Pacts in Europe. New Dynamics*, Bruxelles: ETUI.

Ferrera, M. and Gualmini, E. (1999) *Salvati dall'Europa?*, Bologna: Il Mulino.

Ginsborg, P. (1998) *L'Italia del tempo presente. Famiglia, società civile, Stato*, Turin: Einaudi.

Glyn, A. (ed.) (2001) *Social Democracy in Neoliberal Times: The Left and Economic Policy Since 1980*, Oxford: Oxford University Press.

Golden, M. (1988). Labor Divided: Austerity and Working-Class Politics in Contemporary Italy. Ithaca, Cornell University Press.

—— M. Wallerstein and Lange, P. (1999) 'Postwar Trade-Union Organization and Industrial Relations in Twelve Countries', in H. Kitschelt *et al.* (eds.) *Continuity and Change in Contemporary Capitalism*, Cambridge: Cambridge University Press.

Hall, P.A. (ed.) (1989) *The Political Power of Economic Ideas: Keynesianism Across Nations*, Princeton, NJ: Princeton University Press.

—— and Soskice, D. (eds.) (2001) *Varieties of Capitalism: The Institutional Foundations of Comparative Advantage*, New York: Oxford University Press.

Hancké, B. and Rhodes, M. (2004) 'EMU and labor market institutions in Europe. The rise and fall of national social pacts', *Work and Occupations*, 32(2): 196–228.

ISTAT (2002) *Rapporto Annuale*, Rome: ISTAT.

Kitschelt, H. (1994) *The Transformation of European Social Democracy*, Cambridge: Cambridge University Press.

Ladrech, R. and Marlière, P. (eds.) (1999) *Social Democratic Parties in the European Union: History, Organization, Politics*, New York: St. Martin's Press.

Lehmbruch, G. (1979) 'Consociational Democracy, Class Conflict, and New Corporatism', in P.C. Schmitter and G. Lehmbruch (eds.) *Trends Toward Corporatist Intermediation*, London: Sage Publications.

Lodovici, M.S. (2000) 'Italy: The Long Times of Consensual Re-regulation', in G. Esping Andersen and M. Regini (eds.) *Why Deregulate Labour Markets?*, Oxford: Oxford University Press.

Lynch, J. (2004) 'The Age of Welfare: Patronage, Citizenship, and Generational Justice in Social Policy', *Harvard University Center for European Studies Working Paper Series*, 111: 1–24.

Mandrone, E. (2008) 'Quando la flessibilità diviene precarietà: una stima sezionale e longitudinale', Collana Studi Isfol, 6.

Ministero del Lavoro (2008) 'Rapporto di monitoraggio delle politiche occupazionali e del lavoro', Rome, Online. Available: www.lavoro.gov.it/NR/rdonlyres/09069AB6-8B69-4E16-B525-7FBAC2C28BC1/0/Monitoraggio_2008.pdf.

Myles, J. and Pierson, P. (2001) 'The Comparative Political Economy of Pension Reform', in P. Pierson (ed.) *The New Politics of the Welfare State*, Oxford: Oxford University Press.

Newell, J.L. (2000) *Parties and Democracy in Italy*, Alderscot: Ashgate.

OECD (1994) *The OECD Jobs Study. Facts, Analysis, Strategies*, Paris: OECD.

—— (1999) *Employment Protection and Labour Market Performance. Employment Outlook*, Paris: OECD.

Pizzorno, A. (1978) 'Political Exchange and Collective Identity in Industrial Conflict', in C. Crouch and A. Pizzorno (eds.) *The Resurgence of Class Conflict in Western Europe Since 1968*, London: Macmillan.

Presidenza del Consiglio dei Ministri (1996) 'Accordo per il lavoro', P. d. C. d. Ministri, Rome, 24 September.

Regini, M. (1984) 'The Conditions for Political Exchange: How Concertation Emerged and Collapsed in Italy and Great Britain', in J.H. Goldthorpe (ed.) *Order and Conflict in Contemporary Capitalism*, Oxford: Clarendon.

—— (1997) 'Still engaging in corporatism? Recent Italian experience in comparative perspective', *European Journal of Industrial Relations,* 3(3): 259–78.

Saltari, E. and Travaglini, G. (2006) *Le radici del declino economic*, Turin: UTET.

Schludi, M. (2001) 'The Politics of Pensions in European Social Insurance Countries', *Discussion Paper 01/11*, Köln, Max-Planck-Institut für Gesellschaftsforschung.

Schmitter, P.C. and Grote, J.R. (1997) 'The Corporatist Sisyphus: Past, Present and Future', *EUI Working Paper SPS*. Florence: 22.

Siebert, H. (1997) 'Labor market rigidities: At the root of unemployment in Europe', *Journal of Economic Perspectives*, 11(3): 37–54.

Signorini, L.F. and Visco, I. (2002) *L'economia italiana*, Bologna, Il Mulino.

Simoni, M. (2007) 'The Renegotiated Alliance between the Left and Organised Labour in Western Europe', Unpublished PhD Thesis, London School of Economics and Political Science.

Weitz, P. (1975) 'Labor and politics in a divided movement: The Italian case', *Industrial and Labour Relations Review*, 28(2): 226–42.

18 The crisis of family firms and the decline of Italian capitalism

Raoul Minetti

Summary

After being regarded as a successful model of corporate organization between the 1960s and the 1980s, Italian family firms appear to be unable to face mounting global competition. On the one hand, many tiny family firms are under-sized, reluctant to hire highly qualified personnel and to invest in technological change. On the other hand, the few big families remain trapped in mature and low-growth sectors. What are the prospects of Italian capitalism? How can the limits of family firms be overcome? What role can financial markets and institutions play? What role for the policy maker?

Introduction

The Italian economy is characterized by a massive presence of family firms. This presence is so pervasive that Italian capitalism is sometimes labelled 'family capitalism' in contrast with the 'managerial capitalism' of Anglo-Saxon economies (e.g. United Kingdom and United States). Family firms have developed a mixed reputation among scholars and policy makers in recent decades. While in the past they were often considered a suitable instrument for promoting economic stability and long-term investments, in recent years they have increasingly been blamed as one of the sources of the rigidity and poor growth performance of the Italian business sector.[1] Advocates of the latter view argue that the Italian economy should progressively transit towards managerial capitalism, with a reduction in the concentration of corporate ownership and more professional managers. Between these two polar views, some scholars reject the rigid contraposition between family and managerial firms and argue that family firms should not necessarily be viewed as an alternative to managerial companies. According to this third view, a hybrid system combining elements of family and managerial capitalism would probably be the most suitable for Italy.

In this chapter, I aim to examine advantages and drawbacks of Italian family capitalism, possibly deriving policy implications for the reorganization of the Italian industrial system. In the next section, I investigate the salient features of the Italian corporate sector, with a special emphasis on the patterns of corporate ownership. Also in this section, I compare the Italian case with that of other industrial countries. In the following two sections, I examine in detail the theoretical arguments in favour and against family firms. I then turn to extant empirical and anecdotal evidence on the performance of family firms. I place special emphasis on the Italian experience, trying to draw lessons from the historical performance of Italian family firms. The chapter concludes with a review of the main challenges that the transformation of the Italian corporate sector faces.

The Italian family capitalism

In this section, I assess the role of family firms in Italy by looking at the ownership structure and the identity of firms' main shareholders. In Anglo-Saxon countries, such as the United Kingdom and the United States, the degree of concentration of publicly listed companies is typically low and financial institutions constitute the main shareholders. In Italy, instead, in 2000 the main shareholder of a non-public manufacturing company held roughly 65 per cent of the company on average (Bianchi and Bianco 2008), with this share being even larger for big companies. As for the second and third shareholders, Bianco (2003) and Bianchi and Bianco (2008) report that these held about 25 per cent so that jointly the top three shareholders held almost 100 per cent of firms. Even restricting attention to publicly listed companies, one still finds very strong ownership concentration, with 44 per cent of shares retained by the top shareholder. Another striking difference between the Italian corporate sector and that of other countries, especially Anglo-Saxon ones, is the identity of the top shareholders. For non-public manufacturing companies the top shareholder was a family or an individual in 54 per cent of cases, another firm in 2 per cent of the cases, a foreign company in 13 per cent, and a financial holding in 5 per cent of the cases. For publicly listed companies the state was the top shareholder in 18 per cent of the cases, another company in 10.5 per cent, an individual in 9.5 per cent and a financial holding in only 1.2 per cent of the cases. These figures thus reveal that the role of families and the state in Italian companies is very important. In contrast with the central role of families, in Italy the presence of financial institutions among firm shareholders is very limited. As I elaborate further below, in the past this was due to laws that prevented banks from holding shares in corporations. However, in spite of a recent change in the legislation, the limited role of financial institutions as corporate owners continues to be a distinctive feature of Italian capitalism.

This discussion should not lead the reader to think that family firms have not played a relevant role in other countries as well. In France, until the end of the 1960s families owned virtually all the most important business groups. In Sweden, families have been founders and owners of large banks or corporations (e.g. Ikea). In Switzerland at the end of the twentieth century, 30 per cent of the largest companies were family owned, and in the Netherlands this figure equalled 46 per cent. Family ownership is also typical of countries of the Asian-Pacific region, such as Korea and Taiwan, or of South America, such as Chile. Indeed, even in the Anglo-Saxon countries, traditionally considered as an example of managerial capitalism, family firms have played an important role historically. In England, the family control of the top 200 firms grew from 55 to 70 per cent between the first and the second world wars. In the United States, well-known families such as Mellon and Ford have been founders of economic empires. And even at the end of the twentieth century more than 15 per cent of the largest one hundred US corporations were family owned. However, the contrast between the United States and Italy clearly emerges if one considers that the corresponding figure for Italy was almost 50 per cent.

Theoretical arguments against family firms

Family firms have increasingly been the object of criticism by Italian economists and policy makers. In what follows, I aim to understand the theoretical foundations for this criticism, possibly shedding some light on the Italian case. One of the main problems of family firms is the inefficient allocation of competencies. When a firm grows, the family that founded the firm could lack the competencies needed to sustain its expansion, such as the hiring and selection of highly educated workers. Moreover, when ownership is transmitted across generations, the son, for example, could be less skilled than the father. Therefore, while keeping control inside a family can be an excellent way to guarantee the stability of a firm in the first part of its life it can later become a serious obstacle to the growth of the firm. Caselli and Gennaioli (2006) theoretically explore the problems that can stem from the dynastic transmission of control (dynastic management). In their analysis, they show that if the heir to a family firm lacks the talent needed for managerial decision making, meritocracy can fail.[2] They study the aggregate causes and consequences of this problem and find that the incidence of dynastic management depends on the severity of financial-market imperfections, on the economy's saving rate and on the degree of inheritability of talent across generations. Thus, dynastic management can constitute an important channel through which financial-market frictions and saving rates impact total factor productivity. Caselli and Gennaioli (2006) also employ numerical simulations to demonstrate that dynastic management can be a crucial determinant of observed cross-country differences in productivity.

The problem of the inefficient transmission of control across generations is also at the core of the analysis of Burkart *et al.* (2003). In their model, a founder chooses between hiring a manager and transferring control to his heir and also decides whether to go public (and the amount of shares to issue in the stock market). As in Caselli and Gennaioli (2006), the manager is more efficient at leading the firm than the heir. Burkart *et al.* (2003) study the impact of the legal environment on the founder's decision. Specifically, they find that, when laws prevent the expropriation of minority shareholders, the founder chooses to hire a manager and a widely held corporation emerges. In countries where the protection of minority shareholders is intermediate, management is delegated to a professional, but the family retains a large stake in the company to monitor the manager. Finally, in countries with weak protection of minority shareholders, the founder chooses his or her heir to manage the company and ownership remains inside the family.[3]

Together with the issue of the allocation of competencies, a second major problem of family firms is the separation between ownership and control. In Italy, like in other countries such as South Korea,[4] the retention of control by families is supported by a widespread presence of business groups in the industrial system. In a pyramidal group a family owns a percentage of a company which in turn owns a share of another company, and so forth. Through this chain of participation, the family ends up controlling a large number of firms. The ownership of the family is thus concentrated at the top of the group while the shareholdings of other parties are dispersed across all the affiliates of the group. This system implies that the control exerted by the family goes well beyond the equity it directly holds in the firms of the group. The corporate governance literature (see Shleifer and Vishny 1997 and La Porta *et al.* 2000) argues that when control rights are larger than ownership rights inefficiencies can arise because controlling shareholders can expropriate firm resources (such as enjoying perks and engaging in empire-building activities) but bear only part of the negative consequences of expropriation.[5] This problem is exacerbated by the fact that the pyramidal structure of groups shields firms from hostile takeovers, thus diluting the discipline that the stock market exerts over the firm (through the risk of a change in control). Further, in the Italian context, the lack of discipline of the stock market is allegedly compounded by a limited monitoring of families by financial institutions,[6] attributable, among other reasons, to the scarce presence of financial institutions among firm shareholders (as discussed above).

Theoretical arguments in favour of family firms

Some scholars argue that family firms exhibit a number of advantages relative to managerial ones. For example, family firms may have a longer term horizon than managerial firms. This is particularly beneficial when managers are under the pressure of realizing short-term benefits, for example because their compensation is contingent on short-term results. In a dynamic perspective, this implies that managers may not be interested in introducing new technologies or realizing long-term investments that require a long gestation period before maturing. Families may avoid such a managerial myopia. Indeed, because the company will be controlled by future generations of the family, current owners will have long investment horizons and will maximize long-term value. Interesting anecdotal evidence on this advantage of family firms comes from the experience of the business empire of the Swedish Wallenberg family recently featured by the *The Economist* (2009). According to the *Economist*, the ability of Wallenberg's companies to face the 2008–2009 financial crisis is attributable to the fact that these companies can resist pressure from outside investors, because it is virtually impossible to take them over. A dual shareholding structure also gives the Wallenberg family and their charitable foundations more votes per share than other shareholders, and allows them to retain control over companies even though they only own a quarter of their shares.[7]

A second advantage of family firms is that, by owning a large stake in a company, a family may be willing to monitor the management more than what dispersed owners would be willing to do. In some cases, this benefit could appear marginal because the family tends to manage its company directly. Yet, even in these cases, the monitoring performed by the family may be beneficial because professional managers are likely to be relevant in the decision-making process.

Evidence on the performance of family firms

The theoretical debate provides arguments both in favour and against family firms. One has then to turn to the empirical evidence to shed light on whether the benefits of family control exceed its costs or vice versa. Recently, several papers have begun to analyze the performance of family firms. Let us start with establishing some benchmarks by looking at the performance of family firms outside Italy. The evidence from the United States is mixed. Anderson and Reeb (2003) study a sample of US firms in the S&P 500. They measure firm performance both with accounting (Return on Assets) and market data (Tobin's q). Their main result is that family firms perform better than non-family firms regardless of the way performance is measured. However, when performance is measured with market data, the result holds only if family firms have a CEO who does not belong to the family. Pérez-González (2001) examines 335 successions in listed US family firms. In 122 of the businesses analyzed the successor comes from the family (including marriages among members of the family) while in the remaining 213 cases he/she comes from outside the family. The central result of the analysis is that, on average, the return on assets (ROA)of the firm drops by 17 per cent if a succession occurs within a family while it remains unaltered if the succession occurs outside the family (the results carry through when the performance of a company is measured with the market-to-book ratio). A further study that suggests a negative impact of family ownership on performance is Bennedsen *et al.* (2007). These authors employ a data set from Denmark to investigate how family attributes impact corporate decision making, and the consequences of these decisions on firm performance. They first show that the family characteristics of a departing CEO (e.g. the size of the family and the ratio of male children) have a strong power in predicting CEO successions. They then turn to examine the effect of family successions on performance.[8] The results of the analysis reveal that family successions have a significantly negative impact on performance: profitability falls by 6 per cent in the aftermath of such successions.

Negative evidence on the effect of family ownership comes also from Canada. Morck *et al.* (2000) use Canadian data and offer evidence that family control deteriorates business performance. They find that widely held firms have a better performance than family firms, and this result holds regardless of whether the founder, or one of his or her heirs or a manager act as a CEO. Moreover, Morck *et al.* find no evidence that family firms have a longer horizon and are long-term value maximizers. Indeed, family firms invest less in R&D and have fewer employees than widely held ones.[9] The evidence for Europe is somewhat more favourable for family firms. Sraer and Thesmar (2007) examine French listed companies and find that family firms outperform widely held ones. This, however, does not stem from the dynamic behaviour of firms but from the fact that they can pay lower salaries in exchange for more job security. Barontini and Caprio (2005) study listed European family firms. Although in their analysis there is more about divergence between cash flow and control rights in family firms (because of pyramid structures and dual class shares), family firms obtain better results than non-family firms (regardless of whether one uses accounting or market data to gauge corporate performance).

The Italian experience

As we have seen above, from a theoretical viewpoint the effects of family ownership can be far reaching and, according to several scholars, can explain the slow and limited growth of corporations. Several scholars build on the above arguments and claim that in Italy the scarce reallocation of control induced by family ownership harms dynamic efficiency, hindering the transfer of resources towards the most efficient users.[10] This would imply that small and medium firms do not grow and that instead of entering new sectors that require better competencies they remain confined to their initial sectors of activity. In turn, this would lead entrepreneurs to be over-specialized, operate in the original niches where the firm was born and competencies were developed, and remain closely tied to the territory where the firm was founded, with a limited tendency to export.

In order to understand whether these arguments have ground it is useful to look at the evolution of the size composition of Italian firms over time. Coltorti (2007) reports that the number of medium-sized firms has at most featured a timid tendency to grow in recent decades. The number of medium-sized firms sharply rose by 2577 units from 1971 to 1981, but in subsequent periods this growth significantly slowed down, with only 109 additional units in the decade from 1981 period and 272 between 1991 and 2001. Indeed the mean age of medium-sized firms is about 30 years which testifies the fact that most of these firms were born in the 1970s as a consequence of the crisis of large businesses and of business districts rather than as the result of the expansion of small firms. This observation is corroborated by the fact that most of the birth of medium firms (about two-thirds of the total) during the 1970s occurred in district areas, and that in the following two decades the significantly smaller increases were all concentrated in district areas. Turning to the number of employees, the average number of employees varies very little and has been significantly declining: for example, in the areas where big firms operate it declined from 26 employees in 1971 to 13 in 2001. The limited growth of small firms into medium-sized firms and, in turn, of medium-sized firms into large firms is frequently attributed to family ownership, among other reasons (Coltorti 2007). The ownership of medium-sized firms is largely family based: in more than 70 per cent of cases the owner is a single family or entrepreneur. Furthermore, the dissolution of large firms into medium sized ones occurred in Italy in recent decades is also often attributed to the crisis of large families. During the 1970s and 1980s the form of governance of large Italian firms was allegedly one of the key obstacles to the flexibility of these firms and seriously hampered their performance (Lavista 2007). Even new generations of owners that started to operate in the 1970s and 1980s had to face a sclerotic structure and the strong resistance of their families to a more efficient allocation of control. The experience of Pirelli is one of the most evident cases in which the family governance structure constituted a major obstacle to the internationalization of a big Italian company. In 1970, Pirelli formed an alliance with the British company Dunlop. As a result of the alliance, the interest of the shareholders of Pirelli had now to depend on the decisions of the management of two different companies. The merger would have called for a significant reorganization of the productive structure of Pirelli but this did not occur, eventually causing the failure of the alliance.[11] In turn, the lack of change of the productive structure was mostly due to the resistance to the change of the family ownership structure of Pirelli.

The anecdotal evidence we have discussed is necessarily soft in nature. To further understand the extent to which family firms may have contributed to slow down the growth of the Italian corporate sector we have to rely on more rigorous empirical analyses. The evidence is admittedly more mixed here. Panunzi *et al*. (2006) study the performance of Italian listed family firms in the 1998–2003 period. The study addresses two questions: the relative performance of family firms; and whether such a performance is affected by the type of firm, and in particular whether the CEO belongs to the family or is an outsider. When accounting measures of performance (e.g. ROA and ROE) are employed, family firms appear to perform better than other businesses. This is true not only when the founder is also the CEO, but also when the firm is managed by an heir of the founder or by a professional manager. However, when performance is captured with market data (e.g. stock market returns) no evidence is found of a superior performance of family firms, a result consistent with that obtained by Sraer and Thesmar (2007) for French family firms.[12] Cucculelli and Micucci (2008) deliver more pessimistic findings about the performance of Italian family firms. The authors contrast firms that continue to be managed within the family by the heirs to the founders with firms in which management is instead transferred to outsiders. They find that keeping management within the family has a negative impact on the firm's performance, and this effect is largely borne by the good performers, especially in competitive sectors. The results of Cucculelli and Micucci thus suggest that family firms tend to underperform relative to widely held managerial companies.

Obstacles to the reallocation of control in Italy

Given the growing (though inconclusive) evidence on the limits imposed by family control, it is important to understand what impedes the evolution of Italian family capitalism to a system with more widely held managerial companies. I thus conclude this chapter by examining the causes of the rigidity of the Italian ownership structure. Scholars have identified four main reasons for this sclerotic structure. A first reason relates to the legal environment in which Italian firms operate. As discussed earlier, a broad body of literature argues that laws and regulations influence corporate finance and governance. According to La Porta *et al.* (1998) the judicial systems that provide stronger protection for minority shareholders and creditors are those in which the stock market is more developed, firms easily finance their activity and firm ownership is more dispersed. In fact, in such systems small shareholders feel more protected and are more willing to invest their money in corporations. When, instead, the protection of minority shareholders is poor small shareholders are not willing to invest and controlling shareholders retain a large stake in companies. According to La Porta *et al.* (1999)[13] the Anglo-Saxon countries such as the United Kingdom and the United States are those in which the protection of minority shareholders is strongest. In contrast, Italy does not perform well in this dimension: using the index constructed by La Porta *et al.*, on a scale between 1 and 6, the United States obtains a 5; Italy has only a 1.[14]

A second important issue that can rationalize the strong role of families in Italian companies is the inefficient functioning of the market for corporate control. In Italy, this market is heavily based on the role of banks that should facilitate the reallocation of corporate control from inefficient owners to more efficient ones. However, banks have seldom played this role in the past, as demonstrated by Barca (1994). According to Bianco (2003) a third issue that can explain the scarce propensity of small shareholders to invest in Italian corporations is the political pressure that Italian firms face to target objectives that diverge from value maximization. In fact, controlling shareholders and managers are frequently induced to pursue objectives such as the expansion of firms (empire building), reduce the effects on workers of restructurings, etc.

Finally, a fourth key problem that allegedly inhibits the growth of Italian family firms and the change in the ownership structure has to do with lack of competition in product markets. In a very competitive product market firms face strong pressure to attain positive results, otherwise they risk being excluded from the credit market or to obtain credit only at a very high price. It is generally claimed that competition in product markets is much lower in Italy than in other countries, such as the Anglo-Saxon ones.

What steps have been made to alleviate the four problems we have just discussed? And, therefore, to what extent can we expect Italy to grow out of its traditional, apparently immutable family capitalism in the coming years? The most important change occurred in the last decade certainly with regards to the first of the four problems identified above, the legal environment in which shareholders operate. The reforms of the Italian corporate law and governance enacted in 1998 and 2003 have strengthened the protection of minority shareholders in various manners, paving the way for a stronger involvement of minority shareholders and a reduction in ownership concentration. As documented by Bianchi and Bianco (2008), however, they have not led to dramatic changes in the patterns of corporate ownership of Italian firms in recent years. This could suggest that such a reform of the legal environment cannot produce significant changes if it is not accompanied by a systemic reform that also tackles the other three main problems discussed. The two challenges that the Italian policy makers face thus appear to be (i) promoting an improvement of product market competition and (ii) enhancing the efficiency of the market for corporate control. One can conjecture that to the extent that financial institutions such as banks will become increasingly involved in the ownership and control of Italian firms, this could also facilitate their role in helping firms to reallocate ownership and control efficiently.[15] Indeed, as proved by Caselli and Gennaioli (2006), an inefficient functioning of financial institutions is one of the main reasons that lead to a sclerotic family capitalism. In conclusion, although an analysis of these points is beyond the scope of our study, the general insight one can draw from the Italian experience of recent years is that the recent change in laws and regulations could not suffice to modernize the Italian corporate sector. Indeed, this may require actions that involve a major rethinking of the functioning of product and financial markets.

Notes

1 In 2001, in an interview to *Il Corriere della Sera* (entitled 'Il capitalismo familiare va superato'), the Italian Prime Minister, Giuliano Amato, identified Italian family capitalism as one of the main causes of the poor growth of the Italian economy in the last two decades.

2 In *Italy Today*, Carboni reports the results of a study according to which 92.7 per cent of Italians believe that the leading class (including entrepreneurs) should be chosen on the basis of merit and competence. In contrast, the Italian ruling class, according to Italians, has been chosen on the basis of its economic wealth (68 per cent) and good relations (54.2 per cent), regardless of merit.

3 Burkart *et al.* (2003) show that a crucial problem of family ownership is that it can prevent the firm from growing beyond the financial resources of the family.

4 See the case of South Korean *Chaebols*. More generally, East Asian countries feature an ownership structure very similar to that of Italian firms: a large role of groups in the hands of families with pyramid structures that allow families to keep control without holding much equity.

5 Whereas it is true that, by owning a large block, families can extract private benefits of control, they may not have the incentive to consume them when private benefit extraction entails a deadweight loss. The larger the stake owned by the controlling party, the larger the internalization of the deadweight loss and thus the lower the incentive to divert corporate resources as private benefits of control.

6 The abuse of controlling shareholders may take various forms, such as cash flow appropriation or asset stripping (La Porta *et al.* 1999).

7 In 1917, Knut Wallenberg set up a charitable foundation that has become a repository for most of the family's wealth.

8 To overcome endogeneity issues the authors use the gender of a departing CEO's first-born child as an instrumental variable for successions. This is a valid instrument because male first-child family firms are more likely to transfer control to a family CEO than female first-child firms. In contrast, it is unlikely that the gender of the first child affects firms' performance.

9 Amit and Villalonga (2006) find evidence of superior performance of family firms only if the founder is the CEO or when he or she is the Chairman with an external (to the family) CEO.

10 A further interesting issue worth investigating is whether family ownership could help explain the different economic performance of Italian regions (see, for example Iona *et al.* in *Italy Today*).

11 For a detailed discussion see Lavista 2007.

12 The authors propose an econometric explanation for this discrepancy in the results. They show that the correct econometric model is static (that is, a model where the lagged performance variables are not included in the right-hand side of the regression equation)

when using accounting variables to measure performance, whereas a dynamic model is more appropriate when using market data. When using a dynamic model, the results obtained using market data are similar to those obtained using accounting data.
13 On this see, e.g., Bianco 2003, and Bianchi and Bianco 2008.
14 In Italy one of the main problems is the limited voting rights of minority shareholders.
15 For a theoretical model see Araujo and Minetti 2007.

References

Amit, R. and Villalonga, B. (2006) 'How do family ownership, control and management affect firm value?', *Journal of Financial Economics*, 80: 385–417.

Anderson, R. and Reeb, D. (2003) 'Founding-family ownership and firm performance: Evidence from the S&P 500', *Journal of Finance,* 58: 1301–28.

——, Mansi, S.A. and Reeb, D. (2003) 'Founding-family ownership and the agency cost of debt', *Journal of Financial Economics*, 68: 263–85.

Araujo, L. and Minetti, R. (2007) 'Financial intermediaries as markets for firm assets', *Economic Journal,* 117: 1380–402.

Barca, F. (1994) 'Allocazione e Riallocazione della Proprietà e del Controllo delle Imprese: Ostacoli, Intermediari, Regole', in *Il Mercato Della Proprietà e del Controllo delle Imprese: Aspetti Teorici ed Istituzionali*, Rome: Banca d'Italia.

Barontini, R. and Caprio, L. (2005) 'The effect of family control on firm value and performance: Evidence from continental Europe', *European Financial Management,* 12, 689–723.

Bennedsen, M., Nielson, K.M., Pérez-González, F., Wolfenzon, D. (2007) 'Inside the family firm: The role of families in succession decisions and performance', *Quarterly Journal of Economics,* 122: 647–91.

Bianco, M. (2003) *L'Industria Italiana*, Bologna: Il Mulino.

Bianchi, M. and Bianco, M. (2008) *L'Evoluzione della 'Corporate Governance' in Italia: Meno Piramidi piu' Coalizioni?*, Bologna: Il Mulino.

Burkart, M., Panunzi, F. and Shleifer, A. (2003) 'Family firms', Journal of Finance, 58: 2167–202.

Caselli, F. and Gennaioli, N. (2006) 'Dynastic management', mimeo, London School of Economics.

Cucculelli, M. and Micucci, G. (2008) 'Family succession and firm performance: Evidence from Italian family firms', *Journal of Corporate Finance*, 14: 17–31.

The Econonomist (2009) 'The ties that bind', 22 January.

La Porta, R., Lopez-de-Silane, F. and Shliefer, A.. (1999) 'Corporate ownership around the world', *Journal of Finance*, 54: 471–517.

Morck, R., Strangeland, D. and Yeung, B. (2000) 'Inherited Wealth, Corporate Control, and Economic Growth: The Canadian Disease', in R. Morck (ed.) *Concentrated Corporate Ownership*, National Bureau of Economic Research Conference Volume. University of Chicago Press.

Panunzi, F., Favero, C.A., Giglio, S. and Honorati, M. (2006) 'The Performance of Italian Family Firms', European Corporate Governance Institute – Finance Working Paper No. 127/2006.

Pérez-González, F. (2006) 'Inherited control and firm performance', *American Economic Review*, 96: 1559–88.

Sraer, D. and Thesmar, D. (2007) 'Performance and behavior of family firms: Evidence from the French stock market', *Journal of the European Economic Association*, 5, 709–51.

Index